Ireland–Japan Connections and Crossings

Ireland–Japan Connections and Crossings

Celebrating sixty-five years of diplomatic relationships

Edited by John FitzGerald, Richard Kelly,
Claire Connolly and Hiroyasu Fujisawa

CORK UNIVERSITY PRESS

First published in 2022 by
Cork University Press
Boole Library
University College Cork
T12 ND89
Ireland

Library of Congress Control Number: 2022936361

ISBN: 9781782055150

Book Design and typesetting: Anú Design, Tara

Printed in Poland by BZ Graf.

Cover: Detail from *Tale of Muramatsu* (*Muramatsu monogatari emaki*), style of Iwasa Matabei (1578–1650), 1600–1650. (CBL J 1127.3, © *The Trustees of the Chester Beatty Library, Dublin*)

Japanese affection is not uttered in words; it scarcely appears even in the tone of voice; it is chiefly shown in acts of exquisite courtesy and kindness.

Lafcadio Hearn, *Kokoro* (1922)

貢献者

Contributors

Clothilde Anamizu is a member of the Cistercian community, St Mary's Abbey, Glencairn, County Waterford.

Michelle P. Brown is professor emerita of Medieval Manuscript Studies at the School of Advanced Study, University of London, and visiting professor, University College London.

Claire Connolly is professor of Modern English and Head of the School of English and Digital Humanities, University College Cork.

John FitzGerald is Director of Information Services and University Librarian, University College Cork, and a poet.

Fumihisa Fujinaga is an associate professor in the Department of Literature, Faculty of Literature, Arts and Cultural Studies, Kindai University, Osaka.

Hiroyasu Fujisawa is a professor of English at the Faculty of Literature, Arts and Cultural Studies, Kindai University, Osaka.

Keiichi Hayashi is a Japanese diplomat who served as Japanese Ambassador to Ireland from 2005 to 2008.

Paul Hayes is a freelance Irish composer living in Japan.

Seamus Heaney (1939–2013) was an Irish poet, translator, academic and critic who was awarded the 1995 Nobel Prize in Literature.

Mimbu Kawamura is a professor emeritus of English, Kindai University, Osaka.
Dearbhla Kelly is the Enterprise Engagement Officer with Donegal Education and Training Board, County Donegal.

Richard J. Kelly is a professor in the Department of Literature, Faculty of Literature, Arts and Cultural Studies, Kindai University, Osaka.

Bon Koizumi is the Director of Lafcadio Hearn Memorial Museum and professor emeritus, University of Shimane Junior College (and the great grandson of Lafcadio Hearn).

Michael Longley is a poet, translator and critic living in Belfast, Northern Ireland.

Peter MacMillan is a translator, poet and artist, teaching at the University of Tokyo and Sagami Women's University.

Derek Mahon (1941–2020) was an Irish poet, dramatist, translator and critic.

Akiko Manabe is a professor at Shiga University with interests in Irish and American literatures, especially their relation with *Nogaku*.

Sinéad Morrissey is a poet and professor of Creative Writing, Newcastle University.

John Neary is an Irish diplomat who served from 2010 to 2014 as Irish Ambassador to Japan.

Yvonne O'Conor is a garden consultant and graduate of University College Dublin and The National Botanic Gardens, Dublin.

Patrick O'Riordan is currently Director for China of Enterprise Ireland, having served previously as Director for Japan and South Korea.

Kenzaburō Ōe is a Japanese novelist, short-story writer and essayist who was awarded the 1994 Nobel Prize in Literature.

Ciarán Quinn is a lecturer in English, Kindai University, Osaka.

Mary Redfern is curator of the East Asian Collections at the Chester Beatty, Dublin.

Shaun Richards is professor emeritus of Irish Studies, Staffordshire University.

Paul Ross is the Director of APC Microbiome Ireland at University College Cork.

Hideki Sato is a professor in the Department of Literature, Faculty of Literature, Arts and Cultural Studies and in the Graduate School of Interdisciplinary Human Studies, Kindai University, Osaka.

James A. Sharkey is a former Irish diplomat who served as Ambassador to Japan between 1989 and 1995.

Akiyo Suzuki is an associate professor at the Institute of Human and Social Sciences, Faculty of Letters, Osaka University.

Taketoshi (Toshi) Furomoto was a professor at the Department of International Cultural Studies, Kobe University and at the Department of Literature, Aichi-gakuin University.

Alan Titley is professor emeritus of Modern Irish, University College Cork and former Head of the Irish Department at St Patrick's College, Dublin City University.

Masazumi Toraiwa is a poet and professor emeritus of Waseda University, Tokyo.

Ura-shizuko is a writer who organises the 'Urara literature group' and teaches Japanese classical literature and history.

Akemi Yoshida is a professor in the Faculty of Letters, Kyoto Prefectural University.

The book is dedicated to
the memory of
Lafcadio Hearn (Koizumi Yakumo)
(1850–1904)

Picture contest from *Genji in words and pictures* (Genji kotobae), artist unknown, 1688. (CBL J 1126.2, © *The Trustees of the Chester Beatty Library, Dublin*).

目次

Contents

EDUCATION

HISTORY AND CULTURE

POETRY

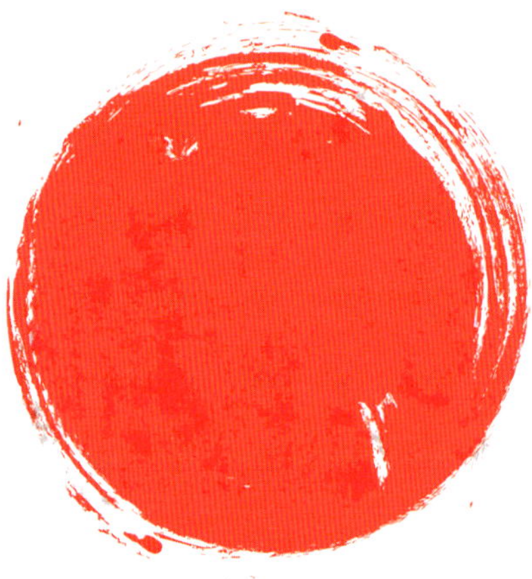

Acknowledgements

謝辞

The editors wish to express their gratitude to those people who, directly or indirectly, have encouraged the production of this book. We wish to thank Professor John O'Halloran, President of University College Cork and Professor Yoshihiko Hosoi, President of Kindai University who have been generous in their encouragement of this project while establishing close ties between our two universities.

Thanks are due to recent Ambassadors of Japan to Ireland and Ireland to Japan, some of whom feature as contributors, notably the current Ambassador of Japan to Ireland, His Excellency Mitsuru Kitano, and current Ambassador of Ireland to Japan, His Excellency Paul Kavanagh. Their support and interest and the assistance of their staff are greatly appreciated.

We wish to express our deep appreciation to Maria O'Donovan of Cork University Press for her stewardship of the manuscript from raw submission to impressive final design, and to Mike Collins, Maureen Fitzgerald and Agnes Nagle of the CUP team.

Grace McGlynn of the Information Services Division at UCC has effectively managed the project from the very start. Her judgement and legendary efficiency have made the job of the editors very easy. Without Grace's involvement, this book could not have been produced and we are profoundly grateful to her.

We are immensely grateful to Dominic Carroll for his assiduous picture research and his valued advice with the manuscript at all stages of its evolution.

Mary Redfern of The Chester Beatty has been a source of valuable advice and imagery and we are grateful to her and The Chester Beatty for their generous support.

We thank all those for their permission to publish their work. To the Gallery Press for permission to publish 'Basho in Kinsale' by Derek Mahon. To Marie Heaney for permission to reproduce *The Pathos of Things* by the late Seamus Heaney.

Finally, and not least, to all the contributors, for sharing their research, knowledge, memories and creativity, and for keeping faith with the project over the past five years.

John FitzGerald, Claire Connolly, Richard J Kelly, Hiroyasu Fujisawa
Cork/Osaka, July 2022

Japanese print *c.* 1900 depicting Europeans visiting Japan, artist unknown. (*World History Archive/Alamy*)

序章

Introduction

John FitzGerald, Richard Kelly, Claire Connolly
and Hiroyasu Fujisawa

Japan has a distinguished record of diplomatic engagement since its first formal international relationship with China some 2,000 years ago. The period CE 600–900 was of special importance, as it saw the advent of Buddhism during the Sui and Tang Dynasties. Korea was to become the other great external influence from the fifth century CE onwards. The Chinese writing system (*kanji*) was introduced to Japan by scribes from the Korean state of Baekje in the early fifth century. The arts of pottery, lacquer ware, silk weaving, music and dance, in addition to advances in arms and armament, architecture, government and administration, are all among the important arrivals to Japan from Korea which originated in the Chinese continent.

The first Japanese international diplomatic mission to New Spain (Mexico) and Europe (France, Italy, Spain) was from 1613 to 1620, led by the *samurai* nobleman Tsunenaga Hasekura (1571–1622). However, on his return in 1620, Japan had entered a period of isolation known as the Edo Period (1603–1868). Japan was not to open to the outside world again until 1868, with the advent of the Meiji Period (1868–1912).

A second diplomatic mission to the West, led by the eminent Japanese statesman Tomomi Iwakura (1825–83) took place over a two-year period from 1872 to 1873, following a round-the-world journey that also included the USA and several European countries. This mission, more than any other, succeeded in bringing Western culture, technology and science into Japan, where they were embraced enthusiastically. Medical books imported from Germany, for example, formed the fundamental basis of modern Japanese medicine. The Japanese parliamentary system, with its upper and lower houses of elected representatives, was adapted from the British system of the time, following this mission.

The political events of the first half of the twentieth century led to upheaval and tumultuous change in relations among most of the major nations of the world. Following the Second World War, diplomacy replaced conflict, as nations and their intergovernmental organisations rebuilt a new economic and geopolitical order. On 5 March 1957, Japan and Ireland established formal diplomatic links between the two island nations, an event that was to celebrate its sixtieth anniversary in 2017. The sixtieth year is a very special celebratory year in the Buddhist tradition, as it is the designated year of retirement: the year in which a parent will pass on to their eldest the title of 'Head of the Household' – a 'Coming of Age' or 'Rebirth', known as *Kanreki* (還暦). To celebrate the 'Coming of Age' and 'Rebirth' between Japan and Ireland in 2017, numerous celebrations and events were held in both countries throughout the course of the year, ranging from art exhibitions and dramatic performances, to official state visits, and even the first ever direct flight between Tokyo and Dublin by Japan Airlines (JAL).

In his book *If You Understand Ireland, You Understand Japan* (2008), Keiichi Hayashi, Ambassador of Japan to Ireland from 2005 to 2008, describes the relationship between Japan and Ireland as natural and complementary. Our book of essays celebrates this natural complementarity. The essays and poems were gathered from 2017 to 2021 as a way of recording and celebrating the remarkable depth and range of the diplomatic, economic and cultural relationship existing between the two nations of Japan and Ireland.

His Excellency, Mitsuru Kitano, Ambassador of Japan to Ireland, highlights the development of bilateral relations over the past years. As a matter of fact, the bilateral relationship has a rich tradition over the last 65 years, marked by various important milestones. One of these was in 2005 when the Emperor and Empress of Japan, Akihito and Michiko Heisei, made a historic four-day state visit to Ireland. During their visit, the Royal Couple dropped in for a cup tea at the country cottage in County Wicklow of the Nobel Laureate Seamus Heaney (1939–2013). This simple gesture still resonates in Japanese national memory because, in the Zen Buddhist tradition, beauty and dignity are both to be found in simplicity.

Seamus Heaney had a lifelong interest in Japan, which is celebrated by him in his contribution on the parallels between Old Irish and Japanese poetry. His friend, Kenzaburō Ōe (1935–), who received the Nobel Prize for Literature in 1994, just one year prior to Heaney's own award, acknowledged in his acceptance speech his indebtedness to the writings of W.B. Yeats and how they inspired his creative work. An extract from Ōe's 'Led by Poets' in *A Novelist's Way of Writing*, translated into English by Toshi Furomoto, affirms this essential influence.

Heaney and Yeats were by no means the only Irish writers to share a fascination with Japanese literature and culture. Jonathan Swift (1667–1745) was the first writer from Ireland to specifically mention Japan by name in Part III of his Gulliver's Travels (1726). Gulliver is going home to Europe from the port of Nagasaki and Swift accurately records the practice of ***fumi-e*** (踏み絵, fumi "stepping-on" + e "picture") – which Gulliver refused to perform, even though his refusal could have had serious (even fatal) consequences for him. Swift's fascination for Japan is described in Richard Kelly's essay on the advent of Christianity to Japan in 1549.

The Irish religious influence on Japan has been considerable. Ireland's contribution to Christianity in Japan can be illustrated through many stories. There is the touching account of John Neary, Ambassador of Ireland to Japan from 2010 to 2014, paying a visit to the Goto Islands in July 2014 to be informed that the church in the picturesque village of Hantomari on Fukue Island was built partly through donations from Ireland in the early 1920s. How this remote island community was connected to Ireland is still somewhat of a mystery; the most likely route was through the Irish College in Paris since the Goto Islands at that time were administered by French missionary priests who had their Mother House in Paris. The influence continues: the headmistress of Sacred Heart International Schools in Tokyo is currently the Irish woman, Yvonne Hayes. This prestigious school has several illustrious *alumni* – including Empress Michiko.

Sr Clothilde Anamizu O.C.S.O. recounts how her quest to deepen her understanding of God brought her from the Trappist monastery nestled in the Rokko Mountains of Nishinomiya in Hyogo Prefecture to Waterford Regional Airport *en route* to joining the Cistercian Community of St Mary's Abbey at

Glencairn, near Lismore, County Waterford. Sr Clothilde recalls how her family recoiled when she converted to Catholicism following a spiritual epiphany while recovering from a serious medical emergency. Today, Sr Clothilde is in her seventies and a vibrant member of the Glencairn Community – happily reconciled also with her Japanese family.

In another connection of the cloth, Ciarán L. Quinn relates the remarkable life of Maura O'Halloran, born in Boston, Massachusetts, USA, in 1955, who moved to Dublin with her parents when she was four years old. Maura entered the Toshoji Temple in Tokyo in 1979 at the age of twenty-four to begin training as a Zen Buddhist monk and completed her formation at Kannonji Temple in Morioka, northern Japan. On her way to Ireland in the summer of 1982, travelling *via* Thailand to establish her own Buddhist monastery there, Maura was tragically killed in a bus accident in Chiang Mai in northern Thailand. Her family published her extraordinary memoirs posthumously in a book entitled *Pure Heart, Enlightened Mind*. Not only did she become an esteemed Buddhist priest called Shoshin (総心) – (a word from Zen Buddhism meaning 'pure heart'), she also dreamed of bringing her appreciation of Japanese monastic culture back to Ireland so that the people there might understand what she had so enthusiastically embraced and mastered. Since her death, a Bodhisattva statue stands in her honour at Kannonji Temple.

The stories of religious connection between Japan and Ireland have an interesting deeper historical context, which is charted by Michelle Brown who goes back to the Early Middle Ages and comparable experiences of reception of incoming literate faiths by the island archipelagos of Britain, Ireland and Japan.

The year 2017 was also the thirtieth anniversary of the Japan Exchange and Teaching Programme (JET). Since Ireland became a participating country in this Japanese Government programme in 1988, 1,390 Irish people have contributed to and enjoyed the programme. Most JET participants work at primary and secondary schools as Assistant Language Teachers, and some work in local government offices as Coordinators for International Relations. The JET Programme brings young Irish people into direct contact with mainstream Japanese society. In rural and urban Japan, the principal merit of the programme has been to have created over 200,000 international cultural ambassadors of Japan in the young men and women who subsequently return to their home countries, including all of the English-speaking world as well as China, France, Germany, Italy, South Korea and Spain.

'Two sages' from 'Part III: A Voyage to Laputa, Balnibarbi, Luggnagg, Glubbdubdrib and Japan' in *Gulliver's Travels* by Jonathan Swift (1667–1745); illustration by Arthur Rackham (1867–1939). (*AF Fotografie/Alamy*)

Ireland's contribution on the JET Programme is described by Dearbhla Kelly in her essay 'Under the Cherry Tree'.

Japan's modern educational system excels in achieving almost 100 per cent literacy in what is undoubtedly one of the world's most complex writing systems. Japanese writing uses three integral character sets that combine pictographic and syllabic meaning: *Kanji, Hiragana,* and *Katakana* –which is reserved for the writing of foreign 'import' words into Japanese. In his contribution, Fumihisa Fujinaga, a specialist in Japanese pedagogy, offers fascinating insights into the Japanese education system (with a special focus on English language learning), which routinely produces Nobel Prize winners particularly in the sciences, engineering and mathematics. This is complemented by an account of a young Japanese man who transitioned from a Western educational experience to the Japanese one. Both accounts illustrate that no one system is perfect: Japan excels in a recall-based system that inculcates memory, whereas the Western model (including Ireland's) develops individuality and critical thinking skills.

The Irish educational sector is deepening its involvement with Japan. Growing numbers of Japanese students opt to study in Ireland for both short- and long-term courses. The number of Irish students in Japanese university campuses is also increasing. Research collaboration between Irish and Japanese universities is visible through research cooperation at faculty and postgraduate level in the sciences and the humanities. Paul Ross presents an invaluable overview of this research collaboration arising from his active involvement in various research collaborations with Japanese researchers such as the Suntory Global Innovation Center in Kyoto, and the Faculty of Life Sciences at Kindai University in Osaka.

Ireland's own voice of Irish horse racing, broadcaster Brian Gleeson, offers a fascinating analysis of the relationship of the world-renowned Coolmore Stud in County Tipperary to Japan. Coolmore gave Japan its most famous racehorse of all time, Deep Impact, out of Wind in Your Hair – both proud members of the Coolmore hall of fame. Deep Impact has become a household name in Japan and the JRA currently has many racehorses stabled in several of Ireland's prestigious stud farms, including Coolmore, and Rathangan, strengthening the sporting ties between the two nations.

The Director of Enterprise Ireland in Japan, Patrick O'Riordan, documents the important wider trading and business connections between Japan and Ireland.

Several major Japanese pharmaceutical and precision engineering companies, such as Takeda and Neriki BBB, have manufacturing bases in Ireland. Technology is represented by Canon, Fujitsu and Mitsubishi Electric, and trading by Marubeni, among others. Ireland, in turn, has some fifty companies currently doing business in Japan. These operate chiefly in the food and drink sector, with Irish dairy products enjoying an ever-increasing presence on supermarket shelves throughout Japan. Irish whiskey and Guinness are established recognised brands in Japan, thanks to the success of the marketing strategies of Diageo and Pernod Ricard and the Irish food-marketing agency An Bord Bia.

No discussion of cultural links between Japan and Ireland can omit the figure of Lafcadio Hearn (1850–1904), to whom this book is dedicated. Hearn is by far the best-known Irish writer in Japan. Born on the Greek island of Lefkada to an Anglo-Irish medical army officer and a Greek mother, he was the first non-Japanese to genuinely understand the uniqueness of Japanese life and culture and to communicate its character to the wider world through his writings. It is a great honour to have his great-grandson, Bon Koizumi, contribute a unique insight into his illustrious ancestor. Uniquely, Hearn combined Western rationalism with Eastern aestheticism in a way not hitherto achieved. He was fascinated by the origins of Hinduism in India and Buddhism in China; and he regarded these as essential to an appreciation of the distinctness between European and Asian mindsets. He wrote two letters to W.B. Yeats in 1901, referring specifically to Yeats's poem 'The Folk of the Air' (1899). Although a reply letter from Yeats is not extant, it is clear from the second letter, where Hearn explicitly expresses his love of things Irish, that the poet and he enjoyed mutual admiration and respect.

The influence of Lafcadio Hearn on Japan is appreciated here from various perspectives, both literary and cultural. Mimbu Kawamura probes the surprising linkages between Hearn's 'Yuki-Onna' and Oscar Wilde's drama 'The Star-Child' and Salomé. Akiyo Suzuki examines the 'Celticisation' of Hearn after his death, in the context of the reception of Irish literature in Japan.

Hearn was much loved by his students at Tokyo Imperial University, and subsequently at Waseda University, mainly because he was fascinated by popular student musical tastes of the day. These were not always to his liking, but the fact that he embraced them demonstrates his characteristic practical modernism. Hearn gave the Japanese word *tsunami* ('a tidal wave initiated by an earthquake')

Actors performing in a *kyōgen* theatre, Tokyo. (*Tibor Bognar/Alamy*)

to the English language in 1904, the year of his death. His remains are interred in Zoshigaya Cemetery, Tokyo, along with other notable internationals who made significant contributions to Japan from the Meiji Era (1868–1912) onwards. In his contribution, Paul Hayes describes the richly allusive context for his own musical adaptation of Hearn's writing.

Akiko Manabe's fascinating account of how Japanese traditional theatre, Noh and kyogen – collectively referred to as Nogaku – have both influenced and been influenced by Yeats and Hearn, and how this influence has been registered also in Ireland. Next to Hearn, William Butler Yeats is the Irish literary figure who has garnered greatest interest among Japan's historically and currently active Irish Studies community. Claire Connolly traces the subtle influence of Japanese culture in some of Yeats's less well-known prose works. Hideaki Sato's study of the influence of 'Cathleen Ní Houlihan' uon 'Sotōba Komachi' demonstrates the curious way in which the two cultures involving Yeats and the great Japanese writer Yukio Mishima influenced each other through Noh, and how Japanese classical drama was effectively reimported into Japan through Yeats to Mishima. Taketoshi Furomoto reveals the strong influence of Yeats's poetry in particular on aspects of Kenzaburō Ōe's fictional trilogy *The Blazing Green Tree.* Shaun Richards explores Yeats's motivations in embracing Noh as a new currency for dramatic expression in the twentieth-century Irish cultural revival, and how well or otherwise Yeats' objectives were met through adoption of Noh.

James Joyce also features prominently in the work of contemporary Japanese Irish Studies scholars, as exemplified in Akemi Yoshida's assessment of a work by Japanese Nobel Prize-winning author Yasunari Kawabata alongside Joyce's *Ulysses* and George Moore's *The Lake.* Bringing many of these literary strands together, Shizuko Ura (Sadako Matsuura) provides a unique account of one eager scholar's journey into Celtic and Irish literary cultures. Religious and literary studies converge in Hiroyasu Fujisawa's fascinating analysis of how the story of Mary Magdalene animated members of the Japanese Irish Studies community during the early twentieth century.

Japan has also established a strong cultural presence in Ireland. The Japanese Gardens at the Irish National Stud in Co. Kildare were designed by a Japanese father and son, Tassa and Minoru Eida, over four years from 1906 to 1910 at the request of Colonel William Hall-Walker. Yvonne O'Conor describes the evolution of this popular amenity and identifies many of its botanical and architectural attractions. The Japanese collection of art, artefacts and scrolls at the Chester Beatty Library in Dublin is one of the finest collections of its kind in the world. Mary Redfern explains the provenance of the collection and recalls a landmark exhibition created from this extraordinary legacy to the Irish nation.

Despite their distance apart and very divergent histories, Japan and Ireland have always granted poetry a special place in society. Alan Titley describes the interconnections between the two writing traditions of Irish and Japanese. The cherished place of poetry has been recognised by the inclusion of poems by John FitzGerald, Michael Longley, Derek Mahon, Sinéad Morrissey, Kenzaburō Ōe and Masazumi Toraiwa. In his essay, James Sharkey, Ambassador of Ireland to Japan from 1989 to 1995, provides a comprehensive overview of all of the literary connections between the two cultures.

There are many aspects of popular culture which are not the subject of articles in *this book,* but which are important to the interconnectedness of Japan and Ireland. The Japan Gaelic Athletic Association, founded in the early 1990s, promotes Irish culture and friendship through participation in Gaelic sports such as hurling and Gaelic football. Irish music and dance are well represented through organisations like Comhaltas Ceoltóirí Éireann (Japan). There are over 130 Irish pubs and branches thereof throughout Japan. Several of these pubs are run by Irish people. They are not only places to enjoy a drink with family and friends, they are important cultural centres for Irish expats where Irish music, dance, sporting events and traditional cuisine can be enjoyed. They serve as a special focus for St Patrick's Day festivals, of which Japan now holds some fourteen in various cities throughout the archipelago, including the main parade in Tokyo.

Irish music is popular in Japan. The Chieftains, Enya, Clannad, Christy Moore, Van Morrison, Mary Black, Riverdance, U2, and Planxty, to name but a few, are all household names in Japan and with attract large Japanese listenership audiences. Performances of Irish drama are staged regularly. A recent performance in Japanese of Samuel Beckett's *Waiting for Godot* at The New National Theatre in Tokyo was very well received, evoking in some reviews the loss associated with the thousands of deaths from the Great East Japan Earthquake of March 2011. One may ask the question: why does Irish culture resonate so powerfully in Japan? Part of the answer lies in the fact that deep in the Japanese psyche is a profound appreciation of beauty in the mysterious – and the writings of Beckett, Heaney, Joyce and Yeats contain these qualities in abundance.

Elements of Japanese sports and culture enjoy a burgeoning popularity in Ireland. Japanese traditional martial arts are represented by Genbukan Ireland, which teaches *ninjutsu* – the art of *ninja*, and *jujutsu* – the art of the *samurai*. These ancient art forms promote the highest levels of technique to ensure survival in times of conflict and peace. This is the essence of the *ninja* and *samurai* spirit. Bonsai Ireland holds various classes and events in the Japanese art of *ikebana* – the skill of Japanese flower arrangement. The annual *ikebana* exhibition is held each year in mid-June at the Chester Beatty Library in the grounds of Dublin Castle. There is a Japanese poetry event held annually at Charlie Byrne's Bookshop in the heart of Galway city in early March. The year 2017 was the tenth anniversary of an event which saw the respected *tanka* poet Hisa Kagawa (1947–) give a reading in Japanese of her own poetic work followed by an English translation by Revd Patrick Towers. The Irish Haiku Society, founded in 2006, promotes the creative writing and aesthetic appreciation of these short-form Japanese poems. *Haiku* were made universally famous by the Japanese poet Matsuo Bashō (1644–1694). This poetic art form has been practised by such renowned Irish poets as Juanita Casey (1925–2012), the first Irish poet to write *haiku* from the late 1960s; Patrick Kavanagh (1904–67); Michael Hartnett (1941–99); Seamus Heaney (1939–2013); Michael Longley (1939–); Gabriel Rosenstock (1949–), and others.

There are many figures of importance in the shared history of these two nations who are not treated in *this book*. It is not widely known that the musical score for Japan's national anthem was composed by an army officer from Kinsale, County Cork: John William Fenton (1828–90). However, Fenton's even more notable legacy is his founding of the marching band tradition in Japan. Today, Japanese secondary schools and universities pride themselves on the quality and excellence of their brass band ensembles and they are now the largest of their kind in the world.

After the Meiji Restoration in 1868, the architect Thomas Waters (1842–98) from Birr, County Offaly, was hired by the Meiji administration and commissioned to design the Imperial Japanese Mint in Osaka. This project was completed in 1870 and he was then invited to Tokyo where he was appointed foreign advisor to the government, with the title Surveyor General. Waters helped design the headquarters of the Japanese Imperial Army, a decorative bridge within the grounds of the Imperial Palace, and a branch of the Imperial Mint in the Ginza District of Tokyo. His most notable contribution to the surviving architecture of the Japanese capital is the three-story Georgian-style shopping promenade in Ginza, which was constructed under his supervision after a fire in 1872. Waters was assisted in this project by his brother Albert Waters and the English architect A.N. Shillingford. This promenade remains one of most fashionable areas of Tokyo to this day, and serves as an enduring symbol of Japanese internationalisation.

A notable person of her generation is Eileen Kato, née Lynn (1932– 2008) from Bangor Erris, County Mayo. An exceptional scholar, poet and translator, she was the wife of a Japanese career diplomat. Kato developed a profound understanding of Japanese *waka* poetry and translated many poems into English and Irish, as well as mastering their composition in English. She also translated Old and Middle Irish poetry into English. After the death of her husband in 1991, she was appointed as a special advisor (*goyogakari*) to the Emperor and Empress of Japan, who are patrons of the *waka* poem society. Eileen Kato held this prestigious position – the only non-Japanese to ever do so – until her retirement in 2007 at the age of seventy-five. Eileen Kato's shy and unassuming nature were qualities wholly compatible

Japanese Imperial Mint in Osaka (opened 1871), designed by Thomas Waters (1842–98) from Birr, County Offaly, Ireland. (*MeijiShowa/Alamy*)

with the Japanese spirit known as *Ki* (Ẽ). She typifies the influence that a number of Irish people have had at the very highest levels of Japanese society.

Not all the interconnectedness between Japan and Ireland involves such celebrity. There is the wonderful story of Sr Julia Canny who was born in Upper Kilbeg, County Galway, in 1893. The story goes that she had difficulty in finding a suitable husband and so she became a Catholic nun, only to find herself stationed in Hiroshima where she survived the atomic bomb of August 1945. She spent the rest of her life in Japan, until her death in 1987 in Tokyo well into her nineties.

Crossings is a celebration of the extensive and very rich connections that exist between Japan and Ireland. It is impossible to document these in their entirety; and this is not the purpose of our book. The articles, stories and poems in this book are a selection from a very wide and deep source. We hope that *Crossings* will encourage readers to continue to read, enquire, and travel into these unique, well-connected islands.

John FitzGerald
Richard Kelly
Claire Connolly
Hiroyasu Fujisawa

Diplomatic

外交

An Optimist's View of the Relationship Between Japan and Ireland

Mitsuru Kitano,
Ambassador of Japan to Ireland

Upward trends in our bilateral relationship

While the whole world, including Japan and Ireland, has been engaged in the uphill battle against Covid-19, the bilateral relationship between our countries is experiencing an upward trend. Despite the disruption caused by the pandemic since 2020, I am delighted to have witnessed a number of notable developments in our bilateral relations over the past few years.

Mutual interests in our respective regions have grown vigorously on both sides of the relationship. Ireland formulated its strategy towards the Asia-Pacific region in January 2020 as an important step for Global Ireland. For Ireland, Japan is a key country to enhance its presence in the region. Ireland House Tokyo, the Irish government's flagship project to upgrade the embassy and the representative office of several Irish governmental agencies, is a clear demonstration of the importance accorded to Japan. The EU also adopted the Strategy for Cooperation in the Indo-Pacific in 2021. Japan has long regarded the EU as an important partner with shared fundamental values such as democracy, respect for human rights and the rule of law.

Ireland's term on the United Nations Security Council from 2021 to 2022 evoked a strong interest within Japan's diplomatic machinery to collaborate with Ireland as a like-minded country with regard to many issues on the international agenda.

Such mutual interests have been substantiated by high-level exchanges. The most recent example is the video conference between Japan's Foreign Minister Yoshimasa Hayashi and his Irish counterpart Minister Simon Coveney TD in December 2021. The conversation covered a wide range of issues from bilateral relations and Japan–EU relations to cooperation in the Indo-Pacific region as well as regional and international affairs.

The Japan–EU Economic Partnership Agreement entered into force in February 2019, providing a solid legal framework for enhancing the bilateral economic relationship. While this set forth a wider framework between Japan and the EU as a whole, Ireland is a clear beneficiary of this new scheme.

The Rugby World Cup 2019 held in Japan was a great occasion for furthering people-to-people relations. Given that Ireland is an enthusiastic rugby-loving country, more than 20,000 people travelled from Ireland to Japan between September and November 2019. This figure is almost the same as the total number of Irish visitors to Japan in the previous year. When Japan's Brave Blossoms (the men's national rugby team) resumed their international activity in 2021 after the disruption caused by Covid-19, they came to the Aviva Stadium twice, in July and November, to play test matches against the Irish national team. Japan's Sakura Fifteen, meaning 'Cherry Blossom Fifteen' (the women's national team) also visited Dublin in November 2021 for a test match against the Irish women's fifteen.

In 2021, the Tokyo Olympic and Paralympic Games further heightened Irish interest in Japan. At the opening ceremony of the Olympic Games, the Irish team surprised the Japanese audience by formally bowing in Japanese style when they entered the stadium, showing deep respect to the host country. The scene immediately went viral on Japan's social media. Both the Irish Olympic and Paralympic teams were warmly welcomed in Japan.

Even in the restrictive environment necessitated by Covid-19, cultural and human exchanges have remained active. The annual Japanese Film Festival fascinated a large Irish audience at in-person screenings held around the country. Despite travel difficulties, the Japan Exchange and Teaching (JET) Programme continues to attract many enthusiastic young Irish people. The 'Edo in Colour' exhibition at the Chester Beatty Library from May to December 2021 was extremely successful. Dr Mitsuko Ohno, Professor Emeritus of Aichi Shukutoku University, received the Presidential Distinguished Service Award for her work translating and promoting Irish literature abroad. Dr Ohno translated the poetry of Nuala Ní Dhomhnaill into Japanese, introducing her work to Japanese literary circles. At the same time, Dr Declan Downey of University College Dublin and Ms Agnes Aylward of the Lafcadio Hearn Japanese Gardens in Tramore were conferred with the Commendation of Japan's Foreign Minister in 2020 and 2021 respectively for their contribution to mutual understanding between both countries.

The two countries also collaborated in response to Covid-19. Japan was one of the countries who supported Ireland in procuring essential equipment, such as ventilators, to deal with the pandemic.

Commonalities between Japan and Ireland

It is not by accident but with good reason that these positive evolutions have taken place. To begin with, Japan and Ireland have many things in common.

First, we have commonalities in geography. While the two countries are located at opposite ends of the Eurasian continent, separated by a distance of 10,000 kilometres, both Japan and Ireland are island countries surrounded by sea. Both share the unique characteristic of being located at the margins of a large continent on one side, and facing a great ocean on the other. This geographical situation is an important determinant in our strategic orientation. Because of this geographical trait, neither could ever be a land power like Prussia or Russia. We are both basically maritime countries, like Venice in medieval Italy, for whom trade and diplomacy are of vital importance. Both Japan and Ireland value being connected to the rest of the world. We like seeing the world safe and stable and are committed to the principle of openness.

Second, we have similarities in history. While one can cite various historical differences, such as the existence or absence of foreign rule, both Japan and Ireland have a long history in common. When Ireland joined the League of Nations in 1923, William T. Cosgrave, then President of the Executive Council of the Irish Free State, called Ireland 'one of the oldest and yet one of the youngest nations'. As for Japan, while the starting point of Japan as a nation is a subject of controversy, few

Japanese Minister Akira Ohye presenting his credentials at Áras an Uachtaráin, Dublin, 1957. (*Irish Photo Archive*)

would question that it has a history of thousands of years. Given that we both have a long history, we are equally proud of having our own unique national cultures, such as hurling and Gaelic football in Ireland and 'sumo' wrestling and other 'budo' martial arts in Japan in the field of sports, for instance. Having our own unique culture and long history allows us to respect each other's history and culture.

Further, both countries also have commonalities in economic history. Japan and Ireland both experienced rapid economic development, the bursting of a bubble economy and recovery from economic depression. Both of us went through these ups and downs within a relatively limited time span. Through these experiences, we have learned some shared lessons: 'Economic policy matters'; 'We have to adapt to the changing external environment'; 'It is important to invest for the future'; 'Human resources are essential.' Having scarce natural resources, we both believe in the importance of self-reliance.

Third, we share the same basic values. Needless to say, one can acknowledge differences in spiritual culture between Japan and Ireland. Christianity is an important part of Irish life, while the strong influence of Buddhism is observed in Japan's culture. However, if we think of such basic values as freedom, democracy, respect for human rights and the rule of law, we see just how alike we are. Both Ireland and Japan are strongly committed to these basic values. In dealing with the current international issues, sharing these values is becoming more and more precious.

Complementarity between Japan and Ireland

Other than these commonalities, there are ample reasons why bilateral links can be mutually beneficial due to complementarity.

For Ireland, Japan's importance partly rests on its location in the dynamic Asia-Pacific region. As is often pointed out, one of the most significant geopolitical trends in recent international relations is the rising prominence of the Asia-Pacific region in the world. In 1980, the share of the Asia-Pacific region's GDP globally, at current values, was approximately 20 per cent. According to the IMF, this is set to double to over 40 per cent by 2025. Amid the economic distress caused by Covid-19, it is the Asia-Pacific region that has shown the most rapid recovery. In world politics, more and more attention is being paid to the tensions between the US and China. Hotspots of their rivalry are in East Asia.

In the Asia-Pacific region, Japan holds considerable weight. It is the second biggest economy in the region, next to China. The share of Japan's GDP in the Asia-Pacific region as a whole is estimated to be around 16 per cent as of 2020. Japan is also home to such global corporations as Toyota, Honda, Sony, Nissan and Canon. Looking at the Foreign Direct Investment (FDI) flow to Ireland from the Asia-Pacific region, Japan is the biggest source of accumulated investment in fields such as aviation leasing, pharmaceuticals and finance as of 2019.

While economic size is important, values also matter. Shared values can be a good basis for having a long-term stable relationship and working together. From this perspective, Japan can be an ideal gateway for anyone planning an outreach to the dynamic Asia-Pacific region.

Another merit and benefit of engagement with Japan is related to the challenges we commonly confront. The global community is facing various challenges – the Covid-19 pandemic, global warming, terrorism and adaptation to new technology, to name a few. Among them, one serious challenge for many countries, particularly among advanced countries, is the issue of an ageing society. In this context, Japan can be considered a frontrunner in facing this challenge. Japan is one of the most aged societies in the world, with a median age of forty-eight, while the equivalent in Ireland is thirty-eight. The median age is the age we are given when we divide a population into two groups of the same size, namely half the people younger than a certain age and half older. It is a single index that summarises the age distribution of a population.

As is well known, an ageing population presents various difficult questions for society to deal with. How to finance the skyrocketing cost of pensions and medical care for the aged population? How to come up with much-needed human resources who can provide care services to the elderly? How to make use of the vitality of the retired population? The reason why I mention Japan as a 'frontrunner' is that Japan is tackling these issues ahead of other countries.

In 1990, thirty years ago, Japan's median age was thirty-seven, almost the same as that of Ireland now. At that time, Ireland's median age was even younger – only twenty-eight. Therefore, Ireland might follow in Japan's footsteps and experience the same kind of social evolution, although the speed of such change is difficult to predict at this stage.

Japan has not always been successful in dealing with these challenges, and it is a process of trial and error. However, it is certain that Japan can share with Ireland lessons learned from its own experience as a 'frontrunner in facing this challenge'.

On the other hand, there is much that Japan can learn from Ireland. First on the list is the entrepreneurial spirit. Irish people are inclined to have a frontier spirit and be disposed to start new things. Ireland is a country with tens of millions of people of Irish descent around the world. Those who left the country included those who had a vigorous frontier spirit to pave a new way forward, while many were obliged to choose that option. Ireland is now one of the most active countries for start-ups, aided by this kind of frontier spirit. It is one of the sources of the dynamism of the Irish economy. Now that the world is changing rapidly both economically and socially, creating new business is becoming more and more important. While Japan's economy is mature and large in size, the Irish economy is vibrant and dynamic. My view is that this vigorous entrepreneurial spirit is one of the things Japan badly needs. In Japan, we have the Japan External Trade Organization (JETRO), a semi-governmental organisation promoting business. One of JETRO's priority areas is

Ireland's leader, Taoiseach Enda Kenny (left) with his Japanese counterpart Shinzo Abe in Tokyo, 2013. (*Reuters/Yoshikazu Tsuno/Pool*)

to support innovation start-ups. I am convinced that the entrepreneurial spirit is one of the things Ireland can offer to Japan.

Another thing Ireland can offer to Japan is an attitude of tolerance towards diversity. In my understanding, Irish people's open-mindedness towards diversity is also related to the experiences of their compatriots who have emigrated to other countries, particularly in the nineteenth century during the time of the Great Famine. Their exposure to different social environments and cultures is no doubt one of the elements forming the background to this openness. In this respect, much has changed in Irish society in the past decades. It has moved to embrace differences and diversity, leaving behind an era when a certain way of thinking dominated the people's way of life. It is illustrative to note that in Ireland, the process of embracing diversity has overlapped with the process of the economy gaining dynamism. In order to advance innovation or creativity, open-mindedness towards embracing differences is important. In my view, this is another example of what Ireland can offer to Japan.

An optimist's view

In view of the commonalities and complementarities between Japan and Ireland, I am optimistic about our bilateral relationship.

In the recent past, there have been several years which have pushed bilateral ties forward to a new height. This was the case in 2013 when there were reciprocal visits by then Prime Minister Shinzo Abe and Taoiseach Enda Kenny. A framework document entitled a 'Partnership for Innovation and Growth' was issued in the form of a Joint Declaration by the two leaders in December of that year. The year 2017 was another remarkable time when the two countries celebrated the sixtieth anniversary of diplomatic relations with reciprocal visits by then Japanese Foreign Minister Fumio Kishida and Irish Foreign Minister Charles Flanagan TD.

Given our common interests and mutual benefit, I am certain we will have more opportunities that will bring our relations to an even higher level in the near future. The year 2022 marks the sixty-fifth anniversary of our diplomatic relations and, in years to come, I would not be surprised to look back on 2022 as another such year of opportunity.

Ireland and My Diplomatic Life: An essay on the occasion of the sixtieth anniversary of the establishment of diplomatic relations between Japan and Ireland

Keiichi Hayashi
former Ambassador of Japan to Ireland

My tenure as Japanese Ambassador to Ireland was not long. Although lasting for just two years and four months between 2005 and 2008, it turned out to be one of the most memorable periods in my diplomatic career. I even wrote a book on the country after completing my ambassadorship, the first book ever published by me. I am often asked by my friends why I ended up writing that book. This is a pertinent question. There were already many good books on various aspects of Irish culture and a few excellent ones on Ireland, including those written by the famous writer Ryotaro Shiba and by Ambassador Yuzo Hatano. They were and still are classics, and it was not my intention to compete with them. However, to put it simply, my experience in Ireland had been so pleasant that I was very keen to share with Japanese readers the pleasure of getting to know Ireland and its people more fully. In order to give briefings to visitors from Japan, I had collected a number of interesting stories related to Irish history and the Irish diaspora, which I included in the book. As it turned out, the book sold more than 10,000 copies and now boasts an electronic version. The fact is that most Japanese people simply do not know much about Ireland, nor about the Irish people. Worse, they cannot make a clear distinction between the United Kingdom and Ireland. So, they are quite intrigued when they read about the two countries' shared history of repression and resistance – a history which, ironically and tragically, led to numerous Irish emigrants making their way to the Americas and Oceania, where their many descendants prosper today.

Soon after I completed my diplomatic career in June 2016, I received a letter from HE Mari Miyoshi, then the Japanese Ambassador to Ireland, informing me of plans for the celebration of the sixtieth anniversary of the establishment of diplomatic relations between Japan and Ireland. While I was still Japanese Ambassador to the UK, she visited me in London to seek my advice concerning that initiative because a decade previously while in Ireland I had organised a series of events to mark the fiftieth anniversary. I found it a great honour that she had taken the time to visit me ten years after the earlier celebration, and I offered any advice I could. At the end of January I had a chance to speak with Foreign Minister Kishida, who was very pleased and proud to tell me that the opening ceremony of the year-long programme of events had been successfully held on the 10 January in the presence of himself and his Irish counterpart. It was the first visit by a Japanese foreign minister in twenty-six years. A historic event, indeed. It is, therefore, a great honour and pleasure for me to have been asked to contribute to the celebration an essay on my relationship with Ireland.

One can safely say that former ambassadors rarely speak ill of the countries where they have served. But then again, not all ambassadors would want to write books, as they recall their postings with different degrees of fondness. In my case, I was so enthusiastic, and my memories of Ireland were so vivid, that it seems as if the book had written itself. The background to my initial contact with Ireland, however, was scarcely idyllic – an epithet often associated with the country dubbed the Emerald Isle. What, then, was my first encounter with Ireland? It started with a bomb. Yes, a real bomb.

Japanese Ambassador Keiichi Hayashi prepares to read from James Joyce's Ulysses on Bloomsday at the James Joyce Centre, Dublin, 16 June 2007. (*Niall Carson, PA Images/Alamy*)

No, I am not old enough to have been involved in the Easter Rising; nor was I so unlucky as to be in Brighton in October 1984. It happened in February 1996, when I had just taken up my post as Political Counsellor of the Japanese Embassy in London. Only a few days after my arrival, the fragile ceasefire came to a close and an IRA bomb went off at Canary Wharf in East London, causing hundreds of casualties. It was my urgent task to follow what was happening and to analyse what was likely to ensue, as there were tens of thousands of Japanese nationals living in or visiting the UK. As it turned out, more bombs would follow. But I was not prepared. After taking up the post, I was supposed to call on my British counterparts, including those in charge of the Irish question, within weeks, but I had met nobody yet. I had only a few telephone numbers provided by my predecessor. After some frantic attempts, I managed to make myself known to a relevant official. In fact, he had just moved from the Northern Ireland Office to a new assignment – fortunately to a closely related job in the Intergovernmental Conference's Secretariat in Northern Ireland – and kindly provided me with useful information and guidance.

In the few days that followed, I was bombarded with queries from Tokyo and from a number of Japanese businessmen based in the UK, who naturally were worried about the resumption of violence in the Northern Ireland conflict. One was the local representative of the biggest Japanese carmaker, which I do not have to name. His problem was that the chairman of his parent company was coming to the UK to attend a UK–Japan 2000 Group meeting, an annual bilateral gathering of leading businessmen, academics and politicians to give advice to the prime ministers of the two countries. He was especially worried that the forthcoming meeting that year was to take place in Northern Ireland for the first time in the group's history, in just about a month's time. The British government had pushed for this choice of location in order to attract Japanese investment there so that more local jobs might be created, which would in turn contribute to easing political tensions in the deeply divided region.

The desperate local representative visited me and asked for my guarantee of personal security for his Japanese VIP visitor, adding that without my words of reassurance he would have to recommend that his chairman not come. The latter happened to be not only the CEO of a major car manufacturing company but also the chairman of the Japanese Federation of Economic Organisations, the most influential business association in Japan. From my perspective, the cancellation of his participation in the wake of an IRA bombing would have been a disaster with regard to the success of the conference itself and to our relationship with the British government because it would have been seen as succumbing to the threat of terrorism. But at the same time it was obvious that I was in no position to guarantee his safety after the IRA's declaration of the end of the ceasefire. Suddenly, I found myself, a novice political counsellor at the Japanese Embassy in London, caught in the middle of the Irish question.

After spending some agonising days hoping in vain that somehow the IRA would change their mind and restore the ceasefire, I came up with the idea of telling the businessman that, while neither I nor for that matter anybody else in the Japanese government would be able to provide a guarantee of safety, I could give my assurance that neither he nor his fellow Japanese would be 'targeted' by IRA terrorists. The carmaker's representative, who must have been in an equally difficult position himself, gratefully took my words as the necessary guarantee. Several weeks later the chairman, accompanied by his wife, came to visit Limavady near Londonderry/Derry for a three-day conference and made a tour of the Giant's Causeway and Belfast, to the great delight of the Northern Ireland Secretary, as well as the other participants of the group, including myself. Two years later, the Good Friday Agreement was reached in Belfast, constituting the very foundation of the process that finally brought peace and stability to the region. However, it took nine more years and many courageous decisions on both the nationalist and the Unionist sides for the agreement to be fully implemented in 2007.

By then I had become Ambassador to Ireland. It was a rather strange feeling to be invited to the Sinn Féin Ard Fheis held in Dublin, where I chatted with Messrs Gerry Adams and Martin McGuinness. When I explained how I had been personally affected by the Canary Wharf bombing, Martin showed evident dismay, not knowing what to say: my remark was the last thing he would have expected from a Japanese ambassador. Of course, my intention was not to embarrass him but to emphasise how much they had achieved. I was truly moved to see the brave and noble decision they and the Unionists had made for their posterity's enduring safety. My involvement in the Northern Ireland peace process seemed to have come full circle when I saw during my ambassadorship (although only on TV) the historic state visit by HM the Queen to Ireland in 2011, the first ever visit by a British monarch since Irish independence.

Subsequently, Prime Minister David Cameron decided that the 2013 G8 Summit, to be hosted by the UK, would be held at Lough Erne, County Fermanagh, in Northern Ireland for the first time. In preparation for Prime Minister Abe's visit on this occasion, which would also be the first visit to Northern Ireland by any Japanese prime minister, I went to Belfast for a 'recce' and to call on the leaders of the Northern Ireland Executive. Normally when an ambassador pays an official call, he or she goes alone or with an embassy aide, but this time I was accompanied by a delegation from the Japanese business community in the UK. I had asked them to come with me because I knew, based on the experience of my first encounter with the Irish question, that what Northern Ireland wanted most from Japan was greater direct investment in business in order to create jobs. But because of the lingering memory of the Troubles and the occasional terrorist acts perpetrated by small splinter groups, major companies based in London almost automatically excluded Northern Ireland from their business plans. Very few Japanese businessmen had bothered to visit the region. I had spoken to the major company executives based in London and found that none of the current leaders of the Japanese Chamber of Commerce and Industry had ever been to Northern Ireland. In the end seven businessmen, each representing the European headquarters of his company, in such diverse areas as trade, banking/financing, shipping, telecommunications and real estate volunteered to come with me. When I called on First Minister Peter Robinson and Deputy First Minister Martin McGuinness of the Northern Ireland Executive, these businessmen joined me and were introduced to them as the 'Seven Samurai' who had come here, totally unarmed, to see firsthand the business potential of the region and to report back to Tokyo. Moreover, there were follow-up business/investment events in the ensuing months, including the first minister and deputy first minister's historic visit to Japan.

During the G8 Summit in June that year, some members of the Japanese delegation were even accommodated in a hotel south of the border, fully appreciating the free movement without any immigration/customs checks, a tangible result of the peace process. Following the summit meeting, Prime Minister Abe stayed overnight in Belfast to carry out a bilateral visit to Northern Ireland, the only one among the G8 Summit foreign leaders to do so. He met with the political leaders together with a number of senior Japanese business executives. Furthermore, Mr Abe flew from there to Dublin – the first visit to Ireland by any Japanese prime minister – before flying to London to give a major speech on economic policy at the Guildhall. Accordingly, I saw him off at Belfast Airport and later welcomed him at London Heathrow. Just before his departure from Belfast I passed a green necktie with a shamrock design to the PM's private secretary, which Mr Abe wore on arrival in Dublin to show his respect for the country. What I had in mind was HM the Queen wearing a green dress on her arrival for the historic state visit there.

It was a moving sequence of events for me, all the more so because I had previously endeavoured to bring another Japanese prime minister to Ireland. After my stint as Ambassador in Dublin, I had been appointed by Prime Minister Taro Aso as Assistant Chief Cabinet Secretary in charge of foreign affairs in September 2008. The most pressing issue then was how to address the world economic crisis triggered by the collapse of Lehman Brothers, and the PM was to attend the G20 London Summit hosted by Prime Minister Gordon Brown at the beginning of April 2009. I managed to persuade PM Aso to take this opportunity to become the first Japanese prime minister to pay a visit to Ireland. The plan was to attend the London Summit and to move on to Ireland, making use of the weekend. The economic summit went smoothly, and we were all set to fly to Dublin, when there was a horrible intervention by North Korea. They announced their provocative plan to launch ballistic missiles over Japan at or after the weekend during which Mr Aso was to visit Ireland. Prudently, but to my great agony, the prime minister decided to fly back to Japan immediately after the G20 Summit, cancelling the Irish visit. The Irish government was obviously as disappointed as I was at this last-minute turn of events, but they understood the decision and took it in their stride. So from my perspective Mr Abe's visit four years later fulfilled, at long last, my frustrated hopes. While the coordination in Ireland was in the secure hands of my successor's successor, Ambassador Atsumi, I felt as if I were somehow associated with the historic visit.

I could enumerate all the pleasant moments I had during my ambassadorship, such as organising fifty cultural and other events to commemorate the fiftieth anniversary, with 'three nos': no extra budget, no extra human resources, no preparation time. These were made possible only by the goodwill and friendship extended by my Irish friends, as well as Japanese supporters who, like me, had simply fallen in love with Ireland and the Irish people. But let me refer to a theme which is very close to my heart as a diplomat. It is the issue of 'reconciliation'.

During my ambassadorship in Dublin between 2005 and 2008, I was happy to observe the historic implementation of the Northern Ireland Peace Process, which had started during my earlier assignment in London. Moreover, I was introduced to the Glencree Centre for Peace and Reconciliation in the Wicklow Mountains. The centre, among its other commitments, aims to apply the experience of overcoming the Troubles as a source of inspiration in order to help bring about reconciliation amidst bitter conflicts in various parts of the world. I was impressed with the Irish willingness to share their difficult experience with others for this noble purpose. Indeed, I learned to view the Northern Ireland Peace Process from the perspective of reconciliation. I was thus gratified to see some Japan-related companies willing to make substantial donations to the centre during my ambassadorship.

I also came to learn about the equally difficult and delicate issue of reconciliation among the Irish people themselves in the context of the Irish participation in the First World War. I was impressed with the brave call of President Mary McAleese in this context for a review of the official neglect or dismissal as traitors of those who had fought on the British side.

Later, when as Ambassador to the UK I took the Seven Samurai on that memorable trip to Belfast, we visited Stormont, where I took them to the garden to see the Statue of Reconciliation, which is a replica of the one in Coventry. The city of Coventry is a symbol of peace and friendship between the UK and Germany because it shared with Dresden the tragedy of indiscriminate civilian bombings. Another replica has been given to Hiroshima for obvious reasons. I explained to the members of the delegation the importance of the reconciliation that has been reached through the prolonged, excruciating process on both sides in order to overcome entrenched hatred and enmity and establish peace and friendship. Indeed, HM The Queen's state visit to Ireland in 2011 was thanks to the strenuous efforts mounted by both sides and was in itself a culminating act of reconciliation in the British–Irish relationship.

As a Japanese diplomat I have been given a rare opportunity to serve in both the UK and in Ireland, not concurrently but separately. I have had the chance to see the two countries from both sides of the Irish Sea and, particularly, to view the unfolding of the entire 1998 Belfast Agreement peace process from the beginning to its fruition. What I have observed has been informed by the spirit of reconciliation, something I learned to treasure through my diplomatic life, especially in relation to Ireland and the Irish question.

Note

I started my diplomatic career in Singapore in 1977. Thirty-two years after the Second World War, strong feelings against the Japanese occupation of the then-British colony were still smoldering.

Ireland/Japan Relations Since 2017: Looking ahead to a bright future together

Paul Kavanagh,
Ambassador of Ireland to Japan

Summary

As we emerge from the global and localised disruptions of the Covid-19 pandemic, the timing is perfect in 2022 to deepen Ireland/Japan relations and bring exchanges to the cusp of a new period of expansion. The enormous promise of the period 2017–19 was followed by worldwide Covid-19-related disruptions. But underneath, the strong fundaments of Ireland's rich ties with Japan have continued powerfully and a further upward trajectory is now in prospect. Trade, investment, cultural and people-to-people ties between the two countries should be primed to take off. A showcase, state-of-the-art new Ireland House in Tokyo will, from 2024, provide a superb platform for projecting all that innovative, creative Ireland has to offer to a land of ancient heritage and culture and the third largest economy in the world – which already, by some distance, gives Ireland its largest trade surplus in the Asia/Pacific region. High-level governmental visits are back on the horizon and the two administrations have many shared views on how, together, we can build a new era of higher ambition and delivery in bilateral ties. Ireland's innovative and digitalised economy is an ideally compatible partner for Japan's own advanced economy. Ireland/Japan relations are strengthened by Ireland's committed membership of the European Union and by the EU's commitment to building a free and open Indo-Pacific in an era where our shared values and attachment to democracy, human rights and the rule of law are more crucial than ever. Having a genuine mutual respect and affection, the Irish and Japanese have a great opportunity going forward to build a bright future together. With the smarts and commitment of the splendid Irish community in Japan also in play, it may even be 'a safe bet' for two countries among whose many close partnerships is that between their respective world-class thoroughbred industries.

Introduction

I am grateful to the distinguished editors of this volume for inviting me to contribute, from the perspective of spring 2022, a 'post script' of sorts to this truly extraordinary compendium of writing that celebrates sixty years and more of diplomatic relations between Ireland and Japan, since their establishment in 1957. My distinguished point of contact, Professor Richard Kelly of Kindai University in Kansai and indeed Cork University Press have been lenient in accepting my piece even as they reached out to activate the print run!

It is a privilege to be read alongside so many distinguished contributors in a volume that features not least hitherto unpublished writing of two Nobel laureates for literature, one Irish, the other Japanese.

This book will, I believe, endure the passage of time as an elegant compendium on Ireland/Japan relations, but also as a work of more general relevance to the continuing journey and development of modern Ireland and of her place in the world. The latter dimension no doubt plays into the wider commemoration of the centenary of the establishment of the Irish state in independence in 1922.

It was in the early autumn of 2018 when I took up my current assignment as Ireland's Ambassador to Japan. I had previously served as Ireland's Ambassador to the United Nations in both New York and Geneva, as Ambassador to France, China, to several countries in The Gulf and at the European Union in Brussels. In the late 1990s, towards the conclusion of a fifteen-year stint with the United Nations Organisation, including nine years in the Cabinet of the Secretary-General, I had spent two years as Director of the UN Secretariat's Office in Tokyo.

It is now twenty-five years since I first came to work in Japan, in 1996. A great deal has happened in the meantime, in this country, in Ireland and on the global and regional canvas, sufficient to fill at least one entire volume. For now, however, allow me to focus on what has transpired in regard to Ireland/Japan relations and exchanges in the half-decade since the sixtieth anniversary in 2017 – and on the strong prospects for their renewed expansion and development in the future.

The Effects of the Global Covid-19 Pandemic

The Covid-19 pandemic that exploded on the world in early 2020 has caused death and disruption on a mass scale. Even if Ireland and Japan managed to avoid the worst, catastrophic effects of the virus, which were experienced by numerous other countries, both countries have nonetheless been seriously affected. They have been obliged to implement intrusive anti-Covid-19 measures. Such restrictive measures greatly impacted society and the economy in each country – as well as the conduct of relations and exchanges between them.

For extended periods during the past two years it has not been possible to undertake bilateral visits at a political level, despite the best of intentions in each capital. Such governmental and parliamentary visits are of vital importance in the regular conduct and development of ties between countries. They serve to crystallise progress achieved over time in building exchanges, while providing a platform from which to launch further advances going forward. They require national administrations, economic agencies as well as business and cultural actors to focus intensively, beyond the normal pattern, on the bilateral relationship between the two countries, and on their own particular place in this matrix. We have missed them!

By the same token, because of anti-Covid-19 restrictive measures, which have affected international travel, it has not been possible generally for business people and stakeholders in cultural and other spaces to undertake in these past two years anything like a normal pattern of visits in either direction between Ireland and Japan.

It is true that new technologies have allowed for interactions to be continued virtually, not least between leading ministers of the governments of Ireland and Japan. Ireland's Foreign Minister Simon Coveney TD has engaged several times virtually and once in-person during the past two years with successive Japanese counterparts Even after the pandemic is more fully mastered across the world, business in the coming years will likely continue to be undertaken on a hybrid basis.

Nonetheless, bilateral interactions between government ministers generally produce optimal outcomes when they are undertaken in person. Furthermore, our own export sector tells us consistently that while existing business relationships with Japanese partners have been largely sustained at long distance during the pandemic, it has proven to be a great challenge in the circumstances to establish new business ties in Japan – a country where personal relations and mutual trust are indispensable prerequisites for doing meaningful business together.

To be sure, spring 2022 appears to be marked by a widespread, if not yet universal, abatement in the Omicron variant of the Covid-19 virus. Governments around the world, including in Ireland and to some extent in Japan, are consequently easing the extensive body of anti-Covid-19 restrictive measures which have been in place. As a result, at time of writing (late February 2022), we expect before long to see a resumption of bilateral visits between Ireland and Japan – in the political space and also in business, cultural, people-to-people and other domains.

There is therefore a degree of excitement in the air as Ireland and Japan prepare once again to accelerate the enlargement of their exchanges with each other. This will build upon and exploit the huge promise for future ties that was showcased in 2017 during the extraordinary, year-long observance of sixty years of our diplomatic relations; and in 2019 in the orbit of a remarkable Rugby World Cup tournament that was hosted so brilliantly by Japan.

Rugby World Cup, 2019

Many important benefits flowed from Rugby World Cup 2019 into wider relations and exchanges between Ireland and Japan. These heralded much promise for the expansion of our ties in the coming period. The tournament proper extended over some six weeks, from late September through early November of that year. But it was on people's minds and on their screens in this country for much longer than that.

Rugby World Cup, Japan, 2019:
Japan versus Ireland in Shizuoka.
(*Elizabeth Cullen/Alamy*)

Some 22,000 Irish citizens travelled to Japan for the tournament itself. They, as well as our national team and delegation, were received over an extended period with warmth and efficiency by the Japanese hosts and people. In turn, they left a positive and widely appreciated impression behind them in Japan. They brought home to Ireland equally positive tales of modern Japan, tales that warmed many subsequent winter evenings.

Now, the official Team Ireland in Japan comprises the embassy in Tokyo as well as strong in-country offices of IDA Ireland, Enterprise Ireland, Bord Bia and, by extension, Tourism Ireland – as well as the Ireland Japan Chamber of Commerce (IJCC). In fact, the dynamic and innovative IJCC is the sole Irish business chamber in the world to be an *ex officio* member of the local, official Team Ireland.

These Irish partners in Japan mounted an extensive promotional campaign across the country to coincide with the Rugby World Cup tournament. This campaign took advantage of the fact that, going into the tournament, Ireland was already prominent in the public eye in Japan – as the top-ranked national rugby team in the world. In addition, all eyes in Japan were on Ireland since our national team would play the very well prepared hosts (the Brave Blossoms) early in the competition, at a time when the ambitions of each side remained intact. At the time it was played, on 28 September 2019 in Fukuroi City, the Ireland–Japan match ('The Shizuoka Shock', as Ireland's friends, Governor Kawakatsu and Mayor Harada have termed it) was the most viewed sporting event of the year on TV in Japan.

To capitalise on this extraordinary exposure, Team Ireland, in their mainly online promotional campaign in Japan, presented Global Ireland – a committed member of the European Union and its single market of some 450 million people – as an ideal place for Japanese people to do business, to invest, research and study in and to visit. Illustrative of this campaign is the four-minute bilingual video that was disseminated by the Department of Foreign Affairs as part of the government's Global Ireland Strategy. This and other posts were seen online many millions of times. Tourism Ireland in particular provided seed funding for market research concerning Ireland among target demographic cohorts and in selected geographical areas. The outcome of this research undertaken across Japan informed content of the promotional campaign.

Also in this fertile setting, but before the tournament began: a major trade mission to Japan, organised by Enterprise Ireland and IDA Ireland, was led by the then minister for enterprise, trade and employment, Heather Humphreys, TD. Similarly, a significant food and agriculture trade mission, organised by Bord Bia, was led by then minister for agriculture, food and the marine, Michael Creed, TD. During the competition, a tourism, transport and sport mission was led by then Minister Shane Ross, TD.

Substantive benefit to Ireland/Japan ties flowed from each one of these sustained, structured engagements with and in Japan. The many participating Irish companies drew benefit from their involvement. To the wider accompaniment of numerous high-profile Irish and collaborative cultural performances in Japan, a platform was laid, not least for the further exploration and development of Japanese tourism into Ireland and, ultimately, of air connectivity between the two countries.

The participation of the cathaoirleach of Seanad Éireann, Denis O'Donovan, in the ceremonies surrounding the enthronement of His Majesty Emperor Naruhito in October 2019, as well as his engagement with the then prime minister and Diet leaders in Japan represented a further important moment in our bilateral ties. In addition, significant visits to Japan by a senior delegation of female members of Oireachtas Éireann and by a wider group of Irish parliamentarians served in the period to further strengthen Ireland/Japan ties.

Unfortunately, after the Covid-19 pandemic broke upon the world in early 2020, it had a progressively damaging effect on the previously extremely bright prospects for accelerated progress in Ireland/Japan exchanges, including in the cultural sphere, which had been so apparent in 2019. Suffice to say that the collapse in international travel and tourism worldwide impacted severely on the plans that had been laid by Tourism Ireland and the wider Team Ireland to advance towards the establishment, in the medium term, of a direct, commercial air connection between the two countries.

Strength And Resilience In Ireland/Japan Exchanges

Despite all of these disruptions, however, the underlying trend in Ireland/Japan ties has long been, and continues to be, strongly upward. That our two countries share common values is well understood and widely appreciated. Let me revert to these shared values a little further along.

Economic Compatibilities

On the economic side, by the time of the Covid-19 pandemic, both Ireland and Japan had long put behind them the worst macroeconomic effects of the global financial crisis. Japan had avoided severe 'peaks and valleys' in its economic performance. Its economic growth through the period had been steady, more measured than robust. Ireland on the other hand had incurred severe setbacks during the crisis a decade ago, only to bounce back in far fewer years than had been anticipated. By the time the Covid-19 pandemic struck, Ireland was again approaching full employment, with her national accounts in surplus and her levels of economic growth consistently among the strongest in the European Union.

As the years passed, it became ever more apparent that the innovative and technology-driven economies of Ireland and Japan are highly compatible. This compatibility has held up through the successive premierships of Abe Shinzo, Suga Yoshihide and latterly Kishida Fumio. Ireland – the innovation island with a science-based and high-end service economy – is an ideal partner for Japan as this country develops a 'new form of capitalism'.

Moreover, in 2020 the European Commission ranked Ireland number one in the EU for the integration of digitalisation into business. Irish companies, universities, research centres and other actors are in turn ideal partners for Japanese counterparts as Japan prioritises her own national strategy of digitalisation. Moreover, Ireland's specialisation in green and sustainable technologies, services and processes provide a further area where close and fruitful partnerships can be developed with Japan's administration, institutions and corporations. In fact, Ireland's National Digital Strategy, that was published by the government in February 2022, specifically stresses that Ireland's green and digital ambitions will complement and reinforce each other.

Of course, Ireland's bilateral ties with Japan are greatly strengthened by the fact that both countries are party to the EU/Japan Economic Partnership Agreement (EPA) which entered into force in February 2019 as the largest trade agreement in the world. Many of the most front-loaded of the trade benefits of the EPA have already helped to increase exports of food and drinks, including such exports from Ireland to Japan.

The EU/Japan EPA is a secure agreement, in the elaboration and conclusion of which Ireland's then EU commissioner for agriculture played a seminal part. Japan and the EU, both as a matter of law and of entrenched political principle, abide by their international treaty obligations. Japan, its government and its economic stakeholders can rest assured that the stability of the EPA is both robust and enduring.

The EPA – alongside the EU/Japan Strategic Partnership Agreement (SPA) – underpins and reinforces further agreements which have been reached at successive, annual summits between the European Union and Japan in recent years, for example in regard to digitalisation, the green economy, connectivity, scientific research and so forth.

Ireland/Japan Trade

In consequence of these and other factors, the value of trade between Ireland and Japan is huge in scale and continues to grow strongly, the deleterious effects of the Covid-19 pandemic notwithstanding.

According to official Irish statistics from CSO.ie, total two-way trade between Ireland and Japan, in goods and services combined, in the calendar year 2019 reached some €14.15 billion, up 12.5 per cent on a year earlier. This large total was the equivalent of 2.5 times Sweden/Japan trade and fully 40 per cent of UK/Japan trade in 2019.

Within this total, Ireland's trade surplus with Japan in 2019 was approximately €8.3 billion. Indeed, once again in 2019, Japan provided Ireland with her largest trade surplus bar none in the Asia/Pacific region. Services exports were the main component.

By 2020, CSO.ie has indicated, total two-way trade between Ireland and Japan, in goods and services combined, had grown to €15.9 billion, once again up some 12.5 per cent on the preceding year. Ireland's trade surplus with Japan meanwhile increased in 2020 to €9.9 billion, once again our largest surplus in the Asia/Pacific region.

Over the two-year period 2019/2020, Ireland's total trade surplus with Japan (goods and services combined) grew by some 19 per cent, from €8.3 to €9.9 billion. By way of comparison, Ireland's trade surplus with China in 2020 was €6.3 billion.

Taking a longer, three-year period (2018–2020), two-way total trade between Ireland and Japan (goods and services combined) grew by 26.6 per cent. In the same period, Ireland's total trade surplus with Japan increased by some 45.5 per cent.

Trade in services, especially exports from the multinational sector in Ireland was once again the largest component. This broad sector includes some 1,500 corporations and employs about 400,000 people in skilled positions in Ireland.

As to indigenous Irish companies, which typically are supported by Enterprise Ireland, those with a representation in Japan now total more than sixty. Meanwhile, over 150 Irish companies export regularly to this country. Their exports grew by some 6.7 per cent in 2019 and by almost 3 per cent in 2020. To have achieved such growth in the face of Covid-19's disruptions represents a significant achievement on the part of these innovative and hard-working companies and their Japanese partners.

In respect of Ireland's food and drinks exports to Japan, with the support of Bord Bia (the Irish Food Board) these grew by *c.*20 per cent in value in calendar 2021, year-on-year. This was a remarkable performance when it is considered that, globally, Irish food and drinks exports in 2021 were a very creditable 2 per cent above their level in 2019, the pre-pandemic year. In Japan, their total value of approximately €180 million breaks down into three more or less equal parts: approximately €60 million in dairy, €60 million in pork and €60 million equally divided between beef, fish and beverages.

Ireland's strong export performance in Japan in the food and drinks sector benefits from the intensive activities of the Bord Bia office and of our embassy's agricultural attaché in Tokyo. Both presences were established in 2019, the year when the EU/Japan Economic Partnership Agreement came into effect. All of these factors coming together support Ireland's world-leading food sector. Our country has a population of some 5 million, but sustainably produces sufficient highest-quality food to meet the needs of about 40 million.

Two-way Investment Flows

When it comes to foreign direct investment (FDI), IDA Ireland indicates that there are about eighty Japanese corporations located in Ireland, of which some thirty-five are IDA client investment partners. These tend to be concentrated in IDA's priority target sectors of Information and Communication Technologies (ICT), Digital and Life Sciences as well as Financial Services. More than 6,000 people are now employed in Ireland by Japanese investment corporations. In recent years Japan has been the largest source of inward FDI investment into Ireland from the Asia/Pacific region, in terms of jobs created.

Growth in the Japanese investment presence in Ireland has been steady and assured over a number of years. Japanese corporates appreciate Ireland's political, economic, financial and business environment stability. They value the strong availability of a highly qualified, innovative, multilingual and multicultural work force. Stability in Ireland's government policies, including in regard to taxation, also has an assuring effect, as does Ireland's committed membership of the European Union and its single market as well as the Eurozone Single Currency Area.

Among the leading Japanese corporations that have made Ireland their home in Europe are Recruit, Alps Electric and Fujitsu in the ICT space, Takeda, Astellas and Nipro in Life Sciences and SMBT, SMBC, JRI and Mitsubishi companies in the Financial Services sector. Meanwhile, the number of people who work in high-quality jobs with innovative Irish companies in Japan now comfortably exceeds 2,000. These are mainly in the Life Sciences and Financial/Fintech sectors.

As with other countries, Ireland's investment profile with Japan is very much a two-way street. This is a result of Ireland's continuous and cumulative economic and technological development within the European Union over the past half-century.

Ireland/Japan Cultural Ties

Elsewhere in this volume, there are eloquent and moving accounts of the range and depth of the myriad connections between our two countries in the fields of literature, music, dance, the performing arts more broadly, film and so forth. I may perhaps be permitted to highlight just a few of these.

In the centenary year of the publication of James Joyce's *Ulysses*, it is fitting to salute the active and longstanding Joyce Society in Japan, which will mark the occasion as well as the annual 'Bloomsday'. By the same token, the Yeats Society of Japan is a venerable partner in hailing our first Nobel Laureate's oeuvre and his close literary ties with Japan. He brought the influence of this country's *Noh* theatre to bear on the establishment of the world's first national theatre, the Abbey in Dublin. Who could not recall and be affected by the seminal opening lines of his poem 'In Memory of Eva Gore-Booth and Con Markiewicz'?

> The light of evening, Lisadell.
> Great windows open to the south,
> Two girls in silk kimonos, both
> Beautiful, one a gazelle.

Seamus Heaney was a frequent visitor to Japan. He prized his interaction with her literature and great contemporary writers. He and his wife Marie famously received Their Majesties the Emperor and Empress in their home in County Wicklow. We look forward here to the ceremony in 2022 that will mark the inaugural Heaney Award for promoting literary ties between Ireland and Japan. With the greatly appreciated support of the late poet's family and estate, our embassy in Tokyo, along with IASIL, will treasure the occasion and the collaboration. IASIL is the International Association for the Study of Irish Literature, which has chapters all around the world. It is as remarkable as it is welcome that the chapter in Japan is the largest in the world – bigger even than that in Ireland itself. What a statement of cultural interaction this is!

A special place in bilateral cultural ties is reserved for the extraordinary bridge-builder, translator and author in his own right, Lafcadio Hearn, also known as Koizumi Yakumo. In a century of remarkable personal journeys, his was exceptional. We are proud of his legacy that brought the culture of pre-Meiji Japan to world readerships through the medium, principally, of the English language. He did so with a delicate and sympathetic pen.

We are gratified by the many partnerships that we maintain for the continuation of Hearn's legacy, not least with his great grandson, Bon Koizumi and his wife Shoko at the Hearn Memorial Museum in Matsue, the author's first home in Japan; as well as at the Hearn Memorial Gardens in Tramore, County Waterford, in Ireland. This exceptional facility is developing very impressively under the direction and curatorship of Agnes Aylward. A tree was planted there in the anniversary year, 2017, by Her Imperial Highness, Princess Takamado, a true and loyal friend of Ireland.

All of these literary ties, and others too, have been well tended and maintained these many years. Many Irish and Japanese people were overjoyed when the president of Ireland named Professor Ohno Mitsuko as recipient for 2020 of the Presidential Distinguished Service Award. He was recognising her many and remarkable achievements over the decades in bringing our two countries closer together in the field of literature, and culture and the arts more widely. If ever such an award was well deserved, it was surely this one!

In the field of music, in particular that of Irish traditional music, ties with Japan are rich and among the most highly developed in the world. Comhaltas Ceoltóirí

Éireann has in Japan one of its most dynamic and well-supported chapters. We are very proud of the many exceptional exponents of Irish music in this country – some of whom have competed over the years in Fleadh Cheoil na hÉireann, with some winning prestigious medals there.

We are delighted too that the annual Irish Book Fair mounted by the leading, nationwide bookshop, Kinokuniya, continues to grow in Japan. Soon, it will resume featuring live readings by contemporary Irish authors.

A further special place is reserved for the Japanese not-for-profit EU–Japan Fest, which has helped to form and enlarge cultural ties between Japan and successive European Capitals of Culture for more than a quarter of a century – including Cork in 2005 and Galway in 2020. With funding generously provided from a blue-ribbon board of leading Japanese corporates, EU–Japan Fest has provided exceptional programme support to Galway 2020. And it has extended the availability and use of these funds by some years beyond 2020, in light of the fact that the Covid-19 pandemic caused the cancellation of many events which were scheduled for Galway's 'year of years'. These are unique friends and partners of Ireland's Embassy in Japan, of Galway 2020 and of Ireland *tout court.*

The New Ireland House, Tokyo

All through the past three years and more, the planning and design phases for the new Ireland House in Tokyo have continued apace. The seminal design emerged in late 2019 from an international competition that was administered principally by the Royal Institute of Architects in Ireland (RIAI). It attracted sixty-eight entries from architects and designers worldwide. The winning design was the work of the Henry J. Lyons practice in Dublin and their Japanese consortium partners, Integrated Design Associates. The selection of the winning design by the international, multidisciplinary jury was unanimous.

The new Ireland House at Yotsuya, Tokyo, will comprise under one roof the embassy, the ambassador's residence, offices for a growing family of Irish economic state agencies, a business/conference facility, a performance space, an exhibition area, a demonstration kitchen to present Irish food and an interactive Irish library. The facility will be a showcase, state-of-the-art platform from which to project across Japan, the third largest economy in the world, all that global and innovative

Ireland has to offer in the economic, financial, scientific research, educational, cultural and people-to-people fields.

This will be the largest capital investment ever made overseas by an Irish government in the 100 years since independence was obtained in 1922. It will do away with the need for the state to rent such facilities in Tokyo going forward. Equally, the renting of outside venues for events to promote Ireland's economic and other interests in Tokyo will cease to be necessary.

The decision to proceed with the design and construction of a new Ireland House in Tokyo was made by the government in the lee of the sixtieth anniversary of the establishment of diplomatic relations between Ireland and Japan. It is expected that construction of the facility will commence in Q2 of 2022 and that it will be commissioned in Q2 of 2024. It will be a major element in the roll-out of the government's Global Ireland Strategy, which aims to double Ireland's footprint and influence overseas by 2025.

Investment in the new Ireland House in Tokyo is rooted in the great strength of existing exchanges between our two countries, some of which I have rehearsed, and the strong prospect for significant growth in these ties going forward. This strategic move by Ireland to expand and deepen its ties with Japan has been warmly and repeatedly supported by successive governments of this country, up to the level of prime minister.

Once it is commissioned in 2024, the new Ireland House will welcome through its doors great numbers of people – Japanese, Irish and international; young and less young –keen to continue to make special and unique contributions to bringing Ireland and Japan closer together. For the luminous architectural creation will be less than it should be if it does not, each day, represent and project a beating heart, eager to bind two peoples closely together.

Those who came from Ireland to this country in the 1950s – including the truly extraordinary dean of our community here, Revd Donal Doyle, SJ of Dublin, professor and friend of the Imperial family – could hardly have imagined when they arrived that the Irish state would be in a position to sustain such a project. Those who worked long and hard in this country but are no longer here to see it will be warmly remembered, not least the remarkable Eileen Kato of County Mayo – discreet adviser, friend and confidante of an Emperor and Empress of Japan.

Fr Doyle, Eileen and others of their special generation are each a role model for Irish women and men of their own time in Japan, for us now and, I am confident, for those who will follow.

Shared Values and Compatible Partners

It is important to recognise wider considerations that bring Ireland and Japan together as partners and friends. Indeed, these dimensions are continually acquiring greater relevance in light of systemic challenges, which have increasingly been a feature of the global situation with its various regional manifestations.

It is more important than ever before to acknowledge that Ireland and Japan share fundamental values as liberal democratic states and societies. We both uphold personal freedoms and genuinely representative government. We both believe that when national leaders lose the confidence of their people, they must depart from office; indeed they should not be in a position to enter government in the first place, in the absence of such freely expressed consent. We are both committed to upholding, promoting and protecting universal human rights which are enshrined in the United Nations Charter of 1945 as well as the Universal Declaration of Human Rights of 1948.

At the international level, Ireland and Japan are firmly committed to the global system that is based on the rule of law, including the sovereignty and territorial integrity of states, with the United Nations at its core alongside a reformed World Trade Organisation. We are also committed to working for a world without nuclear weapons, each in our respective manner.

In light of this, Ireland and Japan have a practice generally of supporting each other's candidacies for membership of the United Nations Security Council, international judicial bodies and so forth. We see Japan clearly as a factor for stability, peace and security in her own region and around the world. It would be gratifying to see Japan join the UN Security Council as an elected member in 2023, upon Ireland's departure from this body at the end of 2022.

Briefly put, Ireland – as a bilateral matter and also as a member state of the European Union – has an interest in seeing stable, peaceful, law-upholding and democratic Japan do well in its own region and more widely. By the same token, Japan has an interest in seeing the European Union, including Ireland, and the wider family of democratic states and peoples in Europe do well as part of the global rule of a law-based international system to which we are all attached.

Little wonder therefore that, during the years (2021/2022) of Ireland's current tenure as an elected member of the UN Security Council, Ireland and Japan have effected a significant strengthening of their bilateral diplomatic engagement and consultation on matters of international peace and security, for which the council has primary responsibility under the charter.

Naturally, even countries that are the closest of friends may differ from time to time. But this is the modern Japan with which Ireland is so keen to build continually stronger ties: in the framework of (a) our government's strategy 'Global Ireland Delivering in the Asia Pacific Region, to 2025', and (b) the European Union's 2021 strategy aimed at achieving a free and open Indo-Pacific. Both of these important documents are commended to readers of the present volume.

Ireland and Japan – Looking Forward to a Bright Future Together

We are very hopeful that senior, political-level – as well as business, cultural and other – visits will resume soon between Ireland and Japan. This will provide a highly valuable blood infusion to ties that have retained all of their strength and promise but whose audible tempo has perhaps slowed somewhat during, and as a consequence of, the Covid-19 pandemic.

The governments of Ireland and Japan already have an extensive meeting of minds as to the scope and content of the closer and stronger bilateral relations and exchanges which they both want to see develop in the coming years. Business, cultural, academic, people-to-people and other stakeholders in each country are already keen to play their own essential roles in this positive future scenario. Irish and Japanese people can look forward with confidence to building a bright future together.

On the Irish side, there is a strong commitment to closer ties with Japan on the part of the taoiseach, the tánaiste and the minister of foreign affairs as well as the entire cabinet. Meanwhile, we know that Prime Minister Kishida and Foreign Minister Hayashi each have 'a soft spot' for Ireland, having both made fruitful visits there in the past.

The new showcase, state-of-the-art Ireland House in Tokyo from 2024 will provide the perfect platform from which to project this higher level of ambition and delivery in our bilateral exchanges with this venerable country, rich culture and advanced economy.

On the people-to-people front, the two governments have already decided to double the number of places available annually in the annual Working Holiday Programme – to 800 in each direction, and to provide for a further doubling should there be sufficient demand among our citizens. As the Covid-19 pandemic recedes, we hope that young people in both Ireland and Japan will step forward to take advantage of this facility and to spend a productive and enjoyable period in the other country.

By 2026, the Japan charity Support Our Kids (SOK) will be winding up. It was founded in 2011 in order to support the recovery and rehabilitation of children and teenagers affected in that year by the Great East Japan earthquake, tsunami and nuclear incident at Fukushima. It will continue until 2026 in order to have assisted those children who entered junior school in 2011, all the way through to their high school graduation in 2026, fifteen years later. The principal international activity of Support Our Kids is to arrange and organise homestays overseas for groups of young people drawn from across the affected Tohoku region. These exposures overseas foster self-sufficiency and indeed leadership qualities on the part of the young participants.

Ireland has provided homestay experiences for such groups of Japanese young people each year, until 2019, after which the Covid-19 pandemic forced an interruption in the annual programme. This has been achieved with the magnificent support of volunteer Irish families and individuals as well as interested educational institutions, public figures and others. The renowned annual Tokyo Emerald Ball has been a constant and highly appreciated pillar of support.

We hope very much that the SOK homestays for these wonderful and deserving survivors of the 2011 disaster will resume in the summer of 2023. Readers of the present volume may wish to consider lending a helping hand. This may be done by reaching out to the Embassy of Ireland in Tokyo. For my own part, it has been my honour to serve since 2018 as International Chairman of Support Our Kids, a privileged position that I inherited from my distinguished predecessor, Anne Barrington.

Through this and many other engagements in Japan, I have frequently come to see the affection that Irish and Japanese people have for each other. One high point has been the strong and ready support that was extended to Ireland by a leading Japanese corporation – with committed backing from no fewer than three Japanese ministries – through the manufacture and supply to Irish hospitals of a significant number of specialised ventilator machines. This sophisticated equipment reached Ireland in quantity, without fuss or fanfare, during some of the darkest days of the Covid-19 pandemic. Thank you, Ogino-san and the entire team at Nihon Kohden corporation.

My colleagues and I received the same warmth in the positive response from all across Japan to the gesture made by the Irish Olympians; during the 2021 Opening Ceremony of the Tokyo Olympiad, they collectively bowed towards the Imperial box high above the splendid stadium. Ireland's team was the only one of some 205 participating teams to make such a thoughtful and considerate gesture to an Imperial family that has itself reserved a special place and friendship for Ireland down the years.

Such mutual respect and affection between Irish and Japanese people will surely continue to be an enormous asset and indeed an engine as our two peoples and countries build a bright future together in the coming years and decades.

Paul Kavanagh
Ambassador, Tokyo
February 2022

From scroll 1 of *Tale of Bunshō* (*Bunshō sōshi*), a 'rags to riches' story, artist unknown, mid-seventeenth century. (CBL J 1186.1, © *The Trustees of the Chester Beatty Library, Dublin*)

The Economy

経済

Ireland's Developing Trade Relationship with Japan

Patrick O'Riordan

Shared Economic Development

Ireland is a trading nation. The opening up and liberalisation of the Irish economy that commenced in the 1950s has led to unprecedented benefits for the country's economy and society over the past seven decades. Ireland's economy has benefited enormously from pursuing a sustained 'twin engine' policy approach of attracting very significant flows of inward investment (FDI) allied to a focused approach of developing a home-grown base of Irish-controlled companies. These indigenous Irish companies are now increasingly ambitious, sophisticated and globally competitive.

Equally, the Japanese economy transformed in a similar timeframe; with Japan's prowess as a manufacturing and technological powerhouse, the country developed at pace into the third largest economy globally.

It is opportune to reflect on the positive experience of the globally minded trade relationships that have benefited both Japan and Ireland's economies immeasurably.

Given Ireland's very small size and location on the periphery of Europe, Ireland might not, at first glance, figure as an obvious trading partner with Japan.

However, when viewed through an Irish lens, our positioning both geographically and culturally as unequivocally European and as an English-speaking nation positions us at the heart of the trading world. Ireland is an important English-speaking economic actor in the trade and investment relationship between the world's largest economic blocs of Europe and the US. The important economic position Ireland holds makes it unsurprising that the country has developed a deep and strong position in the global supply relationship with Japan. In fact, Japan is now among Ireland's top ten global trading partners.

There is much to be positive about in what is a blossoming bilateral trade relationship with values that are deep and mutually respectful. Japan and Ireland adhere to global trade regulations, protection of intellectual property, compliance to technical standards and international credit norms. These shared values strengthen the basis for further bilateral trade and assure stability for current business relationships.

People

Commerce is a people-based endeavour, and Ireland is very fortunate to have a diaspora in all corners of the world. The diaspora in Japan is small in number, but it is also one that is professional, long term and hugely committed to growing a successful Ireland–Japan bilateral relationship in all its facets.

The fulcrum of the Irish diaspora in Japan has roots in an AnCo/FÁS training programme that ran from the 1980s to the mid-2000s. The programme had over 1,000 young Irish engineers experience a language and work placement immersion programme in Japan where many developed a unique combination of excellent language skills coupled with exposure to the work culture in Japanese companies. Several remained on in Japan after their two-year programme ended and many have gone on to have very successful careers in business in both Japan and beyond. Ireland–Japan relations to this day are all the richer for this programme.

In addition, Aldiscon Limited, an exemplar home-grown Irish telecommunications software company founded in Dublin in 1988, was exceptionally successful in Japan. Aldiscon launched the world's first commercial short messaging service (SMS) system platform in 1993. It then entered the Japanese market and was a resounding success before being acquired. Through Aldiscon's internationalisation

Dublin Port. (*Hon Lau/Alamy*)

Yokohama Port, Japan. (*David Ball/Alamy*)

journey in Japan, several young Irish telecommunications and software engineers were on customer deployment assignments, and they have gone on to form part of the early Irish business diaspora in Japan and broader Asia. The development and growth of the Japan Exchange and Teaching Programme (JET) has in more recent years facilitated a substantial cohort of young Irish people to experience time living and working in Japan with some going on to develop deep roots in the country.

Ireland's diaspora, including our affinity diaspora, has been one of the key driving forces of an excellent and very progressive Ireland–Japan Chamber of Commerce that is a very friendly and hugely valuable touch point for any Irish company considering the Japanese market.

The importance of IDA Ireland's work in Japan and the contribution Japanese investors make to the Irish economy can be simply encapsulated by the fact that Japanese investors are the most significant Asian investors in Ireland. In addition, Japanese investors are among the most prized not least because of the quality of their investments but also because they are long-term investments and hugely committed to their Irish operations.

IDA Ireland has had a presence in Japan for several years, and there are currently over thirty IDA Ireland Japanese clients. IDA Ireland Japanese clients directly employed 2,200 people in 2010. By 2020, this number has grown to some 6,000 people through a mix of acquisitions, expansions and new entries. Japanese companies employ across a wide range of industrial sectors from information and communication technologies (ICT), pharmaceuticals and medical technologies to financial services. In a foreign direct investment (FDI) context, Japan's importance to Ireland cannot be overstated.

Over sixty-five indigenous Enterprise Ireland client companies now have a presence in Japan, and these range from small local sales offices and partnerships to larger operations primarily in the digital and life science sectors. This number has ramped up in recent years with exports by Enterprise Ireland client firms tripling in the past decade and now employing more than 2,000 people in Japan in skilled roles. This growth is reflective of a Japanese corporate sector that is cash rich and open to world-class innovation. It also mirrors an increasingly sophisticated base of world-class Irish companies that are globally ambitious and winning in Japan.

The two-way trade and investment between Japan and Ireland is driven by people-to-people relationships; the aggregate experience for both countries has been very positive.

Challenges and Barriers to Entry

There are significant challenges to doing business in Japan for Irish companies and especially so during the Covid-19 pandemic. Japan is a long way from home, with language, cultural and regulatory requirements being significant and with immediate implications for Irish companies. These barriers have upfront cost implications; of all markets, Japan cannot be considered a market suitable for opportunistic endeavour.

If there were a strap line to promote Japan as a market for Irish companies, it could read, 'if you are a world-class company willing to commit long term, please come to Japan'. The scale and sophistication of Japan across sectors means that opportunities for Irish companies are very significant, but it is also a market that has intense competition with very capable domestic suppliers. Thus, any prospective offering by an Irish company must be benchmarked carefully against competition. Irish companies have become increasingly sophisticated in recent years, and these companies are becoming globally ambitious. Japan values innovation and high quality, and there is without question a great fit in many instances for world-class Irish offerings to compete.

The collective experience of Irish companies indicates that entry into the Japanese market is, more often than not, slow, not least because of the depth of due diligence conducted by Japanese buyers. Japanese companies are not transaction oriented; rather, Japanese companies seek to develop long-term, sustainable supply relationships with very exacting technical and servicing standards. To use a tailoring analogy, 'Japanese buyers tend to measure twice and cut once.'

For the increasing cohort of Irish firms in Japan, and there are currently over sixty-five with representation, there are great opportunities to scale and to realise profitable market opportunities.

EU–Japan Economic Partnership Agreement (Free Trade Agreement)

The recent implementation of the EU–Japan Economic Partnership Agreement is very positive news for Ireland–Japan bilateral trade relations.

The Economic Partnership Agreement is already providing a fillip for Ireland–Japan trade relations that will bolster market access between two of the world's largest and most valuable economic blocs. Ireland is benefiting because of lower tariffs and duties in addition to an alignment and mutual recognition of technical standards across some sectors. As an outward looking, trade dependent economy, the opportunities across sectors in Japan, not least for Ireland's indigenous food industry, will be very significant.

It is one of the reasons Bord Bia has in recent years established its thriving office in Japan, developing key buyer relationships and raising the profile of Ireland's offering to this important exemplar market.

Partnering in Japan

Enterprise Ireland's mission is to deliver a major improvement in the international strength of Irish enterprise by transforming the innovation and competitive capabilities of Irish companies. We achieve this by inspiring and supporting ambitious business leaders to increase the scale of their businesses and expand their reach into global markets. Japan is a market we are ambitious for and one that now has natural and positive momentum.

We work closely with our partners at the Embassy of Ireland, IDA Ireland, Bord Bia and a thriving Ireland–Japan Chamber of Commerce to realise our goals that are aligned to the collective objective of further developing and scaling the strong bilateral relationship with Japan.

Potential for Growth

The increasing ambition of founders and management of Irish companies coupled with more globally competitive innovative products and services will undoubtedly ensure Japan figures prominently as a growth market in the coming years.

It is thus appropriate to look forward, with ambition and confidence, to a very bright future in the further development of Ireland's trading relationship with Japan.

Patrick O' Riordan is Enterprise Ireland's Director for Japan.

Ties Between Ireland and Japan in the Sport of Horse Racing and Breeding

Brian Gleeson

The ties between Ireland and Japan in the sport of horse racing and breeding continues to grow and flourish. In fact, the title of this book – *Crossings* – perfectly describes the close relations between our two countries. Japan has always been forward thinking and when the JRA (Japan Racing Association) opened up the prestigious Japan Cup to International Raiders, the Irish mare Stanerra, owned and trained by successful Irish businessman Frank Dunne, won the famous race in 1983. This success ignited a relationship and business of bloodstock between Ireland and Japan that continues to thrive and prosper in terms of equine and humans some forty years later.

Two other Irish thoroughbreds, Persian Boy and Jupiter Island, were to further highlight the success and prowess of Irish thoroughbred breeding to Japanese horse men and women. Soon Ireland was on Japan's radar as a country from which to purchase and import Irish equine bloodlines and improve the Japanese gene pool. Shinko Lady was a daughter of Caerleon – who stood at the magnificent Coolmore Stud, in Fethard, County Tipperary, an equine seven-star hotel – she won the grade-1 mile at Kyoto in 1993 and established course records at both Fukushima and Tokyo racecourses.

At this stage the headlights had been turned on Irish breeding and shrewd Japanese horse men and women went in search of Caerleon stock. Caerleon was trained by one of the world's best trainers, Dr Vincent O'Brien. A very impressive racehorse, he made a significant impact at stud under the guidance of Dr O'Brien's son- in-law John Magnier at his limestone rich Coolmore Stud Farm in County Tipperary. With fillies and mares by Caerleon becoming hot property in Japan, renowned Irish bloodstock agent John McCormack initiated contact with Katsumi Yoshida of the now famous Northern Horse Farm in Hokkaido to see if he would be interested in purchasing Wind In Her Hair.

Wind In Her Hair was registered to John and Sue Magnier and David and Diane Nagle during her racing career, which included a second in the Group 1 Epsom Oaks before securing Group 1 success in Germany. A deal was struck and Wind In Her Hair was sold to Japan. Time proved it an inspired purchase as the Yoshida family had only one mating in mind – breed the best to the best and hope for the best – the Kentucky Derby winner Sunday Silence, already a sire sensation; his dalliances with Wind In Her Hair were to change the landscape of Japanese breeding forever.

In her second breeding season Wind In Her Hair produced a colt who was to make a global impact. He sold as a foal at the JRHA (Japan Racing Horse Association) Select Sale for ¥73,500,000 (€607,110) to Makoto Kaneko. Named Deep Impact, this equine thoroughbred displayed incredible ability, winning the Japan Triple Crown in 2005 – the Japan Derby, Satsuki Sho (Japanese 2000 Guineas) and St Leger. He also won the famous Japan Cup in 2006 and three other grade-1 races and retired after winning twelve of his fourteen starts including two Horse of the Year titles. He retired winning more than ¥1,500,000,000 (over twelve million euro) in prize money. Such was his brilliance on the track that the Yoshida family purchased him back to stand as a stallion at their stunning Shadai Stallion Station and, while his adoring fans were no longer going to see him on the racetrack, it was not long before the racing and breeding community realised they had unearthed a world class stallion. Deep Impact has already made an indelible mark on Japanese racing and is a multiple champion sire.

Little did we know when Frankie Dettori won his first Epsom Oaks in 1994 that it would be the filly who was second place in that fillies' classic that would end

Group 2 'Ireland Trophy' race during the Japan Cup Festival in Tokyo, 2017. (*Photo courtesy of author*)

up having such a global impact. It would have been very difficult to predict the importance of Wind In Her Hair to the horse-racing breed worldwide. Now thirty years old, Wind In Her Hair is retired at the Northern Horse Park in Japan where she remains a popular attraction for equine tourists who wish to pay homage to her place in history as the dam of Deep Impact. In fact, she is held in such esteem and love that Northern Horse Park regularly send out tweets from the Twitter handle @northern_horse.

John Magnier was watching the success of Deep Impact and started sending some of his top broodmares from Ireland to Japan to be covered by Deep Impact. Sending a selection of Coolmore's elite broodmares has already had the desired effect and his foresight has been rewarded in spades as Snowfall's success in the 2021 Epsom Oaks was team Coolmore's third Classic winner by Deep Impact. Snowfall follows Saxon Warrior (himself now a stallion at Coolmore Stud), Fancy Blue and September as a Group 1 performer out of a small number of Deep Impact foals bred by Coolmore. He is referred to as the Japanese Galileo – he has sired seven Japanese Derby winners and over twenty Japanese Classic winners and has topped the Japanese Sires' list nine times. Unfortunately, Deep Impact died in July 2019 at

The paddock at Hanshin racecourse near Kobe, Japan. (*Trevor Mogg/Alamy*)

カシノ
8

Deep Impact, winner of the Satsuki Sho (Japanese 2000 Guineas), the Tokyo Yushun (Japanese Derby), and the Kikuka-shō (Japenese St Leger). These three races comprise the Japanese Triple Crown. (*Wikimedia Commons*)

the very height of his worldwide powers. A neck condition had brought a sudden halt to his covering season weeks before his death, meaning very small numbers in his final crop of foals born in 2020 – luckily for Coolmore they do include colts out of their top-class mares Rhododendron, Hydrangea and Maybe, as well as a filly out of Minding.

Japanese racing is now the envy of other racing nations, not least in terms of massive public popularity for the sport. Japan's top jockeys have celebrity status, and the best horses inspire an enthusiastic fanbase. Deep Impact is one of the best-known horses ever to have graced the beautiful country of Japan. The art and science of the thoroughbred has come full circle thanks to a mare called Wind In Her Hair – bred, born and raised on rich Irish limestone land –whose bloodline would make such an incredible mark on Japanese and world racing breeding through her son Deep Impact. Our two countries will be forever linked in the breeding of the thoroughbred with equine 'crossings' happening on an annual basis as horse breeders from both countries tap into our respective equine genes. There will always be crossings of horses and people between our two beautiful countries and the pursuit to find the next equine champion is on in earnest.

Let Food Be Thy Medicine: A personal perspective on collaborations between Irish food science and the Japanese food industry

R. Paul Ross

Two countries steeped in a food tradition

As two relatively small island nations, both Japan and Ireland share many cultural and human characteristics. These include a true sense of pride and nationalism but overlaid with an overall feeling of modesty and understatedness. Moreover, both countries are steeped in a very deep food heritage that dates back millennia. Both also have a long tradition in dairy, being major consumers and innovators in dairy products. Hard to believe, but the butter market in Cork was once the leading authority with regard to global butter prices based on quality and composition. These traditions continue on both sides. The Republic of Ireland is now the fastest-growing dairy economy in the world, and will be for at least the next ten years. This is partly due to the cessation of European Union (EU) dairy quotas on 1 April 2015, which has allowed milk production to almost double since this lifting.

To give some idea of the potential here, New Zealand quadrupled national milk production to almost twenty billion litres during the time Ireland was subject to EU dairy quotas. But it is not just about milk yield and production, it is more about building a knowledge economy to exploit and add value to this valuable output for the betterment of human health. And this is where our dairy companies come in; companies such as Kerry, Glanbia, Dairygold and Carbery have now become global players supplying dairy products and ingredients across the world. Moreover, Ireland now produces approximately 15 per cent of the total infant-formula exports. From the Japanese perspective, the country has built up very impressive food and beverage industries, with companies such as Meiji Dairies and Suntory being leaders in terms of scale and innovation.

Ireland and Japan have a mutual interest in the role food plays in human health. Here, the ultimate aim is to generate superior foods that not only meet basic nutritional requirements but also contain additional ingredients with the aim of improving health and well-being and reducing the risk of disease. Such foods are known as 'functional foods', a marketing term that, not surprisingly, was initially coined in Japan in the 1980s. The concept was further developed in Japan in 1991 with the introduction of specific legislation to cover this sector – so-called FOSHU foods – or foods for specified health use, and which are licensed to carry a label related to their effect on human health.

Probiotics are an apt example of an ingredient that can raise the status of a food product to a functional one. While the Russian scientist Elie Metchnikoff is often considered the 'father of the probiotic concept', Japan must surely be considered the father of the probiotic and functional foods industry. Indeed, in 1930, the Japanese scientist, Dr Minoru Shirota, was the first to isolate a specific bacterial strain with proven capacity to impart health benefits upon consumption. By 1935, the probiotic-containing fermented milk drink Yakult was launched in Japan. Nowadays, Yakult is a globally marketed product. The Yakult Central Institute was established in 1955 (initially as the Shirota Research Institute) and continues to place significant emphasis on the influence of intestinal bacteria on overall human health. Towards the latter decade of the twentieth century, interest in probiotics and their health-promoting properties, together with the functional-foods concept, had spread from Japan to other regions of the globe, including Ireland, where both industry and academia had taken considerable interest in their

potential both in terms of human health and commercial value. Such interests have been superseded to some extent, however, by the realisation of the importance of the entire community of microorganisms that inhabit our intestine, the so-called microbiome. The necessity to understand how probiotics exert their beneficial effects has now led researchers to place significant emphasis on the make-up and function of the human microbiome. Indeed, the APC Microbiome Institute at University College Cork (UCC) was established on the basis of this principle, and was funded through the foresight of Science Foundation Ireland. The centre, founded in 2003, is now the largest and one of the foremost leading microbiome institutes in the world.

Establishing trust and collaboration in food science and industry

I think it is true to say that the genesis of the more recent relationship in food science between Japan and Ireland came out of a number of governmental missions between the two countries that saw political, scientific and industrial representatives visiting both countries at regular intervals (which continue to this day). Of particular note was a mission I attended in January 2009, when our then Taoiseach, Brian Cowen, set off on a large trade mission to Japan accompanied by the various government ministers, scientists and industry personnel. Such trade missions continued, and in 2012 the Enterprise Ireland trade mission to Japan focused largely on functional foods – another mission I was on. Over that period, I occupied a leadership role in the Food Research Programme at Teagasc, and was delighted to welcome many industrial leaders from the Japanese food industry to Moorepark Food Research Centre and UCC. A key person responsible for building the relationships was Eddie Hughes, the Enterprise Ireland representation in Tokyo at the time; his professionalism and enthusiasm paved the way for the relationships that blossomed from those initial encounters.

Over the last ten years, our research group (headed by Professor Catherine Stanton and myself) has been fortunate to have a number of Japanese post-doctoral researchers from industry performing research at our labs – both at Teagasc and at UCC. The topics of these projects varied from biopreservation (with Professor Colin Hill and Dr Mary Rea) to the influence of food ingredients across the brain/

gut axis (with Professor Ted Dinan and Professor John Cryan). In all cases, we have been very impressed with the level of collaboration with companies such as Suntory and Meiji Dairies and Irish companies such as Dairygold. Although these have been applied projects with an expectation for commercial impact, they have been of a high scientific standard, and their outputs continue to be published in peer-reviewed scientific journals. In my view it is very difficult to force scientific collaboration across different groups; collaboration only works where the two parties benefit from the generation of knowledge that impacts either on the discipline or on industry, or preferably both. This is the case with these projects and, hopefully, will be with many collaborative projects in the future as, together, we develop and understand the role of food and food constituents in human health and disease prevention.

Future collaborations in functional foods across Ireland and Japan

In Japan, FOSHU has been approved by the Consumer Affairs Agency. However, it is restricted to fourteen health benefits, and such foods must provide clinical and nutritional proof of the food and/or ingredient at the intake amount. Perhaps unsurprisingly, probiotics represent a major category of FOSHU products. Moreover, Japan brought in the Foods with Function Claims (FFC) regulation in 2015 in conjunction with FOSHU. FFC is less stringent than FOSHU, accepting systematic literature reviews as evidence, and is open to any health-benefit claim, thereby significantly broadening the functional-foods market. In Ireland and the EU, regulation (EC) no. 1924/2006 governs nutrition and health claims made about foods, and likewise requires scientific evidence of nutritional or physiological effects. However, acquiring an EU health claim for a probiotic has proven virtually impossible owing to the stringency of the regulation. Indeed, the first probiotic to receive an EU health claim was announced in early 2017, despite numerous claims having been submitted beforehand. So the regulatory environments in which the industries operate are very different, with the EU being far more restrictive. There are major learnings here on the European side given the level of innovation and advancement to have been fostered in the retail food industry in Japan through its legislative support.

In recent years, the Irish government has placed huge significance on investing in research and development, and Ireland is now deemed the eighth most innovative country in the EU. Indeed, the state has its sights set on becoming a 'Global Innovation Leader' through its Innovation 2020 strategy, where research and innovation in the agri-food sector is one of its priorities. Similarly, in 2016, Japan launched the 5th Science and Technology Basic Plan with the goal of realising a 'Super Smart Society'.

The Japanese/Irish obsession with the role of food in human health and well-being is perhaps driven by a number of factors, not least the need to meet the demands of a growing world population and the health burden associated with ageing and metabolic disease in populations in developed countries such as Japan and Ireland. Indeed, in Japan the population is rapidly ageing but with decreasing birth rates, while the number of over-sixty-fives in Ireland is predicted to increase by 20,000 a year over the coming twenty years. Foods with the capacity to prevent disease or improve human health will undoubtedly improve quality of life and reduce demands on our health-care systems while also improving nutrition and reducing disease risk in developing nations. The convergence of all these factors opens up huge opportunities for our like-minded nations to come up with knowledge-based nutritional solutions to solve some of the major problems facing humankind with regard to diet, health and disease. As Hippocrates, the father of medicine, said, 'Let food be thy medicine and medicine be thy food'.

A female poet writing the first calligraphy of the new year, by Keisai Eisen (1790–1848), mid-1820s. (CBL J 2011, © *The Trustees of the Chester Beatty Library, Dublin*)

Education

教育

Foreign Language Education in Japan: Context and issues

Fumihisa Fujinaga

Introduction

The Japanese education system comprises the following phases: pre-primary (e.g. kindergartens), primary, lower and upper secondary, and higher education (e.g. universities and colleges). Compulsory education is made up of six years of primary and three years of lower secondary school, starting at the age of six and ending at fifteen. Upper secondary school education, which lasts for three years (or more, in some cases), is optional but the current enrolment ratio is as high as 98.7 per cent, suggesting that most students have opportunities to receive the upper secondary level of education (MEXT, 2016a). Higher education is provided mainly by universities and colleges, which offer four-year programmes for undergraduate students and two- to four-year programmes for graduate students.

Foreign language education formally begins in primary school, and there are a number of schools (in most cases, private ones) that offer foreign language programmes. As regards primary and secondary education, the Ministry of Education, Culture, Sports, Science and Technology (hereafter MEXT) determines the official guidelines called the Courses of Study and stipulates the overall objectives and educational contents, in order to ensure a certain standard of education across the country. All Japanese primary, lower and upper secondary schools, accordingly, are expected to implement appropriate foreign language curriculums in line with the guidelines. Furthermore, the Courses of Study stipulate that English, in principle, should be selected as the target language, and it is, in effect, the only foreign language for most students to learn at the primary and secondary levels.

In the light of this situation regarding Japan's foreign language education, this article focuses on English language education in Japan at the primary and secondary levels, which most Japanese students go through. In the sections that follow, we examine the MEXT's educational policies stated in the Courses of Study and shed light on the issues associated with classroom teaching and learning.

A brief overview of Japanese foreign-language education

Primary school

In 2011, the revised Course of Study for Primary Schools went into effect, and the Foreign Language Activities programme (hereafter FLA) was launched for fifth- and sixth-grade pupils. Since then, English has been a compulsory language to be selected for the activities. The number of classes allocated is thirty-five per year, which is equivalent to approximately twenty-six hours. The overall objective of the FLA is to 'form the foundation of pupils' communication abilities' in English as a foreign language, consisting of the following elements: an experiential understanding of the English language and of cultures in the English-speaking countries, a positive attitude toward communication in English, and familiarity with the sounds and basic expressions of English (MEXT, 2008b, 2010b).

In designing and implementing the learning activities covered by the FLA, the Course of Study requires teachers to help their pupils 'experience the joy of communication in the foreign language', 'actively listen to and speak in the foreign language' and 'learn the importance of verbal communication' (MEXT, 2008b, 2010b). It should be noted here that the goal of the FLA is not to teach language skills themselves but to familiarise students with a foreign language.

What is expected of the FLA is to remove students' learning anxiety and cultivate their willingness to communicate in a foreign language. For this reason, the FLA can be seen as a 'warm-up' for the start of secondary-level English language learning.

Due to this nature of the FLA, English is not taught as a school subject and formal grading (by means of tests, for example) is not conducted.[1] In addition, Japanese homeroom teachers are responsible for the FLA, conducting lessons, in many cases, in cooperation with English-speaking assistant teachers.

Lower and upper secondary school

The implementation of the revised Course of Study for Lower Secondary Schools began in 2012. As is the case with primary schools, English is a compulsory language for foreign language instruction and, therefore, all students are expected to study English as a foreign language. The number of classes is 140 a year (each class lasts 50 minutes), amounting to nearly 120 hours. The overall objective of English education in lower secondary schools is to 'develop students' basic communication abilities such as listening, speaking, reading and writing', with a focus on a deep understanding of language and culture and on the fostering of positive attitudes toward communication using a foreign language (MEXT, 2008a, 2011a). It should be noted here that, in contrast to the FLA in primary schools, lower secondary English education places more emphasis on the use of the four language skills (i.e., listening, speaking, reading and writing), which will be acquired primarily through in-class training.

In upper secondary school education, English as a Foreign Language is divided into the following subjects: Basic English Communication, English Communications 1, 2 and 3, English Expressions 1 and 2, and English Conversation.

Basic English Communication is intended to 'develop students' basic abilities such as listening, speaking, reading and writing, while fostering a positive attitude toward communication through the English language' (MEXT, 2011b). One important feature of this subject is that it serves as a 'bridge' between lower and upper secondary school. It is mainly intended to help first-year students consolidate what they have learned in lower secondary school before taking more advanced subjects, such as English Communication 1.

English Communications 1, 2, and 3 aim to develop students' listening, speaking, reading, and writing skills in English comprehensively by relating the four skills with one another. The overall objectives of the subjects can be summarised as follows (MEXT, 2010a, 2011b):

- To 'develop students' basic abilities such as accurately understanding and appropriately conveying information, ideas etc.'
- To 'enable them to use such abilities in their social lives' (note that this is only for English Communication 3).
- To foster 'a positive attitude toward communication through the English language'.

In these subjects, classroom language activities are supposed to be implemented in an integrative manner: that is, students are expected to speak and write based on what they have heard and read.

English Expressions 1 and 2, in particular, focus on the productive aspects of language, namely speaking and writing. These subjects aim to develop 'students' abilities to evaluate facts, opinions, etc. from multiple perspectives and communicate through reasoning and a range of expressions, while fostering a positive attitude toward communication through the English language' (MEXT, 2011b). To achieve this goal, it is specified that language activities in class should place students in both prepared and unprepared speech situations, including conversation, debate, discussion, presentation and public speech.

The primary focus of English Conversation, as its name suggests, is to 'develop students' abilities to hold conversations on everyday topics' (MEXT, 2011b), while the fostering of 'a positive attitude toward communication' in English is intended at the same time. In this subject, through various language activities, students learn the basic expressions and conversational strategies needed to live or stay in English-speaking countries.

Among the seven subjects mentioned above, only English Communication 1 is mandatory and the others are elective. Each individual school, depending on its circumstances and needs, can decide which elective subjects should be made available to its students. One typical pattern of study would be as follows: students first study English Communication 1 and proceed to English Communications 2 and 3, and, in parallel with these subjects, they study English Expressions 1 and 2.

Minister Hong Bows to the Heavenly Teacher, by Watanabe Kazan; woodblock, 1829 (print c. 1890). (*Jonathan O'Rourke/Alamy*)

In this case, the total hours of study during the three years of upper secondary school will amount to around 500 hours (MEXT, 2010a).

One of the most notable features of the Course of Study for Upper Secondary Schools is the explicit reference to teachers' instructional language. It is required that teachers should use English as the primary medium of instruction for the purpose of 'transforming classes into real communication scenes' (MEXT, 2011b).

Some important aspects of the Courses of Study

Language activities

One important principle of the Courses of Study is that students learn a language by using it in pursuit of meaningful communication, which corresponds to one of the major principles of the Communicative Approach (Richards and Schmidt, 2010). At the centre of classroom teaching and learning, therefore, are not grammar-based drills and exercises but instead communicative activities, in which expressing meanings by means of language is of utmost importance. In designing such language activities, teachers should attend to various facets of language use.

One of those facets is what is communicated through the use of language. It may be thought of as the 'content' which students listen to, speak of, read and write about in a given language activity. In this regard, the Courses of Study mention that language activities should cover such topics as language, culture and students' daily lives (MEXT, 2008a, 2008b, 2010a). Looking at one of the textbooks for English Expression 1, the topics taken up there include friends and family, leisure activities, school life, health issues, and Japanese culture and history (Morita et al., 2016). These topics are chosen in compliance with the descriptions in the Courses of Study.

Language that is used to communicate the 'content' should also be considered. In the Courses of Study, those linguistic components that should be taught – which are referred to as 'language elements' – are described in terms of pronunciation, letters and symbols, vocabulary, and grammar (MEXT, 2008a, 2010a). Take grammar for example: the target items mentioned in the Courses of Study include pronouns, verb tenses, adjectives and adverbs, gerunds, present and past participles, reflexive pronouns, to-infinitives, and auxiliary verbs, among others. For the lower secondary school level, eleven sentence structures (e.g., subject-verb-object structure) are also given as the target items for instruction (MEXT, 2008a).

Concerning vocabulary, the Courses of Study do not provide a specific list. Instead, they mention that this should cover 'frequently used' words, collocations and 'common expressions', which are illustrated with several examples. In addition, they indicate that the number of words that should be taught and learned is 'approximately 1,200' for the three years of lower secondary education and about 1,800 for upper secondary school students who take English Communications 1, 2 and 3 (MEXT, 2008a, 2010a).

Other important facets are 'language-use situations' and 'functions of language'. In the Courses of Study, language-use situations are organised into the following categories (MEXT, 2008a, 2008b, 2010a, 2010b, 2011a, 2011b):

- Situations in which fixed and common expressions are often used (e.g., greetings, self-introductions, talking on the phone)
- Situations that may occur in students' lives (e.g., domestic life, school life, local events) and in social lives (e.g., community activities and workplace activities)
- Situations that involve obtaining information by means of various media (e.g., reading books and newspapers, using communication networks such as the Internet)

Regarding functions of language, the Courses of Study point out the following categories and provide general descriptions (MEXT, 2008a, 2008b, 2010a, 2010b, 2011a, 2011b):

- Facilitating communication (e.g., asking for repetition)
- Expressing emotions (e.g., apologising, complaining, and expressing gratitude)
- Transmitting information (e.g., explaining, describing, and summarising)
- Expressing opinions and intentions (e.g., agreeing and disagreeing)
- Instigating action (e.g., requesting, inviting, and giving orders).

The facets of language use discussed so far should be combined and integrated to create language activities that work. In practice, this may be achieved in this way: if the teacher selects 'students' hometown' as a topic of the lesson (i.e., the content), then he or she will set up a language-use situation and choose a number of language functions associated with it. If the language-use situation chosen is 'asking and giving directions', the possible functions to be chosen as targets may include 'asking questions', 'explaining', and 'expressing gratitude'. In this connection, vocabulary and grammar items to be taught can be specified. Interrogative and imperative sentences, for example, can be possible focal points (e.g., 'Where is ... ?' and 'Turn right at the next corner').

In this way, when designing language activities, teachers need to integrate content, language, language-use situations and functions of language. This should be done 'in a way suitable for the objectives' of the subjects they oversee (MEXT, 2011b).

Osaka. Hotel.

The Osaka Hotel on Nakanoshima Island, Osaka, early 1900s. The Osaka Hotel was Osaka's premier Western hotel, with English-speaking personnel. (*MeijiShowa/Alamy*)

Skill integration

Another important aspect of activity-oriented teaching and learning is the instruction of integrated language skills, which is particularly relevant at the secondary school level. The Courses of Study for secondary schools, in fact, explicitly state that the teaching of the four skills (i.e., listening, speaking, reading and writing) should be done in conjunction with one another. Language activities are supposed to engage students in speaking or writing about 'what they have listened to or read' (MEXT, 2008a, 2010a, 2011a, 2011b). By doing so, the four skills can be 'interlinked for comprehensive learning' (MEXT, 2011b).

One of the defining requisites of skill integration is the use of two or more skills in a given language activity. Consider such a language-use situation as talking on the phone, which is mentioned in the Courses of Study. When you use a phone to talk with someone, you have to say something to convey your message and respond to the person on the other end; you have to listen to and understand what the other person says; and, in some cases, you might have to take some notes while on the phone. Talking on the phone therefore requires the effective use of multiple skills, which are, in this case, listening, speaking, and writing. At the same time, it should be noted here that the successful use of one skill depends on the effectiveness of another. In the example above, failure to comprehend by listening will surely lead to failure to give appropriate responses. Thus, language activities that integrate various skills in class should ensure that students successfully use those skills in a combined and concerted manner.

The 'context' in which skill integration takes place should also be taken into consideration (Johnson and Johnson, 1999). Returning to the example of telephone communication, the skill of listening is used to understand something talked about on the phone, based on which the skills of speaking and writing are also in operation. In this case, the skills involved are connected in terms of one single 'context': the exchanging of information during the phone conversation. Such a link between language skills can make a contribution to the solid manifestations of skill integration in classroom language activities (Kaya et al., 2017).

Another important question related to skill integration is the degree to which the use of multiple skills in language activities conforms to students' real-life language skill use (i.e. the 'authenticity' of skill use). From this perspective, a given integrated language activity could be either very authentic or less so. Suppose the activity engages students in listening to a news story and retelling it to their classmates. It can be argued that this task is 'authentic' in the sense that the students are likely to come across a similar situation outside the classroom. At the same time, however, the activity can be regarded as less authentic if, say, it is obvious that the students are not exposed to news stories in their daily lives. It should be noted here that being 'less authentic' is not necessarily a negative thing in language learning. Even when the simulated language-using scenario does not occur frequently in reality, the activity may still lead to effective language learning (Widdowson, 1990). Teachers, in actual classroom situations, should be able to strike an optimal balance between the 'authentic' and the 'less authentic' in order to create effective language activities.

Problems and difficulties

One major problem with Japanese foreign language education is the disconnection between the MEXT's current policies advocating 'language activities' and 'skill integration' and actual classroom practices. According to a survey of secondary school teachers across Japan, only about 40 per cent said that they were implementing language activities in class to engage their students in speaking and writing based on what they heard and read (MEXT, 2016c). Also, it has been pointed out that Japanese teachers of English tend to spend most of their classroom hours explaining grammar and vocabulary and carrying out related language drills and exercises. One study has revealed that some of the teachers surveyed did not regularly conduct communicative language activities in class, even though they acknowledged the value of these activities (Tahira, 2012).

It seems that this disconnection can be attributed to a number of weaknesses in teaching English through language activities. First of all, the use of multiple skills required by language activities may prevent more focused teaching and learning of a single language skill (Hinkel, 2010). Learning one skill at a time can benefit beginners and low-proficiency students who most likely are not able to use integrated language skills very well.

In addition, activity-oriented teaching could lead to pedagogical attention being paid to each language skill in an unbalanced way. Language activities, as we have seen, place emphasis on expressing meaning through purposeful communication.

In some cases, therefore, a systematic teaching of grammar and vocabulary can be neglected and the quality of students' language production (e.g., accuracy) may receive less attention than it deserves (Hinkel, 2010).

Students' uneven proficiencies across the four skills can also pose difficulties for teachers who implement integrated language activities (Hinkel, 2010). If the students are relatively strong in reading and listening but particularly weak in writing and speaking, their teachers will experience a lot of difficulty eliciting enough language production. This could minimise the effect of language activities, in which active interactions between students play a crucial role.

In terms of the burden on teachers, language-activity-oriented curricula and syllabi focusing on integrated skills are very demanding. Among other things, they should be 'reasonably versatile and well trained' (Hinkel, 2010). While managing many different situations which occur during language activities, they are required to give appropriate feedback and instruction to students on the spot. For this purpose, teachers need to be highly proficient in English and have an adequate knowledge of linguistics, including the relationships between various language-use situations and functions of language. At the same time, they should be able to plan and prepare teaching procedures and materials appropriate for integrated instruction, which is usually laborious and time-consuming (Hinkel, 2010).

However, Japanese school teachers are having difficulty giving adequate time to lesson planning and professional development, due to various extra-curricular and administrative responsibilities (Mondejar, Valdivia, Laurier, and Mboutsiadis, 2012). One of the consequences is implied in the results of a survey on the English proficiency of secondary school teachers across Japan. Only about 30 per cent of the lower secondary teachers surveyed had a CEFR B2 or above level of proficiency; for the upper secondary teachers surveyed, that number was about 57 per cent (MEXT, 2016b).

For primary school teachers, the current situation does not look promising. As mentioned previously, Japanese homeroom teachers are in charge of the FLA. However, most of them are not English language experts, from which it can be assumed that their language proficiency, in general, may not be sufficient for the effective management and implementation of the FLA.

As we have seen, one of the keys to successful teaching is teachers' high level of language competence and pedagogical skills. With this in mind, it is urgent that the present situation should be rectified and improved. More support for teachers is needed so that they may be better prepared to organise language activities and to teach integrated language skills.

Conclusion

This article has discussed some of the current issues in Japanese foreign language education by looking at the Courses of Study for primary and secondary schools. In the course of the discussion, it was shown that the educational policies stated in the MEXT's official guidelines advocate and emphasise the following principle: teaching and learning through communicative language activities that integrate different skills. However, when it comes to putting this principle into practice, there are a number of problems and difficulties that have yet to be overcome. Despite the MEXT's policies, actual teaching practices tend to avoid the frequent use of communicative language activities because teachers are wary of the possible disadvantages of such approaches. In addition, teachers do not have enough time to enhance their skills and knowledge of teaching English in communicative and integrated ways. The current disconnection between policy and practice needs to be bridged for Japanese foreign language education in order to move further ahead.

Note

In Marh 2017, the MEXT published the new Course of Study for Primary School, which came into effect in 2020. It indicates the expansion of foreign language education as follows:

- FLA is mandatory for third- and fourth-grade pupils
- For fifth- and sixth-grade pupils, English as a foreign language is taught as a compulsory school subject.

The MEXT also published the new Course of Study for Lower Secondary School which took effect in April 2021. The new Course of Study for Upper Secondary School was announced in March 2018, which is applied to students enrolled in and after April 2022.

Bibliography

Hinkel, E., 'Integrating the Four Skills: Current and historical perspectives', in R.B. Kaplan (ed.), *The Oxford Handbook of Applied Linguistics,* 2nd ed. (New York, NY: Oxford University Press, 2010), pp. 110–23.

Johnson, K., and Johnson, H. (eds), *Encyclopaedic Dictionary of Applied Linguistics: A handbook for language teachers* (Oxford, UK: Blackwell Publishing, 1999).

Kaya, T., Muto, K, Kito, K., Konno, K., Fujinaga, F., and Ogura, M., 'Eigo 4 ginou no kagakuteki konkyo ni motozuku shidouhou' (Scientific approaches to teaching the four skills), in JACET kyouikumondai kenkyukai (ed.), *Gengo kyouiku ekisupo 2017 yokoushuu* (Language Education Expo 2017 conference proceedings), Tokyo, Japan: JACET kyouikumondai kenkyukai (2017), pp. 12–15.

MEXT (2008a), *Chuugakkou gakushuushidouyouryou kaisetsu gaikokugo hen* (Explanatory comments for the Course of Study for foreign language education in lower secondary schools) (Tokyo, Japan: Kairyudo).

MEXT (2008b), *Shougakkou gakushuushidouyouryou kaisetsu gaikokugo katsudou hen* (Explanatory comments for the Course of Study for foreign language education in primary schools) (Tokyo, Japan: Toyokan shuppansha).

MEXT (2010a), *Koutougakkou gakushuushidouyouryou kaisetsu gaikokugo hen eigo hen* (Explanatory comments for the Course of Study for foreign language education in upper secondary schools) (Tokyo, Japan: Kairyudo).

MEXT (2010b), *Shougakkou gakushuushidouyouryou (gaikokugo katsudou) eiyaku ban (kayaku)* (The Course of Study for primary school [foreign language activities], English translation version [tentative translation]). Retrieved from http://www.mext.go.jp/component/a_menu/education/micro_detail/__icsFiles/afieldfile/2010/10/20/1261037_12.pdf.

MEXT (2011a), *Chuugakkou gakushuushidouyouryou (gaikokugo) eiyaku ban (kayaku)* (The Course of Study for lower secondary school [foreign languages], English translation version [tentative translation]). Retrieved from http://www.mext.go.jp/component/a_menu/education/micro_detail/__icsFiles/afieldfile/2011/04/11/1298356_10.pdf.

MEXT (2011b), *Koutougakkou gakushuushidouyouryou (gaikokugo) eiyaku ban (kayaku)* (The Course of Study for upper secondary school [foreign languages], English translation version [tentative translation]). Retrieved from http://www.mext.go.jp/a_menu/shotou/new-cs/youryou/eiyaku/__icsFiles/afieldfile/2011/04/11/1298353_9.pdf.

MEXT (2016a), *Gakko kihon chousa heisei 28 nendo kekka no gaiyou.* (Report on basic research on school for the year 2016). Retrieved from http://www.mext.go.jp/b_menu/toukei/chousa01/kihon/kekka/k_detail/1375036.htm.

MEXT (2016b), *Heisei 27 nendo eigo kyouiku jisshi joukyou chousa kekka* (Survey on the state of Japan's English education for the year 2015). Retrieved from http://www.mext.go.jp/a_menu/kokusai/gaikokugo/1369258.htm.

MEXT (2016c), *Heisei 27 nendo eigo kyouiku kaizen no tame no eigoryoku chousa jigyou houkoku.* (Report on the survey of English language proficiency among Japanese lower and upper secondary students for the year 2015). Retrieved from http://www.mext.go.jp/a_menu/kokusai/gaikokugo/1377767.htm.

Mondejar, M., Valdivia, L., Laurier, J., and Mboutsiadis, B., 'Effective Implementation of Foreign Language Education Reform in Japan: What more can be done?', in A. Stewart and N. Sonda (eds), *JALT2011 conference proceedings* (Tokyo, Japan: JALT, 2016), pp. 179–91.

Morita, A. Atobe, S., Kaya, T., Sato, Y., Shiozawa, Y., Sugita, M., Suzuki, Y., Nishibori, M., Yamaguchi, T., Yubune, E., Wakaari, Y., and Yoffe, L., *Attainable English Expression 1* (Hiroshima, Japan: Daiichi gakushusha, 2016).

Richards, J.C. and Schmidt, R., *Longman dictionary of language teaching and applied linguistics* (4th ed.) (Harlow, UK: Pearson, 2010).

Tahira, M., 'Behind MEXT's new Course of Study guidelines', *The Language Teacher, 36* (3) (2012), pp. 3–8.

Widdowson, H.G., *Aspects of Language Teaching* (Oxford, UK: Oxford University Press, 1990).

Utilising Personal Experience in Teaching Practice

Jun Nagasaka

I spent three years in a Canadian high school, and now I am teaching English in Kindai high school. I am therefore in a position to put my Canadian experience to good use in a Japanese context. I know both Japanese and Canadian education systems well. Both countries have a great education system and I am endeavouring to exploit the strengths of each system fully. In this essay, I will talk about several things. First, I will talk about attending high school overseas. Second, I will talk about my experience and why I wanted to become an English teacher. Third, I will describe the differences between Japanese and Canadian education systems. Fourth, I will talk about my own teaching style. Finally, I will discuss the uses of ICT in education and I will describe active learning.

I lived in Canada and in the UK for approximately four years. Generally, studying overseas is very common these days. Over the past few decades, globalisation has made studying abroad a common phenomenon. Nowadays, many high schools have their own overseas programmes. In Japan, we have one-month, two-month, six-month and one-year programmes. And a lot of high schools offer advanced English courses. These courses help students to enhance their English skills.

I think participating in school programmes is very important. By doing so, students will gain valuable experiences. In my opinion, students shouldn't hesitate to participate in these overseas programmes. Even if their English is not good enough, I would recommend that they embrace the challenge. I fully enjoyed the challenge while I was in Canada. English proficiency is not so important, although of course it would be good to be proficient. To put it plainly, experience itself is more important than English proficiency. Many students do not have the courage to go abroad and I had a similar feeling initially. But your English will improve while you are abroad! However, you do need to be proactive. In addition, you should cultivate self-discipline in order to succeed.

Going abroad is a great opportunity for students to develop their skills. It enables them not only to develop their English skills but also to gain a deeper insight into what it means to be a human.

I will talk about my personal experiences after returning home. I will describe how my experiences overseas helped me grow and influenced my university life at Kindai. These experiences had a profound impact on my life. This is one of the reasons why I became an English teacher. Needless to say, if I had not had these experiences, I could not have become an English teacher.

There was a particular reason why I chose Kindai after returning to Japan. Kindai offers a resourceful environment for students. There were many courses, and I saw exciting potentials there. I was a member of the Faculty of Literature, Arts and Cultural Studies and I majored in English literature. I studied curatorship too. Within four years, I obtained qualifications in English language teaching and in curatorship. At Kindai, students enjoy a great number of learning opportunities. I took full advantage of these opportunities during my four years there. My major subject was English literature, which exposed me to Western culture. We studied both European and American literature. I focused on Western literature and my undergraduate thesis was on human rights. I drew inspiration from *Gulliver's Travels*, which touches upon the issue of slavery; therefore I focused on labour history and contemporary problems. This includes the problems of child labour and education. My university education enabled me to learn more about English literature and education. Entering this university gave me access to great ideas and opportunities.

I shall now move on to explain my decision to become an English teacher. Having spent some four years overseas, I made up my mind to do what I wanted. At the very beginning, I wanted to find a job where I could put my experience abroad to good use. I was not interested in becoming a teacher until I entered university. One day, I realised that most English teachers had never spent long periods of time living overseas. I am not criticising them, but I thought English teachers should spend at least one or two years abroad. I felt that I was able to contribute to education. There are a couple of reasons why I felt this way.

I had spent the entirety of my high school life overseas. This experience would have a good influence on my students. I would be able to share that real experience, instead of repeating second-hand stories from textbooks. Experience is a great asset. For example, I could clarify the differences between Canadian and Japanese high schools without much difficulty. If I hadn't spent time overseas, I would not have been able to convey this knowledge. Not a lot of teachers have spent time in foreign high schools, so I am pleased to tell them about the differences. I have realised that students are very interested in this topic. Their knowledge is confined to Japanese culture, and many Japanese people don't know what it is like to study in a foreign school. This can be the reason why they find this topic attractive. When I talk about foreign cultures, I not only tell them good stories but also describe any hardships they are likely to encounter in a foreign country. I have undergone many hardships, and it is essential to tell them about these.

The hardships I experienced overseas will be helpful to students who want to go abroad in the future. Living in a foreign country is fun, but it is not easy. Judging from my own experience, the most important thing is adaptability. I lived overseas for about four years, and I was always endeavouring to adapt myself.

To put it simply, I tried to be an enterprising person. There are several reasons why this is important. Obviously, Western and Japanese cultures are different. School culture – from primary school to secondary school – is very different too. Western schoolchildren are much more active than their Japanese counterparts. For example, they play an active role in their school projects. By contrast, in Japan, few students would want to stand out and become the centre of attention. For better or for worse, this is a feature of Japanese culture. When I moved abroad, I tried to be more active. I soon became familiar with foreign customs. I found that sport was the easiest way to communicate. I played ice hockey and it changed me considerably. It is impossible not to talk to your teammates when you play sports. Of course, I had difficulty communicating with my friends, but I never gave up. These opportunities helped me improve my English skills. My best advice is this: even if you are not confident, learning through trial and error is a great way to improve yourself. Don't be shy. Never hesitate to speak up.

The education systems are different. I focus on incorporating the strengths of each system into my teaching. My Canadian experience helps my teaching, and I am able to see things from different angles. Every country has its distinct education style. In Japan, the Ministry of Education establishes guidelines for courses of study. Canada is different.

The Canadian provinces enjoy jurisdiction. This means that the provinces are allowed to establish standards. It gives teachers more freedom to develop inventive lessons. A lot of Canadian teachers demonstrate their individualistic ways of teaching. However, there is not much room for originality in Japan, especially in public schools. The reason is because it is the Ministry of Education which establishes the guidelines. Private schools are not required to follow the guidelines so strictly. Teachers can be more inventive. That is why I am able to introduce Canadian methods of teaching in Kindai high school. I learned these while I was in high school in Canada. I am introducing these methods because they impressed me deeply at that time. I felt that they were completely different to Japanese methods. In Japan, most lessons are unilateral, and students have to listen all the time. It is different in Canada and other Western countries. I find strengths in both teaching styles, however. My advantage is that I have the experience of studying abroad in Canada and the UK. This experience changed my worldview, and I want to share this with my students.

I shall give some examples of my teaching style. When I became a teacher in Kindai high school, I required my students to cultivate independence. I told them: 'Take part in classroom discussions and try to think more. And also, do not be shy when expressing your opinions.' There is a reason why I say this. Students in Japan rarely speak up in class. They don't get to experience an active school life, and most of their lessons are conducted through one-way teaching. I am not criticising this style of teaching, but I want them to understand the Western style too. After being introduced to that style, students undergo gradual changes. They are encouraged to think more and more. One of my aims is to help my students to form a sense of active participation, which enables them to develop their ability to think.

To be concrete, I design very simple lessons. I lead my students into independent actions. For example, I introduce general topics and invite each group to discuss them. After the discussions, they are asked to present their opinions. While I was in Canada, we enjoyed many opportunities of doing research, participating in discussions, and delivering presentations. It is not easy for Japanese students to carry out these activities because they are not often encouraged to do so. To put it another way, they lack a sense of direction in the first place. When they become used to it, they are enthusiastic. In my opinion, sometimes they need to do something different in order to be stimulated.

Now, I will discuss using ICT (Information and Communication Technology) in education. In Kindai high school, there are some interesting resources for students. Every student has an iPad. They have everything on their iPads. For instance, they have an electronic dictionary, and they can use it in class. This is called ICT in education. Basically, teachers are using modern technology to give lessons. Students can concentrate more on their lessons and it will be easier for them to do research. Thus, students will feel a stronger desire to learn. This facilitates their independence. Furthermore, it increases their sense of motivation.

Many people today are using SNS (Social Networking Services). This is another interesting resource available in Kindai high school. They call it a cyber campus. A lot of teachers are pressed for time. After starting to use the cyber campus, my work became more efficient. For example, teachers can upload grammar questions for their students to study. They can access the questions anytime. This means that teachers don't have to go and print hard copies. Therefore, teachers can use their time more effectively. Moreover, this also helps to cut expenses. ICT in education is still developing, and we need to learn by trial and error. In the near future, I think it will become an essential pedagogical tool.

Finally, active learning is spreading throughout the whole of Japan. A lot of English teachers know about this. The passive method has been preferred for a long time, and therefore active learning is becoming all the more important. Now our education system is experiencing a transition period. Our education needs to be more globalised and to respond to the changes of the times. There are many approaches to active learning, and teachers are able to adopt original methods. In my teaching, I attach much importance to communication. For example, I talk to students and try to break the ice. If students feel the strain, active learning will not succeed. I encourage them not to be nervous about taking part in classroom activities. This is very important in terms of developing their ideas and abilities. Needless to say, teacher should find interesting ways to teach and give their students something interesting. If they feel it is interesting, they will try to come up with their own ideas. Although teachers give a lot of advice, students don't always take it. That is why communicating with students is important. Active learning is essential to improve their abilities. It not only helps to enhance their English skills, it also gives them opportunities to present and debate their ideas in front of other people. There are many ways to implement active learning, so teachers can develop their own styles to suit their teaching.

In conclusion, I talked about my overseas experience and the reason why I became an English teacher. After I started to teach, I made full use of my Canadian experience. Thus, I adopted various ways of teaching. Experience is a valuable resource and it can change your life. If teachers have experiences of studying abroad, that will be a useful tool. In addition, students will be interested in foreign topics. In my opinion, teachers need to be interesting, as this helps them impart knowledge more effectively. It is also essential to cultivate students' humanitarian outlook. Now that we are in a transition period, we are forced to realign some of our fundamental attitudes. We will carry on reforming our education system.

What I Knew of Ireland Growing Up

Shizuko Ura (Sadako Matsuura)

Japanese poetry referring to Ireland

Kaoru Maruyama (丸山薫, 1899–1974) was a famous poet in Japan. He was a good friend of Tatsuji Miyoshi and Tatsuo Hori and they were active in the field of modernist poetry. They made up a famous group called Shiki (四季 - Four Seasons). Tatsuji Miyoshi and Maruyama were followers of Sakutaro Hagiwara, who was the greatest master of poetry in the Taisho era (1912–26).

The Taisho era was the Belle Époque of Japan. Sometimes it is referred to as 'Taisho Romanism'. Maruyama became a poet in this time. His masterpiece, which appeared in the Japanese high school Kokugo textbook (the study of Japanese language and literature), was the only Japanese poem that mentioned Ireland before the First World War. The great writer Ryoxtaro Shiba introduced this poem in his famous series, Going on the Highway: Ireland 2 (『街道をゆく 愛蘭土紀行 2』.

'On the Train' (In My Infancy,『幼年』)
by Kaoru Maruyama

On the train, I decided to visit
The countryside, like Ireland,
Where the people are turning around their parasols on the festive days,
Where it rains while the sun is shining.
Let's visit the countryside, like Ireland,
The reflection of my face on the window is my company,
While I cross the lakes and pass through the tunnels.
To meet the strange-looking girls and cattle walking,
Let's visit the countryside, like Ireland
[Newly translated by the author]

When I read this poem in the Kokugo class, my knowledge of Ireland was very poor. The image of 'the countryside like Ireland' left such a vivid impression that I have never forgotten this refrain. But a question was raised: in the early Showa era, c. 1929 (when Maruyama wrote this poem), a substantial part of Japan was still rural. Why write about Ireland then?

In the second year of the Showa period (1927), two years before Maruyama wrote this poem, his master Sakutaro Hagiwara had written a poem entitled「旅上」[Ryojo] ('On the Trip'). In this, Hagiwara wrote of his admiration for France. Apparently, Maruyama was inspired by his master's poem.

But Ireland is even farther away than France! Even for the rich and free Sakutaro, visiting France had been nothing more than a dream. Why should Maruyama focus on Ireland?

To answer this question, we may borrow ideas from the excellent essays by Tetsuji Takahashi in his 1991 book, *A Narrative of Travels on Historical Places in Ireland* (『アイルランド歴史紀行』). We shall return to Takahashi in due course.

Maruyama grew up in Korea, which was a Japanese colony in those days. He often witnessed Korean people being forced to live in poverty and misery, enduring the oppression of the Japanese imperialist government. Is it possible for the colonist to maintain a good relationship with the colonised? Many Japanese people wanted to know how England interacted with Ireland.

As a child, Maruyama had wanted to be a sailor. He eventually gave up, but his admiration for the sea lasted throughout his life. He would have enjoyed sailing to Ireland from Japan.

Karuizawa as Japan's 'Coole Park'

Japan was still very young as a modern country in the Taisho era. Confronted with western civilisation, the Japanese began to spurn their traditional culture. How to rebuild their self-confidence became an important issue.

Yes, in the Taisho era, some intelligent Japanese people wanted to know more about Ireland, especially about the Irish Literary Renaissance led by W.B. Yeats (1865–1939). Young Japan needed a cultural revolution to boost their self-confidence in the face of the Western world.

Takahashi has given me many vital insights. Here I would like to sum up what I have learned from him. There was a 'cultural salon' made up of young Japanese poets and writers: the 'Karuizawa Group'. Karuizawa was a renowned summer resort in Japan, where upper-class people and the cognoscenti gathered. We can say that it was the 'Coole Park' of Japan. (Coole Park was the place where Yeats and his friends pursued their literary endeavours.)

An attractive widow, Hiroko Katayama, was a tanka (traditional Japanese short poetry) poet herself, and the Queen of the Salon. Lady Katayama was an excellent translator of Irish literature, using the nom de plume Mineko Matsumura. Hereafter, we will call her Mineko. She was the Lady Gregory of the Karuizawa Group.

Among the young poets and writers who admired this wise widow, there were famous authors such as Ryūnosuke Akutagawa and Kan Kikuchi.

In the Meiji era (1868–1912), W.B. Yeats was already introduced to Japan. He was the first European writer that demonstrated a strong interest in Japanese Noh plays. His influence on the Karuizawa Group was profound.

Akutagawa actually followed Yeats's creative method in his 'Ohchou-mono' (「王朝物」王朝」); ohchou refers to the Heian period in Japanese history when the famous 'Tales of Genji' (twelfth century) were written. Based on original tales from the Heian period, such as 'Yabunonaka' (「藪の中」), those excellent pieces are often included in our Kokugo textbooks. Akutagawa, a literary genius, was well known as the original author of Kurosawa's famous film *Rashomon* (「羅生門」).

Karuizawa, Japan. The Karuizawa Group was a cultural salon made up of young Japanese poets and writers based in Karuizawa, a renowned summer resort in Japan. (*Kaedeenari/Alamy*)

The Karuizawa Group tried to shape a new Japanese identity by means of a literary renaissance, following in the footsteps of the Irish writers. Thus, as a main member of the Shiki group, Maruyama encountered Ireland in Karuizawa. Mineko introduced the writings of W.B. Yeats, J.M. Synge and other Irish authors to Japan. Japanese Kokugo textbooks are undoubtedly indebted to her work.

Akutagawa fell in love with Mineko, though she was fourteen years older than he was. Their relationship was somewhat similar to that between Lady Gregory and W.B. Yeats. Kikuchi played the role of sponsor, providing money for publishing books about Ireland. He wrote plays which were apparently influenced by J.M. Synge and G.B. Shaw.

One of these, 'The Housetop Madman' (「屋上の狂人」) was published in 1916 in the magazine *Shinshichoun* (『新思潮』): it was first performed in the Teikoku Gekijo (帝国劇場), in 1921, and five years later (26–27 November 1926) it was performed in the Abbey Theatre in Dublin and received favourably by Yeats himself (Akiyo Suzuki (鈴木暁世)『越境する想像力』, Ekkyousuru Souzouryoku, p. 21).

What I learned in Japanese schools

Through the Karuizawa Group, Irish literature became popular in Taisho-era Japan. Maruyama's poem, quoted above, is loved by students even now, because it is a choral piece sung by many on various occasions.

Japanese students also love to sing the Irish song 'The Last Rose of Summer'. The Japanese title is 'Niwa no chigusa' (「庭の千草」: Various flowers in my garden). It was in the music textbooks and has been a favourite of many Japanese people even to this very day.

I was lucky to have a chance to see a performance of J.M. Synge's *Riders to the Sea* in my school days. It was more than sixty years ago, and I was only a fourteen-year-old girl. I saw that drama on a school festival in the beautiful hall of Kobe College Junior and Senior High School in Nishinomiya, Hyogo Prefecture. I still remember the heavy and hopeless atmosphere of that drama, though I was not equipped with any knowledge of the writer J.M. Synge. Nor did I know the location and circumstances of the Aran Islands in those days. Later, I learned that Ireland was a country of poets and thinkers.

Koizumi Yakumo's *Kaidan* (『怪談』, *Ghost Stories*) is quite popular among the Japanese. His tales are not only in the Kokugo textbooks but also in the English textbooks. Now I understand why he was loved by many Japanese people. It is because Ireland and Japan have a similar spiritual background. We still feel the existence of invisible beings, an intimation that predated the modern world. The Japanese believe in fairies, demons and naughty goblins. In Japan, gods or goddesses reside everywhere. We have sacred trees, wells, rivers, mountains and waterfalls. Even now, in Japan, some kinds of animals are believed to have mysterious powers; sometimes they bring happiness, sometimes disasters, and intrude upon human society. They are active only for the people who believe in them. Do we not share a similar ancient faith called 'animism'?

I also encountered Jonathan Swift, the Irish author of Gulliver's Travels (「ガリバー旅行記」, 1728, in my Kokugo class in an essay called 'Jonathan Swift no warai' (「ジョナサンスイフトの笑い」), written by Yoshimi Usui (臼井吉見) in the Chikuma textbook. I did not realise then that this is not simply a joyful tale for children but is a serious satire on human society.

When I was young, I wanted to be an actress, but I never realised this dream. In the end, I became a teacher of Japanese literature at high school. To compensate for my aborted dream, I committed myself to school drama activities as a drama director and sometimes a writer. Privately, I love Western classic music, especially operas, and spend money in the theatres. There, I came across Samuel Beckett.

I love Oscar Wilde, his 「サロメ」 Salomé with Beardsley's strange and demoniac pictures in the Iwanami book. And I saw Wilde in an opera house again.

My encounters with Celtic culture

It was in a Kokugo class that I encountered the word 'Celt'. It was 1974. I was reading an essay titled 'Ishi no shiso' (「石の思想」, 'The Idea of the Stone') in the Kadokawa textbook.

The author of this impressive essay was Takao Aeba (饗場孝男). He insists that we should understand European culture as a tapestry interwoven by different cultures. Among them, there is the famous stone culture (Greek and Roman), but another is older than that: it still exists as an undercurrent of European culture on the continent and the islands, in England and Ireland. This amazing 'wooden

'To meet the strange-looking girls and cattle walking/ Let's visit the countryside, like Ireland.' Ardara, County Donegal, Ireland. (*Richard Wayman/Alamy*)

Tenth-century round tower in the fifth-century monastic settlement of Monasterboice, County Louth, Ireland. (*George Munday/Alamy*)

culture' is known as 'Celtic'.

In 1995, I travelled to the heart of Ireland for the first time. Yes, now I can understand that the spots we visited are not merely tourist attractions, but places you must visit in order to understand Irish traditions and history. I would say it was one of the highlights of my life to travel through this wet and green country. How beautiful the countryside was! In Ireland, I had the best guides ever, and I acknowledge their help with gratitude at the end of this chapter.

I loved the monastic ruins with lovely round towers like Monasterboice. And I was enchanted by those mysterious spirals and knots on the high crosses. They are quite similar to Japanese 'Jomon' patterns, and the world-famous artist, Taro Okamoto noticed this fact and was inspired by Celtic culture.

I loved the Irish countryside, just as Maruyama had admired it. However, when I revisited Ireland in 2005, Ireland was changing under the influences of capitalism and commercialism. Building projects were underway everywhere.

I hope Ireland will make great progress as a member of the EU, but at the same time, I hope she will never lose her natural beauty and the real spirit of her culture. I saw a devout lady 'paying the rounds'. With some wishes on her mind, she was walking round and round a small, ruined chapel and a holy well. The Japanese have the same kind of custom, called Ohyakudomairi. I think the Irish and the Japanese share the same heart!

On my first visit there, I obtained a Claddagh ring as a souvenir. The two hands hold the crowned heart. For me, the crowned heart symbolises love and friendship between Ireland and Japan. May the understanding and respect for each other between the Irish and the Japanese last forever!

Bibliography

Aeba, T.（饗場孝男）'Ishi no Shiso' (「石の思想」, 'The Idea of Stone'). The essay was originally written by him in 1971, titled 'Ishi to Hikari no Shiso' (「石と光の思想」, 'The Idea of Stone and Light' published by Heibonsha. I met him in *High School Modern Japanese Language* 2 published by Kadokawa Shoten in 1974.

Kelly, R., Quinn, C. L. and Furomoto, T. A Look at Ireland: Introduction to Irish Cultural Studies. (Tokyo: Kaibunsha, 2002).

Killanin, L. and Duignan, M.V. *The Shell Guide to Ireland*. Revised and updated by P. Harbison (Dublin: Gill & McMillan, 1995)

Shiba, R. Kaidou o yuku 31(『街道をゆく 31』, *Going on the Highway: Ireland*). Tokyo: Asahi Shimbun Press, 2009.

Suzuki, A. *Imagining Border-crossing: Transgressions of Modernism*（『越境する想像力』）(Osaka: Osaka University Press, 2014).

Takahasi, T. *Ireland rekishi-kiko*. (『アイルランド歴史紀行』)（Tokyo: Chikuma Shobou, 1991).

Usui, Y.（臼井吉見） 'Jonathan Swift no warai' ('Laugh of Jonathan Swift') Original essay was in the magazine, *After the World War*（『戦後』9 (1956), Sengo 9）. I met him in *High School Modern Japanese Language* 1 （『高等学校　現代国語』）published by Chikuma Shobou.

Gratitude

Many thanks to my respectable friends, Satoko Tamura and Kimiko Nakatsuka, for kindly giving advice on my poor English. Special thanks also to my old friends, Richard Kelly and Ciaran Quinn, the best guides in the world, for introducing me to Ireland and Celtic culture.

Priest Yoshida Kenkō, by Utagawa Hiroshige (1797–1858), mid-1840s. (CBL J 2095, © *The Trustees of the Chester Beatty Library, Dublin*)

- Importation of copies of scripture and of imagery and artworks associated with the new religious practice served to give a major impetus to the learning, arts and crafts of the newly converted cultures, combining with their local legacies to form distinctive local expressions of the new religious cultures. These in turn made a major contribution to the wider international cultures of both Buddhism and Christianity.
- The material cultures of both sets of islands is transformed, from the moated tombs of the Kofun era (to 550) in Japan, with their ceramic human and animal effigies and bronze implements, or the migration-period burials of the Germanic settlement period in Britain, with their weaponry, jewellery and utensils, to the aesthetic and technical virtuosity of the Great Buddha of Nara and the Lindisfarne Gospels.
- Temples or churches and monasteries became a new feature of the rural and urban landscape, and fostered the development of architecture.
- Both Buddhism and Christianity introduced socially transformative ideologies and ethical codes, and both survive in distinctive forms in both sets of islands to this day, sometimes even alongside one another.

Christianity in Japan: A story of crossings

Richard Kelly

A curiosity with Japan began for St Francis Xavier (1506–52) when a wayward samurai called Anjiro met with him in December 1547 as the saint was conducting a marriage ceremony in Moluccas (an archipelago of islands within Indonesia).[1] This led Xavier to dedicate the next two years to familiarising himself with the culture and structure of Japanese society. His principal interests were that Japan had an emperor in Miyako (Kyoto), its social structure was feudal, and its universities were influential cultural centres. He strategized that if he converted the emperor to Christianity, the feudal and intellectual elites would soon similarly adhere, thereby rapidly evangelising the whole of Japan.

To realise this aim, he arranged for Anjiro and his compatriots to be taught the essentials of Christian doctrine at a Jesuit college in Goa in the south-western part of India.[2] When they had been adequately instructed in the Christian message, Xavier, together with two Jesuit friars and his Japanese followers, arrived in Kagoshima on the southern tip of Kyushu on 15 August 1549.[3] The local people were generally welcoming towards him to the extent that he was granted an official meeting with the *daimyō* of Satsuma, Takahisa Shimazu; this meeting took place on 29 September 1549. The *daimyō* granted him the freedom to evangelise in the region without any restraints or conditions. The only biblical book that had been thus far translated into Japanese was St Matthew's Gospel. To increase the availability of Christian writings in Japanese, Anjiro set about translating from Spanish *Doutrina Christa* and *Declaracao de Fe*. The Japanese language naturally did not have a Christian vocabulary; therefore, these translations were fundamentally inaccurate.[4] In addition, Xavier's Japanese was so rustic and rudimentary that many local people enjoyed listening to him preach for its pure entertainment value.

As part of his strategy to convert the emperor, Xavier departed for Hirado in late August 1550, leaving Anjiro in charge of the small but committed Christian community in Kagoshima.[5] Once a Christian community had been established in Hirado under the stewardship of Fr Torres SJ, he continued his journey to Kyoto in the company of Br Francisco SJ and a small group of Japanese Christians with the hope of being granted a meeting with the emperor. Upon arrival in Miyako (Kyoto), he was greatly disillusioned to witness a city torn by civil wars, with most of its inhabitants subsisting in abject poverty. The emperor turned out to be a rather powerless figure, and Xavier, who appeared weary and dishevelled after his arduous journey from northern Kyushu, was firmly denied any access to the imperial court.[6] This journey, therefore, proved to be futile, and he became despondent because his strategy to convert the Japanese emperor was never going to succeed.

Xavier's important realisation from this failed mission to Miyako (Kyoto) was that the concept of Christian humility was basically not compatible with the Japanese cultural ethos; he therefore decided upon his return to Yamaguchi to adopt a very different approach when meeting with regional rulers. He assumed the ceremonial role of Viceroy of India and endowed the *daimyō* of Yamaguchi, Yoshitaka Ouchi, with luxurious and exotic bounty.[7] This tactic was highly efficacious, to the extent that the evangelisation of the local lords now became his central modus operandi.

The Jesuits were among Europe's first great teachers of secular as well as religious knowledge – Xavier imparted both during his mission to Japan. The dignity and composure of Br Fernandez SJ when he was spat at while preaching in Yamaguchi inspired evangelisations because those who witnessed it were impressed that he offered no retaliation in the face of this humiliation but, rather, remained composed and steadfast throughout while imparting his Christian message.

The bonzes of the Shingo sect appeared to share a certain affinity with Christian doctrine; however, the use of the term *Dainichi* to signify the Christian God is not wholly compatible in that it also has ambiguous implications with certain unethical undertones. This necessitated the direct transliteration of Christian Latin vocabulary into Japanese; examples are *Kirisuto* (Christ), *Maria* (Mary) *and Baputesuma no Yohane* (John the Baptist).[8] A hostile rivalry with the Shingo sect ensued, yet members of the samurai and the court elites continued to regularly convert to Christianity. Xavier cultivated a genuine respect for Japanese culture and tradition to the extent that achieving this all-important equipoise with Christian beliefs was essential to his mature vision of a Christian Japan.

In August 1551, Xavier received word that a Portuguese ship had arrived in Bungo; this pleased him because he desired to garner current news about the Christian mission in India. He was contemporaneously given an opportune invitation by the *daimyō* of Funai (Oita), Yoshishige Otomo, to officially visit him.[9] In September, he set out for Funai and appointed Fr Cosme de Torres SJ from Hirado to replace him as pastor of the Christian community in Yamaguchi. On his arrival in Funai, he was warmly received by the twenty-nine-year-old Otomo. When this *daimyō* was baptised some twenty-seven years later, he fittingly chose the Christian name Francis. The ship brought no update of any kind from India; therefore, Xavier felt it was his duty to return to India to personally witness and evaluate the state of the Christian mission there. He never set foot in Japan again; he died while doing missionary duty at the Portuguese colony of São João in China on 3 December 1552. His body was finally brought back to Old Goa, India, on 14 March 1554, where it was eventually interred at the Basilica of Bom Jesus, one of India's largest churches.

For some thirty years after Xavier's departure from Japan, the superiority of European cultural values was promoted carte-blanche style in the continual evangelisation of Japan, with little concrete results in terms of significant conversions. Eventually, an Italian Jesuit priest called Fr Alessandro Valignano SJ joined the Japanese mission, and he once more adopted the approach of mutual cultural respect that was the essential trademark of St Francis Xavier. The Christianisation of Japan became reinvigorated, especially throughout the island of Kyushu. By 1582 the Japanese Christian community had become the largest in any country that was independent of European colonial control: it had grown to *c.* 200,000 believers under the stewardship of Valignano.

The Jesuits were not the only mendicant order with a presence in Japan during this era. The Franciscan mission to Japan was initiated from Manila, the Philippines, by Fr Juan Bautista OFM in 1590. The mission was first established in Kyoto, where it founded a hospital for lepers. The order later expanded its presence by establishing friaries in Osaka and Nagasaki. In 1602, a small group of Augustinians arrived in Oita on the west coast of Kyushu, also from the Philippines. Several of their members were publicly martyred at the Hill of Martyrs in Nagasaki in 1637. The Dominicans, under the stewardship of the Spanish St Alphonsus de Mena OP, established the House of the Holy Rosary in Kyoto in 1611; one year later he was reassigned to St Dominic's House in Nagasaki just as the persecution of Christians was gaining momentum. He and his followers were expelled from Nagasaki in 1613 and made their way to Oita, where they established a small but resilient Christian community. St Alphonsus and fellow friar Hernando de Ayala OP eventually decided to return to Nagasaki; on their arrival in the city on 29 May 1617, St Alphonsus was immediately taken prisoner and publicly beheaded by officialdom four days later. He was the first Dominican martyr in Japan.

The Dutch and the English began trading in western Japan from *c.* 1600, and focused solely on this fiscal activity.[10] These two essentially Protestant countries would have considered the Catholic presence in Japan as undesirable to the extent that they would have condoned the suppression of the Roman Church by Japanese officialdom. The Protestant Church during this era did not engage in missionary activity because it was still in its infancy and continuing to establish its firm base in north European territories and societies as it became increasingly politically potent.

Ieayasu Tokugawa (1543–1616) assumed the leadership of Japan in 1600. He intensely disliked Christianity yet just about tolerated it because he wanted to continue trading with Spain and Portugal. The Dutch (and the English to a lesser extent), in contrast, traded commercially with Japan without engaging in any kind of missionary activity. When the Anglo-Irish writer Jonathan Swift (1667–1745) refers to Japan in part three of *Gulliver's Travels* (1726), he describes ***fumi-e*** (踏み絵, fumi "stepping-on" + e "picture"), which is the act of apostatising by stamping on the crucifix or an image of the Virgin Mary.[11] The principled Gulliver refuses to do this defiling act at great peril to his personal safety from both the Japanese and the Dutch, who freely practised ***fumi-e*** (踏み絵, fumi "stepping-on" + e "picture") and had a significant trading base on a series of islands adjacent to the port of

Nagasaki. This sacrilege also illustrates the bitter legacy of the Reformation in early sixteenth-century Europe, which pitted Catholics and Protestants against each other as emboldened rivals.

Why was Swift fascinated with Japan (the only real country that he names; all the others in the work are given fictional names)? The definitive answer to this is not easy to ascertain; however, it is clear from the thematic content of *Gulliver's Travels* that he was clearly interested in cultures that were non-European and which displayed a great deal of political and cultural sophistication independent of any Christian influence.[12] Dutch, along with Spanish, Portuguese and English, were the first European languages to be used for trading and commerce in Japan. The trade to Japan included silver, medicines, furniture and scientific innovation. The trade from Japan comprised silk, pottery, lacquerware, salt, pepper, tea and bamboo.

A Franciscan envoy of the viceroy of New Spain formally requested the shogun of Kagoshima to construct a Spanish fortress in Kyushu. This rivalry between the Jesuits and the Franciscans led to further mistrust of Catholicism in Japan. In later persecution, the Catholic communities in Japan were driven into hiding and became known as *Kakure Kirishitan* (隠れキリシタン) – a literal translation is 'Hidden Christians'.[13] Hideyoshi Toyotomi (1536/7–98) issued a *bateren-tsuihōrei* (伴天連追放令) ('deportation order of Christians') to the Jesuits on 24 July 1587, and placed Nagasaki under his direct rule to take complete control of Portuguese trade and that of the Dutch and English from *c*. 1600. A certain number of Catholic clerics remained illicitly in Japan: eighteen Jesuits, seven Franciscans, seven Dominicans and one Augustinian; the Carmelites were the only mendicant order not to have a presence in initial Japanese evangelisation – their presence in Japan dates from 1930. This suppression was occurring against the backdrop of the thirty years of enduring war between Catholics and Protestants in Prussia (1618–48), which curtailed and even cut off necessary funding and supplies for missionary activity in regions such as Japan. This war was also effective in dividing ruling monarchies in Europe strictly along Catholic or Protestant lines, resulting in ever-more sectarian wars and conflict.[14]

Garnered from a diversity of oral histories from Japanese Catholic communities, Shusaku Endo's (1923–96) internationally acclaimed novel *Silence* (1966; English translation 1969) vividly depicts the acrimonious persecution of Christians and the blanket suppression of the Church. The plot is based on a Jesuit missionary called Sabastião Rodrigues; the character is modelled on an Italian from Palermo,

Sicily, called Guiseppe Chiara (1602–85), who was sent to Japan in the seventeenth century as a Jesuit missionary. Partly composed in the style of a monologue memo by Rodrigues, the theme of a silent God who is omnipresent to a dedicated believer enduring great distress directly echoes Endo's witness of Christian prejudice in Japan, his experience of racism in France, and his lifelong struggle with tuberculosis. The novel opens just after the Shimabara Rebellion (1637–8) with the arrival of Rodrigues on the island of Oshima, which is today part of Fukuoka Prefecture in northern Kyushu; he was eventually arrested in 1643 for evangelisation activity,[15] and died of natural causes in Edo (Tokyo) on 24 August 1685.

Silence was released as an epic historical drama film in late 2016; it premiered in Vatican City on 29 November 2016 and in the US on 23 December 2016. Martin Scorsese directed the production, and it stars Andrew Garfield as Fr Sabastião Rodrigues and Liam Neeson as Fr Cristōvão Ferreira. After a long silence and witnessing appalling suffering borne by anguished Christians, Christ eventually breaks his silence to Rodrigues: 'You may trample, one may trample on the *fumie*. It was to share man's pain that I carried my cross.' Rodrigues then puts his foot on the *fumie*, and it is assumed that Christians are relieved of their sufferings – the climax is left deliberately ambiguous as it is not clear whether this alleviation ever actually happened. The novel expresses a deep moral ambiguity: God suffers with humanity rather than eliminating the causes of that suffering. Endo in *A Life of Jesus* stresses that Japanese culture accommodates such a theme of sharing in suffering due to the centrality of social-group mentality in Japanese culture. The individual and the group are defined by each other; namely, the individual and the group are integrally intertwined. Through this important literary work, Endo illustrates, like St Francis Xavier, that Christianity must be fine-tuned and adapted to the receiving culture, resulting in a Christianity flavoured with certain Japanese mores and norms.

Endo's other great enlightening contribution is that crossings were not just from Europe to Japan. In his novel *Samurai* (1980), he depicts the fictional story of a Japanese diplomatic mission to New Spain (Mexico) and Europe in the early seventeenth century by a Japanese nobleman, and the intriguing cultural and political variances to which this gave rise. The principal character is Rokuemon Tsunenaga Hasekura (1571–1622). During the years 1613–20, Hasekura led a pioneering mission to the Vatican to seek an audience with Pope Paul V (pontificate: 1605–21), travelling there from New Spain.[16] He is essentially the first

Fresco in the Quirinal Palace, Rome, depicting the embassy of Hasekura Tsunenaga, 1615 (painted under the direction of Agostino Tassi, Giovanni Lanfranco and Carlo Saraconi). [Quirinal Palace/Wikimedia Commons]

Japanese ambassador to ever set foot in the Americas and Europe. Japan's next diplomatic venture to Europe did not occur again for over 200 years (1862–3), when it embarked on missions to Great Britain, the Netherlands, Portugal, Prussia and Russia.

Hasekura was baptised Don Felipe Francisco Hasekura at the request of the king of Spain on 17 February 1615; his baptismal sponsor was the duke of Lerma, the de facto ruler of Spain. This was the same year that Galileo Galilei (1564–1642) faced the Roman Inquisition, which berated his theory of geocentricism as being grave profanity.[17]

Hasekura was granted a private papal audience with Pope Paul V in November 1615. He submitted two letters to the pope: one on trade with New Spain and the other for the dispatch of further missionaries to evangelise Japan. These letters were written in Latin on behalf of Masamune Date (1537–1636; ruled Sendai from 1600) by Luis Sotelo in 1613. Pope Paul V granted his request for the dispatch of missionaries, but referred the trade request back to the king of Spain. In addition to evangelisation and trade, issues of a political nature also seem to have been aired. Hasekura put forward the proposal that the sure way to Christianise the entire Japanese archipelago was to establish a special alliance with the ruler of Japan, Masamune Date. This never occurred because by 1614 Christianity in Japan was being actively suppressed.

When Hasekura met again with the king of Spain in April 1616, the monarch refused to sign the trade agreement on the basis that the Japanese embassy did not seem to be officially recognised or sanctioned by the potentate of Japan. Ieyasu Tokugawa (1543–1616) was now the ruler of Japan.[18] He was officially appointed the Tokugawa shogunate in 1603 after a decisive victory at the Battle of Sekigahara in 1600, and was responsible for ordering the widespread persecution of Christians in Japan.[19] Japan wanted to engage in the export trade of fine pepper and lacquerware from regions such as Kyoto and in the import trade of silver from various parts of New Spain. Some of the delegation led by Hasekura remained in Spain and settled in a town near Seville called Coria del Rio, where today some 700 inhabitants use the surname Jopón (originally Hasekura de Japón), identifying themselves as descendants of Hasekura's diplomatic delegation.[20]

In April 1618, the *San Juan Bautista* arrived in the Philippines from New Spain with Hasekura and Luis Sotelo on board. The Spanish colonial government there purchased the ship, which they urgently needed in order to establish a more effective bulwark against incursions from the Dutch and the British. This communiqué of Hasekura to his son dated 28 July 1619 details these specific business dealings:

> The Governor was extremely friendly with the Japanese, and provided them with his protection. As they had many expensive things to buy, they decided to lease their ship. The ship was immediately furbished for combat. The Governor eventually bought the ship, because it turned out

> that it was of excellent and sturdy construction, and available ships of that quality were dramatically few. In favor of your Majesty, the price paid was reasonable.[21]

During his stay in the Philippines among a community of aboriginal Tagalog, Hasekura used the money from the sale of the ship to construct a smaller boat to ferry him home to Japan and to purchase numerous desirous gifts for Masamune Date; he arrived at the port of Nagasaki in August 1620.

He soon realised that Japan had dramatically changed: a decree to eliminate Christianity had been implemented since 1614; Ieyasu Tokugawa died in 1616 and was replaced by his more xenophobic son, Hidetada Tokugawa. Japan had adopted the *Sakokui* policy of national isolation. News of these persecutions was circulating in Europe during Hasekura's sojourn; this resulted in European rulers – the king of Spain to the fore – becoming very disinclined to auspiciously support Hasekura's plans for trade and missionary endeavours with Japan.

Hasekura briefed Masamune Date on his mission once he returned to Sendai. It is recorded that he presented the *daimyō* with a portrait painting of Pope Paul V, one of himself in prayerful meditation, and a set of Ceylonese and Indonesian decorative knives that he acquired in the Philippines (these are now conserved in the Sendai City Museum). Hasekura's briefing was just briefly documented in the records of the House of Masamune Date, with many ambiguous undertones:

> He brought paintings of the king of the Southern Barbarians, and a painting of himself, which he remitted. Many of his descriptions of the Southern Barbarian countries, and the meaning of Rokuemon's declarations were surprising and extraordinary.[22]

The immediate consequence of Hasekura's return to Sendai seems to have been the proscription of Christianity in the Sendai domain just two days later:

> … first, that all Christians were ordered to abandon their faith, in accordance with the rule of the *Shōgun*, and for those who did not, they would be exiled if they were nobles, and killed if they were citizens, peasants or servants. Second, that a reward would be given for the denunciation of

> hidden Christians. Third, that propagators of the Christian faith should leave the Sendai fief, or else, abandon their religion.[23]

It is not known what Hasekura said or did to bring about such a reaction. Later events indicate that he and his descendants remained faithful Christians. Hasekura may have given an account of the power of European countries and their Christian religion that had a chilling effect. He may also have encouraged an alliance between the Church and Masamune Date to take over Japan (an idea promoted by the Franciscans while he was in Rome). Hopes of trade with Spain were dashed when Hasekura communicated that the Spanish king would not enter any pact while persecutions were increasingly occurring in various parts of the country.

Masamune Date – who had been tolerant of Christianity despite the Bakufu's prohibition in the region his administration directly controlled – suddenly chose to distance himself from the religion. The first executions of Christians started forty days later. The anti-Christian measures taken by Masamune Date were, however, comparatively mild, and Japanese and Western Christians repeatedly claimed that they were only undertaken to appease the shogun: 'Masamune Date, out of fear of the Shogun, ordered the persecution of Christianity in his territory, and created several martyrs.'[24]

One month after Hasekura's return, Masamune Date wrote a letter to the shogun Hidetada Tokugawa, in which he makes a very clear effort to evade responsibility for the embassy, explaining in detail how it was organised with the approval, and even the collaboration, of the shogun:

> When I sent a ship to the Southern Barbarian countries several years ago, upon the advice of Shogun Mukai, I also dispatched the Southern Barbarian named Sotelo, who had resided for several years in Edo. At that time, your highness also gave messages for the Southern Barbarians, as well as presents, such as folding screens and sets of armour.[25]

Spain, with a colony and an army in the nearby Philippines, was the greatest threat to Japan at that time. Hasekura's eyewitness accounts of Spanish power and colonial methods in Nueva España (Mexico) may have precipitated the shogun Hidetada Tokugawa's decision to sever trade relations with Spain in 1623 and diplomatic relations in 1624, although other events, such as the smuggling of Spanish priests into Japan and a failed Spanish embassy, also contributed to the decision.

Hasekura's fate is unknown, and there are numerous conflicting accounts of his final years. Contemporary Christian commentators could only rely on hearsay; some rumours claimed that he abandoned Christianity, others that he was martyred for his faith, and others that he practised Christianity in secret. The fate of his descendants and servants, who were later executed for being Christians, suggests that Hasekura remained strongly Christian himself, and transmitted his faith to the members of his family. A certain number of Hasekura's travel companions, such as Shogen Yokozawa, are known to have remained Christian even after their return.

Luis Sotelo, who returned to Japan but was eventually captured and burned at the stake in 1624, gave before his execution an account of Hasekura returning to Japan as a hero who propagated the Christian faith, and passed away shortly after his return:

> My other colleague, the ambassador Philippus Faxecura, after he reached his aforementioned king [Masamune Date], was greatly honored by him, and sent to his own estate, to rest after such a long and tiring journey, where he made his wife, children, servants, and many other vassals into Christians, and advised other nobles who were his kith and kin to accept the faith, which they indeed did. While he was engaged in these and other pious works, a full year after his return, having provided much instruction and a great example, with much preparation, he piously passed on, leaving for his children by a special inheritance the propagation of the faith in his estate, and the protection of the religious [i.e. members of religious orders] in that kingdom. The King and all the nobles were greatly saddened by his passing, but especially the Christians and Religious, who knew very well the virtue and religious zeal of this man. This is what I heard by letters from the very Religious who administered the sacraments to him, and who had been present at his death, as well as from others.[26]

Tsunenaga Hasekura brought several Catholic artefacts back to Japan, but he did not give them to his ruler, and instead kept them in his own estate. He died, according to documented sources, from an illness in 1622; yet the location of his final resting place remains unresolved. Three locations have been traditionally identified: one is near the town of Osata in Miyagi Prefecture, the other is a Buddhist temple in Enfukuji in Miyagi Prefecture, and the third is a Buddhist temple in Kitayama, just north of the centre of Sendai Prefecture, located between Shifukuji temple and Aoba Ginja (Shinto shrine) – this hallowed place also has a memorial dedicated to Padre Luis Sotelo.

The descendants and associates of the Hasekura family, including his son Tsuneyori Rokuemon, were victimised and executed for being Christians or for the suspicion of being so. Tsuneyori was decapitated in 1640 for offering safe passage to two Christian servants called Tarezaemon – this husband and wife accompanied his father on his diplomatic mission to New Spain and Europe. He typifies the concept of the hidden Christian because, although he was the head monk of the Zen temple of Komyji, it was never completely clear if he were Buddhist or Christian – most plausibly he adhered to a fusion of aspects of both faiths. His younger brother, Tsunemichi, luckily managed to avoid certain death by escaping and disappearing after two Dominican friars revealed his name to authorities under the duress of torture.

The Sendai ruling authority confiscated the Hasekura estate and negated all rights associated with it. Some fifty Christian artefacts were seized; these included crucifixes, rosaries, sacred vestments, artworks and sacred writings. Fortunately, they were rediscovered in the late nineteenth century, but unfortunately nineteen codices listed in an 1840 catalogue have been lost. The greater part of these extant treasures is now on display at Sendai City Museum, with a few sporadically housed here and there in smaller local museums in Sendai Prefecture.

The pioneering diplomatic mission of Hasekura was generally circumvented and concealed in Japan until the end of the period of isolation known as *Sakoku* in the late nineteenth century. When the second around-the-world diplomatic mission (1872–3), under the leadership of Tomomi Iwakura (1828–90), reached Europe in 1873, it was shown historical documents in Venice detailing aspects of Hasekura's early-seventeenth-century travels in New Spain and Europe.[27] There are currently public memorials to Hasekura in several locations throughout the world: Acapulco, Mexico; Havana Bay, Cuba; Coría de Río, Spain; the Church of the Holy Japanese Martyrs, Civitavecchia, Italy; Manila, the Philippines; and Tsukinoura, Miyage Prefecture, Japan. The nearby city of Ishinomaki has established a historical theme park commemorating Japan's first diplomatic crossings to the wider world; it also

Urakami Cathedral (St Mary's Cathedral), Nagasaki. Once the largest church in the Orient, it was destroyed by atomic bomb on 9 August 1945 and rebuilt in 1959. [Chris Wilson/Alamy]

contains a replica of the San Juan Bautista because this was the very port from which Hasekura set out from on his pioneering and eventful venture to connect Japan with the wider world order. On his leaving Japan in 1613, the country was still somewhat tolerant of Christianity; but on his return in 1620, it was actively suppressing it because of the real threat it posed to the very foundations of a Japanese identity based on the Buddhist and Shinto traditions.

I would like to conclude this chapter with a personal story. In the early 1990s, I had the privilege of visiting the Amakusa Islands off the coast of Kumamoto Prefecture in south-western Japan, where still resides a considerable Christian community. One picturesque little fishing village called Sakitsu had a special resonance because its Christian community can trace its origins back to 1880, making it one of the earliest after the Meiji government lifted the ban on religious freedom in Japan when it came to power in 1868. The present-day Sakitsu Catholic church is a plain neo-Gothic structure completed in *c.* 1934, under the guidance of a French missionary priest called Fr Halbout, on the site of the residence of the village leader where ***fumi-e*** (踏み絵, fumi "stepping-on" + e "picture") was practised; this church replaced the original simple wooden structure of 1880 that was constructed adjacent to the Sakitsusuwa shrine. The most interesting feature of the church is its *tatami*-mat interior, thereby combining Christian and Japanese design, which would have been totally in keeping with the spirit of St Francis Xavier.[28] This church, together with other historic churches in Kyushu, including the Catholic cathedral of Nagasaki, are currently being officially nominated to become UNESCO World Heritage sites in 2018.

The other reason that church is special to me is that its pastor, who served this remote community of believers from 1982 to 1994, was an Irish Columban priest called Fr Patrick Diamond from Bellaghy, County Derry – one distant region in a crossing with another. We enjoyed chatting about Ireland and Japan, followed by a very personal tour of the historical treasures of the church: these included a Maria Kannon, seashell rosaries and prayer books that were used during the centuries of persecution and suppression.

At that moment, the past and the present eclipsed for me because the Christianity that St Francis Xavier brought to Japanese shores in the mid-sixteenth century still survived, despite the centuries of trials and tribulations it endured; it was still being nurtured in this special place by a gentle and dedicated Irish missionary priest – a true story of crossings.

Bibliography

Bonney, R., *Thirty Years' War: 1618–1648* (London and New York: Bloomsbury, 2002).

Boxer, C.R., *Jan Compagnie in Japan, 1672–1674: Anglo-Dutch rivalry in Japan and Formosa* (Tokyo: Asiatic Society of Japan, 1931).

Boxer, C.H., *The Christian Century in Japan: 1548–1650* (Berkeley, CA: University of California Press, 1967).

Clements, J., *Christ's Samurai: The true story of the Shimabara Rebellion* (London: Robinson, 2016).

Coleridge, H.G. (ed. and trans.), *The Letters of St Francis Xavier*, vols i–ii, 2nd edn (New Deli: Asian Educational Services, 1997).

Cooper, M., *Rodrigues the Interpreter: An early Jesuit in Japan and China* (New York: Weatherhill, 1994).

De Bernoville, G., *The Jesuits* (London, Burns, Oates & Washbourne, 1937).

Endo, S., *Chimoku* (Tokyo: Momumenta Nipponica, 1966).

____, *Silence*, trans. William Johnson (New York: Picador, 2016).

____, *A Life of Jesus*, trans. Richard A. Schuchert (Mahwah, NJ: Paulist Press, 1978).

____, *Samurai* (Tokyo: Shinchosha, 1980).

Galletta, R., *La Darsena Romana: Il porticciolo di Civitavecchia* (Civitavecchia: La Litographica, 2009).

Gonoi, T., *Hasekura Tsunenaga* (Tokyo: Yoshikawa Kōbunkan, 2003).

Endo, S., *The Samurai*, trans. Van C. Gessel (New York: New Directions Publishing, 1997).

Jennes, J., *A History of the Catholic Church in Japan from its Beginnings to the Early Meiji Era (1549–1873): A short handbook* (Tokyo: Oriens Institute for Religious Research, 1973).

Johnson, M.O., M. Kitagaki and P.E. Williams, *Gulliver's Travels and Japan: A new reading* (Kyoto: Amherst House, Doshisha University, 1977).

Kobayashi, T. and T. Watanabe, *Amakusa Kirishitan kikō: Sakitsu, Ōe, Kirishitan yukari no chi* (Fukuoka-shi: Gen Shobō, 2016).

Kume, K., G. Healey, M.B. Jansen and M. Collutt, *The Iwakura Embassy, 1871–73: A true account of the ambassador extraordinary & plenipotentiary's journey of Observation through the United States of America and Europe*, 5 vols (Chiba, Japan: Japan Documents/Richmond: Curzon, 2002).

Laman, C.D., 'Our Nagasaki Legacy: An examination of the period of persecution of Christianity and its impact on subsequent Christianity in Japan', *Northeast Asia*

Journal of Theology, nos 28–9 (March/September 1982).

Laures, J., *Kirishitan Bunko: A manual of books and documents on the early Christian Missions in Japan*, 3rd edn (Tokyo: Sophia University, 1957).

Lee, R., *The Clash of Civilizations: An intrusive gospel in Japanese civilization* (Harrisburg, PA: Trinity Press International, 1999).

Loughlin, J., 'Pope Paul V', *Catholic Encyclopedia*, vol. 11 (New York: Robert Appleton Company, 1911).

Mayer, T.M., *The Roman Inquisition: Trying Galileo* (Philadelphia: University of Pennsylvania Press, 2015).

Moffett, S.H., *A History of Christianity in Asia*, vol. ii (Maryknoll, NY: Orbis Books, 2005).

Nish, I., *The Iwakura Mission in America and Europe: A new assessment*, Meiji Series 6 (London: Routledge Curzon, 2004).

Pérez, L. and C.R. Boxer, *Apostolado y Martirio del Beato Luis Sotelo en el Japón* (Madrid: Imprenta Hispánica, 1924).

Sadler, A.L., *The Maker of Modern Japan: The life of Tokugawa Ieyasu* (Hoboken: Taylor and Francis, 2013).

Schurhammer, G., *Shin-to: The way of the gods in Japan according to the printed and unprinted reports of the Japanese Jesuit missionaries in the 16th and 17th centuries* (Bonn: Schroeder, 1923).

____, *The Great Crusader: A pictorial life of St. Francis Xavier, the apostle of the Indies and Japan* (New York: Catholic Book Publisher, 1924).

____, *Der Heilige Franz Xaver in Japan, 1549–1551* (Schöneck/Beckenried: Administration der Neuen Zeitschrift für Missionswissenschaft, 1947).

____, *Francis Xavier: His Life, His Times*, trans. M.J. Costelloe (Rome: Jesuit Historical Institute, 1973).

Sotelo, L., *Ad Urbanum Octavum Pont. Max. de Ecclesiae Iaponicae Statu Relation* (Rome, 1634).

Suarez Japon, J.M., *Yoko Maeda: Mi amiga Japonesa* (Coria del Río [Sevilla]: Asociación Hasekura DL, 2016).

Suzuki, N., *Seisho no nihongo: Hon'yaku no rekishi*, (Tokyo, Iwanami Shoten, 2006).

Swift, J., *Gulliver's Travels*, ed. A.J. Rivero, Norton Critical Series (New York and London: W.W. Norton, 2002).

Takao, M.H. 'Francis Xavier at the Court of Ōtomo Yoshishige: Representations of religious disputation between Jesuits and Buddhists in la conversione alla santa fede del re di Bungo giaponese (1703)', *Journal of Jesuit Studies*, vol. 3 no. 3 (2016).

Takita, M., *Ōtomo Shiryō: Ōtomo Ke monjoroku* (Ōita: Kin'yōdō Shoten, 1937).

Tanaka, H., *Hasekura Tsunenaga: bushi, Rōma o kōshinsu* (Kyōto-shi: Mineruva Shobō, 2007).

Turnbull, S.R., *Japan's Hidden Christians, 1549–1999* (Surrey: Japan Library; Tokyo: Synapse, 2000).

Varley, P., *Japanese Culture*, 4th edn (Honolulu: University of Hawai'i Press, 2000).

Wicki, J., *Documenta Indica*: *Momunmenta Historica Societatis Iesu*, vol. 70 (Rome: Institutum Historicum Societatis Iesu, 1948).

Wigmore, J.H., *Law and Justice in Tokugawa Japan: Materials for the history of Japanese law and justice under the Tokugawa shogunate, 1603–1867*, vol. 6: *Property: Legal precedents* (Tokyo: University of Tokyo Press, 1981).

Yonehara, M., *Ōuchi Yoshitaka: Meishō ga hanahirakaseta Yamaguchi bunka*, Chūsei Bunshi Sensho 20 (Tokyo: Ebisu Kōshō Shuppan, 2014).

Kōnosuke Hinatsu's portable shrine to the Virgin Mary.
(Iida City Museum/photo courtesy of the author)

'A Book of Mary' Presented by Ryūnosuke Akutagawa to Kōnosuke Hinatsu and Its Unpublished Translation Manuscript

Hiroyasu Fujisawa

Ryūnosuke Akutagawa, Kōnosuke Hinatsu and Irish literature

In an obituary entitled 'Unforgettable People – Ryūnosuke Akutagawa', Kōnosuke Hinatsu recalls his encounter with Ryūnosuke Akutagawa:[1]

> ... It was when Akutagawa, a third-year student at First Higher School (Daiichi Kōtō Gakkō), and I, a first-year undergraduate [at Waseda], met at the Irish Literary Studies Society (Airurando Bungaku Kenkyukai) that he and I came to know each other. The Society had many members, but I thought it was only Akutagawa who was intelligent enough to talk with me. In terms of aesthetic taste and an unquenchable passion for art, Akutagawa was very similar to me.[2]

This comment on Akutagawa indicates how audacious the young Hinatsu was, for he disdained most of the members of the society even though he respected Akutagawa among them. The Irish Literary Studies Society was established mainly by Yaso Saijō and other undergraduates at Waseda, including Hinatsu.[3] They generally met at Saijō's house once a month and discussed the works of Irish writers such as W.B. Yeats and John Millington Synge. Recalling his commitment to the society, Saijō refers to Akutagawa in an essay, 'People of The Mask' ('Kamen no Hitobito):[4]

> Among young literary enthusiasts around Taishō 4 or 5 (1915 or 1916), there were many students who loved mystical literature along with Maeterlinck's mystical thinking and works of Irish literature. For example, Akutagawa contributed an 'Essay on Synge' in the first issue of *New Currents of Thought* (Shinshichō), visited my house with Makoto Sangū or Kōnosuke Hinatsu for the meetings of the Irish Literary Studies Society and used to tell us ghost stories.[5]

Irish literature as discussed at the society played an important role in forging connections between the two influential writers of the Taishō period, Ryūnosuke Akutagawa and Kōnosuke Hinatsu.

In this chapter, I discuss Akutagawa's present for Hinatsu, 'A Book of Mary,' and Hinatsu's unpublished translation of the book. I discovered the latter manuscript in a local library in Nagano Prefecture, where Hinatsu spent the last few years of his life.

Akutagawa's 'A Book of Mary' presented to Hinatsu

In the early years of the Taishō period, Akutagawa sent a postcard to Hinatsu, promising to present to him 'a book of Mary':

> I don't have any copy of Kokuchō because I lent it to someone else. I will send you a copy of Gesta Romanorum. I will humbly present to you another one, a book of Mary, because it would be much more profitable to the world for you to have it than for me to keep it. I hope you will receive it with a smile. Now I am terribly busy writing novels.[6]

But what does Akutagawa mean by 'a book of Mary'? Scholarly uncertainty has prevailed and even Iwanami's authoritative *The Complete Works of Ryūnosuke Akutagawa* does not answer this question. A close examination of *The Complete Works of Kōnosuke Hinatsu*, however, can help. Hinatsu tells us about his relationship with Akutagawa in his short essay, 'Concerning Akutagawa's Literature as a Will' ('Akutagawa no Isho Bungaku'):

> With him [i.e. Akutagawa] I did not play a mah-jong; nor did I talk about a horse race or women's appearances. Yet I did talk with him about rare books or, what is called, well-known kohon [a book of which only one copy has survived] much more than anyone else. ... In terms of the unknown Italian author's *The Life of Mary Magdalene*, he came to my bleak house in Sakanoshita after teaching at the Naval Engineering College, and left it on my small desk, which appeared to be that of a kid, and which I had borrowed from a fisherman.[7]

This passage provides some clues. The author who wrote 'a book of Mary' is, in Akutagawa's words, 'the unknown Italian author', while 'Mary' refers to Mary Magdalene, rather than to the Virgin Mary. These clues enable us to identify, among many books on the saint, a possible candidate in *The Life of Saint Mary Magdalen*, published by John Lane at the Bodley Head in 1906.[8] The book's title page shows that it was translated from the Italian into English by Valentina Hawtrey, with an introduction by Vernon Lee, and that its author is 'an unknown fourteenth-century writer' (Sheet 1).

Kōnosuke Hinatsu's collection of books is currently owned by the Iida City Central Library in Nagano Prefecture. Carrying out research at the Hinatsu Library (Hinatsu Bunko) at the end of July 2016, I came across a copy of *The Life of Saint Mary Magdalen*. The back cover of this book shows what appears to be Ryūnosuke Akutagawa's handwriting, 'Akutagawa Library' (芥川文庫, Akutagawa Bunko). It is in black Indian ink, made with a Japanese writing brush. The handwriting indicates that this was the very book Akutagawa gave Hinatsu.

But the book also carries other precious materials. What is most surprising is that a section of Hinatsu's unpublished translation of *The Life* is found between its pages. The manuscript is written in black ink, perhaps with a fountain pen, and

(Sheet 1) the first sheet of Hinatsu's translation manuscript. (*Photo courtesy of the author*)

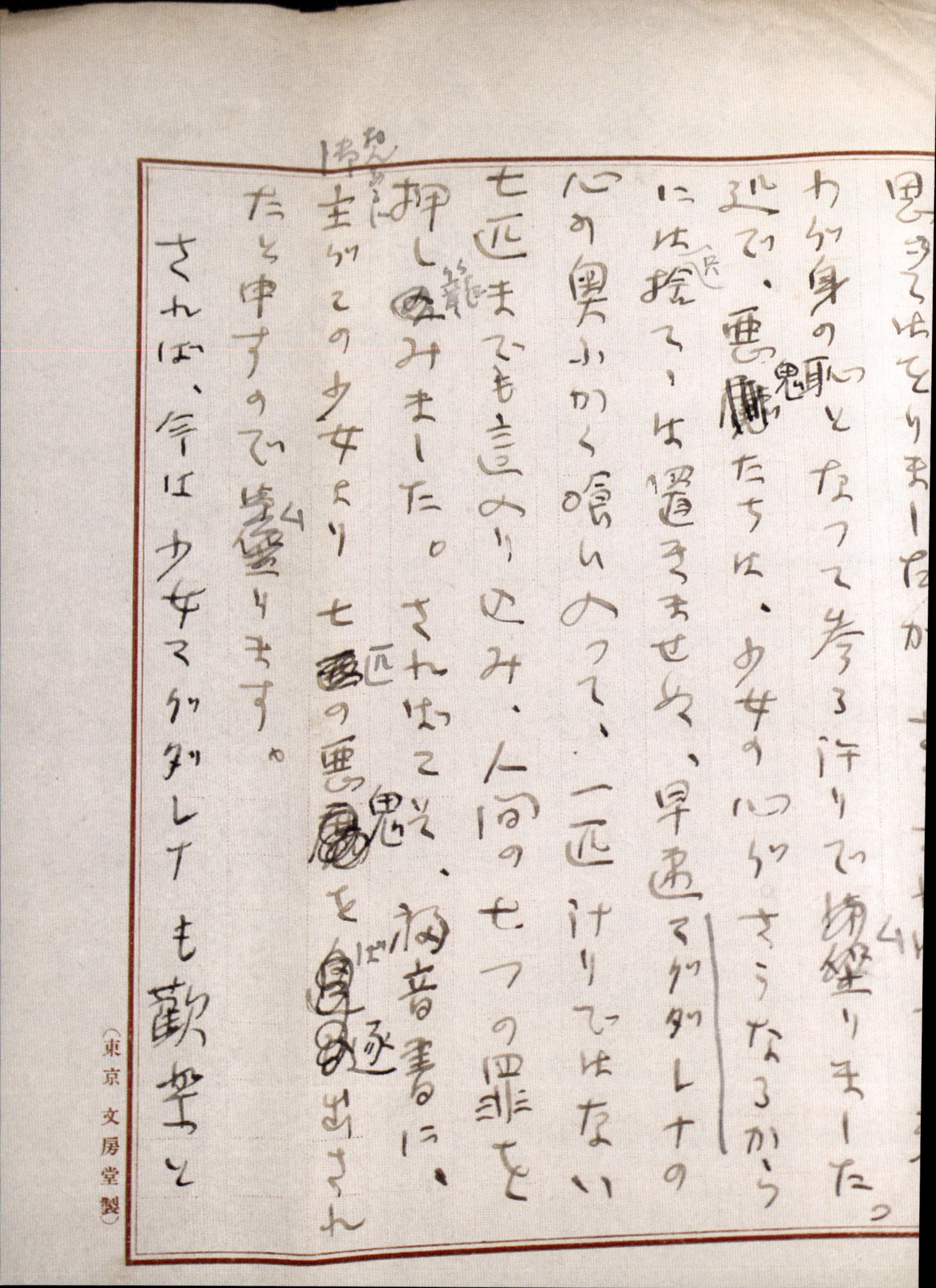

思って居りましたが
わが身の恥となって参る許りで御座りました。
迄で、悪鬼たちは、少女の心がさうなるから
には捨ては置きませぬ、早速マグダレナの
心の奥ふかく喰ひ入って、一匹許りではない
七匹までも這入り込み、人間の七つの罪を
押し籠みました。されば御経書に、
主がこの少女より七匹の悪鬼を追ひ出された
たと申すので御座ります。
されば、今は少女マグダレナも歓楽と

（東京　文房堂製）

從從えん少女が上に戻る。さて

作者の考へでは、マグダレナに於いては、
歓楽が再びとわが手にもどつては来らぬものなるを見
てとつたね、云ひ知らぬ寂しさ遣る瀬な
くつい棄て鉢となつて、向ふ見ずな自堕落
にわれとわが身を持ち崩すやうに相成りました。
ので、己が身をも焼き盡す熾ふ
ての悲みを免れんものと、誘惑、快楽の數々を
妖しき快楽や喜びを暮らしを日に夜に趁わて
淫らな女となり果てました。とうかして今は憎い
る者ヨハネ名スに荷心かけてゆりんしもの宿と

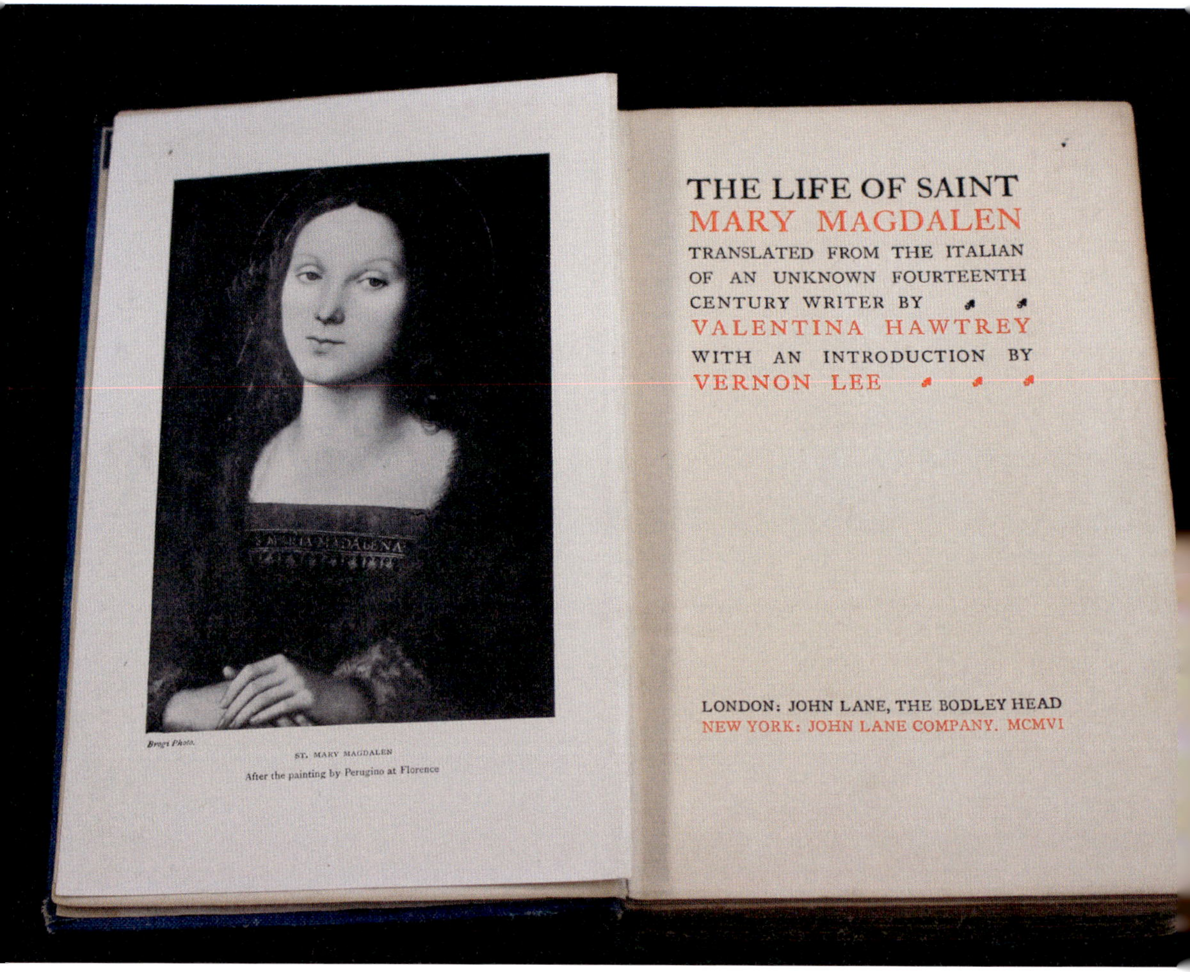

(above) Frontispiece in *The Life of Saint Mary Magdalen*, unknown author, translator Valentina Hawtrey, 1906. (*Photo courtesy of the author*); (opposite page) Memo by perhaps, Kinji Shimada(?) (*Akutagawa Library/photo courtesy of the author*)

consists of ten sheets of manuscript paper ruled off into 400 squares (see Sheets 1 to 10). In addition, a memo handwritten by 'Kinji Shimada,' (島田 謹二, professor of comparative literature at the University of Tōkyō at that time), contains instructions on how to find the sources of pictures portraying Mary Magdalen in *The Life*: i.e., by consulting the supplementary volumes of the *Century Dictionary* that deal with proper nouns in history. This also appears to be a response to Hinatsu's inquiry into

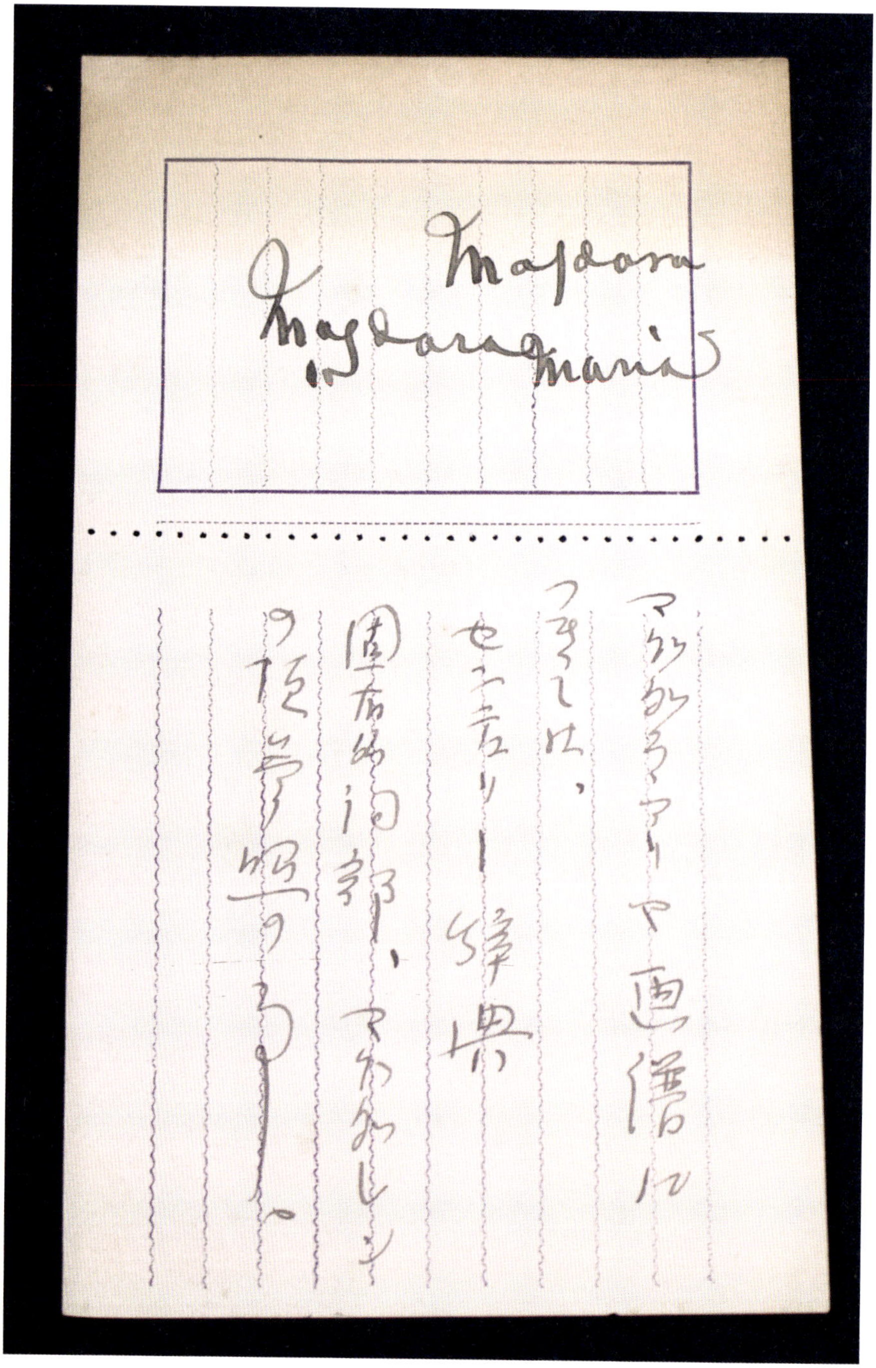

(opposite page) Kinji Shimada's instructions to Kōnosuke Hinatsu on how to investigate the Mary Magdalen images. (*Photo courtesy of the author*)

those sources. This memo, trivial as it might seem, sheds valuable light on Hinatsu's scholarly friendship with Shimada.

Curiously, the title of *The Life of Mary Magdalene* (「マグダラのマリア傳」, Magudara no Maria Den) also appears in an advertisement for Hinatsu's forthcoming books, attached to the end of his second collection of poems, *Virgin Mary Draped in Black* (Kokui Seibo, 1921).[9] And then, four years later, the third issue of the second volume of *The Sabbath* (Sabato) – a literary journal of which Hinatsu was a general editor – announced that a translation of a part of *The Life* would appear in future issues. In 1927, Hinatsu did indeed publish a translation of the first few pages of *The Life* in the first issue of the fourth volume of *The Sabbath*, under the title, 'A Strange Story: The Life of Saint Mary Magdalene' (「椿説 嘛煦陀羅、聖尼瑪利亜伝」, 'Chinsetsu Magudara Seini Maria Den'). To these sources we can also add an announcement of the publication of Kōnosuke Hinatsu's translation of *The Life* in a book series called the Sabbath Nanka Series (Sabato Nanka Sōshō); this would be entitled *A Strange Story: The Illustrated Book of Saint Mary Magdalene* (『椿説 まぐだら聖尼まりあ絵詞』, Chinetsu Magudara Seini Maria Ekotoba). These facts show that Hinatsu seriously intended to publish in a book form his translation of *The Life of Saint Mary Magdalen* by regularly translating parts of it for *The Sabbath*, and that the seventeenth volume in the Sabbath Nanka Series was intended to be a book containing the pictures of Mary Magdalene, with verbal interpretations (Ekotoba) literally means 'a book or a scroll explaining pictures'). The changing titles indicate that Hinatsu was a writer who continued to revise his work and further suggests that he did not hesitate to use difficult Chinese terms.

A close examination of *The Life* in comparison with Hinatsu's manuscript reveals not only that the content of pages 6 to 11 of *The Life* corresponds to that of Hinatsu's translation, but that these pages also dovetail with the translation published in the first issue of the fourth volume of *The Sabbath*.[10] Judging from these facts, it is safe to say that *The Life of Saint Mary Magdalen* is the 'book of Mary' mentioned by Akutagawa and Hinatsu.[11] It can be concluded that Hinastu planned to publish serially his translations of several pages of *The Life* in the

Akutagawa's signature in *The Life of Saint Mary Magdalen*, unknown author, translator Valentina Hawtrey, 1906. [Photo courtesy of the author]

periodical he was editing, a plan which was nevertheless interrupted because the journal ceased publication in 1927.[12]

II *The Life of Saint Mary Magdalen*

Vernon Lee praised *The Life of Saint Mary Magdalen* as 'among the most remarkable' of 'the Italian devotional romances of the Middle Ages'.[13] She said that the book was 'printed in certain editions of Frate Demenico Cavalca's well known charming translations of St. Jerome's "Lives of the Saints"'.[14] A careful comparison of *The*

Life with Domenico Cavalca's *Vite dei Santi Padri* reveals that the former does not correspond to the latter at all, but that it shares similarities to an Italian book by Cavalca: *Vorgrizzamento delle Vite de' Santi Padri*, published in 1854.[15] Valentina Hawtrey must have used a different Italian book from Domenico Cavalca's *Vite dei Santi Padri* to translate *The Life* into English.

The unknown fourteenth-century author of *The Life of Saint Mary Magdalen* first identifies the 'Mary' who followed Jesus in Bethany as Mary Magdalen, though descriptions of her in the Gospels slightly differ from each other. According to the author, Mary Magdalen is disappointed with John the Evangelist, who refuses to marry her in order to become a disciple of Jesus. He depicts her degradation, which results from despair, and the cold shoulders that are turned upon her. Yet, Jesus' visit to Bethany, where she lives with her brother Lazarus and her sister Martha, transforms her life. Jesus expels seven devils from the Magdalen and turns her into one of his devoted followers. Mary and Martha are fascinated by Jesus' miracles, including the raising of Lazarus, and they faithfully follow his words and even decide to sell all of their belongings in order to 'minister to the poor and the sick'. Then the Passion of Jesus is meticulously represented: frantically, Mary Magdalen sees Jesus experience his cruel punishment, whereas the Virgin Mary weeps like the Magdalen but somehow remains calmer than she. What is conspicuous in the representation of Mary Magdalen is that when they come back to Bethany soon after Jesus' execution, she accuses his disciples of hiding themselves for their own security during the Passion. The book ends with an illustration of Mary Magdalen's encounter with the resurrected Christ. She anoints him with a special ointment concocted by her.

Hinatsu's translation of *The Life of Saint Mary Magdalen*

As the changing titles of Kōnosuke Hinatsu's translation of *The Life* suggest, Hinatsu tended to refine his writings by using as many difficult Chinese characters as possible, to the extent that most Japanese readers today will find it difficult to read his works. The newly discovered manuscript seems to manifest this particular feature of his revisionary process.

It is beyond the scope of this essay to examine comprehensively Hinatsu's choices of words in the manuscript, but we can at least point out some characteristics.

The first point I would like to make is that Hinatsu uses furigana (ふりがな) as effectively here as he does in his other writings.

Kana (かな) denotes the Japanese syllabic writing system, and furigana is a type of kana that is written on the right side of Chinese characters: it helps readers to pronounce difficult Chinese characters. For example, Hinatsu does not pronounce 「普通」 'futsū' (ふつう) as many Japanese readers would; rather, he pronounces it 'arikitari' (ありきたり, common). Furthermore, he gives furigana, 「わたし」(watashi, meaning 'I', at the beginning of Sheet 1) to 「作者」(sakusha, meaning 'the author'). These are typical examples showing Hinatsu's way of defamiliarising the language he uses. The second characteristic of Hinatu's translation is that he uses uncommon Chinese characters to represent fairly simple ideas. For instance, he deletes a common word, 「読者」(readers), in the middle of Sheet 3, replacing it with a new word 「看官諸子」, which is seen in Chinese classics. We should also note that Hinatsu supplies a very common furigana meaning 'everyone' (みなさま). On the left side of Sheet 6, Hinatsu similarly crosses out 「風俗」(custom and manners) and opts for 「時勢粧」(basara, indulgence in worldly pleasures), which even the literati of his times would have found it difficult to pronounce. These details suggest that Hinatsu was a translator who did not expect all of his readers to understand his work, and who spoke selectively to intellectuals who could truly appreciate his play on words.

Akutagawa, Hinatsu and Namban culture

How, then, do we account for this rather bizarre Japanese? Kōnosuke Hinatsu's representative work, *The History of Meiji-Taishō Poetry*, gives us a clue. In the headnote to this monumental study, Hinatsu explains the reception of Christianity in Japanese poetry:

> The inventors of Christianity-influenced Japanese poetry were Bin Ueda and Ariake [Kambara]. Then, [Mokutarō] Kinoshita and Hakushū [Kitahara] followed them. This was the extraordinary artistic and literary fervor at the end of the Meiji period or at the beginning of the Taishō period which came to infect [Kōnosuke] Hinatsu and [Ryūnosuke] Akutagawa, and its enthusiasm is comparable to the Dunhuang fervor in Kyōto later.[16]

This brief but precise summary of their writing illustrates that Akutagawa and Hinatsu were influenced by their predecessors, such as Hakushū Kitahara or Mokutarō Kinoshita, who had aggressively attempted to draw upon *namban* culture (*namban bunka* refers to Spanish-Portuguese cultures as they were first introduced to Japan).

Although Hinatsu emphasised that both Akutagawa and he were merely 'laymen' in terms of their religious attitudes towards Christianity, they incorporated Christian elements into their writing by weaving together Japanese and Spanish-Portuguese cultures: in Akutagawa's case, this is evident in seven short pieces of work written in his later years, conventionally called *kirishitanmono* (a group of writings that deal with Christian topics); in Hinatsu's case, this can be seen in his *Kokui Seibo* (Virgin Mary Draped in Black) and other poetical works.

Akutagawa, Hinatsu and their worship of the Virgin Mary

Speaking of the interweaving of Christianity and Japanese culture, it is also worth noting that both Akutagawa and Hinatsu worshipped the Virgin Mary in their own ways. It is well known that Akutagawa cherished a statue of Maria Kan'non (the Virgin Mary disguised as a Kan'non in order to evade persecutions of Christians in Japan), which he had obtained during a journey to Nagasaki. Like Akutagawa, Hinatsu devoted himself to the Virgin Mary, displaying in his study a portable Marian shrine, which his friend Daigaku Horiguchi is said to have purchased in Brazil and presented to him. Akutagawa's Maria Kan'non may appear to have nothing to do with Hinatsu's Brazilian Virgin Mary, but in fact they share important common ground, both being products of cultural hybridity.

In the context of the two writers' Marian worship, it should be pointed out that Akutagawa appropriated the title of Hinatsu's *Virgin Mary Draped in Black* for a short story of his own.[17] Akutagawa's 'Kokui Seibo' is a strange story in which a Maria Kan'non grants a woman's wish that her sick grandson would live for as long as she lives. Yet as soon as the woman passes away, her grandson also dies. The story ends on a bewildering note when the narrator observes a smile around the statue's mouth soon after the child's death.

Both Akutagawa and Hinatsu found not only sacredness but also something mysterious, something dark or even profane, in the Virgin Mary.

Akutagawa, Hinatsu and Mary Magdalene

As for Mary Magdalene, Kōnosuke Hinatsu mentioned her only sporadically in his works and did not leave any substantial comments on her, apart from his translation of *The Life*.

Compared with Hinatsu, Ryūnosuke Akutagawa appears to have been much more profoundly inspired by the saint from the beginning of his literary career. Akutagawa wrote an unpublished short dialogue between two Romans who wonder why Mary Magdalene became a follower of Jesus.[18] He also supported Ritsujirō Wake (1888–1975) in publishing a Japanese translation of Maurice Maeterlinck's *Mary Magdalene*.[19] Above all, in Akutagawa's short story, 'The Christ of Nanjing' (1920), a young Chinese prostitute, Jin Hua, reminds us of Mary Magdalene.[20] Infected with syphilis, she, being a good Christian, hesitates to subscribe to the widely held belief that a prostitute will recover from the disease once she has passed it on to her customers. However, she eventually has sex with a foreign visitor who looks like Jesus Christ. And then miraculously, she recovers. The story ends with a Japanese tourist wondering whether he should tell Jin Hua about George Murry, a mixed-race Japanese-American who boasts of having sex with a prostitute without paying. When she notices that she is cured, she says to herself, 'Then, that man was Jesus Christ,' and kneels down. Akutagawa describes her thus: 'She … knelt on cold flagstones and began to say her prayers as if she had been a beautiful Mary Magdalene who had talked with the resurrected Lord.'[21] The characterisation of Jin Hua highlights the connection between her and Mary Magdalene, who, despite being a social outcast, personally witnesses the resurrection of Christ. That Jin Hua is a sex worker also reminds us of the prevalent belief that Mary Magdalene was once a prostitute. Her sexual intercourse with a foreigner who resembles Jesus Christ is also reminiscent of the belief that Mary Magdalene was a lover of Jesus Christ.[22] Finally, Akutagawa briefly comments on Mary Magdalene in a work of quasi-aphorisms written towards the end of his life, 'The Man in the West' ('Saihō no Hito'):

> **15 Women**
>
> Many women loved Christ. Above all, Mary Magdalene forgot about being attacked by the seven devils because she had met him once, and she began to feel even poetic love, regardless of what she does for a

> living. After Christ's life was over, it was such a power of love that made her first look at him. Christ also loved many women – above all, he loved Mary Magdalene. Their poetic love still smells sweet like an iris' flowers. His loneliness was alleviated whenever he saw her. Later generations – or men in later generations – have been indifferent to their poetic love. Yet women in later generations were always jealous of this Mary.
>
> 'Why didn't Christ show his resurrection to his mother Mary, prior to anyone else?'
>
> It was the most hypocritical sighs that they have given.[23]

This passage shows that Akutagawa regarded Mary Magdalene as a woman special to Christ, special in the sense that it was she, not the Virgin Mary, who was the first woman to see the resurrected Christ. These textual examples suggest that Akutagawa was attracted by the story of Mary Magdalene: her being possessed by the seven devils, the possibility of her having been engaged in prostitution, Christ's love for her, and so forth. Unlike the Virgin Mary, in whom he saw both profanity and selfless love, Akutagawa seems to have been deeply interested in the coexistence of sacredness and mundanity in Mary Magdalene.

III Akutagawa and Hinatsu in our age: a historical irony

This chapter started with Hinatsu's obituary for Akutagawa, and it is appropriate to conclude by considering a passage that follows what I quoted earlier. After writing about their frequent rendezvous in Kamakura, Akutagawa's hatred of dogs, and other reminiscences, Hinatsu launches his criticism of certain aspects of Akutagawa's life. He abruptly says:

> I didn't like Akutagawa being on good terms with Kan Kikuchi. I often said to him, 'If you associate with such a worldly person, you will reap unfavourable consequences.' Yet Akutagawa was a sociable man and played with silly people in the literary world, ingratiating himself with them.[24]

A 'worldly person', Kan Kikuchi (1888–1948) was a novelist and founder of the prestigious Japanese publishing company, Bungeishunjū. Although harshly criticised in most of Hinatsu's obituaries for Akutagawa, Kikuchi was to establish the Akutagawa Ryunosuke Prize (Akutagawa Ryūnosuke Shō or, simply, Akutagawa Shō) in order to sustain Akutagawa's reputation and to promote serious literature on his behalf. Still Japan's most coveted literary prize, it continues to publicise the works of emerging novelists, fostering the careers of internationally popular authors such as Shūsaku Endō or Kenzaburō Ōe.

Given this fact, we cannot but sense the historical irony of the two literary giants of the Taishō period. The reputation of the communicative Ryūnosuke Akutagawa has flourished even into our age. He is still being commemorated through the Akutagawa Prize and the annual conferences organised by the International Society of Akutagawa [Ryunosuke] Studies, not only in Japanese but also in many other languages. On the contrary, the scholarly and reclusive Kōnosuke Hinatsu has been forgotten even by Japanese intellectuals. This irony reminds us of Hinatsu's translation of *The Life*, the manuscript of which lay unexplored in the archives of the Iida Central Library despite his profound influence upon contemporary writers. I hope this chapter has shed new light on the connections between Akutagawa and Hinatsu, revealing how they struggled to reinvent Japanese literature under the influences of *namban* culture or, needless to say, Irish literature.

Transcription

Sheet 1 Now let us return to her

I think to myself that when the Magdalen saw that he could not be brought back to her, being in despair because of her loneliness, she gave herself up to a reckless life: she pursued pleasure and diversion so as not to die of grief, and she was glad to do him dishonour, but we must own that she did it still more to herself. And the devils seeing her heart thus prepared, entered there, not one but seven, with seven mortal sins; for the Gospel says that our Lord cast out from her seven devils. So the Magdalen now began to seek pleasure (and amusement …)

Sheet 2

(So the Magdalen now began to seek pleasure and amusement,) and to go forth to feasts and places of diversion, showing herself in deed and attire not modest. And I think that at first her kindred, who loved her dearly, were glad that she should seek distraction and not die of grief; they did not expect that the evil would grow so widespread as it afterwards did, nor would they have wished it.

And they say in the story of St Martha that no one believes that she yielded to such shame, that it would not have been suffered, that her brother, her kindred, and her friends (would have imprisoned her, for they would have reclaimed her.)

Sheet 3

(... and her friends) would have imprisoned her, for they would have reclaimed her. And it is not to be believed that she squandered her temporal goods, as it is said in the songs of the blind; but it is quite enough that she had sin in her desires, and would have consented thereto, if it had not been for this restraint put upon her.

And here one might ask: 'Now why was she held a sinner in all the city, and had lost her fair name, and why was she esteemed an evil-doer in the eyes of all good people?' And I answer and think to myself that such was the virtue of all good women at that time, that if any yielded to dishonesty she was abhorred and scorned by all who knew her; (and Mary was a great lady, and known to many ...)

Sheet 4

(and Mary was a great lady,) and known to many; she was most fair in form, and for this also was I known, and her tongue was glib with words of unseemly merriment; and she was such that all good and virtuous women covered their faces when they saw her, for so great was the virtue of all good women in those days that, as we know, one taken in adultery was condemned by the law to be stoned. This is in the Gospel, but nowadays it not so.

And we know that when women went to churches and to festivals, the men went by one road, and the women by another. And this also is in the Gospel, for when Messer Jesus Christ was (lost at the festival ...)

Sheet 5

(for when Messer Jesus Christ was lost at the festival) it is said that His mother thought He was with Joseph, and Joseph thought He was at home with His mother, before they perceived that He was lost. And then, you see, choirs were made in the churches, that is, a wall in the middle between the men and the women, and that is still done to this day. But I believe these choirs were differently made, for there were different entrances for men and women, and a woman would never have entered by that of the men, or she would have been held worse than a sinner, and would have been hunted out as a demon; such was the virtue of women.

And not a hundred years ago widows who were about to return to the world, remained shut up until they received the ring and changed their mourning garments; and all this I saw done in my childhood …

Sheet 6

(… all this I saw done in my childhood;) and if there were any young women who stayed over long at the windows, ill was spoken of them, and they were thought immodest; and this also I remember well. And if I have said so much about the honesty of women, I have done so for the reason that thus the Magdalen's sinfulness is aggravated; for certainly I have thought many times of the women of today, seeing their graceless carriage, that had they lived in the time of the Magdalen, they would have been called more than sinners; but because these customs are common to all, it seems that people are heedless thereof.

Sheet 7

Certain I am that the Magdalen did not uncover her bosom as they do. I know well that the Magdalen had that sin in her heart, but I cannot believe that she yielded to it, as many will have it said; but her brazen ways and the other sins that she committed were quite enough to render her infamous.

Now let us tell of Martha, according to what is said in the legend. Martha was ill, and for her illness there was neither physician nor physic. She had a handmaiden whose name was Martilla, who I think had first been with their mother, and had helped to bring up these children, and she dwelt with them to be a mother to them, and as housekeeper and guardian of all their things. She was very wise and experienced, and loved this family,

Sheet 8

(She was very wise and experienced, and loved this family,) though she loved best to be with Martha, for she was the youngest and was ill, and was good and pious and wise; and they grieved much for the Magdalen, and took shame to themselves for the evil fame that she bore, and especially when this holy woman sometimes went round about for things of necessity, and found that the good women, and perhaps also the good men were saying, 'What scandal is this? Now what a thing is this to let a maiden act in such a way that all the city speaks of her? And Lazarus does not seem to perceive it. Why do ye not rather hold her captive?'

Martilla shrank from their words (and did not know what to say…)

Sheet 9

(Martilla shrank from their words and did not know what to say;) and she could not excuse her, for she herself was much distressed by such ways. And returning home she would confer with Martha concerning these words, and many times they wept together in great sorrow.

And I think that sometimes they called Mary and told her of these sayings, and chid her severely; then I think that Mary would begin to laugh and sing and would run away from them, and would not stay to hear, so that they were left in far greater grief.

And there came some of their kindred, and of their great friends, men and women, who said sadly, 'What is to be done with her? and in what way will ye hinder her? She has lost her fair name in all the city, and is called a sinner by all virtuous people, …

Sheet 10

(She has lost her fair name in all the city, and is called a sinner by all virtuous people,) so that there are few who call her by her real name, and we are all ashamed to speak of her ill repute; people wish that she should be kept captive, and marvel that *Lazarus should suffer her.'

And Martha and Martilla wept; and I think that Martilla said, 'Lazarus is young, and he is of the world, and does not believe these things, nor are they told to him as much as they are to us; and it seems that it pleases him to go with her to seek amusement, for he loves her much, so that there seems to be no remedy for this trouble. But tell it to him, and we also will tell him, to see if he will help.'

*Lazarus
Hinatsu attached a small sheet of paper to his manuscript in order to furnish a note on Lazarus: 'Lazarus. A brother to Mary and Martha. Christ's friend. It is said that Christ raised Lazarus from the dead.'

A Visit to the Irish Church on the Goto Islands

John Neary

The Goto Islands are a group of about sixty-three islands in the East China Sea approximately 100km west of Nagasaki (and 200km from the Korean coast). From the eighth to the twelfth century, the islands flourished as the last stop for traders and diplomatic missions travelling from Japan to China. Nowadays, the economy rests on agriculture, fisheries and tourism.

The main island is Fukue Island, where more than half the total population resides. The islands form one administrative unit headed by a mayor based in Goto City, the capital of Fukue Island. The islands are part of Nagasaki Prefecture. They are unusual in Japan in that around a quarter of the population is Catholic, compared to less than 1 per cent in Japan as a whole.

I visited the Goto Islands on 2 July 2014 to see the church in Hantomari, a small village on Fukue Island, which was built with a donation from Ireland in 1920.

The Christianisation of the islands began in the sixteenth century when the Christian faith expanded in western Japan following the arrival of Francis Xavier in 1549. The local lord, Uku Simusida, invited Christian priests to Fukue Island, and before long there were some 2,000 Christians, who were given permission to build churches. However, in the late sixteenth century an edict was issued expelling the missionaries and ordering the destruction of churches. The ban on Christianity was extended when Toyotomi Hideyoshi ordered the execution of twenty-six martyrs in Nagasaki in 1597 (one of whom, John of Goto, was from the islands). The religious ban was further extended under the Tokugawa shogunate: priests were expelled from the country, churches were destroyed, and Christianity was forced underground. From then on, the 'hidden Christians' (called *kakure kirishitan* in Japanese) practised and passed down their faith in secret.

In 1797, around 3,000 Catholics fled to the Goto Islands to escape poverty and persecution in Sotome in the Ōmura domain (in present-day Nagasaki Prefecture). While they continued to experience hardship due to the barren soil and conflict with local inhabitants, they did manage to keep their faith.

Following the Meiji Restoration in 1868, the hidden Christians continued to suffer persecution until, under international pressure, the Meiji government officially lifted the ban on Christianity in 1873. At that stage, the Christians on the Goto Islands began to practise their faith openly and to build churches on the islands. According to a handbook on the Goto Islands' churches produced by Nagasaki Prefecture, the church in a small village called Hantomari in the north of Fukue Island was built with a donation from Ireland in 1920. The construction of the church commenced in 1919 and was completed in 1922.

The churches and Christian sites in Nagasaki have now been designated as UNESCO World Heritage sites since June 2018. There are twenty-two in all. Following contact with the city authorities in Goto in advance of my visit, it was arranged that Ms Masako Yamaguchi from the Junrei Centre, a not-for-profit organisation set up to promote the candidature of the 'Churches and Christian Sites in Nagasaki' for UNESCO World Heritage status, would escort me to the church in Hantomari and to some of the other churches on the island.

When I arrived on the island on 2 July, accompanied by my wife, we were met by the mayor of Goto City, Mr Ichitaro Noguchi; the deputy mayor, Mr Motoki Nakano; a member of the local assembly, Mr Kiguchi; the priest who celebrates Mass in Hantomari church, Fr Iwasaki; as well as Ms Yamaguchi. Ms Satoko Wakana, from the tourism-promotion section of Goto City Hall, was also present to act as interpreter. They provided a car to bring us around the island, and invited us to lunch in the city.

Interior of Sakitsu Catholic Church, Amkusa Islands, Kumamoto Prefecture, Japan. (*Photo courtesy of the author*)

Our first stop was Dozaki church, the first Western-style church built on the island following the 1873 abolition-of-persecution decree. It is a small, red-brick Gothic structure that is now used as a Museum of Christian History, although Mass is still celebrated there. It has exhibits from the time of the early evangelisation, through the era of persecution up to the revival of the faith, including the bones of St John of Goto, one of the twenty-six martyrs. Nearby we were shown the site of an orphanage built by the first pastor for children whose families were too poor to support them.

We then drove on a narrow road over the heavily wooded mountains to Hantomari church, located in a picturesque inlet beside the beach. We were greeted by Fr Iwasaki and the three remaining 'believers', as they are called on the island: Mr Kiichi Miyagawa, a local fisherman, and his wife Tsutae, and Mrs Yoshino Hamaguchi, who, with her husband Takashi, owns the café next door. Our guide, Ms Yamaguchi, explained that when the first settlers came to this place, there was too little land to support all of them, so half of them stayed while the others moved on. Hence the name Hantomari, which means 'half stayed'.

The church is a small wooden structure designed and built by Tetsukawa Yosuke, the architect and builder of many of the churches on the Goto Islands. Inside, there is little decoration, although the light-blue colour of the walls gives it a light and airy feeling. Outside, the church is surrounded by a high wall built with stones collected from the beach to protect the building from typhoons, which are common in this area.

We were escorted into the church by the three parishioners, and I was presented with a bouquet of flowers by Mrs Miyagawa. Mr Miyagawa, a thin, wiry-looking man of eighty-three, told us that the money from Ireland was used to buy the wood for the church. It was sourced on Kamigoto Island, north of Fukue, and it took five days to bring it by rowing boat from there to Hantomari. Mr Miyagawa and his wife are clearly devoted to their church and worry about who will take care of it when

Sakitsu, Amakusa Islands, Kumamoto Prefecture, Japan
(Photo courtesy of the author)

they are gone. They told us that the church had been damaged during a typhoon thirty years earlier, when all the walls, with the exception of the altar area, were flattened. It was rebuilt with the help of their neighbours from Uragashira church.

Mr Miyagawa told us that he goes to the church every morning to pray before he goes out fishing, which he has been working at since he was eight years old. He and his wife had nine children, five of whom live on the Goto Islands and four in other parts of Japan. He was moved to tears that the Irish ambassador had come to visit, and expressed regret that he did not have more notice of the visit so that he could have caught some shrimp to offer as a gift.

After visiting the church we all moved to the café next door, which is located in the former school, now closed. Mr Miyagawa said that when he was young

there were sixty children in the school. Now there are only five households in the area, comprising nine people in total. The café owner, Mr Takashi Hamaguchi, is from Tokyo but came to this place, which is where his wife is from, to find a more congenial place to live. He runs the café, which he says gets around 1,000 customers a year, as well as working to revive rural villages and in eco-friendly farming. We were served coffee and cake before bidding farewell.

In the afternoon we visited two more churches: Kusuhara and Mizunoura. Kusuhara is the second-oldest church on the island and is a fine solid red-brick structure, reminiscent of many country churches in Ireland. Located close to it are the remains of Kusuhara prison, where 'believers' were imprisoned at the beginning of the Meiji era (before the ban on Christianity was lifted). Mizunoura church is a very pretty white church, with a convent beside it and a graveyard with white crosses on the hill behind.

On our way back to the port, our guide told us that the mayor was attending a sitting of the assembly, and she asked if it would be all right if he were to inform them of the visit by the Irish ambassador. Before we left, I was asked to record a message about my visit for the local newspaper. After we boarded the boat for departure, we saw the mayor and several other assemblymen arrive at the quayside to bid us farewell.

We were unable to discover how the connection between Ireland and the church in Hantomari came about. The only information Ms Yamaguchi could give us was that the funding for the church had been organised by a Fr Combaz in Nagasaki. An Internet search reveals that he was a member of the Société des Missions étrangères de Paris, a French missionary order that sent priests to Japan after the ban on Christianity was lifted. Fr Combaz became bishop of Nagasaki in 1912 and died there in 1926. It is not clear whether he received the funding from the Church in Ireland (the most likely option) or from some other source.

There are few enough connections between Ireland and Japan in the Meiji period, and the link with this church is, accordingly, especially noteworthy. It would be nice to maintain and develop the relationship with the Goto Islands, although, given the dwindling community in Hantomari, it is not at all certain that the church there will survive beyond the lifetime of the current parish community.

Nevertheless, it would be worthwhile for the embassy to maintain a relationship with the people on Fukue Island, and it would be good to revisit the church in a year or so to keep up contact with the local community.

The Ghosts of Lafcadio Hearn and Karlheinz Stockhausen: Crossings and re-crossings between Ireland, Japan (and beyond) in contemporary music – a personal view

Paul Hayes

'Buckley and Hayes should leave it all to the Japanese.' I will always remember that line written in a review in the *Hibernian* magazine in Dublin in the 1970s when John Buckley and I were composition students of James Wilson at the Royal Irish Academy of Music. It was written by the music critic Fanny Feehan when reviewing a concert of the Association of Young Irish Composers at Dagg Hall, where both Buckley and I had had new pieces performed. At that stage I had no idea I would end up living in Japan. I found it difficult to work out how my composition could be compared to Japanese music. This first serious contemporary classical piece of mine, in a strange way, anticipated the Japanese music I was to encounter when I finally ended up living in Tokyo.

The composition critiqued by Fanny Feehan was a trio for clarinet, cello and piano which I called *Construction Work*. The formal plan was to build a final melody from notes with very long durations, which I whittled down rather like a stonemason would until the melodic pitches and rhythms came closer and closer together. After a short introduction that diverts the listener away from the main idea of the piece, there is a long, slow middle section that metamorphoses into a translucent melodic finale. I use the Fibonacci series of numbers 0, 1, 1, 2, 3, 5, 8, 13, whereby the next number is the addition of the two numbers before. I started with the higher numbers and worked the series backwards, eventually going into fractions at the end. I wanted to create a sense of stasis in my music, and it was not until I heard *gagaku* music in the Imperial Palace in Tokyo that I realised that there were connections.

Even though Ireland has a small population, it is well represented in the classical and contemporary classical-music arena in Japan. The pianist John O'Conor has performed many recitals here and has been a jury member of the Hamatsu International Piano Competition. James Kavanagh, the trumpeter and conductor, has worked with both the Japanese Philharmonic Orchestra and the Tokyo Oratorio Society. Seóirse Bodley represented Ireland at the ISCM (International Society for Contemporary Music) World Music Days Festival in Yokohama in 2001. Paul Roe, the clarinettist and teacher, has given performances of Japanese and Irish music in Tokyo and Nagoya, as well as clarinet masterclasses. He has also lectured in Japan on Irish traditional music, and has collaborated with Japanese composers.

The flautist and shakuhachi player Philip Horan has a master's degree in ethnomusicology focusing on shakuhachi acoustics and Japanese aesthetics. As a performer, Horan covers a wide range of genres, including both Japanese traditional styles such as *honkyoku* and *sankyoku*, Irish and Celtic music, contemporary pieces and jazz. He plays shakuhachi with the Japanese-Irish harpist Junshi Murakami, and has fostered a small shakuhachi community in Ireland. He actively promotes the shakuhachi and makes his own instruments (both the *ji-nashi* and *ji-ari* variety). As he says himself, his shakuhachi 'are ideal for Zen meditation or blowing Zen'. In January 2017, Horan performed at the opening ceremony for the celebrations of the sixtieth anniversary of the establishment of diplomatic relations between Ireland and Japan in Iveagh House in Dublin. For the fiftieth anniversary in 2007, Horan gave a concert with Bill Dowdall (flautist), John Feeley (guitarist) and Junshi Murakami (harpist) in Dublin Castle. This programme included a version of 'The Last Rose of Summer', popular here in Japan under its Japanese title, 'Niwa No Chigusa' (A Thousand Different Grasses in the Garden). Tōru Takemitsu's 'Toward the Sea' was performed at the same event. I met Takemitsu at a reception in Suntory Hall before he died. The British conductor and composer Oliver Knussen was also present, having just conducted the Tokyo Metropolitan Symphony Orchestra in the first performance of his own Horn Concerto. The contrast between the demeanours of the two composers was evident. Knussen was talkative and enthusiastic, while Takemitsu stood apart from the crowd. As I gave Takemitsu my name card, I felt a certain aura of placidity. People in Japan relate to music as an extension of nature.

In Ireland in the 1970s, there was a 'rush' to catch up with the modernists of Central Europe. Seóirse Bodley, one of my university professors, had already admitted a certain amount of modernist elements into his music. The music of Schonberg, Berg, Webern and Stockhausen came to be considered more progressive than that of the Irish and English composers of the first half of the twentieth century. Stanford, Moeran, Vaughan Williams, with their pastoral arrangements and imitations of English and Irish folk music, had been the mainstay of the modern elements of the orchestral and chamber concerts at that time. I remember the excitement when the composers Messien, Stockhausen and Eliott Carter came to Ireland for the Dublin Festival of 20th Century Music. Younger composers felt that a new era had begun.

I feel that serialism and the 'total serialism' of the mid-twentieth century was too abstract for the Irish temperament. The lack of musical narrative in these pieces went against the natural tendency of the Irish for storytelling: we needed a drama to elaborate upon. Our Gallic nature leaned more towards the French and the Mediterranean composers than the Austro-Germanic music of Central Europe. The electronic music of Stockhausen was a tour de force of sonic innovation that instilled new life into the serial expressionism of the mid-twentieth century. This struck a chord, so to speak, with Irish experimental composers such as Roger Doyle, who ended up writing almost exclusively in the electro-acoustic idiom. Two Irish composers, Gerald Barry and Raymond Deane, studied with Stockhausen in the late 1970s at the same time as the South African composer Kevin Volans. Volans subsequently came to live in Ireland and became an Irish citizen. He taught the composer Jennifer Walshe, who realised that there was no avant-garde as such in Irish contemporary classical music. She 'invented' one by writing a 'history' of the Irish avant-garde as a piece of creative writing that blurs the lines between the various artistic disciplines and changes the way we identify ourselves. It is an extraordinary feat of creative ingenuity. When Walshe came to Tokyo in September 2016, I accompanied her to Kita Senju, where she gave a presentation to Tokyo University of the Arts students. Subsequently, she gave a performance of a new collaborative work with the Japanese composer Tomomi Adachi on the roof of the German Institute in Roppongi, which concluded with quasi-operatic singing in a bath full of water. Here indeed was a narrative of sorts.

In May 2005, when I met Stockhausen at a concert in Tokyo, he seemed happy to be there again. He also told me he had been given the Freedom of the City of Belfast at the Sonorities Festival the year before. He then invited me to a festival of his music in his hometown, Kurten, that summer. It was at that festival that Stockhausen gave a 'live performance' of his *Telemusik*. This was an electronic composition Stockhausen had composed on his first visit to Japan in 1966, commissioned by NHK Radio. It was one of those fascinating moments in musical history when everything just seems to coincidently come together. As Stockhausen said, 'I have learned, especially in this country [Japan], that tradition does not simply exist; it must be created every day'. Stockhausen wrote subsequently in 1972, 'Until *Telemusik* I have tried to refuse to let anything come into my music that would be identifiable …'. He also wrote in 1996 that 'In *Telemusik* you can study what modern genetics seeks: namely, to cross living things which do not cross in nature so that odd hybrid types arise.' The work was recorded at NHK Electronic Music Studio in Tokyo in 1966, and included ethnic music from around the world, the chanting of Japanese monks, and recordings of Japanese gongs.

To celebrate the sixtieth anniversary of diplomatic relations between Ireland and Japan, I was asked to compose a piece for the Japanese pianist Satoko Inoue for tape, piano and actor, based on a story by Lafcadio Hearn. The Hearn story I chose was that of Shaka and Nanda, which is a digression within an account of silkworms in his book *In Ghostly Japan*. When I visited the Lafcadio Hearn Garden Centre in Tramore, County Waterford, I was given a tour of the centre by Agnes Aylward. She told me the story of how it was on Tramore beach that Lafcadio Hearn heard from his father that he was leaving him behind with an aunt and returning to Greece. Hearn was only seven years old at the time.

Lafcadio Hearn. (*The Reading Room/Alamy*)

I always consider a new composition as a new adventure. It is like a journey and, as far as possible, I take the scenic routes. I like to wander, and Lafcadio Hearn was a wanderer. The two things that Hearn and myself had in common was that we had holidayed in Tramore in our childhoods and we both ended up living in Japan. In my preparatory work for the piece, I meandered through Hearn's writings and letters, and I came across 'Dust', the last and strangest article written by Hearn for *The Atlantic* magazine in 1896. David Barber, writing in *The Atlantic* more than a hundred years later, in 2003, called it 'an intensely mystical [article],

The Boy Who Drew Cats, Japanese Fairy Tale Series No. 23, translated by Lafcadio Hearn, illustrations by Suzuki Kason, published by Hasegawa, T., Tokyo, 1898. (*British Library/Alamy*)

14

He painted a great many cats upon the screens; and then he began to feel very, very sleepy. He was just on the point of lying down to sleep beside one of the screens, when he suddenly remembered the words: "*Avoid large places; — keep to small!*"

The temple was very large; he was all alone;

From *The Boy Who Drew Cats*, Japanese Fairy Tale Series No. 23 (page 14), translated by Lafcadio Hearn, illustrations by Suzuki Kason, published by Hasegawa, T., Tokyo, 1898. (*British Library/Alamy*) a lush meditation on Buddhist spirituality and cosmology'. 'Dust' is almost avant-garde and surreal in its musings: 'I an individual – an individual soul! Nay, I am a population –a population unthinkable for multitude … Generations of generations I am, eons of eons! Countless times the concourse now making me has been scattered, and mixed with other scattering.' Stockhausen conveyed the same sensation when he wrote about composing *Telemusik*. He felt he was 'going one definite step further in the direction of writing not "My" music but a music of the whole world'. There is a sense of the negation of the self in 'Dust' and *Telemusik*.

In Hearn's collection of Japanese ghost stories, *Kaiden*, there is a curious little tale with the title '*Hi-Mawari*'. He recalls hearing the Thomas Moore song 'Believe Me If All Those Endearing Young Charms' played by an itinerant Welsh harpist. 'He made you cry', says Hearn's friend Robert at the end of the episode. This song would have been a well-known drawing-room or parlour song during the nineteenth and twentieth centuries. It was my pathway into the soundtrack, so to speak, of Lafcadio Hearn's life. I decided to use other songs that Hearn would have been familiar with from the mid-nineteenth century onwards as points of departure for the texture of the music. The problem was how to utilise these songs so as not to destroy their original integrity, and the answer I came up with was to recreate them into a twenty-first-century tapestry of ephemeral memories, both my own and Hearn's. I did not want to quote the song directly, so I deconstructed the music rather like a visual artist breaking down form into abstract coordinates.

In order to achieve these rearrangements and recreations of Japanese and Irish songs, I used a technique quite familiar in the compositions of Stockhausen and other avant-garde composers called 'octave displacement'. The idea is to take the notes of melodies and/or harmonies outside of their original containment and throw them into different octaves. I use rhythmic transformation, truncation and elision, overlapping certain melodies and harmonies to give a kind of reinterpretation of familiar music. I hope this conveys a sense of fleeting shadows floating on a 'sorrowful world', the region of cyclical death and rebirth in Buddhism. In Japanese the homophone of the word *ukiyo*, as well as meaning 'floating world' can also mean 'sorrowful world'. I imagined 'ghosts' disappearing and reappearing in the uncertainty of timelessness – Hearn calls it 'This sense of the voidness of things'. I wanted to create the same stillness and artlessness that is evident in the elegance of *gagaku* music. In his article 'Out of the Streets; Japanese Folk Songs', also written for *The Atlantic* in 1896, Hearn says of these street songs: 'The real art of them, in short, is their absolute artlessness.' It is this seemingly 'artless' nature of Japanese art that conveys to me a sensation of universality.

In the story, Shaka, the Buddha, sees Nanda's love for a girl as vulgar, and wants to teach him a lesson. The idea of Paradise and beauty is the overarching theme of my musical setting. The notion that Nanda should have to make retribution for the indulgences of his rebirth into the Second Heaven of Desire is an interesting subtext within the story itself. In the end I let the music return to the Second Heaven, but this time it is the idealised childhood notion of Paradise without the temptation of the heavenly maidens. The ludicrous and the seriousness of the story coexist for me as if in *ukiyo-e*, a painting of the 'floating world' or, as its homophone suggests, the 'sorrowful world'.

Johnathan Cott called his biography of Lafcadio Hearn *The Wandering Ghost*. As Hearn says: 'I have the double sensation of being myself a ghost and of being haunted, haunted by the prodigious luminous Spectre of the World.' Elizabeth Bisland in *The Life and Letters of Lafcadio Hearn* refers to a 'pellucid simplicity' that appears in Hearn's writings after he assimilated into the Japanese ways of living and thinking. I feel it was the 'ghosts' of Stockhausen's youth in Germany in the 1930s and 1940s that made him reconsider his way of thinking and espouse universality rather than the specificity of German and European music. This process began here in Japan with *Telemusik*.

For the celebrations of the sixtieth anniversary of the establishment of diplomatic ties between Ireland and Japan, a number of contemporary classical concerts took place. The Japanese pianist Satoko Inoue gave a series of concerts in Ireland – in Donegal, Dublin and Waterford – in the summer of 2017, which included my composition *The Second Heaven of Desire in Old Tramore*. The concerts also featured other new pieces on the stories of Lafcadio Hearn composed by two Japanese composers, Yuji Itoh and Akemi Naito, and Irish composer John McLachlan. These pieces were performed in the autumn in Tokyo.

The Irish pianist and composer Martin O'Leary gave lecture recitals in October at Rikkyo University based on Irish contemporary piano music, which included my piece based on a quotation from Yeats called *The Agony of the Red Piano in Old Cambodia*.

To conclude, Jennifer Walshe has made a mythology out of the absence of the avant-garde in Irish contemporary music and, in so doing, has confronted our notions of identity and universality. Looking back on my undergraduate years in Ireland, I am glad I did not, as the critic Fanny Feehan suggested, 'Leave it all to the Japanese', and I attempted to cross the lines between imitation and innovation and bridge the imaginary universal *Yamato-e* clouds between the Occidental and the Oriental.

Lafcadio Hearn's 'Yuki-Onna' and Oscar Wilde's 'The Star-Child' and *Salomé*

Mimbu Kawamura

There is a tale entitled 'Yuki-Onna' (Snow-Woman) in Lafcadio Hearn's *Kwaidan: Stories and Studies of Strange Things*, a collection of short stories written in English and published in 1904, the year of his death. Originally intended for an American readership, the book was later translated into Japanese. 'Yuki-Onna' is a weird but beautiful border crossing story shaped like a folktale. Whereas it has often been interpreted in the context of the entire collection, this essay proposes to read it alongside Oscar Wilde's short story 'The Star-Child' in *The House of Pomegranates* (1891) and his play *Salomé* (1894).

'Yuki-Onna' begins thus: 'In a village of Musashi Province, there lived two woodcutters: Mosaku and Minokichi.' Mosaku was an old man and Minokichi his 18-year-old apprentice. Every day they went to a forest to fell trees for commercial purposes. The forest was situated five miles away from their village, and they had to be carried across a wide river by a ferryman. One winter evening, they were caught up in a snow storm on the way home and could not cross the river, the ferry being moored on the other bank. They were obliged to stay in the ferryman's hut for the night. They tried to sleep with their straw rain-coats on. It was not particularly cold at first but as the snow storm gathered force, temperatures began to drop. The old man fell asleep soon; after a while the young man was asleep too. However, it became so cold that the young man woke up. He found, 'by the snow-light', that the entrance door had been forced open; in the room there was a woman in white bending over Mosaku and blowing her breath upon him 'like a bright white smoke'. Then she turned to Minokichi and stooped over him, her face almost touching him. The woman was very beautiful, but her eyes frightened him. She intended to 'treat' him as she did the old man but took 'pity' on him: she said, 'because you are so young … You are a pretty boy, Minokichi; and I will not hurt you now.' However, she ordered him not to tell anybody about what he had seen that night, not even his mother; if he should break his promise, he would be killed. Having said this, she left. It was then that Minokichi found Mosaku frozen dead.

After being rescued by the ferryman, Minokichi fell ill and ceased to work, but as soon as he had recovered, he resumed his work in the forest alone. One evening in the following winter, Minokichi overtook a girl on his way home. She was 'a tall, slim girl, very good-looking', and she greeted Minokichi in a sweet voice, like 'a songbird'. While they were walking together, the girl said that her name was O-Yuki, and that having lost her parents, she was on her way to Edo to work for her relatives there, even though there had not been any pre-arrangements. Soon Minokichi was 'charmed' by 'this strange girl' and asked her whether she was married or engaged. Her answer was no, and she asked him the same question. He told her 'that although he had only a widowed mother to support, the question of an "honorable daughter-in-law" had not yet been considered, as he was very young …' After these polite exchanges, he brought the girl to his house, where she was warmly welcomed by his mother. Instead of going to Edo, she settled there as an 'honorable daughter-in-law'.

As she served her mother-in-law well, O-Yuki was much loved. When five years had passed, her mother-in-law died. Before her death, the narrator reports her praise of O-Yuki and calls her a 'wife', rather than a 'daughter-in-law'. After that, O-Yuki bore Minokichi ten boys and girls, 'handsome children all of them, and very fair of skin'. However, because she remained as 'young and fresh' as ever, the

Yuki-Onna, *the Lady of the Snow*, a spirit in Japanese folklore, by Evelyn Paul (1883–1963), 1912. (*Niday Picture Library/Alamy*)

village folk began to wonder whether she was 'by nature different from themselves'.

One night when their children had gone to sleep, and while O-Yuki was sewing 'by the light of a paper lamp', Minokichi looking at her said: 'To see you sewing there, with the light on your face, makes me think of a strange thing that happened when I was a lad of eighteen. I then saw somebody as beautiful and white as you are now – indeed, she was very like you.'

Instead of stopping him, O-Yuki invited Minokichi to tell the story. Minokichi therefore told her what had happened in the hut that night, and though he did not know whether it had been 'a dream or the reality', he emphasised that it was the first and only time he had seen any woman as beautiful as O-Yuki was: it was as if O-Yuki were the very same woman he had seen. Not being able to bear it any more, O-Yuki cried, 'It was I – I – I! Yuki was I.' Thus revealing her own identity, she had to kill Minokichi because he had broken his promise. But she could not do this, thinking of her own sleeping children. Therefore, asking him to take good care of their children lest she should return and 'treat you as you deserve', O-Yuki evaporated through the smoke-hold on the ceiling, her voice becoming 'thin, like a crying of wind' and herself melting 'into a bright white mist'. O-Yuki again crossed the border and returned from the human world to her own realm, nature.

The above is a synopsis of 'Yuki-Onna'. I shall come back to the essential points of this story while discussing Oscar Wilde's 'The Star-Child'. For the time being, I shall turn my attention to Masaru Toda's study on the ways in which Hearn's 'Yuki-Onna' has been interpreted.

Toda explores the question of whether there is a written ur-story upon which Hearn modelled his 'Yuki-Onna'. He sums up two main streams of studies that have been carried out so far and concludes that there is no written ur-story of the snowwoman preceding Hearn's 'Yuki-Onna,' but that it was Hearn's work that provided the original model on which many other Japanese tales about the snow-woman have been based.[1] On the one hand, Toda regards Shinichi Matsumura's 'Hearn's "Yuki-Onna" and the Ur-"Yuki-Onna" as representing one of the two streams of discussion regarding the Ur-"Yuki-Onna"'.[2] Matsumura insists on the existence of a mountain folktale known as 'A Snow-Woman of Hakubagatake', which was widely circulated in the border district between Ecchu and Echigo (cited in Sazanami Iwaya's *Daigoen*, vol. 7), and he believes that this was the story that informed Hearn's 'Yuki-Onna'. On the other hand, Toda sees Yoko Makino's

'Lafcadio Hearn's 'Yuki-Onna' and Baudelaire's 'Les Bienfaits de la Lune' as representing the other stream.[3] Makino highlights the influence of Baudelaire's prose poem 'Les Bienfaits de la Lune', which Hearn read as a young man, and which he then translated. Makino suggests that Hearn created his 'Yuki-Onna' by bringing Baudelaire's poem to bear upon a fragmentary oral tradition surrounding the snow-woman. Through his research and fieldwork, Toda has concluded that Makino's argument is more convincing than that of Matsumura. Namely, Hearn's 'Yuki-Onna' is the first written story on which various other literary productions – translations and adaptations – are based. And it is these latter derivative works that have made up the large corpus of stories about the snow-woman that many children are reading today.

Toda also responds to Makino's assertion that 'Yuki-Onna' was informed by Hearn's memories of his mother and of his birthplace, Greece. Toda observes that Hearn deprives the story of a paternal figure – the pillar of Japan's patriarchal social structure – and that he gives pride of place to maternal figures, who play a predominant role from the beginning to the end of the story. Toda emphasises the fact that at the beginning of the story the snow-woman appears and kills the old woodcutter Mosaku but refrains from killing Minokichi because he is young and handsome. Toda indicates that Hearn projects his childhood self-image onto Minokichi, and the image of his beautiful mother onto the snow-woman. Toda also points out that Minokichi's mother is alone at home, his father being absent. Moreover, Toda says that the story is dominated by the mother–child relationship from the beginning to the end. Although the snow-woman blames Minokichi for his betrayal, she does not kill him; rather, she requests that he should take good care of her children and returns to nature as a mist. Thus, Toda argues that the story is told solely from Minokichi's point of view at the beginning and the end of it, and that Minokichi's existence is wiped out during the intervening span, i.e., the period that covers the ten children's births and their growing up – to say nothing of the five years during which Minokichi's mother lives with her daughter-in-law. During that five-year period, Minokichi appears to be neither a husband nor a father, his fictional existence becoming tenuous; this is because Hearn deliberately distances the story from Minokichi's viewpoint.

In this way, according to Toda, Hearn creates a new story which reverses Japan's traditional patriarchal social order, in favour of a predominant maternalism. Toda suggests that it is the memory of his mother that leads Hearn to devise this social reversal. Hearn's mother Rosa stooping over him and gazing upon him lovingly – this may be the image Hearn projects onto the snow-woman when Minokichi first encounters her.

However, whether Japanese society was traditionally patriarchal or not is a question to be reconsidered. Whereas European society seems to have been essentially patriarchal, in Japan a maternal order was in fact dominant. I have explored this question in *The Imagination Directed towards the Mountain-Top*; see also Hayao Kawai's *The Pathology of Japan as a Maternal Society*. Perhaps Hearn found matriarchal Japan more congenial than patriarchal Europe.

As we have seen, Toda argues that the story adopts Minokichi's point of view only at the beginning and the end, and that Minokichi's perspective vanishes during the period from O-Yuki's moving to Minokichi's house to her departure. In relation to this argument, a few words must be said about Sukehiro Hirakawa's Japanese translation of 'Yuki-Onna'. There are some places in Hirakawa's translation where the original English is so simplified as to wipe away the nuance of some English words.

Take, for example, one detail already mentioned above: Minokichi tells O-Yuki that his mother has not yet had an 'honorable daughter-in-law'. Hirakawa translates this phrase as 'yome' in Japanese. But Hirakawa also translates the phrase 'his wife' as 'yome' in that scene where Minokichi's dying mother expresses her thanks to O-Yuki and calls her 'his wife' for the first time.[4] The English phrases 'honorable daughter-in-law' and 'wife' have significantly different meanings. The former emphasises a woman's domestic role in the family she marries into ('yome' in Japanese), while the latter highlights a woman's role in relation to the man she marries. In this story, it is only when her mother-in-law dies that O-Yuki becomes Minokichi's 'wife', bearing him ten children.

Toshiaki Komura has paid critical attention to the significance of O-Yuki being called a 'daughter-in-law,' as distinct from a 'wife'.[5] Komura argues that in order for O-Yuki, whose 'strange' existence is alien to the human world, to dwell with humans, she needs someone who can give her a sense of belonging: this is supplied by the figure of the mother or mother-in-law, as Julia Kristeva says.[6]

Komura suggests that Minokichi's mother performs an anchoring function: for O-Yuki, to be embraced by her mother-in-law is to begin to belong to the human world. For O-Yuki's part, what she should do in order to be accepted as a member of the village is to serve her mother-in-law as well as she can. She does achieve this aim. However, as Komura says, O-Yuki's assimilation into the human world is confined to the span of her mother-in-law's existence. After her death, O-Yuki forfeits support, and her 'strangeness' begins to attract suspicion: despite having given birth to ten children, O-Yuki is as young and beautiful as ever, and the villagers begin to refer to her as 'a wonderful person, by nature different from themselves'. Hirakawa translates 'a wonderful person' into Japanese as 'subarasiihito,' which means a splendid person, but it should in fact be translated as 'fusigina-hito' (a person full of wonder).

As Komura goes on to observe, O-Yuki's increasingly obvious strangeness leads to Minokichi's breaking the promise that he would never tell anyone about his encounter with the snow-woman. Komura's argument is convincing. However, I do not see the period between the death of O-Yuki's mother-in-law and her return to nature as merely representing a process whereby her strangeness becomes apparent. The fact that this is also the period during which ten children are born should be emphasised. It seems that only after her mother-in-law's death does O-Yuki become a 'wife': while her mother-in-law lives, nothing is said about giving birth to children. The number of the children suggests how intimate the relationship between O-Yuki and Minokichi is. The acceptance of O-Yuki as an 'honorable daughter-in-law' in the human world hinges upon her mother-in-law, but after the latter dies, O-Yuki's acceptance is further confirmed by her becoming Minokichi's 'wife' and bearing him ten children.

Thus, O-Yuki performs two different roles in Minokichi's domestic sphere: to serve her mother-in-law as her 'honorable daughter-in-law' and then to serve Minokichi as his 'wife' by giving birth to, and bringing up, his children. In this way, Hearn differentiates between 'house' and 'individual'. The roles O-Yuki performs in the human world represent her best efforts to find acceptance in that world. However, even her children – quite apart from the villagers – must be aware of their mother's strangeness. The snow-woman's destiny is preordained – she will eventually have to leave the human world and her beloved children. This behaviour of O-Yuki seems to be the epitome of the present women's way of life in that since it is Minokichi himself who breaks the promise, she will not permit him to retain his lingering attachment, even if the woman in the past is the same as O-Yuki herself. Thus, her border-crossing journey comes to a tragic close.

I shall now proceed to read 'Yuki-Onna' from the perspective of comparative literature: that is, the story can be interpreted as a 'myth'. Scholars have identified a 'Nature Myth', which symbolises the cycles of nature. Take the myth of Demeter and her daughter Persephone, for example.[7] Demeter, the goddess of agriculture, asks to be allowed to bring back her daughter Persephone from Hades. Persephone is given permission to return to the earth only for a limited period of time each year. Her brief sojourn coincides with spring. After the autumnal harvests, she is forced to return to Hades, and that is when winter arrives. There is also a 'Prophetic Myth': a particular event is to come to pass as foretold. For instance, the myth of Quetzalcoatl predicts Hernando Cortés' conquest of the Aztecs.[8]

Winter is placed at the beginning of Hearn's 'Yuki-Onna', and snow represents a dominant element of nature which presides over the entire story. The snow-woman – as an embodiment of snow – blows her breath over Mosaku and freezes him, but she refrains from doing the same to Minokichi. Predicting that they will meet again, she disappears. Here snow has two levels of significance. First, snow conjures up winter, which is the severest part of the seasonal cycle. Mosaku's death is, as it were, a sacrifice to winter; in other words, he is subsumed under the cycles of nature. Second, snow necessarily prepares for spring; it covers and protects living things that have gone into dormancy until they are revived in spring. Thus, nature's apparent cruelty in fact ushers in the vernal season. The snow-woman in 'Yuki-Onna' embodies these two aspects of snow: death and revival.

To further explore these two aspects of snow, I shall compare Hearn's 'Yuki-Onna' with Oscar Wilde's short story 'The Star-Child' (1891).[9] At the beginning of his story, Wilde, like Hearn in 'Yuki-Onna', introduces two woodsmen who are travelling home from a forest in a snow storm. There is a dialogue here between animals and birds. The green Linnets say, '… the old Earth is dead, and they have laid her out in her white shroud'. The 'white shroud' is, of course, snow, which here symbolises death. By contrast, the Turtle-doves say, 'The Earth is going to be married, and this is her bridal dress.' For the Turtle-doves, the Earth, rather than being dead, wears the white 'bridal dress' of snow, which promises new birth and the arrival of spring. Here, Wilde juxtaposes the contrasting symbolic workings of 'snow.' These birds' very different views of snow shed light on the symbolic workings of this natural element in Hearn's 'Yuki-Onna'.

In addition to these contrasting understandings, 'The Star-Child' elucidates

Oscar Wilde, photographed by W. and D. Downey (studio photographers), 1889. (*Granger Historical Picture Archive/Alamy*)

three different ways to cope with snow. This points towards the practical – as distinct from mythological – aspect of Wilde's story, which differs from Hearn's 'Yuki-Onna'. In 'The Star-Child', the Wolf regards the two views of snow mentioned above as nonsense. He says, 'I tell you that it is all the fault of the Government, and if you don't believe me I shall eat you.' The Wolf attributes the bad weather, which deprives him of food, to the government's flawed policies. The Wolf's opinion is politically tinted. Next, the Woodpecker displays a philosophical bent of mind when he says, 'I don't care an atomic theory for explanations. If a thing is so, it is so, and at present it is terribly cold.' This is an attitude of resignation. The third attitude – exemplified by the Owls – is to welcome the cold as it is: 'Tu-whit! Tu-whoo! Tu-whit! Tu-whoo! what delightful weather we are having!'

In what follows, I shall consider how the two woodsmen in 'The Star-Child' come across the Star-Child and what happens to him subsequently. At the same time, I shall explore the parallels between 'The Star-Child' and 'Yuki-Onna' from the perspective of comparative literature.

Unlike Hearn's story, the two woodsmen in Wilde's story are not in a master–apprentice relationship; nor are they father and son (as the two male characters become in various adaptations/translations of Hearn's story). They are simply poor woodsmen, each with many children. As they were plodding on in the snow storm, they lost their way and were horror-struck; the narrator portrays their feelings: 'for they knew that the Snow is cruel to those who sleep in her arms'. The snow is here feminised, whilst the ice is referred to as the 'Ice-King'.

Believing that St Martin would protect them, they finally arrived at the margins of the forest and spotted the lamplight of their village far below in the valley. They rejoiced and compared the earth to a flower of silver, and the moon to a flower of gold. However, the joy soon gave way to sadness again, for they remembered they were poor. They complained of 'Injustice', which created social inequalities, and thought that it would have been better if they had died in the forest. This remark picks up on the Wolf's political response to the snow at the beginning of the story, and it also corresponds to the theme of poverty and death at the beginning of Hearn's 'Yuki-Onna'.

While they were thus bewailing their 'misery', something strange happened. A bright and beautiful star crossed the sky and seemed to fall behind 'a clump of willow trees that stood hard by a little sheep-fold near them'. The sheep-fold has a Christian connotation, and as we will see, since this story can be read as a prophetic myth, the star can be said to have a symbolic meaning of prophecy. The two woodsmen thought that 'a crock of gold' had fallen from heaven and hurried to the spot. There was indeed gold lying on the snow. But it was not 'a crock of gold' but 'a cloak of golden tissue, curiously wrought with stars'. Wrapped in it was no treasure of gold but a sleeping child.

One of the woodsmen said that he already had many children, and that an additional child would be of no use. The other did not want to leave the child in the snow, saying that though he was very poor and had many children to support, and though his wife might complain, he would ask her to take care of it. This scene shares parallels with Hearn's 'Yuki-Onna', where the snow-woman does not kill the young and beautiful Minokichi but allows him to live.

The name of the woodsman who brought the child home is not known. He rejected the other's proposal to share the golden cloak, regarding it as belonging to the child. His wife complained that it was not actually gold in the cloak but a child who might be 'a changeling' and therefore bring about 'bad fortune'. She did not want to subscribe to her husband's belief that this was 'a Star-Child'. At that time 'a bitter wind from the forest came in through the open door and made her tremble'. Then her husband said, 'Into a house where a heart is hard cometh there not always a bitter wind?' She was moved. Hugging and kissing the child, she took it to the bed where her own youngest child was sleeping. Here we sense the woman's motherly instinct. Likewise, in Hearn's 'Yuki-Onna', the snow-woman spares the young Minokichi. Moreover, as mentioned above, critics have pointed out that the snow-woman is in some respects a motherly figure to Minokichi.

The woodsman and his wife found 'a chain of amber' round the Star-Child's neck and stored it in a chest together with the golden cloak. The child became even more beautiful as he grew up, 'white and delicate as sawn ivory', and he looked like 'the narcissus of a field'. In Hearn's 'Yuki-Onna', O-Yuki's children resemble her: 'handsome children all of them, and very fair of skin'. At this point in Wilde's story, the Star-Child does not know who his mother is, but he is like O-Yuki's children, 'beautiful', 'white and delicate as sawn ivory'. His physical features distinguish him from the 'swarthy and black-haired' children in the village. The reader can guess that his mother is not an ordinary woman.

In both Hearn's and Wilde's stories, there is a strange power working from a realm beyond the ordinary world. Hearn's 'Yuki-Onna', as many critics say, is 'a story of hetero-species marriage' – here I wish to add that this may have something to do with the fact that, as Edward Larocque Tinker observes in *Lafcadio Hearn's American Days*, Hearn himself was a product of 'miscegenation': 'the young Lafcadio was a queer sort of human cocktail, having a little dash of everything – English, Gypsy, Irish, Greek, Arab and Moor ... heir to all the antagonistic qualities of these illy-assorted races'.[10] Notwithstanding their many similarities, Wilde's 'The Star-Child' differs from Hearn's story in that it can be regarded as 'a story of a wandering noble man', employing the narrative pattern underlying the stories of Okuninushi in Japanese mythology, of Hikaru Genji (the hero of *The Tale of Genji*, who is sent from the capital city to Suma in rural Harima Province), and of the wandering Odysseus, all of whom are high-born heroes who stray from their origins and overcome hardships with the help of animals and women.

The 'beautiful' Star-Child is compared to 'Narcissus', who is self-absorbed. Springing from a Star, he is 'noble', and he made other children of 'mean parentage' serve him, treated animals and birds badly, and took no pity on others. One day 'a poor beggar woman' in 'her garments torn and ragged' passed through the village. Finding her resting under a chestnut-tree, the Star-Child instigated his companions to throw stones at her to drive her away. Realising what the child has done, the woodsman scolded him: 'Surely thou art hard of heart and knowest not mercy, for what evil has this poor woman done to thee that thou should'st treat her like this wise?' The word 'treat' here reminds us of the same word the snow-woman in Hearn's story uses when she says at her final departure, 'if ever they have reason to complain of you, I will treat you as you deserve!' 'The Star-Child' was written and published earlier than 'Yuki-Onna'; if we take some of the similarities mentioned above into consideration, it seems probable that Hearn was influenced by Wilde's story.

In 'Yuki-Onna' Hearn gives O-Yuki's children no other descriptions that indicate their connection with the snow-woman than their being 'handsome' and 'very fair of skin.' Wilde's 'The Star-Child' picks up the story where Hearn leaves off, describing the Star-Child growing up to be a man. Thus Wilde constructs 'a story of a wandering noble man'; in other words, 'a short story' in the western style, while Hearn's story was created by borrowing some elements of Japanese folklore and by incorporating his own early memories; if the relationship between the snow-woman and her children had been consciously established when they had grown up, as it was in Wilde's story, the snow-woman could not have remained as mother and would have erased herself from this world, too, as it is the rule of 'a story of hetero-species marriage'.

Although the settings at the beginnings of both stories share some common ground, Wilde's 'The Star-Child' departs from the paradigm of the 'hetero-species marriage' and goes on to develop 'a story of a wandering noble man'. When the female beggar heard the woodsman say 'I found thee in the forest', she screamed and fainted. When she regained her consciousness, she asked the woodsman whether the child had been found in the forest ten years before, and when he said yes, she again asked whether the child had had 'a chain of amber' around his neck and had been wrapped in 'a cloak of gold tissue broidered with stars'. Answering yes, the woodsman took them out of the chest and showed them to the woman, who wept for joy and said, 'He is my little son whom I lost in the forest … in search of him have I wandered over the whole world.'

The woman told the child that she had given birth to him in the forest, but that he had been seized by robbers. Showing him her mementoes, she implored him to come away with her. But the child did not want to accept her as his mother. He rejected her final request for a farewell kiss and asked her to leave. The woman went into the forest, crying. After she had left, the child felt glad and went back to his companions. However, they noticed that the child had changed: he now looked 'as foul as the toad, and as loathsome as the adder'. They 'drove him out of the garden', just as Adam and Eve were expelled from paradise.

Then he became aware of his physical transformation and realised that he had sinned. The ten-year-old boy now went on a journey to ask his mother to forgive him. The journey in search of the mother is a theme closely related to Hearn's endeavours to reunite with his mother, from whom he was separated early in life. I shall return to this detail when I discuss Baudelaire's 'Les Bienfaits de la Lune', a poem which Hearn loved and translated.

Travelling through the forest, the boy asked the animals and birds whether they had seen his mother. As the boy had mistreated them, none of them offered help. He went away, weeping. When he emerged from the forest, the village labourers did not allow him even to stay in the sheds. No one took pity on him. For three years he travelled through a merciless world, reaping the consequences of his own pride.

One evening, he arrived at 'the gate of a strong-walled city that stood by the river'. Just as forests are where mysterious things happen, so literary rivers are sometimes symbolic borders which must be crossed in order to gain a new life. We have already seen Hearn's woodcutter Minokichi and the snow-woman crossing the river that separates the forest and the village. For the Star-Child, he has to cross the river and enter the city to find his mother.

The Star-Child entreated the guards to let him enter the city, but they scorned him for his beggarly appearance and drove him away. But 'an old and evil-visaged man' passed by and bought the boy for 'the price of a bowl of sweet wine'. The boy was brought to the man's house in the city and was imprisoned in the dungeon.

The man turned out to be 'the subtlest of the magicians of Libya', and the name of the city Giaours means infidels. The magician ordered the boy to go into the forest near the city to find gold. On the first day, he had to bring back the white gold. Should he fail, he would be given a hundred stripes and cast into the dungeon again. There would be no food for him.

The boy went into the forest outside the city. The forest appeared beautiful, but once inside, he was surrounded by briars and thorns, nettles and thistles. The white gold was nowhere to be seen. When evening came, he was obliged to head back. On the outskirts of the forest, he found a little hare in a trap and set it free. The grateful hare told the boy that the white gold was hidden inside the cleft of a great oak. The hare said, '… as thou dealt with me, so I did deal with thee'.

When he came back to the city gate with the white gold, the boy saw a leper. Taking 'pity' on him, the boy gave him the gold. When he returned to the magician empty-handed, he was beaten and thrown into the dungeon. We have already examined the significance of the word 'pity' in 'Yuki-Onna', where the snow-woman takes pity on Minokichi.

The following day, the boy was asked to go and find the yellow gold in the forest. He could not find it anywhere and had to head back when evening came. But the little hare he had rescued appeared again and told him to go and look for it in a pond. When the boy returned to the city gate with the gold, he came across the same beggar. As on the previous day, the boy took 'pity' on him and gave him the yellow gold. Again, he was beaten by his master and thrown into the dungeon without any food.

On the third day, the boy was asked to bring back the red gold from the forest. This time, the hare told him to go and find it in a cave. Once again, he gave the gold to the beggar at the city gate. As the boy had been told he would be killed should he fail to bring back the red gold, his heart was heavy. Much to his astonishment, however, the people of the city began to follow him, chanting 'How beautiful is our lord!' The priests and high officers of the city also came to praise him: 'Thou art our lord for whom we have been waiting, and the sort of our King.'

Seeing his face reflected on a warrior's shield, the boy realised that he had regained his beautiful look. This miracle happens because the boy has shown 'pity'. It is 'pity' that makes this transfiguration possible. The priests and high officers of the city told the boy that the advent of this day had been prophesied; this is therefore an example of 'prophetic mythology.'

But the Star-Child refused to be crowned. He said he had embarked upon this journey, not to be a king, but to find his mother and to beg her 'pardon'. Then he spotted his mother among the crowd. He dashed to her, knelt down and kissed her injured feet. In tears, he said, 'Mother, I denied thee in the hour of my pride. Accept me in the hour of my humility.' But she did not speak. The child asked the leper standing beside her to intercede. The leper, too, was silent, and the child began to sob again, entreating them to allow him to return to the forest where he had first been found. Finally, the female beggar and the leper together ordered him to 'rise'. When he rose, they transfigured themselves into 'a King and a Queen'.

The king and the queen kissed the child, led him to the palace, clothed him in fine garments, placed the crown on his head and the sceptre in his hand. The new king showed 'much justice and mercy' to all, banished the evil magician, sent many presents to the woodsman and his wife who had brought him up, and conferred high honours on their children. He would not 'suffer any to be cruel to bird or beast, but taught love and loving-kindness and charity' and gave bread and clothes to the poor. Thus 'peace and plenty' reigned in that land. However, as he had endured many sufferings, he ruled for only three years and died. 'And he who came after him ruled evilly.'

The above is a synopsis of 'The Star-Child'. We have seen how 'nature mythology' embodies the cycles of nature: that is, winter signifies both death and potential rebirth. In what way can we bring this mythological model to bear upon the latter part of the story? In Wilde's story, the cycles of nature, particularly the seasonal transition from winter to spring, are juxtaposed with human social cycles:

in other words, human society has to undergo severe trials in order for goodness to prevail, and when goodness has had its day, evil takes over again.

At first sight, this cyclical view of history may be seen as manifesting Wilde's cynicism. However, if in nature, no one is able to escape from winter until the arrival of spring, in human society, no one can avoid tribulations until the advent of goodness.

Before he is crowned, the Star-Child experiences trials and tribulations on his journey in search of his mother, and this process takes place in nature, where spring follows winter, and where winter reigns again after the harvest season. Regarding the theme of 'death and rebirth,' both Wilde's 'The Star-Child' and Hearn's 'Yuki-Onna' can be said to draw upon nature mythology. Underlying both stories is winter's double-edgedness: annihilation and the promise of rebirth. It is the differences beneath this shared pattern that are particularly interesting. We have already noted that Wilde's is 'a story of a wandering noble man', while Hearn's is that of a 'hetero-species marriage'. It is significant that while Hearn's story comes to a close when the snow-woman leaves her children and disappears, Wilde has the child set out on a journey to find his mother. The two stories seem to complement, or complete, each other in this regard.

There is a further similarity from another point of view. In Wilde's 'The Star-Child' the female beggar and the leper transform themselves into a queen and a king, moving from death and decay to beauty and life. In Hearn's 'Yuki-Onna', too, the snow-woman, who embodies deathly winter, turns into a beautiful girl. Both stories transfigure horribleness and death into beauty and life. Both works elucidate the two aspects of nature: 'Natura Maligna' and 'Natura Benigna', as Theodore Watts-Dunton explores them in *The Coming of Love and Other Poems.*[11]

II

We have compared and contrasted Hearn's 'Yuki-Onna' and Wilde's 'The Star-Child.' Now I shall revisit Makino's comparative study on Hearn's 'Yuki-Onna' and Baudelaire's 'Les Bienfaits de la Lune' and bring Wilde's play *Salomé* into the picture.

Makino regards 'Yuki-Onna' as a story developed from unwritten Japanese folklore and mixed with Hearn's memory of his mother. The composition of the story, according to Makino, owes much to Baudelaire's prose poem 'Les Bienfaits de la Lune', which was a favourite of Hearn's. Hearn translated the poem into English for an American journal and wrote an essay on it. When he came to Japan, Hearn used the poem in a lecture, along with his own interpretation of it.

Makino maintains that it was Baudelaire's characterisation of the moon that fascinated Hearn. However, she only quotes Hearn's English translation, without providing the original French text; this, as we shall see, potentially leads to a problem. As Baudelaire's original text is important for our purposes, it is worth quoting it in full here:

Les Bienfaits de la Lune

La Lune, qui est le caprice même, regarda par la fenêtre pendant que tu dormais dans ton berceau, et se dit: 'Cette enfant me plaît.'

Et elle descendit moelleusement son escalier de nuages et passa sans bruit à travers les vitres. Puis elle s'étendit sur toi avec la tendresse souple d'une mère, et elle déposa ses couleurs sur ta face. Tes prunelles en sont restées vertes, et tes joues extraordinairement pâles. C'est en contemplant cette visiteuse que tes yeux se sont si bizarrement agrandis, et elle t'a si tendrement serrée à la gorge que tu en as gardé pour toujours l'envie de pleurer.

Cependant, dans l'expression de sa joie, la Lune remplissait toute ta chambre comme une atmosphère phosphorique, comme un poison lumineux; et toute cette lumière vivante pensait et disait: "Tu subiras éternellement l'influence de mon baiser. Tu seras belle à ma manière. Tu aimeras ce que j'aime et ce qui m'aime: l'eau, les nuages, le silence et la nuit; la mer immense et verte; l'eau informe et multiforme; le lieu où tu ne seras pas; l'amant que tu ne connaîtras pas; les fleurs monstrueuses; les parfums qui font délirer; les chats qui se pâment sur les pianos et qui gémissent comme les femmes, d'une voix rauque et douce!

'Et tu seras aimée de mes amants, courtisée par mes courtisans. Tu seras la ruine des hommes aux yeux verts dont j'ai serré aussi la gorge dans mes caresses nocturnes; de ceux-là qui aiment la mer, la mer immense, tumultueuse et verte, l'eau informe et multiforme, le lieu où ils ne sont

> pas, la femme qu'ils ne connaissent pas, les fleurs sinistres qui ressemblent aux encensoirs d'une religion inconnue, les parfums qui troublent la volonté, et les animaux sauvages et voluptueux qui sont les emblèmes de leur folie.'
>
> Et c'est pour cela, maudite chère enfant gâtée, que je suis maintenant couché à tes pieds, cherchant dans toute ta personne le reflet de la redoutable Divinité, de la fatidique marraine, de la nourrice empoisonneuse de tous les lunatiques.
>
> Charles Baudelaire: 'Petits poèmes en proses – Le spleen de Paris', 1869.[12]

By quoting Hearn's English translation, Makino observes:

> We can easily recognize a dramatic construct common to that of the first, impressive scene of 'Yuki-Onna.' Moonlight, just like snow, creeps into a dark room at night, and mysteriously lit up in such light, a personification of the moon appears. She is a beautiful but frightening figure, all in white. She comes to the baby who is lying in the cradle, lowers her face, and, kissing it, speaks to it in half blessing, half cursing words. From that moment on, her words control the destiny of the child. And the infant, whose cheeks turn pale, is both frightened and fascinated, just as Minokichi was by Yuki-Onna. (Makino, p. 239)

Makino suggests that Baudelaire's moon goddess is 'characterized as a typical fin-de-siècle "femme fatale"', that she 'has a double face: one beautiful and tender, the other destructive and dangerous', and that she is also 'the ruler of a powerless young man's destiny'.

Makino's assertion that the moon goddess of Baudelaire's poem is 'a fin-de-siècle femme fatale' and that Hearn modelled his snow-woman on this figure is very interesting. It reminds us of Wilde's play *Salomé*, in which the moon is also suggestive of Salomé as a femme fatale with 'a pale face'.

However, it is wrong to identify (as Makino does) the infant visited by the moon as a boy. In the original text, Baudelaire calls the sleeping infant 'cette enfant' (feminine), and 'the lover thou shalt never know' is originally 'l'amant que tu ne connaîtras pas' (masculine). Makino may have simply followed Hearn's translation, but then why did Hearn, who is said to have been very well versed in French, change the infant's gender? It seems unlikely that this was unintentional.

In his essay on Baudelaire's prose poem, Hearn uses his own translation, referring to the scene where the moon goddess enters the chamber of the infant and whispers in 'his dreams'. Discussing this passage, Makino quotes again Hearn's phrase: 'the woman thou shalt never know'.[13]

Makino argues that there is a reason why Hearn preferred this poem to many other poems featuring femmes fatales in Western literature: 'He probably identified with the infant asleep in the cradle and saw his own loving but afflicted mother in the opening scene of "The Moon's Blessings."' This may indeed be the reason why Hearn changed the infant's gender, perceiving a maternal impulse in the moon goddess. As Makino points out, Hearn was separated from his mother early in his childhood: Baudelaire's poem may well have intensified his longing for his mother and for his mother's home. If Makino is right, can we not also say that Wilde's 'The Star-Child' is a story about the protagonist's quest for his lost mother and her country? And was it not Hearn himself who set out on a home-searching journey, first leaving Ireland, then sojourning in America and finally arriving in Japan, where his dream came true?

However, Makino also observes that Hearn's memory has 'a double, ambivalent significance': its 'idealized charm' and its 'fearful futility that gnaws the heart'. Hearn cannot rest contented with the recovery of the memory of his lost mother and her homeland. As Makino argues, 'Yuki-Onna' reflects the ambivalence of Hearn's memory: because Minokichi articulates a memory that should never be recalled, he has to sacrifice something enshrined in that very memory.

I shall now turn my attention to the characteristics of the moon goddess as a femme fatale in Wilde's *Salomé* and in Baudelaire's 'Les Bienfaits de la Lune'. As mentioned above, Makino maintains that Hearn favours Baudelaire's moon goddess over other femmes fatales in Western literature, and if this is true, Hearn would also have had a special feeling for Wilde's *Salomé*. Wilde's Salomé is typical of the fin-de-siècle femme fatale. What should we make of Salomé's moon-like, 'pale' appearance, which reminds us of Baudelaire's moon?

The first scene of the play presents some soldiers leaning over a balcony to look at the moon. One of them, Queen Herodias' page, says: 'Look at the moon. How strange the moon seems! She is like a woman rising from a tomb. She is like a dead woman. One might fancy she was looking for dead things.'[14] In response, a young Syrian captain says: 'She has a strange look. She is like a little princess who wears a yellow veil, and whose feet are of silver. She is like a princess who has little white doves for feet. One might fancy she was dancing.' Here the moon is implicitly identified with Princess Salomé with her yellow veil; the feet of silver and little white doves may refer to the white clouds under the moon, and Salomé is destined to dance.

Thus, from the beginning Salomé is likened to the moon. The young Syrian captain entranced by Salomé fixes his eyes on her 'pale' face – 'How pale the Princess is! Never have I seen her so pale. She is like the shadow of a white rose in a mirror of silver.' As the play unfolds, the complexion of Salomé and the moon will change, and the Syrian captain's words – 'a white rose in a mirror of silver' – have a significant meaning. The image here is not that of a real rose but that of a reflection, and the word 'shadow' makes the reflection even more tenuous. Death is implicit in this image: it is both Salomé's destiny and something with which the moon is associated.

Later on in the play, King Herod, who is enamoured of Salomé (his daughter-in-law) sees her changing and says: 'Never have I seen her so pale.' Moreover, listening to her guests talk about miracles and angels, Queen Herodias draws upon old proverbial lore and says: 'These men are mad. They have looked too long on the moon. Command them to be silent.' Indeed, the Syrian captain who gazes upon Salomé commits suicide.

Why then does Salomé look as 'pale' as the dead? It is because she is fascinated by the voice of Jokanaan the prophet (who is imprisoned in a cistern) and by his 'ivory'-like body. And as she is driven by her desire to obtain Jokanaan, her 'paleness' grows. In addition, she is a virgin possessing the moon's characteristics.

King Herod asks Salomé to dance in order to satisfy his lust, and he promises to give her anything she desires. What Salomé wants is Jokanaan's head. Herod refuses. But Queen Herodias intervenes, for she does not want Herod to fall in love with Salomé (Salomé's father was Herodias' former husband, Herod's brother, who was killed by Herod).

Herod eventually gives Jokanaan's head to Salomé, who confesses that nothing can quench her desire for Jokanaan, the only man she has ever loved, and for his

The Toilette of Salome; illustration by Aubrey Beardsley (1872–98) for Oscar Wilde's *Salomé*, 1907 edition published by John Lane. [World History Archive/Alamy]

ivory-like body, and that she has offered her 'virginity' in return for his head: 'I was a virgin, and thou didst take my virginity from me.' While saying this, Salomé kisses Jokanaan's mouth, but the taste is 'bitter'. At this moment, Herod orders his soldiers to kill Salomé, while 'A great cloud crosses the moon and conceals it completely.' Thus the moon and Salomé both lose their light.

Salomé, the femme fatale in Wilde's play, has something in common with Hearn's Yuki-Onna: she possesses both irresistible charm and a deadly power. Moreover, so far as Baudelaire's 'Les Bienfaits de la Lune' is concerned, the moon, or the moon goddess, is, needless to say, a 'virgin', and owing to this she cannot have her own offspring; therefore, she transfers her own characteristics to the female infant, turning her into her surrogate. So, in Wilde's play, Salomé is 'a virgin' and the only man to whom she wishes to lose her virginity is Jokanaan. This happens in her imagination, like 'the shadow of a white rose in a mirror of silver' at the beginning of the play. However, we, as readers, know that in the world of literature what happens in the shadowy, illusory worlds can be more real and more impressive than what happens in the real world.

Finally, it must be admitted that it is unclear whether Hearn read Wilde's 'The Star-Child' and *Salomé*. There is no reference to the matter in his *A History of English Literature* (5th revised edition, Hokuseido, 1941), nor in John Erskine edited version of *Books and Habits from The Lectures of Lafcadio Hearn* (1922), nor in John Erskine's *Lafcadio Hearn, Interpretations of Literature* (c. 1928). However, 'The Star-Child' was included in Wilde's collection of short stories, *A House of Pomegranates* (1891), which followed his famous *The Happy Prince and Other Stories* (1888), and in 1892 *Salomé* was banned from the stage by the Lord Chamberlain (the ban lasted forty years). It was first published in French in 1893 and one year later the English text was published. Since *Salomé* was a play that caused a scandal in the literary world, it seems almost impossible that Hearn, another writer with an Irish background, did not know of it, even if he was at that time far away from his home country (he began to live on an island in Asia in 1890).

Lafcadio Hearn's Dictionary (Kobunsha, 2000) cites a revealing remark by George Hughes, a former visiting professor at the University of Tokyo: Hearn used to talk about Wilde's American visits, but he ceased to do so later because of some of Wilde's frivolous behaviours (I have recently been guided to this reference by Bon Koizumi).[15] Since Hearn was deeply interested in fin-de-siècle literature, he would have paid much attention to Wilde and his works as he did to the Pre-Raphaelites and Willkie Collins, etc. As George Hughes points out, both Wilde and Hearn, living in the fin de siècle, challenged conventions and represented new ways of thinking from peripheral regions: Wilde went against mainstream sexual norms, whilst Hearn situated himself in the liminal realm between the East and the West.[16]

Bibliography

Baudelaire, Charles, 'Les Bienfaits de la Lune', http://www.beverymatherne.com/Blessings-of-the-moon.html.

Erskine, John (ed.), *Books and Habits from The Lectures of Lafcadio Hearn* (1922).

Erskine, John (ed.), *Lafcadio Hearn, Interpretations of Literature* (New York: Dodd, Mead & Co., 1915).

Erskine, John (ed.), "Studies on Extraordinary Prose', in *Interpretations of Literature* (New York: Dodd, Mead & Co., 1915).

Hearn, Lafcadio, 'Yuki-Onna', in *Kwaidan: Stories and Studies of Strange Things* (Kegan Paul & Co., 1904).

Hearn, Lafcadio, *A History of English Literature*, 5th revised ed. (Hokuseido,1941).

Hirakawa, Sukehiro (ed.), *Koizumi Yakumo's Kwaidan & Kidan* (Koudansha, 2013).

Hirakawa, Sukehiro (ed.), *Lafcadio Hearn's Dictionary* (Kobunsha, 2000).

Hughes, George, *Looking Forward and Looking Back: Essays on Hearn and Teaching in Japan* (Hiraishi Takaki & Tamai Akira trans. Tokyo: Kenkyusha, 2002).

Kawai, Hayao, *A Pathology of the Maternal Society Japan* (Tokyo: Chukososho, 1976).

Kawamura, Mimbu, *The Imagination Directed towards the Mountain-Top* (Tokyo: Eihosha, 1996).

Komura, Toshiaki. '"Translations and Transformations of Snow Women as Exiles: Lafcadio Hearn's "Yuki-Onna" and Anne Sexton's "Snow White and the Seven Dwarfs"', *Department of Literature Bulletin*, 51, 2014, Fuji Women's University; NII-Electronic Library Service, pp. 1–30.

Kristeva, Julia, *Strangers to Ourselves, trans. by* Leon Roudiez (New York: Columbia University Press, 1991).

Leeming, David, *Mythology (*Tokyo: Kinseido,1984).

Makino, Yoko. '"Lafcadio Hear's "Yuki-Onna" and Baudelaire's "Les Bienfaits de la Lune"', *Comparative Literature Studies*, vol. 28, no. 3, East–West Issue,1991, Penn State University Press.

Tinker, Edward Larocque, *Lafcadio Hearn's American Days (*New York: Dodd, Mead and Company, 1924).

Toda, Masaru, *A 'Transmigrating' Story – the World of Koizumi Yakumo's Kwaidan* (Shinyosha, 2011).

Wilde, Oscar, 'The Star-Child', http://www.eastoftheweb.com/short-stories/ UBooks/StaChi.shtml.

Wilde, Oscar. *Salomé*, in Aldington, Richard & Weintraub, Stanley(eds), *The Portable Oscar Wilde* (London: Penguin Books, 1981).

The Cultural Correspondence of Japan and Ireland through Patrick Lafcadio Hearn

Bon Koizumi

Patrick Lafcadio Hearn (1850–1904), whose father was Irish, lived in Dublin for around ten years from the age of two. Having spent time in the United States and Martinique, at the age of thirty-nine he travelled halfway round the globe to live in Japan. Here, he perceived that folklore constituted the country's fundamental cultural strata; he retold Japanese folktales and wrote essays about them. He seems to have felt an affinity between the traditional cultures of Japan and Ireland.

Hearn married Setsu Koizumi, a daughter of a samurai family from Matsue, and while on honeymoon he had a strange dream: a woman of Izumo – 'a Province of the Gods', as Hearn put it – began to sing a sorrowful song in a place that resembled the precincts of a twilight temple. The song reminded him of a Celtic nursery rhyme he had heard as a child; and the woman's dark hair fell spiralling onto the stone. Significantly, he had this dream on the night of the Bon Festival, when, once a year, all souls are said to return to this world from the Otherworld. The Izumo

Lafcadio Hearn with his wife, Setsu, and son.
(*Photo courtesy of the Koizumi family*)

woman's spiralling hair conjures up the spirals ubiquitous in Celtic ornamentation, just as the Bon Festival is reminiscent of its Celtic counterpart, Samhain.

After this dream, Hearn continued his honeymoon journey for a while, and at Mihonoseki in Matsue he wrote a letter to Basil Hall Chamberlain (dated 27 August 1891) in which he commented on the 'very charming influence upon life' of 'this creed of pre-existence and transmigration with its promises for future births, and its fearlessness about journeying to the Meido'.[1] His dream may have prompted him to subscribe to metempsychosis, an idea shared by the Japanese and the Irish. William Butler Yeats wrote that 'All nations believed in the rebirth of the soul and had probably empirical evidence like that Lafcadio Hearn found among the Japanese.'[2] The evidence Hearn gathered seems to refer to the four rebirth stories he retold during his time in Japan: 'The Story of Mochida-no-ura', 'The Rebirth of Katsugoro', 'The Story of O-Tei' and 'Riki-Baka'. Writing to Yeats from Tokyo in September 1901, Hearn says that as a child he had a wet nurse – Catherine Costello from Connacht – who sang him nursery rhymes and told him fairy tales. Celtic culture, as it existed in an oral tradition inherited and channelled by an Irish speaker, seems to have awakened in him a deep affection for Ireland and cemented his spiritual bonds with the country. I met Mr Oisín O'Connor in Spiddal, west Galway, in 2014, who told me that his grandmother was also called Catherine Costello, and that there were a great many Costellos in that area. Further west is a village called Costello, where almost all the villagers were Costellos. So it is tempting to guess that Hearn's wet nurse might have come from that neighbourhood.

Hearn gathered and retold many kwaidan stories, often with a deep affection, towards the close of his Japanese years. Works such as 'The Story of Mimi-Nashi-Hōichi', 'Kosodate-Yūrei – The Child Raising Yūrei' and 'Urashima-Taro' have their Irish counterparts: the first story is similar to 'The Magic Fiddle', and the latter two resemble the stories of Oisín. Irish folktales such as 'Three Wishes' and 'Animal Language' have been circulated in my family ever since Hearn's time. That these stories have been passed down from generation to generation in the family would seem to indicate Catherine Costello's profound influence on Hearn. It does not seem to be a coincidence that the cultural features that most attracted Hearn in Japan – the tales about yōkai (apparitions), the idea of metempsychosis, and the belief in the spirituality of water and trees – should also be the distinct features of Irish folklore.

As many scholars have observed, Japan and Ireland are located at the extremities of the Eurasian continent, and their fundamental cultures have much in common. Hearn seems to have been aware of this fact, even though he did not discourse on it at length. He may be said to have been a writer who embraced both Ireland and Japan. Having inherited a sixteenth part of my blood from my great grandfather Hearn, I always feel honoured and pleased to see his name included in any friendly exchanges between Japan and Ireland.

In this chapter, after first considering Hearn's place in current Japan–Ireland cultural exchanges, I wish to show how such exchanges may further profit from his memory in the future.

Lafcadio Hearn Gardens in Tramore

In June 2015, the Lafcadio Hearn Gardens[3] were opened in Tramore, County Waterford. Prior to this – in December 2013 – I was invited to Prime Minister Abe's official residence, where I had a conversation with Prime Minister Enda Kenny during the dinner party. We discussed the proposed Lafcadio Hearn gardens, and Kenny said reassuringly that the gardens would provide a new basis for cultural exchanges between Japan and Ireland. I was delighted when, just a year and a half later, the gardens were opened.

Tramore is a village about 200km south of Dublin, on the coast of the Celtic Sea. Hearn's great aunt Sarah Brenane, who brought him up, loved that sea and had three houses there. Hearn often spent his summer holidays there, where he learned to swim and was fascinated by his nurse Catherine Costello's fairy tales and gothic stories. His experience in this small seaside village had a significant impact on him: he maintained a strong attachment to the sea and to supernatural stories throughout his life. For a long time Hearn was little known in Tramore, but he was eventually commemorated through a bronze bust in Tramore's public library, created by John Coll. In 2012, during a visit to Tramore with my wife after an interval of eighteen years, the idea of the Lafcadio Hearn Gardens was born.

Agnes Aylward, a historian in Tramore, knew of a hectare of land under municipal ownership, and proposed that the gardens should be developed there. The plan was proposed under the aegis of the Tramore Development Trust, an existing not-for-profit organisation; responsibility was placed with the Lafcadio Hearn Project within the Trust. With the support of the JECFUND (Japan World Exposition Commemorative Fund) and the Irish government, the project was brought to

A pencil sketch by Lafcadio Hearn published in *Letters from the Raven: Being the Correspondence of Hearn with Henry Watkin*, ed. Milton Bronner (New York: Brentano, 1907). (*The Reading Room/Alamy*)

fruition within two and a half years. The opening ceremony was held on 27 June 2015. During the ceremony, Agnes Aylward said, 'Like Hearn, the gardens will be more like Japan as the years go by', and Chihiro Atsumi, Japanese ambassador in Ireland, said, 'The gardens will be a good venue for further strengthening the ties between Ireland and Japan.' Brendan Howlin TD, minister for public expenditure, commented on how 'important culturally he [Hearn] was as the link between Western civilisation and Japan, the human link embracing both countries'. In my own speech I expressed my pleasure at the gardens being established in a place where Hearn had fond memories of his childhood, and my belief that the gardens would become a cultural resource for Tramore. Those present acknowledged that the Lafcadio Hearn Gardens were not like those Japanese gardens usually found in foreign countries: for our gardens were based on Agnes Aylward's vision and were created by an Irish gardener, Martin Curran, benefitting from his rich imagination. As a result, the gardens embody Hearn's spirit. Kazumi Kusumi, a gardener in Kyoto, visited the place on three occasions, and offered advice concerning the relationship between the Japanese and stones.

The Lafcadio Hearn Gardens express Hearn's life. There are nine gardens, each of them having its own theme: Beginnings: Patrick Lafcadio Hearn's Tramore Connection; the Transition Garden: Imagining the Future; the American Journey;

Chin Chin Kobakama, Japanese Fairy Tale Series No. 25, translated by Lafcadio Hearn, published by Hasegawa, T., Tokyo, *c*. 1903. (*Agefotostock/Alamy*)

the Greek Garden; Arrival in Japan; the Stream Garden; Woodlands; the Garden of Peace and Harmony; and the Story of a Living God. Though in some ways they resemble Japanese gardens – with a path around a central pond and surrounded by trees – the gardens are also reminiscent of Greece, South America and England, reflecting Hearn's various cultural experiences throughout his life. They are intended to articulate the vision of 'Hearn's open mind' soaring in and beyond Tramore, a place deeply rooted in his spirit.

Around 4,000 people visited the gardens in the first three months – mainly from Ireland, but also from England, Germany, Sweden, America, Japan and elsewhere. The gardens have also become a venue for wedding photographs. They are expected to become both a tourist attraction and a cultural resource for Tramore.

The *Coming Home* exhibition and reading performance in Dublin

One hundred and fifty years have passed since Hearn left Ireland, but little had been done to commemorate him in the form of memorials or exhibitions. In this respect, 2015, with its focus on Hearn, was an epoch-making year for exchanges between Japan and Ireland.

Coming Home: The Open Mind of Patrick Lafcadio Hearn

The first exhibition, *Coming Home: The Open Mind of Patrick Lafcadio Hearn*, was held at the Little Museum, Dublin from October 2015 to January 2016. Simon O'Connor (curator of the museum), John Moran (a journalist at *The Irish Times*) and Paul Murray (Hearn's biographer) were the driving forces behind the exhibition. The exhibition developed from a project entitled *The Open Mind of Patrick Lafcadio Hearn* (initiated in 2009), which celebrates Hearn's 'open mind' and his spirituality. The exhibition has visited Athens, Matsue, New York and New Orleans – cities deeply connected with Hearn, Matsue being especially important. The Little Museum's own exhibition featured fifteen items usually kept at the Lafcadio Hearn Memorial Museum in Matsue, including Hearn's first editions and family photographs. The exhibition attracted many Dubliners.

Prior to the opening, four Hearn scholars from Ireland, the United States and Japan – myself included – delivered lectures to a large audience, emphasising the importance of cultural exchanges between Japan and Ireland with Hearn at the centre. Among the fifty guests at the opening of the exhibition were Jimmy Deenihan, minister of state for the diaspora, and Chihiro Atsumi, Japanese ambassador to Ireland.

Lafcadio Hearn reading performance: Maraudo – visitors from the world beyond

The Lafcadio Hearn Reading Performance consists of readings, music and lectures. Shiro Sano – an actor born in Matsue, Japan – is the scriptwriter and reader, guitarist Kyoji Yamamoto is responsible for the music, and I supervise the production and deliver a lecture prior to the performance. The performance is held every year – with changing themes – in Matsue, Tokyo, Leucas and Corfu in Greece. Most recently, in Maraudo, we combined episodes from Hearn's childhood and material from his work with Irish folktales, and we wanted to bring this back to his homeland, Ireland. The audience were able to immerse themselves in the works Hearn had created during his time in Japan.

The performance was held in three cities: Dublin, Waterford and Galway. Lafcadio Hearn would have appreciated being so warmly welcomed by his fellow Irish people. In Dublin, St Ann's church was the venue. Lafcadio's great-great-grandfather Daniel Hearn had worked there, and this made me feel connected to the place. The reading performance aims to represent in spoken words Hearn's literary achievement, as well as the 'open mind' his works embody, and the combination of reading and music was well received.

Matsue and Ireland

Matsue was the first place in Japan where Hearn lived and where he worked as an English teacher for one year and three months. In 'The chief city of the province of gods' – a chapter in his first piece of work in Japan, *Glimpses in Unfamiliar Japan* – Hearn described the charms of Matsue as he had experienced them with his own five senses.

Thanks to Hearn's cultural legacy, Matsue's Castle Town (in Sanin Province) began to communicate with Ireland in the late 1980s. The winner of the first prize in the annual Lafcadio Hearn Contest is presented with the Irish Ambassador Award and invited to give a speech and to visit Ireland, with the support of the Japan International Cooperation Centre. An international committee member – somebody born in Ireland and permanently resident in Matsue city – introduces elementary and junior high school pupils in Matsue city to Irish culture; moreover, the pupils are sometimes regaled with Irish cuisine, such as Irish stew.

In 1994 the Sanin Japan–Ireland Association was established. They are committed to the dissemination of Irish culture, including the Irish language, Irish literature and Irish films, and they have also formed a traditional Irish music band called Ceol agus Craic. Furthermore, the association, together with Matsue city, holds the Irish Festival on the second Sunday of March each year, and organises the St Patrick's Day Parade, which consists of two elements: a land parade and a parade in a pleasure boat circulating the castle moat; there is also the Shamrock, a contemporary Irish pub opening only for two nights, as well as a market selling Irish products, amongst many other events.

In 1995 President Mary Robinson visited Matsue as a guest of Shimane prefecture and planted an oak tree – a tree sacred to the Irish – in front of the Lafcadio Hearn Memorial Museum. In 2007, when the world athletics championships were held in Osaka, the Irish track and field athletes were offered accommodation in Matsue.

Since 2008, the Matsue Ghost Tour has never stopped, inspired by the popular Dublin Ghost Bus Tour. On each Matsue Ghost Tour, participants walk for two hours in the places featured in Hearn's ghost stories, whilst enjoying the kwaidan stories told

Coming Home: The Open Mind of Patrick Lafcadio Hearn exhibition, The Little Museum of Dublin, October 2015 to January 2016. (*The Little Museum of Dublin*)

by professional storytellers. By late November 2016, nearly 5,000 people had attended 291 tours, mainly on Saturdays in the summer months. Recently, participants from Tokyo, Osaka and further afield have outnumbered local people on the tours: such is the popularity. As a result, kwaidan has become recognised as a Matsue cultural resource.

Thus, thanks to its connection with Hearn, Matsue has become a city closely associated with Ireland, presiding over cultural exchanges at both national and local levels. Future development of this connection should be carried out with an eye to cultural resources.

Conclusion

The significance of Hearn's legacy seems to lie not only in the appreciation of his literary works but also in the transformation of his works and outlooks into cultural resources for contemporary society. Cultural resources refer to local culture as a whole; they are not limited to cultural assets protected and appreciated by administrative bodies. This sometimes unappreciated local culture contains within it a potential for cultural reinvigoration and for tourism by excavating the buried culture of a locality and recreating it in a new form. To understand the concept this way is to follow what Hearn devoted himself to throughout his life: excavating old stories and recasting them for the contemporary world.

Tramore's Lafcadio Hearn Gardens tap into the concept of cultural resources, partly by expressing Hearn's 'open mind' in figurative art and partly by reshaping it into a new cultural resource. This realisation in the form of gardens is indebted to the tireless work of many scholars and to readers' efforts to perpetuate and celebrate Hearn's achievements. I hope that Hearn's literary legacy will continue to serve as a cultural resource facilitating the friendly exchanges between Japan and Ireland.

In 2017, the Lafcadio Hearn Memorial Museum, together with the Dublin Writers' Museum, opened an exhibition on the theme of Irish literature and Hearn. In addition, Hearn's works were performed in Ireland in the form of Kyogen, a traditional Japanese art.

From Tír na nÓg, Lafcadio Hearn must be observing with pleasure the abiding friendship between Japan and Ireland.

The Reception of Irish Literature and the Image of 'Celts' in Modern Japan: Lafcadio Hearn's writings and 'national characteristics'

Akiyo Suzuki

1. Race and literature: Lafcadio Hearn's assessment in Japan and the 'Celts'

After moving to Japan in April 1890, Lafcadio Hearn (1850–1904) wrote travel accounts and reflections on the country, and retold Japanese legends under the pen name Koizumi Yakumo. In 1914, ten years after Hearn passed away, Kikuchi Kan (1888–1948), in his article 'Thinking of Lafcadio Hearn', urged people to reassess Hearn: 'I think that a person is being forgotten in the Japanese literary world – someone that no Japanese person should forget. It is nobody but Lafcadio Hearn, also known as Koizumi Yakumo.'[1] He went on to say that 'It is rumoured that the Okuma cabinet is going to recognize Hearn, and I am waiting for this rumour to become a reality many times more than the likes of the abolishment or reduction of taxes'.[2] In November 1915, upon the enthronement of the Taisho emperor, Koizumi

Lafcadio Hearn, aged sixteen. (*Historic Images/Alamy*)

Yakumo received the honour of the junior fourth rank (jushii). We find Japanese documents from the beginning of the twentieth century which define Hearn's race as 'Celt' and which assert that his writing was shaped by his Celtic background. A discussion of Hearn in connection with the Celts may serve to clarify some of the characteristics of modern Japan's literary history.

Bon Koizumi, when describing the influence of Celtic oral culture on Hearn, wrote that 'The motifs of and spirit that comprise the cultural background of the Japanese folk tales that Hearn enjoyed retelling are often shared by Celt mythological tales and Irish folk tales'.[3] Scholars have also been exploring the relationship between Hearn and Ireland, as well as between Hearn and Yeats: for example, Paul Murray on the correspondence between Hearn and W.B. Yeats,[4] George Hughes on Yeats and Hearn regarding the concept of 'ghosts',[5] and Nishi Masahiko on Hearn's lectures on Yeats at Tokyo Imperial University.[6]

As Barbara Hayley has noted, the Hearn family (the family of Lafcadio Hearn's father) were Anglo-Irish and arrived in Ireland in the seventeenth century.[7] Hearn's father Charles was a doctor in the British army, and his mother Rosa was from the Greek island of Kythira. Hearn was born in 1850 on another Greek island, Lefkada, and at the age of two moved to his father's native Ireland. When aged nineteen he moved to the United States and lived in Cincinnati and New Orleans. He then moved to Martinique in the Caribbean, where he continued to engage in reporting and writing. After arriving in Japan, Hearn became an English teacher at the Tottori Prefecture Normal Secondary School and the Kumamoto Fifth Higher Secondary School. He also worked at the *Kobe Chronicle*. In September 1896 he became a lecturer of English literature at Tokyo Imperial University's Humanities College. He resigned from Tokyo Imperial University in 1903 and began teaching at Waseda University. He passed away in September of the following year.

Hearn is a multidimensional author.[8] However, in Japan he began to be associated with Ireland and the Celts around the 1910s, the time during which he began to be reassessed. Honma Hisao (1886–1981), a literary critic and scholar of English literature, stated in his 1914 article 'Recent currents in thought: a new theory regarding Lafcadio Hearn' (published in *Waseda Bungaku*) that Lafcadio Hearn presented Japan as a 'country of dreams, a country of illusions' rather than 'as it existed in the real world':

> Hearn did not compare and observe Japan like many Westerners do through the perspective of cultural superiority and inferiority. He saw Japan as a country of dreams, a country of illusions … This passage by Michael Monahan is, as its title indicates, an explanation of the Celtic disposition of Lafcadio Hearn … He argues that Hearn's writing is sensuous and ghostly because of his Irish blood. His Disillusionment of Japan was, in short, because he was a Celt … If, as Taine emphasizes, racial characteristics cannot be possibly removed from a person regardless of the power involved, then we can easily surmise that Lafcadio Hearn's thought is also no exception. In this sense, I think that Monahan's

> interpretation is an especially useful reference for understanding and appreciating Lafcadio Hearn.[9]

The article by Michael Monahan that Honma Hisao quoted is 'The Celtic strain in Lafcadio Hearn', published in the May 1915 issue of *Forum* magazine. In this article Monahan asserts that Hearn's writings were influenced by his Celtic disposition. Furthermore, in reference to Monahan's statement that Hearn's 'Irish blood' is the reason why his writing is 'sensuous' and 'ghostly', Honma asserted that Hearn's disposition as a member of the 'Celtic race' shaped his work. Honma's view was influenced by Hippolyte Adolphe Taine's *Histoire de la littérature anglaise* (1863), which held that literary phenomena can be explained by the three elements of 'race, milieu, and moment'.

In Japan Taine's literary history was actively adopted at the end of the nineteenth century. Upon his death in 1893, the literary critic and author Tsubouchi Shōyō described his considerable influence in Japan: 'Taine's contribution in Japan is many times more than Renan. His *Histoire de la littérature anglaise* is currently a textbook at twelve private schools and is the most enlightening English literature history work that circulates in contemporary Japan'. In fact Mikami Sanji and Takatsu Kuwasaburō reference Taine's theory – that 'The French erudite scholar Taine compiled a literary history of his country, researching its psychology' – in their 1890 *Nihon bungakushi* (Japanese Literary History), which they proclaimed to be 'truly the beginning of literary history in our country'. They asserted that since 'in a country's literature, a nation's unique thought, emotions, and imagination are written with its language', literary history is important as it 'can get a glimpse of the nation's hearts and minds'. In the context of a rapidly modernising Japan, they saw the importance of researching Japanese literature as a way of solidifying national identity. Mikami and Takatsu thought that if a country's literature could be explained by race, it would help clarify 'the nation's hearts and minds'. In other words, they saw Taine's theory regarding literary history as useful. In this way Japanese literary scholars discussed literature in connection to race in the latter half of the nineteenth century; this gave rise to the idea that authors' national identities appear in their writing. It was in the context of this understanding of literary history that Honma Hisao and others focused on what they saw as the characteristics of the Celtic race when discussing Lafcadio Hearn's literary works.

A stone to mark the site of the last residence of Lafcadio Hearn, in Shinjuku, Tokyo. (*Damon Coulter/Alamy*)

At a memorial event in Matsue for the twenty-fifth anniversary of Hearn's death, Doi Bansui (1871–1952), a student of Hearn as well as a poet and a scholar of English literature, wrote the following tanka: 'Fondly remembering the drive [ishi] of you, who received hot blood from your father of the Celtic race'.[10] Doi perceived Hearn's 'hot blood' and 'drive' as coming from the 'Celtic race'. In the same way, in his *Koizumi Yakumo* (Waseda Daigaku Shuppanbu, 1914), Hearn's student Tanabe Ryūji (1875–1957) stated that Hearn's 'passion' was from the 'Celts'. It was primarily Hearn's students who said that he had a passionate personality due to his Celtic heritage. Based on this view, they saw his writings as sensuous and ghostly. From where did this perception of Celts originate, and why did Hearn's 'Celtic' nature become an object of discussion?

2. The reception of Irish literature in early twentieth-century Japan

The discourse focusing on Hearn's Celtic background first appeared in the 1910s. This seems to have been due to the popularity of the plays by the Irish writers W.B. Yeats, John Millington Synge and Augusta Gregory, which drew people's attention to Ireland and 'Celtic culture'. In an article of *Bunshō sekai* (January 1914) it is reported how, 'Led by Yoshie Takamatsu, members of the magazine *Kamen* are holding the "Irish Literature Society", which will widely research the civilisation of not only Ireland but all Celtic race.'[11] Several prominent writers and poets were also part of the Irish Literature Society, including Ryūnosuke Akutagawa, Sangu Makoto, Hinatsu Kōnosuke and Saijō Yaso. We can see that, at the time, the interest of students and young writers from the English Literature departments of Tokyo Imperial University, Kyoto Imperial University and Waseda University in Irish literature was growing.

Like Akutagawa and Sangu, Kikuchi Kan belonged to the coterie surrounding the magazine *Shinshichō*, which energetically introduced Irish literature to Japan, and he used it as a source of inspiration when writing his own plays and novels. Looking back on the 1910s, he would later state that 'research on Irish literature was actually becoming a general trend in literary circles at the time'.[12] It appears that, when discussing the Celts, he referred to W.B. Yeats's 'The Celtic element in literature' (1897). At the beginning of this piece, Yeats presented several characteristics of the Celts as discussed by Ernest Renan in *The Poetry of the Celtic Races* (1854).

> Ernest Renan described what he held to be Celtic characteristics in *The Poetry of the Celtic Races*. I must repeat the well-known sentences … 'It has worn itself out in mistaking dreams for realities,' and 'compared with the classical imagination the Celtic imagination is indeed the infinite contrasted with the finite.' 'Its history is one long lament, it still recalls its exiles, its flights across the seas.' 'If at times it seems to be cheerful, its tear is not slow to glisten behind the smile. Its songs of joy end as elegies; there is nothing to equal the delightful sadness of its national melodies.' Matthew Arnold, in *The Study of Celtic Literature*, has accepted this passion for nature, this imaginativeness, this melancholy, as Celtic characteristics, but has described them more elaborately.[13]

The words of Renan that Yeats quoted here would again be quoted by literary scholars such as Kikuchi Kan when discussing the Celtic people. Yeats stated that Renan remarked on how Celtic literature 'has worn itself out in mistaking dreams for realities'. This phrase is found in the following passage in Renan's *The Poetry of the Celtic Races*: 'So is it with the Celtic race; it has worn itself out in taking dreams for realities, and in pursuing its splendid visions'. Yeats also presented the following two characteristics identified by Renan: 'Its history is one long lament, it still recalls its exiles, its flights across the seas', and 'If at times it seems to be cheerful, its tear is not slow to glisten behind the smile. Its songs of joy end as elegies; there is nothing to equal the delightful sadness of its national melodies.'

Next, Yeats quoted Matthew Arnold's 'The study of Celtic literature' as a refined version of Renan's image of Celtic-ness, and then proceeded to modify it:

> Matthew Arnold has said that if he were asked 'where English got its turn for melancholy and its turn for natural magic,' he 'would answer with little doubt that it got much of its melancholy from a Celtic source, with no doubt at all that from a Celtic source is got nearly all its natural magic.' I will put this differently and say that literature dwindles to a mere chronicle of circumstance, or passionless phantasies, and passionless meditations, unless it is constantly flooded with the passions and beliefs of ancient times, and that of all the fountains of the passions and beliefs of ancient times in Europe, the Sclavonic, the Finnish, the Scandinavian, and the Celtic, the Celtic alone has been for centuries close to the main river of European literature.

Yeats first observed that Arnold accepted and expanded on the qualities of the Celtic people pointed out by Renan (for example, passion for nature, imagination and melancholy). Regarding Arnold's theory, Yeats remarked that 'I will put this differently and say that literature dwindles to a mere chronicle of circumstance, or passionless phantasies, and passionless meditations, unless it is constantly flooded with the passions and beliefs of ancient times', which modified his perception of the Celts. He then stated that out of 'all the fountains of the passions and beliefs of ancient times in Europe … the Celtic alone has been for centuries close to the main river of European literature', thus asserting that the Celts are the very people who have continually maintained the source of ancient Europe's passions and beliefs. In other words, by arguing that the elements presented by Arnold are not particular to the Celts but can also be found in the passion and beliefs of other ancient European cultures, he resisted the view that the Celts were a group of people whose culture was different from the rest of Europe. However, the Celtic characteristics presented by Renan and Arnold that Yeats cited and modified in 'The Celtic element in literature' were again quoted by scholars of literature in Japan, and would be used when discussing Yeats himself and Hearn – for example, Honma's attributing Hearn's 'sensuous' writing to his 'Celtic disposition', as well as Doi Bansui and Tanabe Ryuji stating that Hearn showed a 'passion' that was inherited from the Celts. These descriptions recall Renan's and Arnold's discussions of Celtic traits, which led to the perception among Japanese literary scholars that the Celts were a unique ethnic group.

3. The focus on Ireland and Japan's cultural similarity

Kikuchi Kan stated that in the Irish writer John Millington Synge's plays there are many examples of Celtic characteristics; he later also attributed these characteristics to Hearn as an author.

> In general, Irish people are descendants of ancient Britons, the so-called Celtic people. All ethnic groups that politically decline have a poetic and lovable personality. The Celts are no exception: instead of being practically-oriented or intellectual, they are extremely fantastical and passionate. It is said that therefore half of the myths and legends in Europe were produced by the Celts. The reason that the poems of English literature are outstanding is that the Anglo-Saxon race borrowed various beautiful elements from the Celts.
>
> …
>
> Koizumi Yakumo Sensei, who carried on the blood of the Celtic race, translated the *mono no aware* of the Japanese people as the 'ah-ness of things'. Of the races of Europe, the only nation that knows *mono no*

Bust of Lafcadio Hearn, also known as Koizumi Yakumo, near his home in Matsue, Japan. (*Photo Japan/Alamy*);

Lafcadio Hearn, *c.* 1906. (*Photo courtesy of the Koizumi family*)

> *aware* is the Celts. It is said that the Celts actually see life through a mist of tears, and that Celts' songs of joy end as elegies.[14]

It is clear that Kikuchi's statement that 'the reason that the poems of English literature are outstanding is that the Anglo-Saxon race borrowed various beautiful elements from the Celts' is based on Arnold's 'The study of Celtic literature'. Furthermore, the statement 'It is said that the Celts actually see life through a mist of tears, and that Celts' songs of joy end as elegies' was based on Renan's statement in *The Poetry of the Celtic Races* that 'its songs of joy end as elegies'. Kikuchi thus recapitulated those Celtic characteristics identified by Arnold and Renan – precisely the same characteristics Yeats referred to in his aforementioned article. Kikuchi, who had a strong interest in Irish literature, learned these 'Celtic' characteristics from Yeats, and brought these to bear upon his evaluation of Synge and Hearn as 'Celtic-like' authors.

Furthermore, Kikuchi's remark on the Irish people's Celtic characteristics (that is, 'All ethnic groups that politically decline have a poetic and lovable personality. The Celts are no exception: instead of being practically-oriented or intellectual, they are extremely fantastical and passionate') is based on a binary understanding of the Anglo-Saxons and the Celtic people: the former is seen as politically powerful and logical, while the latter are more passionate. This view resonates with Arnold's statements:

> Sentimental, – Always ready to react against the despotism of fact; that is the description a great friend of the Celt gives of him; and it is not a bad description of the sentimental temperament; it lets us into the secret of its dangers and of its habitual want of success. Balance, measure, and patience, these are the eternal conditions, even supposing the happiest temperament to start with, of high success; and balance, measure, and patience are just what the Celt has never had … (p. 82)

As 'in material civilisation he has been ineffectual, so has the Celt been ineffectual in politics'.[15] Kikuchi maintained that Hearn, who 'carried on the blood of the Celtic race', had a good understanding of Japan – the Celts are the only group of Europeans fully capable of this, he suggests. In other words, Kikuchi was arguing that the sadness and melancholy that characterise the Celtic people are similar to the *mono no aware* of the Japanese people, and that the Celts were the only Western people who would be able to understand Japanese culture. Kikuchi claimed that since Hearn was a Celt due to his Irish ancestry, he could appreciate Japanese culture.

In 'Literature chat: the Irish and the Japanese', Kikuchi indicated that he was sympathetic to Ireland's effort to gain independence from England: 'I express sincere sympathy for Sinn Féin'. And he goes on to describe the similarities between the Irish and the Japanese:

> It is impossible to place Ireland, which has such grand and outstanding literature, under the rule of a different ethnic group. The Irish, who are of the Celtic race, are completely different from the English in terms of temperament, disposition, and lifestyle ... They [the Irish] are very similar [to the Japanese] even in essential aspects. Easily emotionally excited yet despite this not attached to their habits, quick to quarrel, and deeply superstitious: they are the group of European people most similar to the Japanese. They are also similar to the Japanese in that they feel the beauty of nature and understand *mono no aware*. Did Lafcadio Hearn not love and understand Japan as much as he did because he had half Irish blood?[16]

With regard to the issue of Ireland's autonomy/independence from England, Kikuchi stated that since the Irish are completely different from the English not only in terms of race, religion and tradition but also in terms of disposition, temperament and lifestyle, it would be impossible for England to rule Ireland, a nation that boasts a 'grand and outstanding literature'. Furthermore, he argues that the Irish owed their literary achievements to the characteristics of the Celtic race – namely that they are 'Easily emotionally excited yet despite this not attached to their habits, quick to quarrel, and deeply superstitious'. He goes on to claim that in this regard the Irish – more than the other European peoples – resemble the Japanese. Culturally speaking, the Irish, like the Japanese, feel the 'beauty of nature', and they understand the Japanese concept of *mono no aware*. According to Kikuchi, Hearn was able to 'love and understand Japan' because he was half Irish.

Kikuchi stated that while he cannot feel an affinity with the lives and characters depicted in English, French and Russian literature, the lives of farmers in Irish plays 'touch us profoundly'. Kikuchi conjectured that this was because the Irish and the Japanese had a similar disposition: like their Japanese counterparts, Irish mothers are 'unconscious' (mujikaku) and self-sacrificing, in contrast to English mothers, who 'have an abundant intellect characterized by a strong ego'. This binary view is derived from Matthew Arnold. Kikuchi applied the image of the Celts – as it was shaped by Renan and Arnold – to his appreciation of Irish drama.

In modern Japan, which saw an influx of Western merchandise, national identity became an urgent issue. This led to the reassessment of Japan's literary history. To propagate the view that Japanese literature enshrines the uniqueness of the Japanese people was, in a way, to secure literature's place in a modern, logic-oriented Japan. At the beginning of the twentieth century, Ireland's struggles for autonomy/independence were extensively covered in the news: that was exactly when Japanese literary scholars turned their attention to Irish literature. Furthermore, the image of the 'Celtic race' which had been shaped by Ernest Renan and Matthew Arnold was imported into Japan through Yeats. In the context of a new interest in Irish literature (and particularly in Yeats and Synge), literary scholars in Japan adopted Renan's and Arnold's stereotypical image of the Celts. In this milieu, the 'Celt' Lafcadio Hearn was rediscovered, and discussion of his writings was often informed by the stereotypical characteristics of the 'Irish' and the 'Celtic' people. Kikuchi saw the culture of Ireland, a 'Celtic' country, as a unique 'Other' different from the other Western cultures; he also emphasised the similarities between Ireland and Japan. By doing so he implicitly gave an equally unique place to Japanese culture. Kikuchi therefore used Irish culture and Celtic characteristics to demonstrate the uniqueness of Japanese culture and its people. By arguing that Japan shared affinities with a nation that had a rich literary history, he was able to claim that Japanese literature was both distinctive and similar to its Western counterpart.

Bibliography

Hayley, Barbara, 'Lafcadio Hearn, W.B. Yeats and Japan', in Robert Welch and Suheil Badi Bushrui (eds), *Literature and the Art of Creation* (Totowa, NJ: Barnes, 1988), pp. 43–60.

Hughes, George, 'W.B. Yeats and Lafcadio Hearn: Negotiating with ghosts', in Sukehiro Hirakawa (ed.), *Rediscovering Lafcadio Hearn: Japanese Legends, Life & Culture* (Folkestone: Global Books, 1997).

Kannotō, Akio, 'From modern national literature studies to Japanese literature scholarship in an age of internationalization: Understandings of Japanese literature', *Atomi University Literature Forum*, 4 (2006).

Kimura Ki, *A New View of Comparative Literature* (Yagi Shoten, 1975).

Miyoshi, Miyuki. 'The image of Celts in England', in The Institute of Cultural Sciences, Chuo University (ed.) *The Celtic Renaissance* (Tokyo: Chūō University Press, 2001).

Suzuki, Akiyo, *The Cross-Border Imagination in the Reciprocal Influence of Japanese and Irish Literature* (Osaka: Ōsaka University Press, 2014).

The Pure Cold Light: Yeats's and Hearn's influence on the contemporary performing arts in Japan and Ireland

Akiko Manabe

In the late nineteenth and early twentieth centuries, two literary figures, William Butler Yeats and Lafcadio Hearn, created innovative works through their encounters with Japan, leaving a legacy that continues to influence us today. Both writers breathed new life into folktales that captured the souls or spirits in traditional Irish and Japanese cultures. Yeats notably used Japanese traditional theatre, *Noh* and *kyogen* – collectively referred to as *Nogaku* – to reinvigorate his theatrical repertoire. This, in turn, led to a Renaissance-like literary encounter between Japan and Ireland, and more generally, between the East and the West.

I have recently been assisting in the production of professional performances inspired by Yeats's work both in Japan and in Ireland. Marking the sixtieth anniversary of the establishment of diplomatic ties between Ireland and Japan, Yeats's play *The Cat and the Moon* (hereafter, *C and M*) and Lafcadio Hearn's

The Cat and the Moon, by Yoko Akino. (© *Yoko Akino*)

Chin Chin Kobakama will be performed in a traditional *kyogen* style by the prestigious Sengoro Shigeyama *kyogen* group in Ireland in the summer of 2017. The performances will take place in Smock Alley Theatre in Dublin, the Factory Performance Space in Sligo, and Garter Lane Arts Centre in Waterford.[1] In March 2017 I also took part in the production of a reading performance of Hearn's writings in an old Zen temple (Seiryoji, in Hikone, Shiga) for the Light and Art Festival: Dramatic Legacy – Stories of Historical Heritage in Hikone and Taga. These performances by contemporary Japanese artists reveal the universal values of Yeats's and Hearn's works, transcending both time and space. In this paper I will explore Yeats's and Hearn's works and their contribution to this Irish–Japanese literary renaissance.

Early in their lives, both Yeats and Hearn were fascinated by folklore and orally transmitted stories. Yeats was raised in Dublin, but during his summer visits to his maternal grandparents in Sligo he was exposed to local fairy tales; similarly, the tales told by Hearn's nurse enriched his life in Dublin (Koizumi, Murray). In this way Irish folktales fostered their childhood imagination, and both writers developed a strong interest in the otherworld. They were so immersed in these traditional stories that the actual sights and sounds of Sligo and Dublin faded into the background. For them, fairies and ghosts were all too real. Both writers envisioned a parallel reality that coexisted with ours.

In the late nineteenth- and early twentieth-century Ireland and Japan, mythical creatures were an endangered species. Ireland's folktales – which had been passed down from generation to generation, and which reflected the spirit of the country – were losing their grip, as was the Irish language. Similarly, Hearn was dismayed by Japan's rush toward a modernity defined by Western standards while neglecting their rich tradition of folktales and songs. By collecting Irish and Japanese folktales and rewriting them in beautifully inflected English prose, both Yeats and Hearn tried to bring back the endangered mythical creatures. Though they both wrote in English, the soul of Ireland was faithfully captured in Yeats's lyrical reframing; the same was true of Hearn's writings on Japan.[2]

I shall now turn my attention to Japan's classical theatrical forms, *Noh* and *kyogen*, both of which were developed in the fourteenth century. It was through these theatrical traditions that Yeats was able to create a series of plays for the Abbey Theatre. While *Noh* plays generally deal with serious or tragic matters, *kyogen* plays are primarily comical or farcical and are performed between individual *Noh* plays.[3] *Noh*'s subjects are taken from history, mythology and classical literature. It is a highly stylised form of drama, performed on a simple, minimalist stage. *Kyogen*, with laughter at its centre, presents what the common people encounter in their daily lives on the same simple stage on which *Noh* is performed, and with the simplest possible stage setting. Yeats commented on the new drama he had created following his encounter with *Nogaku*: 'this form has no need of scenery that runs away with money nor of a theatre-building' (*Early Essays*, p. 173). This is precisely the kind of stage *kyogen* relies on. For example, during the three-day theatrical event I organised – 'Modernization of Hikone City; Symposium and *Kyogen*' – *kyogen* plays were performed on the small stage in Shiga University's auditorium, which can accommodate 200 to 300 people.[4] Each symposium had a *kyogen* performance that matched its theme. The existing *kyogen* plays, composed mostly before the Meiji Restoration, explore issues that are still relevant today (and these were discussed at the academic symposia). Yeats must have perceived *kyogen*'s universal contemporariness. In this way, though *kyogen* is usually performed on the *Noh* stage, as long as there is space *kyogen* players can perform anywhere; that is why performances are possible in Ireland, even though there is no traditional *Noh* stage there. In addition, the only prop used for *C and M* is a simple chair covered with a piece of black cloth. The three theatres in Ireland where our *kyogen* will be performed – Smock Alley Theatre, Factory Performance Space, and Garter Lane Arts Centre – can accommodate 150, 80 and 150 people respectively. These theatres are more spacious than what Yeats had in mind when he wrote *At the Hawk's Well*, his first play composed after his encounter with *Nogaku*. 'I have written a little play that can be played in a room for so little money that forty or fifty readers of poetry can pay the price' (*Early Essays*, p. 163). In fact, some fifty people were invited to its premiere performance in the drawing-room of Lady Cunard's house in Cavendish Square on 2 April 1916, but the second performance on 4 April attracted 200–300 people. Our performance will be staged in a more intimate space, which Yeats would surely appreciate (Ewick, p. 2).

Kyogen characters are anonymous, unspecified common people, like servants and peasants who have a very real persona. This was congenial to Yeats, who said 'I love all the arts that can still remind me of their origin among the common people'

Photo by Yoshiko Eryu, @ Ku no Tabibitosha.

(*Early Essays*, p. 164). Often at the beginning of a *kyogen* play, an actor would say, 'I am the person who lives in this neighbourhood.' This means they could be anyone in the audience. Often the servants or other common folk appearing in *kyogen* productions are witty and wise, and it is easy for the audience to identify with them. Intuitively they plot to trick their masters or make fun of them. This triggers laughter and brings satisfaction to the audience.

Occasionally, *kyogen* plays deal with folktales as their subject matter. This makes sense as folktales feed the collective consciousness of a people. Yeats deeply appreciated the literary gems hidden in Irish folk memory. He hated the idea of a 'mob' or 'common people' contaminated by contemporary realism and journalism, but he nevertheless appreciated the idea of a 'common people' unfettered by realism. Therefore, it was an urgent matter for him, along with Lady Gregory, to collect and preserve Gaelic folklore, which was vanishing.

In 2012 I organised a performance in a small temple, Shorakuji, at the foot of a mountain in Shiga prefecture, where a *kyogen* entitled *Tsurigitsune* (Foxhunt) originated in a local folktale.[5] The performance took place in the small main inner sanctuary of the temple. The distance between the audience and the stage was less than half a metre, so it was an intimate space. As the photo shows, the priest of this temple was in the audience, and a flute player sat next to the fictional priest on the stage; every so often the physical distance between the actor who played the priest and the real priest was considerably shortened. The invisible border between the world of the play and the real world was there, but the physical proximity of these two priests served to lure the audience into the imaginary world. In this particular *kyogen*, when the protagonist – the priest – takes off his human mask and his priest's costume, he is transformed into a fox, his real existence. He wears a fox mask and his body is covered with yellow fur. Without any stage setting, *kyogen* players are able to create these highly dramatic scenes by means of the sheer mastery of their theatrical craft – exactly the kind of theatre Yeats was searching for. Based on a folk legend belonging to a small Japanese village, this *kyogen* raises ethical issues about killing animals, ecological issues about the balance between animals and humans, and economic issues about sustaining our lives – all of them universal ideas that remain relevant today.

C and M – which Yeats intended 'to be what the Japanese call a "Kiogen" and to come as a relaxation of attention between, let us say "The Hawk's Well" and

"The Dreaming of the Bones"' – is based on stories about St Colman's well, a well near Yeats's residence, Thoor Ballylee (*Variorum*, p. 805). The two main characters in the play are a Blind Beggar and a Lame Beggar. The former carries the latter on his back, just like the *shite* (the protagonist) and the *ado* (the supporting role): two recurring theatrical types in traditional Japanese *kyogen*. Once he has regained his eyesight thanks to the Saint's mythical powers, the Blind Beggar begins to hit with his stick the man who has served as his 'eyes' for over forty years. Cruelty towards the physically challenged is a major motif in *zato mono*, a group of *kyogen* plays that deal with the blind (*zato* in Japanese means a blind person).[6] After the cured Blind Beggar disappears from the stage, the blessed Lame Beggar begins to dance with the Saint on his back, although he is still actually physically disabled. Using an old folktale from Galway, Yeats follows the conventions of *kyogen*'s stage setting, character development, theatrical structure, music, singing and dance to achieve something unique in this play. The final dance by the Lame Beggar and the Saint culminates in a cathartic moment. Amazingly, when I saw the *kyogen* version of this play (produced by the Shigeyama Sengoro Family), I found myself visualising an Irish landscape, even though nothing on the stage seemed to suggest Irishness, except perhaps for the words exchanged by the three actors.[7] At the beginning, the Saint, wearing a black mask of Daikoku – the god of wealth – appears on the scene singing the first 8 lines of Yeats's poem 'The Cat and the Moon' in a kyogen chant, called *kouta*, which, with its peculiar musicality, brings the audience immediately into the world of *kyogen*. The tonality and the phrases of the chant – which are authentically Japanese – have a mesmerising effect upon the audience. Then, the Blind Beggar makes his appearance, with the Lame Beggar on his back. The three of them, in traditional Japanese *kyogen* costumes, weave through an imaginary Irish landscape on the stage while reciting modern Japanese words in a traditional *kyogen* style, accompanied by music. In a sense this epitomises the ideal combination of East and West, which transcends time. A case in point: I think one of the reasons why Yeats and *kyogen* are so well suited to each other is that both evince a positive outlook in responding to harsh realities with laughter, and it is in this very outlook that their universality consists. Folklore is deeply rooted in its local milieu, but at the same time it confronts universal issues everyone in the world can identify with.

Next, I would like to introduce a brand new *kyogen*, *Chinchin Kobakama*,

Shiro Sano and the musician Kyoji Yamamoto in a Lafcadio Hearn reading perfomance. (*© Photo taken by Masaki Sugihara*)

composed in 2017 by Sengoro Shigeyama XIV; it is based on Hearn's tale and originates in a Japanese folktale passed down from generation to generation. The process whereby Hearn's work was transformed into a *kyogen* play is interesting given our discussion above. Hearn's wife Setsu heard this Japanese folktale in Japanese and then transmitted it to Hearn in her Japanese English. Hearn's marvellous command of English enabled him to fashion the tale into a literary work. Hearn was familiar with Hiberno-English, American English, the pidgin English spoken in Martinique, and British English – therefore with his linguistic

versatility he was able to create a style perfectly suited to the story, paying tribute to its original sense of locality. Though Hearn wrote in English, he also understood the essence of Japanese literature. His English translations of Japanese folktales are faithful to the originals. In fact, many Japanese people, like myself when I was a child, without knowing that it is actually a translation from English, have assumed that his *Chinchin Kobakama* is an original Japanese work. Using this Japanese translation, Sengoro XIV created a new play which captures both its light-hearted humour and the ethical issues it raises. Sengoro XIV has transformed the play into a classic *kyogen* performance, using a traditional theatrical form or style (*kata* in

Japanese). Amazingly, many different processes were intertwined in this new *kyogen* piece. With only two characters – a *samurai* warrior and his wife – the actors' language and movements conjure up hundreds of fairies on stage. Neither props nor special effects are necessary – the actors' mastery of their roles, a thoughtfully written script, and the audience's imagination are all that is needed.

I will conclude by referring to an idiosyncratic reading performance of Hearn's work at a modern arts event. The Lafcadio Hearn Reading Perfomance, held annually for the past ten years, is done by the actor Shiro Sano and the musician Kyoji Yamamoto (they have been friends since their high-school days in Matsue, Japan).[8] This performance is supervised by Hearn's great-grandson, Bon Koizumi, and produced by his wife, Shoko. In 2006 Sano began this project in his hometown of Matsue, the place that had stimulated Hearn's imagination and become a major source of his creativity during his one and a half years there. Sano selects a theme annually – such as 'Encounter,' 'Promise' and 'Nostalgia' – for which he chooses seven to ten pieces of Hearn's work, eventually integrating them into a coherent whole, with Yamamoto's music as an essential element of the production. They have given performances in various places in Japan – Matsue, Tokyo, Toyama and Yaizu – and on the international stage in Greece and Ireland. I was among the audience on three occasions during their Irish tour in 2015, where I saw the audience completely dazzled and spellbound, regardless of linguistic barriers. Sano read in Japanese while Hearn's original text was shown on the screen, which Shoko Koizumi skilfully operated. Sano's dramatic reading enlivened Hearn's work, overcoming the barrier between the English and Japanese languages. Thanks to the power of his reading, mingled with Yamamoto's poetic music, the Japanese text almost became a universal language – just as the *kyogen* version of *C and M* eliminates the differences between Japanese and Irish cultures. In a sense, Sano succeeds in reinforcing the long and rich oral traditions of both Ireland and Japan. He tells stories just as the ancient bards did, with Yamamoto's music employing fili's harp, except that Sano does not carry his 'harp' on his back. Hearn's work is transformed into a musical score, as these two artists, like old bards, reinvent a classic performance style.

The reading performance I produced in March 2017 at Seiryoji Temple in Hikone, entitled 'Nostalgia – Eternal Home of the Soul', was of a similar quality. The temple is located at the foot of Mount Sawayama, which used to be the centrepiece of a medieval castle town that played a significant role at a turning point in Japanese history, just before the long Tokugawa regime of the Edo Period (1600–1867). The temple is especially well known for housing the graves of the feudal Lords Ii of Hikone. It is also known for the legend of the 'Seven Mysteries of Seiryoji Temple'. In this special atmosphere, a statue of Kwannon, the goddess of mercy, guards the legends and history surrounding this ancient temple.

Against this historic backdrop, both artists delivered a brilliant performance, bringing Hearn's work back to life in a unique fashion. At the end of the evening the protagonist of the final story, *Kwashin Koji*, climbed into a boat floating on the water of Lake Biwa (Japan's largest lake, located in Shiga) on an eight-piece folding screen which depicted the Eight Beautiful Views of Shiga, Omi Hakkei. It felt as if the *tatami*-floored room where the performance was taking place had been transformed into the fictional room in the story. The instant Kwashin Koji's boat disappeared into the screen, the audience experienced that magical moment when the border between this world and the other world vanished. Hearn's work captures something perennial and universal in the human condition; one could not but be overwhelmed by a cathartic serenity when imagining the two brothers dying, covered with white snow, as if with a *futon* blanket, at the end of 'Tottori no Futon'. The catharsis was truly felt when the souls of the two brothers were taken to heaven, with the statue of Kwannon in the background shining in a beam of light, thanks to the skilful effects created by the stage director Nobuyuki Nishikori. Hearn's work also raises ethical issues that continue to be debated in today's world, such as human beings' unconscious bias against outsiders, a theme Hearn often revisited, as in one of his best-known stories, 'Yuki-Onna' ('Snow Woman').[9]

To conclude, Hearn's work continues to give inspiration to artists everywhere. Similarly, Yeats's *C and M* stimulated many Japanese artists, such as Yoko Akino, born and raised in Kyoto and currently working in Ireland, where she has created a series of prints called 'The Cat and the Moon'. Indeed, both Yeats and Hearn will continue to stir our innermost feelings, just as when Minnaloushe, the cat, looks up at the moon and reflects:

> The pure cold light in the sky
> Troubled his animal blood (*Collected Plays*, p.461).

Bibliography

Ewick, David, 'Notes toward a cultural history of Japanese modernism in modernist Europe, 1910–1920, with special reference to Torahiko Kori', *Annals of the Institute for Comparative Studies of Culture*, Tokyo Woman's Christian University, vol. 77 (Tokyo: Tokyo Woman's Christian University), pp. 1–17.

Hearn, Patrick Lafcadio [Koizumi, Yakumo], *Chin Chin Kobakama*: *Japanese Fairy Tale Series*, no. 25 (Tokyo: Takejiro Hasegawa, 1903).

___, 'Yuki Onna,' *Kwaidan: Stories and Studies on Strange Things* (Boston: Houghton Mifflin, 1904).

Koizumi, Bon, 'Lafcadio Hearn's reception and succession of oral culture', *Celt no Suimyaku* [*Water Vein of the Celt*] (Tokyo: Chuo University Press, 2006), pp. 429–63.

Matsumoto, Kaoru, 'On directing *The Cat and the Moon*,' paper given at the 1st International Yeats Symposium, held in Barcelona, December 2016, 'Yeats & Asia: Imagining Asia Through Yeats' (trans. Akiko Manabe).

Murray, Paul, *A Fantastic Journey: The Life and Literature of Lafcadio Hearn* (Ann Arbor: University of Michigan Press, 1993).

Yeats, William Butler, *The Collected Plays of W.B. Yeats* (London: Macmillan, 1985).

___, *The Collected Works of W.B. Yeats, Vol. I, The Poems*, ed. Richard J. Finneran (New York: Scribner, 1996).

___, *The Collected Works of W.B. Yeats, Vol. II, The Plays*, eds David R. Clark and Rosalind E. Clark (New York: Scribner, 2011).

___, *The Collected Works of W.B. Yeats, Vol. IV, Early Essays*, eds George Bornstein and Richard J. Finneran (New York: Scribner, 2007).

___, *The Collected Works of W.B. Yeats, Vol. XIV, A Vision*: rev. 1937 edn, eds Catherine E. Paul and Margaret Mills Harper (New York: Scribner, 2015).

___, *Neko to Tsuki* [*The Cat and the Moon*], *Yeats Gikyoku Shuu* [*Complete Plays by W.B. Yeats*], trans. Tetsuro Sano et al. (Kyoto: Yamaguchi Shoten, 1980), pp. 206–10.

___, *The Variorum Edition of the Plays of W.B. Yeats*, ed. Russell K. Alspach, assisted by Catarine C. Alspach (London: Macmillan, 1966).

___, *A Vision* [1937] (London: Macmillan, 1981).

http://snowwomanfilm.com/

https://www.youtube.com/watch?v=xWr-yYyLV34

W.B. Yeats and Yukio Mishima: A study of the influence of 'Cathleen Ní Houlihan' on 'Sotōba Komachi'

Hideaki Sato

W.B. Yeats (1865–1939) could not have known Yukio Mishima (1925–70), who was deeply influenced by him. Yet, Yeats was interested in Japanese Noh and wrote plays that show its influence. Mishima similarly adapted Noh into modern plays.[1] We can say, therefore, that the two cultures that nourished Yeats and Mishima influenced each other through Noh. It is very curious that Mishima was introduced to Japanese classical drama through Yeats although it is also true that too much emphasis on the textuality of a literary work can lead to errors in performances. We can untangle the complexities of this literary influence by focusing on specific texts. This chapter investigates Yeats's influence upon Mishima's 'Sotōba Komachi' in his Modern Noh Plays, considering what Mishima, under Yeats's influence, intended to convey in the play.

In May 1945 Yukio Mishima was enlisted to work at the Kōza naval arsenal in Kanagawa prefecture. Though he had volunteered for military service, his application had not been accepted due to an erroneous medical diagnosis. However, he knew that he would eventually be enlisted if the war continued. At the Kōza naval base he was given a relatively uncomplicated office job and was able to indulge in his literary pursuits in his free time. In a letter to Fumio Shimizu (his former teacher at Gakushūin High School), Mishima wrote: 'Now I am translating Yeats's one-act play into Japanese … I translate all of it in a classical style of Japanese letter writing (Sōrōbun).'[2] Later, having read an essay in which Shimizu quoted this letter, Mishima said, 'This is completely wiped out from my memory. I wonder if the translation might have been that of "At the Hawk's Well" if I had really attempted to translate any of Yeats's works.'[3] The manuscript of Mishima's translation has not been discovered; nor is there any reference to it in his other writings. Yet he also wrote in the same essay,

> Yeats is not easily connected with the age at the end of the War. I did not strive to connect those I could not connect but concentrated on abstracting realities at that time. I no longer have any chance of participating in literary circles and I seem to have been immersed in as small, solitary, aesthetic tastes as possible.[4]

This quotation shows that the young Mishima was indulging himself in private literary endeavours, which enabled him to escape temporarily from the pressure of the war.

Three months after he wrote the letter to his teacher, the Second World War ended. Writing to Utarō Noda, the editor of the journal *Literature and the Arts* (Bungei), on 2 September 1945, Mishima said: 'All of us deeply regret that the Japanese have trampled their nobility and beauty for themselves and with their own hands to such a miserable extent as this'; in a postscript to this letter, he added, 'I would like to follow W.B. Yeats's spirit of the Irish Literary Renaissance.'[5] Here, Mishima does not regard Yeats merely as an author who satisfies his literary taste, but as a representative of Ireland's national literature. In spite of his enthusiasm for literature, Mishima at that time was only an obscure student writer; the manuscripts he submitted to publishers and editors of literary journals were not warmly received.

Six years later, following the success of *The Confession of the Mask* (Kamen no Kokuhaku), Mishima was finally regarded as a professional author, and he began to write plays. He fully exploited Noh's essence and wrote one-act plays which were subsequently collected in an edition called *Modern Noh Plays*. The play 'Sotōba Komachi' was first published in *Gunzō* in January 1952; it is among Mishima's representative plays, and I will discuss it further in this chapter. In 'A Preface to Sotōba Komachi', he wrote: 'In writing the Modern Noh Plays, I was inspired by various sorts of motives such as my experience of reading poetical plays influenced by Yeats's Noh, of being impressed by Torahiko Kori's "Kanawa", "Dojō-ji", and "Kiyohime", and my interest in Noh since childhood.' This illustrates Yeats's considerable influence upon him. Yeats's significance for Mishima had shifted after the war: no longer merely a writer whose works catered to Mishima's 'solitary aesthetic tastes', Yeats had now taught Mishima how literature could express the spirit of a country.

It was through Ezra Pound that W.B. Yeats came to know Japanese Noh. From 1914 to 1916, Pound served as a secretary to Yeats (whom he respected), while arranging Ernest F. Fenollosa's manuscripts on Noh in order to publish them. Fenollosa was an American who taught philosophy and other subjects at the University of Tokyo. He had wide-ranging interests, and he was highly thought of in academic circles, especially in the field of Japanese art history. Fenollosa had learned Noh from Minoru Umewaka, a Kanze-style Noh player. He asked Tokuboku Hirata, editor of the journal *Bungakukai* (*The Literary World*) in the Meiji period, to translate Noh songs (Yōkyoku) and Noh and to annotate them. According to Keiko Wells, who has investigated Fenollosa's notes in the Beinecke Library at Yale University, 'Japanese lyrics of Noh songs are written in Roman letters and each of those words is underlined and their meanings are explained in English … Some of them are given notes, and others have memos attached to them about performers' behaviours and settings of the stage.'[6] Pound was very interested in Fenollosa's notebooks, and Yeats – who was collecting Celtic myths – also shared this enthusiasm. Frowning upon modern realistic drama such as Ibsen's plays, Yeats was fascinated by Noh's methods of freely manipulating time and space, its simple stage settings, and its masks and stylised behaviours. Yeats wrote four plays inspired by Noh: 'At the Hawk's Well', 'The Only Jealousy of Emer', 'The Dreaming of the Bones' and 'Calvary'. 'At the Hawk's Well' was first performed in Lady Emerald Cunard's house in 1916. Michirō Itō – a Japanese student of Irish dance – played the role of the hawk-like woman. Yeats was apparently pleased with this performance.

I hesitate to describe these four plays as Noh because Yeats does not seem

Yukio Mishima, author, poet, playwright, actor and film director, during a failed coup d'etat attempt known as the 'Mishima Incident', 1970. (*CPA Media/Alamy*)

to have fully understood Noh's dramatic form. Noh does not involve dialogues between characters; nor does it necessarily create dramatic oppositions between characters. Rather, Noh's major characteristic is that each play is narrated by a shite (protagonist).[7] In 'At the Hawk's Well', three characters – the Young Man, the Old Man, and the Guardian of the Well – articulate the oppositional framework of the play. Mario Yokomichi's 'Takahime' was a Noh version of 'At the Hawk's Well': Yokomichi transformed Takahime (the Guardian of the Well) into a shite and removed the oppositional structures that govern Yeats's characters. Yet it was not Yeats's Noh that attracted Yukio Mishima. Like Yeats, he was not content with realistic drama, and sought to adopt Noh's free manipulations of time and space. Stimulated by the plays of Yeats and Torahiko Kori, who did not strictly follow the form of Noh, Mishima was flexible in his appropriation of Noh for his Modern Noh Plays. A comparison between Mishima's Modern Noh Plays and the plays of Yeats and Kori makes this clear.

We may ask which of Yeats's dramatic works had the greatest influence on Mishima. There seems to be no obvious trace of the influence of Yeats's 'At the Hawk's Well' upon Mishima's plays, but what is most interesting is the relationship between Yeats's 'Cathleen Ní Houlihan' and Mishima's 'Sotōba Komachi'. There is no reference to 'Cathleen Ní Houlihan' in Mishima's essays, and neither is it clear whether he actually read the play. There are, however, evident similarities between these two plays. In order to analyse them, I will first explain the content of the Noh song 'Sotōba Komachi' before discussing Mishima's play. I will then compare both with 'Cathleen Ní Houlihan'.

'Sotōba Komachi' was first composed by an eminent Noh playwright, Zeami Motokiyo, in the fourteenth century. It begins with an old female beggar sitting upon a sotōba.[8] A Buddhist priest of Mount Kōyasan passes by and criticises her blasphemous behaviour, asking her to leave. The Old Woman retorts and even composes a song for the occasion. Astonished, the priest asks her name. Replying that she was once a legendary beauty, Ono no Komachi, she tells the story of how she has turned into a ninety-nine-year-old beggar. Suddenly, Komachi is possessed by the ghost of Fukakusa no Shōshō (Captain Fukakusa), a courtier who was in love with her. When she regains her consciousness, she determines to be a pious Buddhist forever.

In his 'Sotōba Komachi', Yukio Mishima presents several lovers whispering to each other on a bench in a park when a ragged old woman – a spider-catcher – appears on the scene. She asks the lovers to yield their bench. Seeing this, a young poet asks her why she has interrupted them: they love each other and are so happy that it seems as if they could reach the stars. While leaving the stage, the lovers are conversing about mundane things: 'We might miss the last train', 'I wonder whether the chicken will lay eggs tomorrow', and "That necktie doesn't suit you.' Watching them, the Old Woman rejects the Poet's view that the lovers are living meaningful lives. Baffled by the Old Woman's comment, the Poet asks who she is. She replies that she was once called Ono no Komachi. The inebriated Poet playfully suggests that he will play Fukakusa no Shōshō. All of a sudden, the Old Woman is transformed into a beautiful young lady. The stage setting instantly changes to the garden of the Rokumeikan (Rokumeikan Hall), and ladies and gentlemen are praising the woman for her beauty. Komachi, however, warns them that they should not say she is beautiful because all men who have done this have died. She tells the Poet that he should observe her wrinkles, her tattered and stinking clothes, and her dirty breast. In spite of this, however, he says 'You are beautiful', and then he dies. The act ends with the Old Woman collecting cigarette butts, as if nothing ever happened.

In Mishima's 'Sotōba Komachi', the Poet's words – 'The bench on which the Old Woman is sitting looks like a sotōba' – hark back to the original Noh song. Yet the Buddhist message in the original composition has been jettisoned. There are two striking arrangements in Mishima's play that are worth noticing here: first the park in the present metamorphoses into the garden of the Rokumeikan eighty years ago, and second, the same actor plays both the Old Woman and the young lady. In the original Noh song, as we have seen, the Old Woman does not change into her younger self. In the play, the actor is transformed in front of the audience, crossing the boundary of time within an instant. Another interesting point is that the drunken Poet – who at first criticises the Old Woman – develops a passion for her, to such an extent that he ends up losing his life. The play gives its actors much freedom to interpret their roles and is very popular not only in Japan but also in Europe and the United States.

Let us now turn to 'Cathleen Ní Houlihan' and consider its similarities with Mishima's 'Sotōba Komachi'. I should first point out that when Cathleen arrives on the scene, she is also a homeless old woman; she then changes into a beautiful young woman, just as the Old Woman in 'Sotōba Komachi' does. In Yeats's play, people in Gilen's house are busy preparing for their son Michael's wedding the following day. Having successfully obtained morning coats and a dowry, they are enjoying themselves. But an uninvited old woman arrives. Explaining that she has no home, and that she has been deprived of 'four beautiful green fields', the woman says that many men have died because they loved her so much. She adds that this will continue to happen. Michael's father says that he can provide her with food or silver coins, but she declines. Then she says, 'Those who try to save me must try their life. They should determine to give everything to me.' The father wonders who she is, and his wife asks the old woman her name. She answers, 'I am Cathleen, a daughter of Houlihan.' Cathleen says that she must go and welcome those who have come to save her, and Michael says that he should go with her. At the port, many ships and French soldiers are landing. Regardless of his parents and fiancée, Michael leaves the house to join the French army. In response to his father's reference to the old woman, Michael's younger brother says that she is a young, rather than old, woman, walking as stately as a queen.

It is obvious that 'Cathleen Ní Houlihan' and Mishima's 'Sotōba Komachi' have much in common. In his study of Mishima's 'Sotōba Komachi' and W.B. Yeats, Takako Abe finds similarities between the two plays in the relationships between the characters and the development of the plots, pointing out Yeats's influence on 'Sotōba Komachi'.[8] Abe's argument centres on three points. First, in each play, an old woman is transformed into a beautiful youth. Second, Komachi's words – 'All the men who said I was beautiful have already died' – resonate with what Cathleen says: 'a lot of men died because they loved me'. Third, both plays present a scenario where 'a young man is forced to choose one of the two different values'. The plots of both plays revolve around an old woman who entrances a young man. In the case of Mishima's 'Sotōba Komachi', the Old Woman tries to restrain the Poet, to no avail. Takako Abe's argument regarding the similar plots of the plays is very convincing. Another similarity is that in both plays an old woman appears on the scene as an unknown figure. Because of this, the other characters have to ask her who she is. In both plays, then, the audience gradually unravel the mystery of the old woman. A further observation is that in each play a young man risks his life for an old woman. In 'Cathleen Ní Houlihan', Michael is to participate in an uprising, and his death is foretold by Cathleen. As mentioned above, nowhere in his writings did Mishima mention 'Cathleen Ní Houlihan'. Yet, given the similarities in their dramatic settings and plots, there is little doubt that 'Sotōba Komachi' was written under the influence of Yeats's play.

On the other hand, could it be possible that 'Cathleen Ní Houlihan' was influenced by Zeami's Noh play, 'Sotōba Komachi'? I would think so, because there are clear parallels between Komachi and Cathleen in terms of characterisation. Among them are the Old Woman's intelligence – surprising given her unkempt appearance – crafty eloquence, strong will and arrogance towards the other characters. In addition, I would also point out that 'Sotōba Komachi' is included in Fenollosa's *The Classic Noh Theatre of Japan*, edited by Ezra Pound. However, this does not support the hypothesis, since it was not until 1914 that Yeats knew Pound was editing Noh plays, while 'Cathleen Ní Houlihan' had been published in 1902.

Both Yeats's and Mishima's plots are astonishing, in that each portrays a physically weak old woman who exerts a tremendous emotional power over a young man, and who succeeds in seducing him. Rather than being confined to realism, the old woman in each play carries larger symbolic meanings: through these figures, age is sanctified and idealised. Cathleen Ní Houlihan is a legendary figure in Ireland, and it is generally accepted that the play is based on this national symbolism. Ono no Komachi is similarly a folkloric existence that has come down in history. Yukio Mishima identified similarities between the two legendary figures and perceived in both the universal image of the Old Woman. In Mishima's 'Sotōba Komachi' the dramatic devices function effectively to suggest that the Old Woman's disturbed state of mind results from her being spiritually possessed, as depicted in the original Noh song, while in 'Cathleen Ní Houlihan' the transformation of the old woman is implied in the words of Michael's brother. In 'Sotōba Komachi', Mishima portrays the supernatural old woman as a substantial character with a powerful personality.

The Old Woman in 'Sotōba Komachi' criticises the Poet, who admires the lovers. Yeats also frequently depicted the gulf between the young and the elderly. For instance, in 'Sailing to Byzantium' an old man says, 'That is no country for old men.' He also says that 'an aged man' looks just like 'a tattered coat upon a stick'. This reminds us of the appearance of the Old Woman in 'Sotōba Komachi', who is a repulsive beggar wearing 'tattered clothes'. What is represented in 'Sailing to Byzantium' is an old man who seeks eternal ideals beyond a 'sensual' world

W.B. Yeats, *c.* 1920s.
(*Archive Pics/Alamy*)

subjected to the relentless cycles of procreation and death. Komachi, who has lived to be ninety-nine years old, observes the lovers in the park and, just like the old man in Yeats's poem, distances herself from them; she says 'They are dead while they are doing things like that', which apparently corresponds to the old man's view in 'Sailing to Byzantium':

> ... The young
> In one another's arms, birds in the trees,
> – Those dying generations – at their song,
> The salmon-falls, the mackerel-crowded seas,
> Fish, flesh, or fowl, commend all summer long
> Whatever is begotten, born, and dies.[9]

The old man in the poem strikes a note similar to that of the ninety-nine-year-old Komachi. We cannot prove that Yukio Mishima had 'Sailing to Byzantium' in mind, but in reading the play it is impossible to ignore the two old people's common state of mind.

Though they both observe young people from a distance, the old man in 'Sailing to Byzantium' and Komachi in 'Sotōba Komachi' have different outlooks. Yeats's old man dreams that a 'form' made of 'hammered gold and gold enamelling' or an 'artiface of eternity' should be where the soul belongs. Mishima's Komachi finds the essence of life in everyday chores which apparently make people look bored. It is as though it were Mishima's intention to bring forth a perception of life that is different from Yeats's, although he agrees with Yeats's poem in seeing the young people's lives as nothing but delusions. Neither Yeats nor Mishima, however, disapprove of emotional intensity. Rather, they both recur to a sense of life's upheavals in the end.

In that scene in 'Sotōba Komachi' where the young lovers rehearse their daily routines and worries, there is a conversation between the Old Woman and the Poet:

Old Woman:	At last – they've come back to life.
Poet:	The skyrockets have gone out. How can you say they've come back to life?
Old Woman:	I know what the face looks like of someone who's come back

> to life – I've seen it often enough. It wears an expression of horrible boredom, and that expression is what I like … Long ago, when I was young, I never had the sensation of being alive unless my head was all awhirl. I only felt I was living when I forgot myself completely. Since then I have realized my mistake.[10]

This is a view of life that the Old Woman intends to maintain, and her words here touch upon the main theme of 'Sotōba Komachi'. This view is also what Mishima was determined to uphold. He explained that the main theme of 'Sotōba Komachi' was 'The author's determination to live as an artist'. What does this mean? Mishima was twenty-six years old when he wrote 'Sotōba Komachi'. The young Mishima was physically weak. It was natural that he should have turned to the solitary pleasures afforded by literature. Later, he recalled:

> In my boyhood, when disliking the sun constituted a rebellious act against the times, I singularly favoured Novalis' night and Yeats's Irish Twilight and wrote some works about the night in the Middle Ages. From the end of the War onwards – for that was a turning point – I gradually felt that the time was coming when making the sun an enemy to us was truckling to the trends.[11]

In a sense, Mishima – like the protagonist in Thomas Mann's *Tonio Kröger* – began to hate his boyhood self, a former existence untouched by the brightness of youth. When he was thirty years old, he undertook body-building with the help of a trainer. In addition, he learned kendō, iai sword-drawing and karate, and he even underwent recruit training organised by Japan's Self-defence Forces. Mishima called these activities 'self-remodelling' (jiko kaizō). His discontent with his physical weakness led to his commitment to maintaining good health. A month after writing 'Sotōba Komachi', he left Yokohama for a round-the-world trip, and enjoyed the sun while at sea. He had eventually welcomed sunshine into his daily life. Turning his back on his unhealthy literary pleasures, he embraced his body and life itself. He was determined to *live* as an artist, and this new focus is behind his characterisation of the Old Woman.

'Sotōba Komachi' does not merely represent Mishima's private consciousness, for it is placed within a much larger framework. The play is considered to be an allegory. Komachi, who was proud of her beauty when she was young, now insists on continuing to live despite her ugliness. The secret to her longevity lies in her forbearance and her determination to carry on living her everyday life, boring as it may be. My hypothesis is that the play can be understood as an allegory of Japan in the post-war period. A developing country, Japan was too proud of itself in the face of competing Western European countries, and challenged them in the Asia–Pacific War, ending up completely devastated. Komachi says, 'The worse the liquor, the quicker you get drunk.'[12] The young Komachi lived 'in the midst of my drunkenness, in the midst of those sentimental feelings and tears'. Pondering her former situation, she says, 'I was dying.' Then she concludes: 'Since then, I have made it a rule not to be drunk. This is the secret to my long life.'[13]

The ninety-nine-year-old Komachi remembers that she was at a ball at the Rokumeikan eighty years ago. This suggests that she was born around Meiji 1 (1867), taking into account that the Rokumeikan period is dated Meiji 16 (1883) to Meiji 20 (1886).[15] Komachi's life, therefore, perfectly corresponds to the progress of modern Japan. The characterisation of Komachi suggests that she is a symbol of modern Japan. Needless to say, the Rokumeikan was a place for socialising, established to break off unequal treaties with Western European countries. It has also come to symbolise Japan's rush towards modern civilisation, as well as its attempt to bend other countries to its will by sleight of hand.[15] The Rokumeikan represented in 'Sotōba Komachi' has some kind of national connotation. Or we can regard the old Komachi as a symbol of post-war Japan, or of Japan unspecific to any historical period, considering that the Komachi legends have persisted from the Heian period to our age.

On 21 November 1951 Yukio Mishima finished writing 'Sotōba Komachi'. This came after 8 September 1951, when the Japanese government signed the Treaty of San Francisco, and before 28 April 1952, when the peace treaty came into effect. The treaty allowed Japan to recover its sovereignty after six years and eight months' suspension, and restored the country's independence, releasing it from the occupation of the United States. The Old Woman's words 'they have finally recovered' are reminiscent of the end of US occupation. The park in 'Sotōba Komachi' – Hibiya Park – was returned to Japan after the US had withdrawn. The chief objective of Japanese politics under the age of occupation was to raise the people's living standards. Prime Minister Shigeru Yoshida aimed to withdraw from the protection of the US and to disassociate Japan from US interests.[16] Yoshida lay aside national pride so as to improve the people's standard of living. The Old Woman in 'Sotōba Komachi' suggests that to live is not to live for one's own purposes. Rather, to continue to live – this itself is meaningful. This seems to be the Old Woman's way of saying that the hard task of surviving is more important than the abstract ideal of living to achieve one's own ends. Her attitude perfectly corresponds to that which underpinned the reconstruction of post-war Japan.

One might think Mishima's suicide on 25 November 1970 contradicts this message in 'Sotōba Komachi'. The forty-five-year-old Mishima declared to members of Japan's Self-defence Forces that this should be the nation's army, but when it became clear that they were not in agreement, he protested by committing suicide in front of them. Mishima's point seems to have been that the Japanese should reform their constitution, which stipulated the renunciation of war, and that Japan should be independent of the United States. The twenty-six-year-old Mishima made a realistic choice, adopting a lifestyle aligned with Japan's post-war recovery. Yet such conservative politics would not have exerted influence on his contemporaries when Marxist ideas were dominant among the intellectuals. The larger framework of 'Sotōba Komachi', which suggests how Japan can survive in the post-war period, was hidden, so that its allegorical message went unnoticed by the audiences. It was ten years before Mishima's political ideas were transformed and actualised.

Allegory might restrict a text's meaning. Deciphering allegorical symbols can reduce the inherent complexities of a text. However, previous studies of 'Sotōba Komachi' have ignored the political framework of the play. This results from their understanding of Mishima during his mid-thirties as a romanticist, or as a novelist who sympathised with the notion of art for art's sake, and as someone not engaged with the relationship between literature and politics. They had not paid attention to his literary expressions regarding politics. We need, therefore, to further explore the young Mishima's political expressions. It is well known that 'Cathleen Ní Houlihan' was described as a 'patriotic play', and that Cathleen symbolises Ireland.[17] The event depicted in 'Cathleen Ní Houlihan' was an armed uprising that ended in failure. In 1801 Ireland was united with Britain. It was not until 18 April 1949 that Ireland became fully independent of the United Kingdom. This news was only briefly reported in Japanese newspapers; just four years after the war, Japanese readers were not keenly interested in foreign affairs, and the newspapers generally ran to only one or two pages, their foreign desks remaining closed.[18] It is not clear whether Mishima read about this, but it is very likely that he knew of Irish nationalism through Yeats. We can imagine Mishima adapting the nationalistic allegory of 'Cathleen Ní Houlihan' into 'Sotōba Komachi', but it is impossible to prove this. It is obvious, however, that Mishima's 'Sotōba Komachi' has much to do with Yeats's 'Cathleen Ní Houlihan' in that both one-act plays present an old woman as the symbol of the repressed homelands of the respective playwrights.

The meaning of nationalism varies according to a nation's historical and social conditions. Among the factors that define its meaning are, first, resistance and insistence; second, joy, antipathy and obedience; third, the strengths and weaknesses of the country and its forms of existence; and, fourth, the extent of its introversion and extraversion. Therefore, we cannot argue about Yeats and Mishima in the same way. What we can do is try to understand what it is like to be a member of each of these countries and to partake in an abstract sense of belonging. The evident similarities between Cathleen and Komachi seem to prove the influence of W.B. Yeats upon Yukio Mishima to a much greater extent than we may have expected.

Kenzaburō Ōe and W.B. Yeats

Taketoshi Furomoto

In Ōe's trilogy of *The Blazing Green Tree*, each of the three volumes has an episode with death at its core. In the first, O-baa the grand-mother, who is a sort of 'miko' or prophetess, has inherited the stories and legends circulated around her village on Shikoku Island. She wants to ensure that the tradition will be passed down to the next generation. Her death takes place fairly early in the volume (one third of the way through). In spite of being over ninety years of age, her groans resound across the valleys and through the forest: strange, tremendous sounds that are sometimes unbearable, and at other times indistinct, depending on the direction of the wind. The tale is repeatedly told among the villagers. After her death, there is a special funeral conducted by the 'fireworm children': groups of children carrying torches go to the mountain separately, with one group carrying the urn to bury it at the foot of a tree known only to them.

One legend told by O-baa is about the villagers resisting the government army which attacked the place in order to destroy its autonomy, typical of the Meiji era's forced modernisation. The villagers chose to die in the open ground down in the river valley, rather than waiting to perish in the remote mountains. O-baa taught these lofty deeds to the three young men in the family. One of them becomes an ambassador and travels all over the world. The next becomes a novelist and lives in Tokyo. The third also studies in Tokyo and gains as much cultural knowledge as the other two; he returns to the village to pass on O-baa's teachings and devotes himself to healing the villagers by means of 'touch'. But this first Brother Gee is killed by those who misunderstand his healing power and religious teaching.

The three young men share an interest in languages and read Dante and Yeats, whose works were in the library of the murdered guru.

In this family, Takasi, the son of the ambassador ('the Consul General'), inherits the tradition as the second Brother Gee. In the second volume, the retired 'Consul General', who suffers from cancer, returns to the village to die. His son has already started treating the villagers. A memorable episode involves a dialogue between Takasi and a boy. The boy suffers from an infantile cancer and complains about the unfairness of life. Takasi suggests a way to fight back against his fate: to outlive it by one second. There is a similarly impressive passage in Joyce's short story, 'A Painful Case' in *The Dubliners*, which shows what it is like to be an 'outcast from life's feast'.

Brother Gee suggests that the mind should be disciplined, first by absorbing the idea of eternity and second by being 'trained in things spiritual'. The former made me think of this formula of the total sum of arithmetic progression:

$$1 + 2 + \ldots + n = S$$
$$N + (n-1) \ldots +1 = S \qquad S = 1/2 \times n(n+1)$$

When I was taught this formula in high school, I was strongly impressed by its simple precision. And there is a resemblance between the formula and Brother Gee's explication of the brevity of our life compared with eternity. The n in the formula symbolises an endless, shapeless continuity of time extending infinitely, while the natural number 1 or 100 etc. suggests a definite span of time, which is always brief and ephemeral. Thus, Brother Gee suggests to the boy that his anxiety arises from his inability to understand eternal infinity. The inability is caused by uncertainty, together with uneasiness, impatience, anger and fear.

The other hint – to be 'trained in things spiritual' – may sound strange to our ears. But its extraordinariness may suggest that the hero's decisiveness and passion for his work are far greater than those of ordinary people.

Kenzaburo Ōe. (*Lucas Vallecillos/ Alamy*)

Having returned home, the 'Consul General' attempts to write an autobiographical novel, imitating his novelist relative, 'Uncle K'. He draws inspiration from Yeats's *Collected Poems*. The first chapter of the second volume is entitled 'Led by Yeats', and it quotes amply from the *Collected Poems*. The 'Consul General' confesses that his references to Yeats are explicitly biographical (p. 10). Yet he reads far more of Dorothy Wellesley than a casual reader would, and his biographical approach to the poet is by no means uncommon.

One of the most memorable biographical allusions is made by the Consul General:

> All that I have said and done,
> Now that I am old and ill,
> Turns into a question till
> I lie awake night after night
> And never get the answers right.
>
> (*The Man and the Echo*, Ōe (vol. II, pp. 15, 16, 17))

The following is a list of quotations from Yeats in *The Blazing Green Tree*:

> Ōe Vol. II chap. I, 'Easter 1916'; p. 8, 'What Then'; p. 10, '1919'; p. 28, 'Gyres' II, p. 30; 'The Tower', p. 36; 'Politics', p. 50; 'Magic' (Essays and Prefaces) chap. II: p. 59, 'Lapis Lazuri'; p. 75, 'Vacillation'; p. 136, 'The Second Coming'.

The words used in these quotations constitute a resounding lexicon. Words such as gay, joy, rejoice, repentance, memory, imagination, meditation, violence, frenzy, and terrible carry biographical connotations. That is one reason why Yeats is attractive.

Another feature of the Consul General's literary allusions is the apocalypse. First, the title of the novel is derived from an image in the Welsh mythological cycle, *The Mabinogion*. Then there is another experience of Yeats himself, described in 'Vacillation', verse IV.

> My fiftieth year had come and gone,
> I sat, a solitary man,
> In a crowded London ship,
> An open book and empty cup
> On the marble table-top.
> While on the shop and street I gazed
> My body of a sudden blazed;

> And twenty minutes more or less
> It seemed, so great my happiness,
> That I was blessed and could bless.
>
> (Ōe, vol. III, p. 22)

I quote these passages to substantiate the image of eternity in the dialogue between Brother Gee and the boy with cancer.

In his sermons, Brother Gee confesses in the following way. The words are spoken mainly to a dying man: 'I sometimes think your life seems to me more precious than mine' (p. 240). And he explains that if his life is more or less meaningful, it seems to him solely to utter these words to you. The Consul General was also trying to give the same significance to his own life, which is suggestive of Brother Gee's late tragedy.

Brother Gee's words and action seem to tell us that what humans can do is to try and alleviate their sufferings, in what ever little way they can.

In volume III, the cult group is plunged into sectarian conflicts. Its members have forgotten the original aim of Brother Gee (to be trained in things spiritual) and are now solely preoccupied with increasing their numbers. Brother Gee realises what has gone wrong and burns the gigantic cypress, the symbol of the cult, thus dissolving the group. He seeks to carry on with his spiritual work in a solitary way. But just before his departure, he is attacked by some radical group members. He dies unresistingly, true to his own teaching, 'to respect others' lives more than one's own' (p. 353).

Brother Gee has two aims: one is to prove that God really exists, and the other is to answer the question 'Are you a saviour?' Both of these issues are theological but, as we shall see, they do not necessarily have to be answered in a theological way.

The second chapter of volume II (entitled 'Void in the Centre') alludes to an anthropologist friend of the novelist Uncle K. The implication of the allusion is as follows: as a peculiarly Japanese phenomenon, we can find a void in the middle of the governing power, a void which blurs social responsibility. The partial explanation, but not defence, given by Brother Gee is that our concentration on the cocoon – the substantial form outside – can give us a sense of tangibility. In this way the original amorphousness gradually assumes a concrete shape. Following

The Ishiteji Temple, Matsuyama, Ehime Prefecture, Japan.
(*Christopher Ayumu Nakahara/Alamy*)

this logic, he says, praying to a supernatural being gives us the satisfaction of having done something on our part, and whether our prayers are answered depends on the being we pray to, rather than on our own responsibility (p. 73). Brother Gee says 'It is not for us to catch God, but for Him to catch us' (pp. 132–3). To directly answer the question of whether God exists is merely to give God our self-made image.

In this context, it is worth mentioning Yeats's play, *Where There is Nothing*, which provides an interesting key clue to his attitude towards occultism. Paul Ruttledge, the protagonist of the play, comes to believe that all institutions – state, church and property – must be utterly destroyed, spiritually if not physically: 'We must destroy the World; we must destroy everything that has Law and Number, for where there is nothing, there is God' (ll. 357–8). This play shares parallels with those poems of Yeats which foretell apocalyptic destruction and the birth of a new order, such as 'Leda and the Swan', 'The Second Coming', 'A Prayer for My Daughter', and 'Nineteen Hundred and Nineteen'. Here, the Revelatory Incident, or epiphany, is described as visiting us when we are unprepared; where 'there is nothing' is where there is no temporary sequence, no expectation, no conjecture of cause and effect.

In Brother Gee's order, there is a training objective called Concentration, which can be explained in the same way. Like an epiphany, the being to whom we pray cannot be fully grasped. It comes spontaneously and catches us, though it cannot be caught by us; it is not bound by any human notions of action. The training is occasionally criticised as eclecticism or syncretism, but it is a way of expressing an important truth. It is a sort of editing of the scriptures, or a collection of collaged meaningful texts like Auden's *A Certain World* (Oe liked Auden). In the same way, Simone Weil's words are suggestive (Weil is another of Ōe's favourite writers): the aim of studying or praying is not to know what God is, but to arrange our minds so that God can descend upon us as much as possible. Ōe also shows an interest in the steps of training whereby the Dark Night of the Soul leads to union with God. To conquer the difficulty of this mental process is analogous to climbing physical steps – both require constant efforts and patience, as well as an unfailing sense of purpose (Simone Weil, Waiting for God).

It was from his mother that Ōe learned to concentrate and to be attentive. She asked him questions about the books he was reading, which prompted him to read more carefully and to take notes. Ōe has told us a story about his son, who had difficulty speaking at first. The first thing he uttered was a corncrake song. Ōe was so surprised that he could not believe his ears. He describes how anxiously he waited for the bird to sing again and for his son to imitate it, to make sure that he had not been imagining the song. He is so sympathetic to the souls crying in the dark (figurative of his son's suffering) that this sympathy applies to those souls crying in the dark on the Day of Judgement (*Me in the Obscure Japan*, p. 63 quoting from Blake's *Four Zoas*).

One similar example can be found in *Dark Rain* by Masuji Ibuse. The protagonist prays for a rainbow to appear as evidence of his niece's recovery from radiation poisoning. Ōe seems to be interested in the tensions of waiting. This type of concentration depends on acquiring the habit of purifying the mind, rather than on any verbal conventions. It is the way to approach the supreme being.

Ōe says he put almost every thing he wanted to write about in this novel (*Me in the Obscure Japan*, p. 132). The intensity of waiting for the corncrake to sing again is so vividly described that the reader can imagine it sympathetically even without hearing the song. Ōe confesses that his is a liberal mind unfettered by any particular religious faith, but he believes that there are times when a supreme being may visit even a mind that subscribes to free will and free judgement (p. 77). What is significant is not whether our prayers are answered but our being aware of our ability to concentrate. Quoting from Gaston Bachelard's *Air and Dreams*, Ōe mentions that the liberation of the imagination is a moment when certain images lead to a revelation of new experience: when the whole set of letters, images, experiences, memories and habits replaces human existence itself as one new entirety (*For New Literature*, p. 82).

The aforementioned training by Ōe's mother was not only for reading, but also for literacy itself, the crystallisation of literary experiences, and actualisation of the past.

Ōe's story of three generations of course has precedents in English novels familiar to Japanese readers, such as *Wuthering Heights* or *The Rainbow*. And the prophetess O-baa is succeeded by Sacchan, who also inherits the role of tribal storyteller as the bearer of her family blood. She is uncommonly androgynous, like Tiresias, who knows the experience and psychology of both sexes. This structure is a little too artificial. Yet, Ōe's reading of Western literature has surely enriched his perception of the world.

As for the image of the blazing green tree in 'Vacillation', there can be no doubt about its Welsh source, but we can discuss the origin of this allusion. The image is so impressive that it is hardly surprising that Matthew Arnold used it in *On the Study of Celtic Literature*. Yeats perhaps used Arnold's translation in 'The Celtic Element in Literature'. Both Arnold and Yeats describe the episode from a plural perspective – 'they saw a tree…' – while Lady Charlotte Guest's translation from the original Welsh is 'he saw…' This may seem trivial, but the difference is in fact significant. The plural pronoun 'they' suggests that the experience is more or less objectively affirmed by more than one person, while the singular 'he' hints at a subjective experience, like a vision that cannot be shared with others. Ōe's tendency to enlarge the personal into the collective may have something to do with these literary precedents.

As I have mentioned, there is a tendency in Yeats to conquer time. This is expressed in two ways. One is vertical: to be removed from the flow of time and thus to be dissociated from the chain of cause and effect. The other is horizontal: to recover the past and to penetrate into the future so as to extend the span of time both ways. By these means, we are able to overcome the despotism of time even if it is just for a short while.

Here I would like to further explore Yeats's 'Vacillation', which Ōe quotes more than once. Verse VII of the poem contains a dialogue between the soul and the heart, but it suggests an irreconcilable conflict between the saint and the poet, the sacred and the profane, the holy and the secular:

> *The Soul.* Seek out reality, leave things that seem.
> *The Heart.* What, be a singer born and lack a theme?
> *The Soul* Isaia's coal, what more can man desire?
> *The Heart* Struck dumb in the simplicity of fire!
> *The Soul* Look on that fire, salvation walks within.
> *The Heart* What theme had Homer but original sin?

'To do things spiritual' belongs to the task of a prophet or a saint, while to engage with the complexities of the heart is the fate of a poet. The former seeks to renounce various desires, the latter to yield to them so as to verbalise them. The former aspires to a unified simplicity, while the latter embraces diversity. The same contrast is described in another poem, 'A Dialogue of Self and Soul', in which the self is a synonym for the heart. Both poems end with an utterance by the Heart (or Self) without expecting a response from the other speaker. No wonder Ōe quotes 'A Dialogue' and emphasises its significance:

> Measure the lot; forgive myself the lot!
> When such as I cast out remorse
> So great a sweetness flows into the breast
> We must laugh and we must sing,
> We are blest by everything,
> Everything we look upon is blest.
>
> (Ōe, vol. III, p. 21)

The Yeatsian word 'remorse' refers to a dissatisfaction that arises in one's life, and in seeking heaven the effort compels one to become worthy of salvation. However, one should not rest contented with joy; nor should one be entirely subjected to asceticism. But the poet embraces everything, even unhappiness such as unrequited love, untimely death, pain, jealousy, and anger. He tastes joy in finding the truth of life; he does not abandon remorse, but to 'cast out remorse' is to confront it and break free from it. Religious men are eager to remove the pain, while the poet looks for the awakening of the dual nature of life. The Soul aims for blessings beyond the grave, whereas the poet stives to be alive to reality. The poet regards this as a 'blessing', but it is a blessing drastically different from that sought by the Soul.

In 'Vacillation', there is a moment when both come into close contact, but they separate themselves in the end. Thus, the final part of verse VIII expresses the Heart's perspective:

> Must we part, Von Hugel, though much alike, for we
> Accept the miracles of the saints and honour sanctity?
> The body of Saint Teresa lies undecayed in tomb,
> Bathed in miraculous oil, sweet odours from it come,
> Healing from its lettered slab. The self-same hands perchance

Eternalised the body of a modern saint that once
Had scooped out Pharaoh's mummy. I – heart might find relief
Did I become a Christian man and choose for my belief
What seems most welcome in the tomb – play a predestined part.
Homer is my example and his unchristened heart.
The lion and the honeycomb, what has Scripture said ?
So get you gone, Von Hugel, though with blessings on your head.

Salvation (Blessing) in Christianity or in any other religion is beyond physical liberation or its joy. But once in a while, we come across descriptions of a miracle, such as a saint's body that retains a special fragrance years after his (or her) death. Yeats seems to have been particularly attracted to such experiences. The story of Samson in the Book of Judges in the Old Testament tells of the miracle of honey coming out of a lion's carcass (an example of the sweet coming out of the strong), a riddle given to the Philistines to solve, as an unfathomable union of contradictory elements. So far as it is a riddle, it is unsolvable and unfair. In the stories about Samson, after several betrayals by his consorts the hero perishes with his tribe's enemy, and the tragedy of revenge is told only to show the justice of Jehovah, with the protagonist as a tool. But here the Heart sticks to its 'predestined part', not the tool destined in heaven. The combination of 'the lion and the honeycomb' is a sample of wisdom unfathomable to men, yet of inevitable transformation destined in heaven.

The Heart does not choose that way but the reality of inevitable change and diversity, of the poet's shouldering mundane principles.

Brother Gee's sermons lead the audience to the cross-roads of these two choices, but he seems in the end not definite on the last choice. This is the reason I guess Ōe did not quote positively the last passage of the Self. Neither he nor anyone can be so sure about the last moment of arrival at the destination, however sympathetic with the process of arriving at it. Ōe seems to say that to stay at this critical point is as important as the final decision.

Bibliography

Ōe, Kenzaburō, *The Blazing Green Tree* (Shinchousha I 1993)
____, II (1994)
____, III (1995)

Pagination in the text is of these editions.

Accidence and Incoherence: Yeats and the novel

Claire Connolly

> Long ago, before the earliest stone of the pyramids was laid, before the Bo tree of Buddha unrolled its first leaf, before a Japanese had painted on a temple wall the horse that every evening descended and trampled the ricefields, before the ravens of Thor had eaten their first worm together, there lived a man of giant stature and strength named Dhoya.

So begins W.B. Yeats's strange short fiction *Dhoya,* published in 1891 alongside his novel *John Sherman* under the pseudonym 'Ganconagh'. Yeats uses the craft of Japanese painting to figure a remote past and to prepare readers for an occult world in which a young mortal man grows to be a giant and falls in love with a fairy. Alongside the pyramids of Egypt and a legendary warrior from Germanic mythology, Japanese art helps to give shape to Yeats's fantastic plot. Together, these disparate images create what Yeats would later call a 'phantasmagoria': an obscure but powerful invocation of an ancient past that anchors his fiction in time and space.

The setting of Dhoya is the Bay of Ballah, set on the western shores of a mythological Ireland: a lightly disguised Sligo Bay. We find a further reference to Japan in the same volume, this time as part of Yeats's longer prose fiction *John Sherman*. An early description of the protagonist's home in the fictional west of Ireland town of Ballah (again, a fictionalised Sligo) describes the home Sherman shares with his mother in 'one of those bare houses so common in country towns'. Alongside heavy mahogany chairs 'with horsehair cushions worn at the corners' is a table:

> On the round table was somebody's commentary on the New Testament laid like the spokes of a wheel on a tablecover of American oilcloth with stamped Japanese figures worn half away.

Where *Dhoya* evokes ancient autochthonic accomplishments, *John Sherman* offers us an everyday commercial artefact, shabby from use. These two very different inscriptions of Japanese imagery can be seen to represent vital but opposing forces

The Quay, Sligo, Ireland, c. 1900–39. (*National Library of Ireland*)

in Yeats's thought: remote and auratic art forms on the one hand, and the mundane world in which the artist must move on the other. As phrased in 'The Choice':

> The intellect of man is forced to choose
> Perfection of the life, or of the work.
> And if it take the second must refuse
> A heavenly mansion, raging in the dark.

In 'A General Introduction to My Work', Yeats imagines the distinction between the life and the work via a contrast between prose fiction and poetry. In the account Yeats gives of the life of the poet, novels are the stuff of 'accidence' and 'incoherence', while it is poetry that possesses the power to knit experience into meaningful, passionate and archetypal patterns:

> A poet writes always of his personal life, in his finest work out of its tragedies, whatever it be, remorse, lost love or mere loneliness; he never speaks directly as to someone at the breakfast table, there is always a phantasmagoria. Dante and Milton had mythologies, Shakespeare the characters of English history, of traditional romance; even when the poet seems most himself, when he is Raleigh and gives potentates the lie, or Shelley 'a nerve o'er which do creep the else unfelt oppressions of mankind', or Byron when 'the heart wears out the breast as the sword wears out the sheath', he is never the bundle of accident and incoherence that sits down to breakfast; he has been reborn as an idea, something intended, complete. A novelist might describe his accidence, his incoherence, he must not, he is more type than man, more passion than type.
>
> (Yeats, *Collected Works,* vol. v, p. 204)

Yeats's description of the world of accidence, incoherence and breakfast seems to summons up Mrs Sherman's tablecloth. In the novel her 'tablecover of American oilcloth' is described as 'seldom used', adorning as it does a table in the drawing room where the rector's wife takes tea. When John Sherman eats breakfast in the house, he sits down to eggs boiled by his mother that sustain him through days spent reading, gardening and fishing; he longs, however, for a higher calling.

The novel as a whole can be read as John Sherman's quest to be 'reborn as an idea, something intended, complete'. That journey towards artistic selfhood may take its bearings from Japanese art and Germanic mythology, but it begins at breakfast, a routine event reimagined in terms of the everyday mystery of an oilcloth with 'stamped Japanese figures worn half away'. In what follows, I consider Yeats's achievements in writing a poetic prose that makes 'a phantasmagoria' of real and imagined places, connected to one another via water.

John Sherman

The beginnings of *John Sherman* lie in the encouragement given to Yeats by his father 'to write something which would reflect real life'. As R.F. Foster remarks, however, 'the author's voice was still uncertain: ironic social and psychological observation alternates uneasily with romantic introspection' (Foster, I, p. 68). Uneasiness is manifest in the book's plot, which sees John Sherman, a young man with powerful but undefined artistic ambitions, go to London as apprentice to his merchant uncle and try to learn the shipping trade. As Foster puts it, it is 'the Yeats/Pollexfen dichotomy which provided the theme of the book' even as 'Provincial Ireland is balanced against metropolitan London' (I, p. 111).

John Sherman concerns a search for artistic and individual identity, expressed in highly self-conscious ways via a debate about the meanings of place. The novel opens 'in the west of Ireland, on the 9th December, in the town of Ballah, in the Imperial Hotel.' A visiting Protestant curate named William Howard finds himself 'in Ballah among the barbarians', and enjoys a pleasant sense of superiority over the inhabitants of 'this half-deserted town': 'Here everybody lives in the eighteenth century – the squalid century! Well I am going tomorrow you know. Thank Heavens I am done with your grey streets and grey minds!' (p. 8). Accused by the curate of 'vegetating' in this provincial west-of-Ireland town, Yeats's protagonist, the young John Sherman, replies:

> No, I am seeing the world. In your big towns a man finds his minority and knows nothing outside its border. He knows only the people like himself. But here one chats with the whole world in a day's walk, for

Market Street, Sligo, Ireland, *c*. 1890–9. (*National Library of Ireland*)

> every man one meets is a class. The knowledge I am picking up may be useful to me when I enter the great cities and their ignorance.
>
> (p. 9)

Sherman's sense that 'every man one meets is a class' in the west of Ireland resonates with John Millington Synge's observations regarding 'the absence of any division of labour' on the Aran Islands and 'the correspondingly wide development of each individual, whose varied knowledge and skill necessitates a considerably activity of mind'.

The great Yeatsian critic T.R. Henn wondered if

> Perhaps, also, to understand fully these poems one needs to have been born and bred in one of the western Irish towns; to remember how it was the centre of your world, how the mountains and river and the woods become a portion of your life forever; to have loved with a sense of possession even the roadside bushes where the cotters hung their clothes to dry. That sense of possession was the very centre of the matter.
>
> (p. 78)

W.B. Yeats (photogravure), by Alvin Langdon Coburn (1882–1966). (*National Portrait Gallery Collection, Smithsonian Institution*)

John Sherman counters such a case in the character of the self-satisfied Anglican curate. Howard is a cosmopolitan who has 'read much, seen operas and plays, known religious experiences and written verse to a waterfall in Switzerland' (p. 7). He regards Sherman as a 'mercenary' young man who, living only in a small town dominated by 'facts', fails to take nature for his 'compass' (p. 9). Where Howard looks over the bridge at the river and imagines it bound to his own consciousness by a 'web of thoughts' ('Some meaning sure it must have'), John Sherman stands on the bridge and baits his fishing hooks. Howard's easy praise for the charms of the place ('this beautiful river, these stars, these great purple shadows') is answered only by Sherman's purposeful setting of his lines. The novel teases out a distinction between the Englishman Howard's shallow admiration for Swiss waterfalls versus Sherman's deep knowledge of his own west-of-Ireland place. Yeats referred to the novel as 'this Sligo story' in a letter to Augusta Gregory in 1901 (Foster I, p. 111), while the river in which Sherman fishes arises in a lough with an island called Inniscrewin, the name of which Yeats changed in his *Collected Works* to Innisfree.

The conversation ends with Sherman turning from abstract talk of nature to the simple act of baiting his hooks. When John Sherman introduces the act of fishing, it is in relationship to his home town:

> 'You need some occupation peculiar to the place,' said the other, baiting his hooks with worms out of the little porringer. 'I catch eels. You should set some night-lines too. You bait them with worms in this way, and put them along the weeds at the edge of the river. In the morning you find an eel or two, if you have good fortune, turning round and round and making the weeds sway. I shall catch a great deal after this rain.'
>
> (p. 8)

While the curate stares intently at the water, spinning a web of connections from the water to himself – 'Some meaning must it have' he thinks – John Sherman is content to fish. The association of fishing with a slow-paced, immersive and authentic relationship to place is familiar from Yeats's later great poem 'The Fisherman', published alongside 'September 1913' in the 1914 collection *Responsibilities*, and echoed in its turn by 'Casualty', Seamus Heaney's elegy for his eel-fishing friend

Louis O'Neill. A century earlier, Thomas Moore's poem 'Let Erin Remember the Days of Old' also invokes the figure of the fisherman in relation to place and past:

> On Lough Neagh's bank, as the fisherman strays,
> When the clear, cold eve's declining,
> He sees the round towers of other days
> In the wave beneath him, shining.

George Bernard Shaw disliked Moore's lines for their problematically romantic politics and wrote a memorable parody: 'Let the fisherman who strays on Lough Neagh's bank when the clear cold eve's declining be thrown into it. And then Ireland will have a chance at last' (p. 8).

Shaw may have distrusted Moore's easy invocation of past glories, but there are reasons to give close consideration to the ways in which Yeats directs our attention to the flow of the water. Towards the end of *A Vision,* in the section entitled 'Gates of Pluto', Yeats speculates, with reference to fishing once more, on the relationship between lived experience and abstraction:

> Much of this book is abstract, because it has not yet been lived, for no man can dip into life more than a moiety of any system. When a child, I went out with herring fishers one dark night, and the dropping of their nets into the luminous sea and the drawing of them up has remained with me as a dominant image. Have I found a good net for a herring fisher?
>
> (Yeats, *Collected Works* XIII, p. 206)

Referring to 'Yeats's system of contraries', Eve Patten argues that *John Sherman* contains the essences of division and quarrel, and of the 'contemplative spirit that can master them' (Patten). She compares the opening of *John Sherman* to *A Vision*, with Sherman and Howard prefiguring the dialogue between Owen Aherne and Michael Robartes, or Will and Mask (Patten).

In the novel the protagonist John Sherman has a rough passage over what his mother calls the 'uneasy water' that separates London from Ballah. He leaves Ballah by sea, sailing on a cattle ship, the SS *Lavinia*, via Tory Island, for London, where he finds work as a clerk in his uncle's shipping firm. There, he courts but finally resigns the affection of a young woman, Margaret Leland, who eventually marries the self-absorbed curate, Howard. Midway through the novel, John Sherman makes a journey home, arriving in Ballah by rail, having connected from Euston via Holyhead and Dublin. On this occasion he tells his childhood friend that Mary Carton is to be married and returns to London. There, however, he remains dissatisfied. Sherman finally returns to Ballah, where he is first rejected, then accepted, by Mary.

John Sherman is not simply a book that contrasts Sligo and London but also one that gives consideration to the experience of being between places. This aspect of the book is most notable in its depiction of John Sherman's travels on the Irish Sea. Crossing to Liverpool on a 'cattle boat', on which his mother has insisted that they must travel in order to save money, she suffers below while he is 'pretty happy on deck'. There, John Sherman listens to squealing pigs and has to sit in close proximity to an old woman and the geese she is bringing to market in Liverpool. On other sea journeys Sherman watches gannets striking the water and porpoises gleaming in the sun. Sherman's own state of suffering is realised in close relation to the human and non-human environment that surrounds him, and he writes a letter describing his 'desolation' as he watches puffins sleeping on the waves: 'each one of them had its head tucked in a slightly different way. "That is because their characters are different," he thought.'

On his final return to his homeplace, Sherman travels again on the SS *Lavinia*, this time, because on the return journey, with 'no cattle but many passengers'. On board ship Sherman engages in close observation of his fellow passengers: restive cattle dealers, a consumptive clerk from Liverpool, a nervous governess with her luggage heaped around her. Sherman subjects these human figures to his scrutiny, just as when on the first journey east he had contemplated the characters of puffins sleeping on the waves. The narrative describes the boat's journey via the north-western islands of Tory and Rathlin, with some care, noting how the Donegal cliffs come into view. We might note here that 'The Speckled Bird', an unpublished autobiographical prose fiction that exists in outlines and variant versions written by Yeats between 1896 and 1902, began when the publisher A.H. Bullen gave Yeats advance royalties of £2 a week and some travel expenses for him to write a 'long novel' about Tory Island.

When Mary Carton finally accepts Sherman in what Foster calls '[t]he book's hasty but striking finale' (I, p. 68), we are reminded that this is a novel that is

Knocknarea, County Sligo, Ireland. (*Leo Swan – The Discovery Programme, Ireland*)

highly unstable in tone: almost as if narrative itself mirrors Sherman's ascent of Knocknarea before his return to Mary and his anxious pacing along the 'gritty and barren roads' of home. Just as Sherman's movements are attuned to the material conditions of life on Irish roads, boats and trains, so the natural world also shapes his journeys. Reflecting on his own passage at a crucial point in his London time, Sherman decides that 'I am not going forward; I am at present trying to go sideways like the crab.' The novel is unusually detailed in its depictions of passage over water and even in its attention to aspects of marine life. It reminds us that the younger Yeats was an avid reader of Charles Darwin and Alfred Russell Wallace, and recalled in *Autobiographies* that his 'favourite book' as a boy was 'a small green-covered book given to my father by a Dublin man of science; it gave an account of the strange sea creatures the man of science had discovered among the rocks at Howth or dredged out of Dublin Bay' (Yeats, *Collected Works* III, p. 59).

John Sherman seems to strive for an ethical relationship to place in its fullest sense: an environment that has emerged over time, and where 'the whole world' includes non-human as well as human others. When John Sherman first visits Mary Carton's schoolhouse (following the mysterious guidance offered by a beetle in his garden), they sit watching a mouse carrying away a crumb. His time as a shipping clerk seems largely spent absorbed in the activity of inspecting the movement of fourteen flies on the ceiling of his office. Meanwhile, he gardens: in Sligo, we encounter John Sherman checking his tulip shoots, forcing sea kale, and sorting seeds; while in London he tackles dock leaves, dandelions and 'patches of untimely grass'.

Lonely in London, John Sherman finds himself considering his own artistic past, as preserved by his fond mother. As he ponders practical questions of artistic education, John Sherman's mind turns to home and to the memory of the cruelty of a peasant child towards a dog. The prose sequence is beautifully arranged:

> Round the walls were one or two drawings, done by him at school. His mother had got them framed. His eyes were fixed on a drawing of a stream and some astonishing cows.
>
> A few days ago he had found an old sketch book for children among some forgotten papers, which taught how to draw a horse by making three ovals for the basis of his body, one lying down in the middle, two standing up at each end for flank and chest, and how to draw a cow by basing its body on a square. He kept trying to fit squares into the cows. He was half inclined to take them out of their frames and retouch on this new principle. Then he began somehow to remember the child with the swollen face who threw a stone at the dog the day he decided to leave home.

For John Sherman the problem of how to represent animals is connected to the issue of how to treat them: together, these issues help to bolster the ethically informed relationship to place that culminates in a return to Ballah and marriage to Mary Carton.

The question of where and how to live is closely connected with Sherman's journeys on the Irish Sea, just as the journey towards personal and artistic fulfilment in the novel is often realised in terms of uncertain boundaries between water and land. T.R. Henn remembers Jack Yeats's discussion of the way in which Sligo's Garavogue River makes its brief journey from Lough Gill through Sligo town before discharging into the Atlantic:

> It was Jack Yeats, the painter, who told me of an ancient piece of myth: that where a great mass of water meets the sea by way of a short river, a kind of magic is generated and spread upon the whole neighbourhood.
>
> (Henn, p. 77)

Part of the magic generated by *John Sherman* is to bring into view the question of Ireland's oceanic identity. In *Dhoya*, 'the faint murmurs of the western sea' determine the lives of its fated protagonists. Rather than simply offering contrasting accounts of provincial Ireland and metropolitan London, *John Sherman* offers a remarkable instance of the inscription of Ireland's oceanic identity in literature. The novel frames its depiction of the search for artistic selfhood in ways that seem to call for a fuller understanding of Ireland's relationship to its coastline and the seas that surround the island. In its opening evocation of homeland experienced beside a Sligo river and through its strange scenes of homesickness at sea, the short novel imagines an ethical relationship to place in its fullest sense: as an environment that has emerged over time, made up of non-human as well as human subjects.

In London, Sherman follows pathways along the edge of the Thames and thinks of Sligo, like London, a settlement shaped by an estuarine relationship between river and sea. In one remarkable prose sequence, *John Sherman* revisits and rewrites Yeats's poem of 1888, 'The Lake Isle of Innisfree':

> He was set dreaming a whole day by walking down one Sunday morning to the border of the Thames – a few hundred yards from his house – and looking at the osier-covered Chiswick eyot. It made him remember an old day-dream of his. The source of the river that passed his garden at home was a certain wood-bordered and islanded lake, whither in childhood he had often gone blackberry-gathering. At the further end was a little islet called Inniscrewin. Its rocky centre, covered with many bushes, rose some forty feet above the lake. Often when life and its difficulties had seemed to him like the lessons of some elder boy given to a younger by mistake, it had seemed good to dream of going away to that islet and building a wooden hut there and burning a few years out, rowing to and fro, fishing, or lying on the island slopes by day, and listening at night to the ripple

> of the water and the quivering of the bushes – full always of unknown creatures – and going out at morning to see the island's edge marked by the feet of birds.

The Chiswick eyot (the latter an Old English term for an islet) is a small, narrow, uninhabited island in the River Thames. Its covering of osier, a type of willow used to weave baskets, suggests the wattles of 'The Lake Isle of Innisfree', while the wooden hut in which the hero might live even more clearly echoes Yeats's famous poem. Rather than an imagined journey from 'the pavements grey' of London to a lonely island in Lough Gill, however, the transition undertaken by *John Sherman* is from one abandoned waterway to another.

Seen from boats, bridges and quays, Ballah is a place pervaded by water. When the curate first leaves his hotel in *John Sherman* and walks to the bridge (past the fish market), the entire town seems waterlogged – soggy with rain that promises well for John Sherman's eel trapping:

> The town was dripping, but the rain was almost over. It was the hour of ducks. Three or four had squeezed themselves under a gate, and were now splashing about in the gutter of the main street.

When Mary finally accepts John Sherman, it is as a fellow castaway: she says, 'We have been shipwrecked. Our goods have been cast into the sea.' As London becomes 'a reef' upon which his protagonist is cast away, the oceanic identity of Britain's imperial capital comes into view.

The references to Japan in *John Sherman* and *Dhoya* with which I opened may be accidental, but they are not incoherent. Both prose fictions express Yeats's yearning for new forms that must find expression within 'the indifferent world'. Rather than suggesting the tensions between art and environment, however, the novel seems to seek out the lineaments of a fuller world, one defined by its proximity to water. Both the cave of the Japanese painter and the drawing room of John Sherman's mother are realised within prose fictions whose every turn of plot depends on the movement of lake, river and sea, and whose narratives cross and connect human and non-human alongside environmental and cultural histories.

Bibliography

Foster, R.F., *W.B. Yeats: A life* (Oxford: Oxford University Press, 1997).

Henn, T.R., 'The Place of Shells', *Yeats, Sligo and Ireland: Essays to mark the 21st Yeats International Summer School*, ed. A. Norman Jeffares (Totowa, NJ: Barnes & Noble Books, 1980). pp. 73–88.

Shaw, George Bernard, 'On Throwing Out Dirty Water', *Irish Statesman*, vol. 1, no. 1, 15 September 1923, pp. 8–9.

Yeats, W.B., *Autobiographies: The collected works of W.B. Yeats*, vol. 3, ed. William H. O'Donnell and Douglas N. Archibald (New York: Scribner, 1990).

——, 'Introduction (1937) for the never-published Charles Scribner's Sons' 'Dublin Edition' of 'W.B. Yeats'; published in *Essays and Introductions* (1961) as 'A General Introduction for My Work', *The Collected Works of W.B. Yeats,* vol. 5, ed. William H. Donnell (New York: Scribner, 1994), pp. 204–16.

——, *A Vision: The original 1925 version. The collected works of W.B. Yeats*, vol. 13, ed. Catherine E. Paul and Margaret Mills Harper (New York: Scribner, 2008).

——, *The Collected Works of W.B. Yeats. Vol. 1: The poems*, ed. Richard J. Finneran (Scribner: New York, 1997).

'Distinguished, indirect and symbolic': Yeats and the Noh

Shaun Richards

In his 'Introduction' to *Certain Noble Plays of Japan* (1916), edited by Ezra Pound from the translations and notes by Ernest Fenollosa, W.B. Yeats said that, helped by the four *Noh* plays in the collection (*Nishikigi*, *Hagoromo*, *Kumasaka* and *Kagekiyo*), he had 'invented a form of drama, distinguished, indirect and symbolic and having no need of mob or press to pay its way – an aristocratic form'. This was opposed to realism, 'created for the common people … without the memory of beauty and emotional subtlety.'[1] The rejection of realist theatre in favour of a subtle and symbolic one was already an established theme in Yeats's work. In 1893, he attended the first London production of Ibsen's *A Doll's House,* and in 'The Tragic Generation' (1922) recalled how he had 'hated the play', especially resenting the dialogue, which reproduced modern educated speech so closely that there was no music and style. Indeed, in 'The Reform of the Theatre' (1903) he concluded that 'the theatre must be reformed in its plays, its speaking, its acting, and its scenery. That is to say, I think there is nothing good about it at present.' Given these feelings about the debased state of contemporary theatre, he came to believe that, as he wrote in 'The People's Theatre' (1919), the poetic theatre he desired was not possible unless he excluded 'the artisan and small shopkeeper' in favour of 'leisured and lettered people' who would be more receptive to his 'mysterious art'.

Although Yeats had succeeded, with Lady Gregory and J.M. Synge, in establishing the Abbey Theatre, Dublin, in 1904, by 1910 he gave vent to his frustration with the theatre in 'The Fascination of What's Difficult':

> My curse on plays
> That have to be set up in fifty ways,
> On the day's war with every knave and dolt,
> Theatre business, management of men.
> I swear before the dawn comes round again
> I'll find the stable and pull out the bolt.

Apart from the stress of dealing with 'every knave and dolt', the success of the Abbey was, as he wrote to Lady Gregory in 1919, 'a discouragement and a defeat' in that it was founded on the prosaic art of realism and attracted what he regarded as an undiscerning, popular audience. *Noh*, however, as described by Ezra Pound in *The Classic Noh Theatre of Japan* (1916), was a theatre 'of allusion, or the love of allusion … made for the few; for the nobles; for those trained to catch the allusion.'

This chapter will examine the development of Yeats's interest in *Noh*, reading his *Noh*-inspired *Four Plays for Dancers* (*At the Hawk's Well* (1916); *The Only Jealousy of Emer* (1919); *The Dreaming of the Bones* (1919) and *Calvary* (1921)) as the culmination of his belief in a poetic drama that had been evolving even prior to his encounter with symbolist theatre during his sojourns in Paris in the 1890s. Yeats came to *Noh* frustrated by the perceived failure of his own ambitions for a poetic theatre and, as argued by Daniel Albright, 'The Noh … as far as Yeats is concerned is less a Japanese invention than a distant echo of what the Irish national theatre ought to be.'[2] It was, as Yeats said in the 'Introduction', 'natural that I go to Asia for a stage-convention' for he had already formulated a theory of theatre for which he sought confirmation. In this he was not unlike Antonin Artaud, for whom a performance by Balinese dancers in Paris in 1931 crystallised his concept of the Theatre of Cruelty, whose First Manifesto was published in 1932; or Bertolt Brecht, whose meeting with the Chinese actor Mei Lan-Fang in Moscow during

1935 informed his essay 'Alienation Effect in Chinese Acting', which was written in the following year. Yeats, like them, 'was already armed with a formulated theory and a synthesising concept, and did not rest content with a description of what met his eye; he was eager to interpret what he saw in the interests of his own theory'.[3]

It is clear that Yeats admired Japanese art well before his reading of the works of Pound and Fenollosa. In 'A Symbolical Drama in Paris' (1894) he placed his recollection of a Japanese picture of cranes flying through a blue sky at the head of the hierarchy of works that were his references for artistic quality. In 1904, he wrote to Lady Gregory rejecting a stage wing designed by her son Robert, saying that the kind of thing he wanted was the type of tree found in Japanese prints. He declared in 'The Theatre of Beauty' (1911) that, as he was a writer of poetic drama and tragic drama, he wanted to keep to symbolism and pattern like the Japanese. And in his 'Introduction' of 1916 he noted that some of the plays included by Pound reminded him of a Japanese screen painting he had seen at the British Museum.

Yeats was not alone in his *Japonisme,* the term coined in 1872 by French art critic Philippe Burty to describe the interest in the culture that, from the 1870s to the 1920s, influenced the arts in London and Paris. As R.F. Foster notes:

> *Noh* theatre was being performed in London in the mid 1870s and discussed in *The Times* by the 1890s ... Symons, always attuned to the current vogue, had some time ago led him to the Japanese prints in the British Museum, which strongly influenced WBY's notions of stage-settings. He knew Binyon's commentaries on Japanese art by 1909, and long before his *Savoy* days, had met Osman Edwards, who published on Noh drama in 1901. In the Spring of 1914 Yone Noguchi had lectured on Noh theatre in London.[4]

Noguchi, who had known Yeats since 1903, advanced arguments in favour of *Noh* that anticipated Yeats's own views, particularly in terms of its refutation of the tenets of realist drama, stating in *The Spirit of Japanese Poetry* (1911) that it would be ideal if *Noh* drama could be introduced to the West as it would be not only a protest against the norms of the Western stage but it would also stand as an example for those people, such as Yeats, who were disillusioned with contemporary theatre practice. While Yeats was then inspired by *Noh* theatre, it was in a context

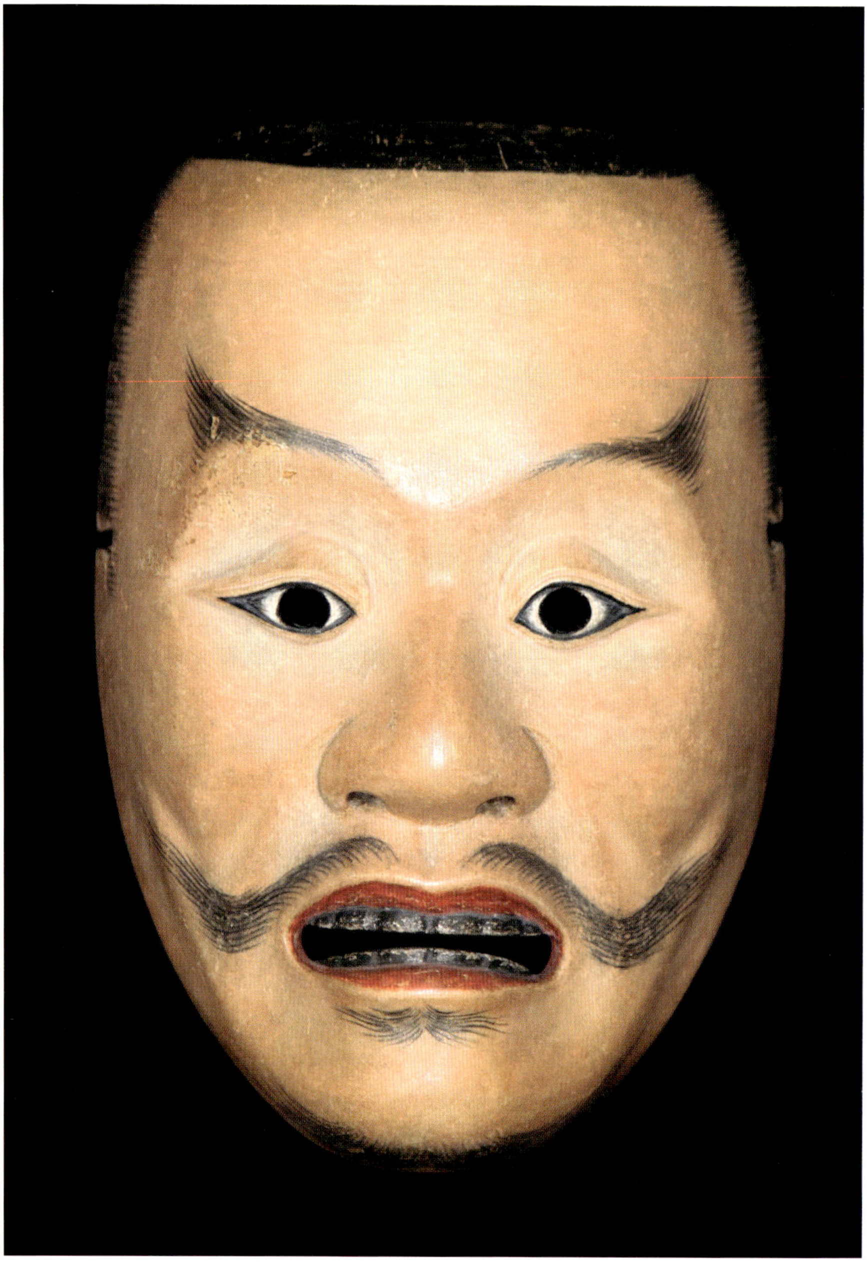

Noh mask. (*Photo courtesy of the author*)

in which Japanese culture was already influential in the artistic circles in which he moved and, as R.F. Foster observes, it was Yeats's friend and mentor Arthur Symons who introduced him to the prints in the British Museum, which he recalled in his 'Introduction' to *Certain Noble Plays of Japan.*

Symons was also instrumental in providing Yeats with an entrée to the European avant-garde. In 1894, the two men attended the premiere in Paris of Villiers de l'Isle-Adam's symbolist drama *Axel*, 'behind which', said Yeats, 'glimmered a spiritual and passionate mood, as the lamp glimmers behind the dusky blue and red glass in an Eastern lamp'. Symons also introduced Yeats to the drama of Maurice Maeterlinck, which, for Yeats, revealed 'truths come out of a solitary and mysterious ideal' revolving around 'invisible and impalpable things'. As Maeterlinck wrote in his essay 'The Tragical and Daily Life',

> I have grown to believe that an old man, seated in his armchair, watching patiently, with his lamp beside him, giving unconscious ear to all the eternal laws that reign about his house ... does live in reality a more human and more universal life than the lover who strangles his mistress, the captain who conquers in battle, or 'the husband who avenges his honor'.[5]

The aim of this 'static drama', as Symons observed in 'Maeterlinck as a Mystic', 'is not only to render the soul and the soul's atmosphere, but to reveal the strangeness, pity, and beauty through beautiful poetics'.[6] *The Symbolist Movement in Literature* (1899), the collection in which the essay appeared, was dedicated to Yeats as the chief representative of symbolism in the country, for it is clear that exposure to the theatre in Paris refined Yeats's orientation towards the symbolic, esoteric drama he later found in *Noh*. Indeed, as he noted in his 'Introduction' to *Certain Noble Plays of Japan*, he had already 'simplified scenery' in *The Hour Glass* (1903), playing initially in front of green curtains before setting the play among the ivory-coloured screens that had been invented by Gordon Craig. That production was in 1911, when Craig had become a major influence on Yeats's theatrical imagination – one that, however, only directed him ever more certainly towards *Noh*.

In 1900, Craig had attended a performance in London of the company run by Kawakami Otojirō, which toured Europe in this period and added to the fascination with Japanese culture. Although its repertoire was a hybrid form that mingled aspects of Western theatre with Kabuki rather than *Noh*, it did introduce Craig to the Japanese use of colour as an expression of emotion and character, and *The Mask*, the journal he founded in 1908 'to change the whole theatre', contained significant articles and reviews on Japanese art and drama, especially *Noh*, which Craig described in 1910 as offering 'supreme examples of brevity and fine tradition'. Yeats's objective, as he stated in 1902, was to reduce the visual and gestural importance of theatre in order 'to restore words to their sovereignty'. Craig's concern, however, as he outlined in 'The Art of the Stage, the First Dialogue' (1905), was that the theatre should harmonise scene, costumes, verse, prose and the theme of the play, stressing that audiences 'flock to *see*, not to hear, plays'. But these apparently divergent views were more a question of emphasis than opposition. Yeats had anticipated Craig's position on the harmony of all the elements in a work of art, declaring in 'The Symbolism of Poetry' (1900) that the ideal was to harmonise the relations between sound, colour and form so that they were able to 'evoke an emotion that is made out of their distinct evocations and yet is one emotion'. This impulse towards an intense crystallisation of artistic experience also accords with Pound's definition of the image in 1913 as 'an intellectual and emotional complex in an instant of time'. United in their rejection of superfluity in expression, the three men looked to *Noh* as a living embodiment of the form of art to which they aspired. Above all, Yeats and Craig were opposed to the commercial theatre of realism, and as Arthur Symons observed in his essay, 'A New Art of Theatre', 'The whole art of Mr Craig is a protest against realism, and it is to realism that we owe whatever is most conspicuously bad in the mounting of plays in the present day.'[7]

Undoubtedly, Craig was a major influence on Yeats as he moved to a more complex modernist technique, and at the time he was collaborating with Craig on the production of *The Hour Glass*, Yeats published 'The Tragic Theatre' in which he outlined a conception of theatre that anticipated his *Noh*-inspired work: 'If we could give our theatre the dignity of a church … we must have a scene where there is no realism, no objects represented in mass. We shall have made possible once more a noble, capricious, extravagant, resonant, fantastic art.' The article appeared in *The Mask* in 1910, and the influence of Craig on Yeats' thinking at this time is made evident in the fact that all that summer Yeats had been absorbed in playing with a model stage set that allowed him to experiment with various scenes. The miniature set had been provided by Craig, and it propelled Yeats to think beyond the proscenium arch stage and an audience's expectation of a realist set. Moreover, the screens that Craig devised for *The Hour Glass* were folded and unfolded on stage in front of the audience, a concept that Yeats adapted in all the *Four Plays for Dancers*, which open and close with the unfolding and refolding of a cloth. In addition to the screens, Craig also designed masks for the Fool and the Blind Man in *The Hour Glass*, which so delighted Yeats that he told Lady Gregory that he would like the Abbey to be the first modern theatre to use masks. Masks were a staple element in *Noh* and were already part of the symbolist aesthetic. In 'The Truth of Masks' (1891) Oscar Wilde elevated the mask to a metaphysical realm of 'truth'. In his 'A Note on Masks' (1910) Craig asserted that masks were an integral part of a drama that 'takes us beyond reality'. The mask, then, only added to Yeats's commitment to a ritualistic style of performance that eschewed the transitory social concerns of realism and engaged instead with the timeless and the universal. When Yeats was then introduced to the *Noh* plays by Pound in 1913, he responded to a form that seemed to embody his own theatrical ideals as they had been progressively refined through his exposure to symbolist theatre and work with Craig on the 1911 production of *The Hour Glass*.

The collaboration with Craig and the evolving interest in masks was followed by the period Yeats spent with Ezra Pound at Stone Cottage, Sussex, in the winters of 1913 to 1916, when he engaged with Pound's editing of Fenollosa's translations of *Noh*. However, while Yeats was attracted to *Noh* by the time of this encounter, it was not enough to move his interest from theory to practice. As Yeats acknowledged, it was in seeing Michio Itow dance in London that he glimpsed the possibility of producing a *Noh*-style play of his own. Yeats and Pound saw Itow dance at Lady Cunard's in 1915, and Yeats began writing *At the Hawk's Well* in the winter of that year; by 4 February 1916 he had decided on an appropriate form, and on 16 February he started to plan its production. This took place in the drawing room of Lady Cunard's London home on 4 April 1916, with Itow dancing the part of the Guardian of the Well.

The irony was that Itow was antipathetic to *Noh*, not trained in its rigorous discipline, having initially left Japan for Paris to study opera. There he was inspired by seeing Nijinksy and the Ballet Russe in 1911, and moved to Germany to train in dance with Émile Jaques-Dalcroze. The advantage, however, was that Itow was sympathetic to the symbolist impulses of the European avant-garde, and contributed that sensibility to Yeats's production uninhibited by adherence to any pure sense of *Noh* performance. This has contributed to a critical view as to Yeats's flawed conception of *Noh* and the subsequent failure of his plays. Richard Taylor's *The Drama of W.B. Yeats: Irish myth and the Japanese No* (1976) asserts that the work of Pound on which Yeats based his drama was arbitrary, almost haphazard, and misleading, while In *Yeats and the Noh* (1990) Masaru Sekine and Christopher Murray conclude that the plays were an heroic failure.

However, this is to assume that Yeats wanted to produce *Noh* plays rather than create a *Noh*-style theatre. As he stated in his 'Introduction' of 1916, he had 'invented a form of drama' but never claimed that the plays were *Noh*. Rather, all *Four Plays for Dancers* are in a *Noh* style as defined by Yeats, having a chorus, music, masks and dance in dramas that focus on moments of extreme emotion. The storyline of *At The Hawk's Well* is derived from the *Noh* play *Yoro*, and that of *The Dreaming of the Bones* on *Nishikigi*, albeit with significant non-Japanese amendments, and while both plays were worked on by Pound, only the latter was included in *Certain Noble Plays of Japan*. But these adaptations of the plays were only part of Yeats's objective. As he wrote in the notes to *At the Hawk's Well*, he had found his 'first model' for a theatre where 'a room full of people share the one lofty emotion' in 'the "Noh" stage of Japan'. It was, then, as a model for a theatre rather than strictly as a style of drama that Yeats turned to *Noh*, although clearly the formal elements of plays cannot be entirely disassociated from the place in which they are to be performed.

'We should distrust bodily distance', Yeats declared in his 'Introduction', arguing that it was only through proximity to Itow's performance in all its 'separating strangeness' that audiences could enter 'the deep of the mind' and become aware of 'some more powerful life', a realisation of Yeats's ideal of theatre as capable of transcending mortality and the mundane. This physical proximity to the performance was clearly the opposite of the distance between stage and auditorium in the conventional theatre, while the 'separating strangeness' reversed normal expectation of empathy and identification between audience and actor/character. These radical changes were to be achieved by ritual, stylisation, music and the formalisation of the dance. Accordingly, as noted in the stage direction for *At the Hawk's Well*, 'The stage is any bare space before a wall against which stands a patterned screen', while the lighting is that which 'we are most accustomed

A *Kabuki* actor, c. 1890–1909, hand-coloured albumen print. (*New York Public Library*)

to in our rooms'. The instructions are similar for the other three plays: in *The Dreaming of the Bones* 'The stage is any bare place in a room close to the wall', for *The Only Jealousy of Emer* 'the stage as before can be against the wall of any room', while *Calvary* adds that it is a 'bare place, round three sides of which the audience are seated'. Yeats noted that *At the Hawk's Well* 'was played upon the floor, and the players came in through the same door as the audience', for this absence of a formal stage meant that the same space was occupied by both actors and audience, and they, referred to by Yeats as comprising only 'fifty people', are consequently in the required 'distanced intimacy' with the performance's 'separating strangeness', for 'These masked players seem stranger when there is no mechanical means of separating them from us.'

Yeats went into the first performance of *At the Hawk's Well* in a buoyant mood, writing to his friend and patron, the New York lawyer John Quinn, that he was 'as lucky as a Japanese dramatic poet at the Court of the Shogun' with the privacy from press intrusion and lack of commercial constraints with which the play was to be performed. And his hopes were apparently fulfilled as he commented in his notes for the play that 'the audience and the players and I myself were pleased'. However, he was less content when it was performed just two days later in 'Lady Islington's big drawing room at Chesterfield Gardens', as he commented that 'my muses were but half welcome'. The reason would appear to be that the ideal conditions of audience proximity to performance were not met. 'None of my friends were there', Yeats said, meaning it was not the invited audience of fifty that had gathered for the first production. Moreover, it was performed on a 'platform', around three sides of which 'were three hundred people including Queen Alexandra'. In addition to the queen, Princess Victoria, Grand Duchess George of Russia, the Princess of Monaco, the Ranee of Sarawk, the Duchess of Marlborough and Lady Randolph Churchill were also present. In his 'Introduction' of 1916 Yeats wrote, 'I have written a little play that can be played in a room for so little money that forty or fifty readers of poetry can pay the price', but, as he noted, the drawing room at Lady Islington's was 'big' and the 300-strong audience 'fashionable', an elite in terms of their social position rather than their poetic sensibility.

If the ideal conditions for *At the Hawk's Well* had been found once, albeit for one performance only, the first productions of the other three plays indicate that performances in 'the bare space before a wall' were not to be achieved again. As

Yeats said in his notes for *Four Plays For Dancers*, *The Only Jealousy of Emer* was written for performance in 'a private house or studio', Yeats believing it 'unsuited to a public stage'. However, it was premiered 'on a public stage in Holland', which necessitated that Yeats 'retold the story in prose', which he 'tried to make very simple'. 'I do not say', he continued, 'that it is always necessary when one writes for a general audience to make the words of the dialogue so simple and so matter-of-fact; but it is where the appeal is mainly to the eye and to the ear through songs and music.' *The Dreaming of the Bones* received its premiere in a Sunday-night-only performance at the Abbey Theatre in December 1931, and while Yeats was pleased with the ceremonial movement in the performance, the conventional stage/auditorium spatial relationship in the theatre would not have permitted 'distanced intimacy'. *Calvary*, the last of the four plays to be written, was not staged in Yeats's life time. As he prophetically noted in the introduction to *Four Plays for Dancers*, 'In writing these little plays I knew that I was creating something which could only fully succeed in a civilisation very unlike ours.'

In his 'Introduction' to *Certain Noble Plays of Japan*, Yeats said, 'I have asked Mr. Pound for these beautiful plays because I think they will help me to explain a certain possibility of the Irish dramatic movement', but that possibility is yet to be realised, certainly as far as the National Theatre is concerned. *At the Hawk's Well* was last produced at the Abbey Theatre in 1989, *The Only Jealousy of Emer* in a one-night rehearsed reading in 2010, *The Dreaming of the Bones* in 1989, and *Calvary* in 1986, all in the 130-seat Peacock Stage rather than the larger auditorium. But as Richard Allen Cave commented on the Coca-Cola-sponsored Yeats cycle directed by James Flannery in 1989, which included *At the Hawk's Well* and *The Only Jealousy of Emer*, 'Yeats's writings on theatre and its practice demonstrate that he envisaged a dedication and a discipline akin to Graham's, Grotowski's and Wilson's as essential for the proper handling of his plays.' The inclusion of Yeats in a roll call of dance and drama innovators such as Martha Graham, Jerzy Grotowski and Robert Wilson testifies to the standing in which Cave held Yeats as a major figure in both European and American theatre. However, as he concluded,

> It was disheartening for anyone believing in Yeats's genius as a dramatist to read the reviews in the Dublin press the morning after the opening of the cycle, where the disappointment of critics generally expressed itself

> as a continuing doubt about the viability of the plays as theatre. The production failed, not because the plays are inherently poor but because Yeats's exact and exacting prescriptions for their performance were not met. Until they are, audiences have no right to condemn the playwright out of hand.[8]

In his *Irish Times* review of the cycle, Fintan O'Toole said that it was staged 'for coherence rather than concentration, for a longer, less passionate line of action, for something that is closer to narrative than to ritual'. The rejection of ritual, the essence of Yeats's conception of *Noh*, was further emphasised in that there were no masks. Moreover, a soft-rock-music score had replaced drum, gong and zither. This threatened at times to overwhelm the words, but, O'Toole observed, 'words are not primarily what this production is about' as this was Yeats for an audience more familiar with *Star Wars* and *Batman.*[9]

In *Noh: The classical theatre*, Yasuo Nakamura states that *Noh* acting is a family tradition in which 'a Noh actor begins the training of his own sons at about the age of seven' (*Noh* acting is an exclusively male preserve) after which 'he must continue and practice all his life'.[10] Such dedication is unlikely in a theatre tradition where realism of performance is the dominant concern, and in that respect even Yeats's *Noh*-styled plays are unlikely to be performed as Yeats required, let alone that theatres could survive with his non-commercial imperative that productions would cost 'so little money that forty or fifty readers of poetry can pay the price'. In his notes to *At the Hawk's Well*, Yeats declared 'I need a theatre … My blunder has been that I did not discover in my youth that my theatre must be the ancient theatre can be made by unrolling a carpet or marking out a place with a stick, or setting a screen against the wall'. That cry still resonates in an Irish theatre that, while less bound to realism than in the past, still has no place for a poetic, ritual drama of 'Beautiful, lofty things'.

A Comparative Reading of Yasunari Kawabata's *The Lake* (Mizuumi, 1955), James Joyce's *Ulysses* (1922) and George Moore's *The Lake* (1905)

Akemi Yoshida

Introduction

By reading *The Lake* (Mizuumi), a novella by Yasunari Kawabata (1899–1972), a Nobel Prize-winning Japanese novelist, alongside *Ulysses* by James Joyce (1882 1941) and *The Lake* by George Moore (1852–1933), this essay attempts to shed new light on the formative process of what is called Makai (literally, 'magical world' or 'demonic world'), a term Kawabata adopted from the words of Sōjun Ikkyu, a renowned Zen priest in the Muromachi period (Tomioka, p. 13), to characterise his own fictional world. 'To discuss Kawabata is to discuss Makai', Koichiro Tomioka says, and also 'the entire work of *The Lake* constitutes Makai' (p. 155, my translation). Kawabata's *The Lake* may be summarised as:

> a story of a perverted pursuer of beauty, in which a male protagonist,

> who has an inferiority complex because of his ugly, monkey-like feet, is driven by impulse to follow any beautiful woman he encounters, and which depicts not the transgression of moral or ethical laws but the magical power that lurks within minds that pine for beauty.
>
> (Tomioka, p. 13)[1]

Tomioka continues: "Makai is not merely the intangible mystery of the workings of the human mind; nor is it a psychological term referring to a subconscious "drive"' (p. 13).

Nevertheless, it seems to be an undeniable fact that among Kawabata's chief concerns in writing *The Lake* is the question of how to faithfully represent psychological reality. The narrative exposes to the reader's eye cruelly and crudely the stream of consciousness in the mind of the male protagonist, Gimpei Momoi, who is relentlessly driven by his sexual impulses. Events actually happening in the external world are interwoven with his subjective fancies. This narrative seems to presuppose that reality can only be represented by faithfully reflecting what is sensually and mentally perceived by a subject. I would argue that the influence of certain Irish writers plays a greater role than hitherto recognised in Kawabata's construction of the narrative. Specifically, I strongly suspect that Kawabata has borrowed some motifs from Joyce's *Ulysses*.

The influence of *Ulysses* on Kawabata has already been studied by critics such as Sharif Mebed and Kyoichi Kawaguchi. Early in his career, Kawabata was fascinated by Joyce's internal monologues and his daring approach to human psychology (Mebed 2003, p. 8). In 'The Crystalline Phantasmagoria' (Suisho-Genso, 1931), Kawabata imitates Molly's monologue in the 'Penelope' episode to describe the mind of his female protagonist, who is the wife of an embryologist.[2] In both *Ulysses* and 'The Crystal Phantasmagoria', the flow of associations that constitutes the stream of consciousness is triggered by verbal cues, and all the thought processes are verbalised in a conversational style, even though the monologues are ostensibly addressed to nobody but the speakers themselves. It seems as if all the internal thoughts are organised and woven into one linear form conveyable through language. James Joyce was not the inventor of this style: it was George Moore who introduced him to the interior monologues developed by the French writer

Kawabata Yasunar, 1968. (*Archive PL/ Alamy*)

Édouard Dujardin (Kawaguchi, p. 67), in whose *The Bays are Sere* (Les Lauriers sont coupés), all the unspoken thoughts and feelings inside the male protagonist's mind are verbalised.

Dujardin admittedly owes this prose style to Wagnerian operas, whose technique he defines as:

> the life of the soul expressed through the incessant emotion of musical motifs, coming up to speak, one after the other, undefined and in

George Moore, by Édouard Manet (1832–83), 1879. (*Classic Paintings/Alamy*)

> succession, the 'states' of thought, feeling, impressions, brought into existence … in no logical order, in the form of bursts of thought rising from the depth of the self, from what we today would call the unconscious or subconscious.
>
> (Dujardin, 'Interior Monologue', p. 135)

Accordingly, many of the episodes in *Ulysses*, written under the influence of *The Bays are Sere*, are characterised by the 'incessant' succession of thoughts and feelings bubbling up without any visibly logical order. The same could be said of Kawabata's *The Lake*.

In *The Lake*, however, Kawabata employs a different kind of stream of consciousness than the one used in 'The Crystalline Phantasmagoria' and *Ulysses*. In this novel, a third-person narrator faithfully conveys the movements and developments of images inside the male protagonist Gimpei Momoi's mind, without furnishing any authorial comment or moral judgement. While not all the inward thoughts, which may take the form of purely visual images, have necessarily to be verbalised in the mind of the protagonist, the third-person narrator translates these images into verbal descriptions for the reader. What strikes me is that the narrative style of Kawabata's *The Lake* bears an intriguing resemblance to the 'melodic line' adopted by George Moore in novels such as *The Lake*; and what is more, there are curious coincidences in the titles and in their symbolic meanings. Is it possible that Kawabata was aware of George Moore's work and paid homage to this Irish writer by adopting the same title? Though there is little evidence that Kawabata ever came into direct touch with this text, the resemblances are noticeable;[3] and even if Kawabata did not actually know Moore's work, a close comparison helps to show how these writers of different times and countries came to embrace similar views on novelistic narratives – possibly because they shared similar reading and thinking experiences.

On the other hand, even though Kawabata differs from Joyce in the narrative method he adopts for *The Lake*, there are resonances of *Ulysses* both in its plot and in its characters. In this essay, I will first elucidate these similarities and then focus attention on the affinities between Kawabata's *The Lake* and Moore's work of the same title.

I. Magical Magnetism between the temptress and the tempted: the 'Nausicaa' episode of *Ulysses* and Kawabata's *The Lake*

As the back cover of the Shincho Bunko edition of Kawabata's *The Lake* says, the male protagonist Gimpei Momoi is 'what is called a "stalker" in modern terms'. Obsessed with the distorted, ugly toes he has inherited from his father, and seeing them as a sign of his own abnormal sexuality, Gimpei is also endowed with an aesthetic sensibility especially susceptible to feminine beauty. When fascinated by a beautiful stranger, Gimpei, as if hypnotised, loses control and follows her almost unconsciously. In the passage quoted below, he follows Machie, a girl of 'miraculous sensuality' he has seen for the first time (p. 90, my translation), along a deserted street:

> This time also, there was only one pedestrian, a girl who was pulling a Shiba Inu dog walking up the slope. No, there was another one, Gimpei Momoi, who was following that girl. Yet, since Gimpei was so totally enamoured of the girl as to lose any sense of himself, it is questionable if he counted as one.[4]

I conjecture that Kawabata here intentionally lets his protagonist commit the deeds which Leopold Bloom in *Ulysses* imagines but never dares to carry out. In the 'Calypso' episode of *Ulysses*, Bloom impatiently waits for the butcher to process his order, secretly desiring to chase after the attractive female customer before him if she walks slowly enough to allow him to do so (4: 171–2). And the illicit relationship between Gimpei and Hisako in Kawabata's *The Lake* is comparable to the clandestine, nonverbal erotic communion between Leopold Bloom and Gerty MacDowell in the 'Nausicaa' episode of *Ulysses*; furthermore, it can be argued that Kawabata gives the characteristics of Gerty to the three female characters stalked by Gimpei – Hisako, Miyako and Machie – and also to Gimpei himself.

In the 'Nausicaa' episode, Gerty and Bloom, without exchanging a word, succeed in communicating their mutual sexual attraction by various nonverbal signs. The defective leg of Gerty, whom Bloom calls 'that little limpy devil' (13: 851–2), seems to have inspired the ugly distortion of Gimpei's toes. Irmela Hijiya-Kirschnerect has argued that in the literary world of Kawabata, 'beautiful and able-bodied characters are counterposed to those who are defected, diseased, or handicapped and who evoke disgust, antipathy, corruption, or foreshadowings of death' (p. 167, my translation), but in *The Lake*, the defected and the beautiful are simultaneously opposed to and connected with each other. The ugliness of Gimpei's toes seems to be the very reason why he appreciates beauty in others, as if he were seeking to compensate for his own inherent defect.[5] 'Is it the ugly part of his flesh that pines for beauty? Is it an act of Providence that the ugly feet should follow beautiful women?' (p. 39) Gimpei wonders. Gerty in *Ulysses* also shows extraordinary aesthetic sensibilities, which find expression specifically in her underwear.

There are also resemblances in the ways the profound solitude experienced by the male flâneurs in both stories betrays itself to the women targeted by them. That feeling of isolation, or thirst for life, drives these male protagonists to strangers who seem able to fill the void in their existence. Gerty detects 'the story of a haunting sorrow' (13: 422) written across Bloom's face, just as Miyako, having struck Gimpei in the face with her handbag, remembers that 'the man seemed to be conscious of his sorrow' (p. 73).

Gerty attracts Bloom's attention through a 'magnetic influence' (13: 984–5) so that 'he never [takes] his eyes off of her' (13: 495–6) and:

> Her woman's instinct told her that she had raised the devil in him and at the thought a burning scarlet swept from throat to brow till the lovely colour of her face became a glorious rose.
>
> (13: 517–18).

Likewise, Kawabata's *The Lake* suggests that Hisako, Gimpei's female pupil, gloats over her victory over him: 'By being followed by him yesterday, Hisako might have become aware of her devilish charm [masho] and she trembles with secret pleasure. Gimpei was electrified by this mysterious girl' (p. 36). Both texts describe mutual sexual attraction in terms of an electronic reaction.

There is also a striking common motif of secret communication and planned reunion. On leaving the seashore, Bloom wonders if he will see Gerty again by returning there the next day: 'Will she come here tomorrow? Wait for her somewhere for ever. Must come back' (13: 1,253–4). Also, he feels tempted to 'Write

James Joyce's *Ulysses*. (*Koerie/Stockimo/Alamy*)

a message for her' (13: 12,567) on thc sand. Hc actually starts to do so but soon decides to efface the letters, thinking: 'We'll never meet again' (13: 1,272). Though Bloom lets his consciousness play freely with erotic fantasies, his secret desires are not allowed to encroach upon visible reality; rather, they are banished by social norms to the realm of fantasy.

On the other hand, as I have mentioned earlier, Kawabata has his protagonist put into practice what Bloom merely imagines. Because of their improper relationship, both Gimpei and Hisako (teacher and pupil) are expelled from their school and are separated. But they still try to stay in touch with each other by leaving messages in chalk on a concrete wall (p. 119), a detail which recalls Bloom's aborted attempt on the sand. Later in his life, Gimpei, this time fascinated by the ethereal beauty of Machie, dreams of the voyeuristic pleasure of secretly and daily watching the girl, who would walk her dog along the same route every day, 'forever coming up toward Gimpei, who would hide at the top of the slope' (p. 96). The next day, he actually waits in ambush for her at the place where he first saw her (p. 126).

There are other motifs in *The Lake* which Kawabata seems to have borrowed or adapted from *Ulysses*. Both Bloom and Gimpei are afraid of dogs. On seeing Machie's Shiba Inu dog, 'the feeling of gripping a dead rat, still warm' (p. 91) revives in him: he is reminded of the rat killed by the Japanese terrier kept by the family of Yayoi, Gimpei's female cousin and his first love. The sight of a dog accompanied by a girl thus evokes the memory of another dog associated with another girl who had a profound influence upon his life and personality. This scene is reminiscent of the recurring dog images in *Ulysses*. The festive night of firefly hunting in *The Lake* also shares parallels with the night of fireworks in the 'Nausicaa' episode – indeed, the fireflies thrown up from the tower and then 'powerlessly falling down' (p. 151) are compared to 'fireworks about to go out' (p. 151). Further, I believe Gimpei's act of hanging a 'cage of fireflies' (p. 107), which dimly illuminates the belt round Machie's waist, originates in an image in the 'Nausicaa' episode: 'the glowworm's lamp at his belt gleaming here and there' (13: 1,170–1).[6] And besides their dog-phobia, Bloom and Gimpei share one crucial characteristic, that is, the guilt they feel about the child they have lost. Though the circumstances are quite different – Bloom's only son, Rudy, could not live due to his fragile constitution, whereas Gimpei deserts his illegitimate child at the entrance to a brothel (where he is supposed to have impregnated a prostitute), having no idea whether it is dead or alive – both are haunted by spectral images of their children years after their separations. Masaya Shimokusu points out that the image of the 'unbaptized child' that is believed to often 'come back as [a] [revenant]' is repressed in *Ulysses*, 'among the thick layers of imagery given to the Rudy in "Circe"'. In both works, the infant figures, forever suspended in indeterminacy, refuse to rest or remain suppressed in the domain of the unconscious and repeatedly slip back into the consciousness of the living.[7] The usage of such a recurrent motif can be traced back to the Wagnerian 'leitmotifs' adopted by Dujardin in fictional narratives, 'motifs which reappear in the drama every time the same emotion appears' (Dujardin, p. 111).

As we have seen, many elements in Kawabata's *The Lake* indicate that this novel owes much to Joyce's *Ulysses*. Transposing and transforming these elements and motifs, Kawabata differentiates his own work from Joyce's not only by employing a different narrative method but also by letting his protagonist, Gimpei, actually commit the improprieties, which in *Ulysses* remain contained within the mind of the protagonist. What does Kawabata aim to achieve by this means?

While appreciating the significance of Joyce's stylistic experiment – through which external realities and inward visions are seamlessly displayed – Kawabata attempts to carry that experiment one step further: he wants to blur the boundaries even more, to let internal visions invade exterior realities. And this is the very characteristic that defines what is called Makai (magical/evil world).

II. Irish and Japanese Namesakes, *The Lake*: A distant resonance or a convergent evolution?

As I have said, the narrative style Kawabata adopted in *The Lake* is not the same as the internal monologues employed in *Ulysses*: it is a third-person narrative drawing upon stream-of-consciousness techniques.[8] Shin'ichiro Nakamura says, 'the first amazement that struck me about this work was the beauty of the description of the 'stream of consciousness' of the protagonist' (p. 183, my translation). Why, again, did he differentiate his style from *Ulysses* while borrowing motifs from it? I would like to pay attention to Gimpei's words to Hisako:

> Even if you were to spend twenty-four hours a day with Miss Onda and keep telling her whatever comes to your mind, it would still be impossible for you to keep no secret from her at all.
>
> (p. 34)

Can this statement indicate Kawabata's awareness of the impossibility of fully verbalising mental images and processes, as well as his suspicion of the limits inherent in the internal monologues in the 'Penelope' episode of *Ulysses* and in Dujardin's *The Bays are Sere*? The style Kawabata adopts in *The Lake* is in fact similar to what is called the 'melodic line' of George Moore. Moore was a close friend of Dujardin's, and according to Anthony Suter, his 'records of random thoughts are in flashes reminiscent of interior monologue' (Suter, p. xii). When *The Bays are Sere* was published, Moore, while appreciating Dujardin's attempt at exploring human psychology, did not entirely approve of his narrative technique: 'Your story is very good, uncommonly good: the daily life of the soul unveiled for the first time, a kind of symphony in full stops and commas. All I am afraid of is monotony. We shall see; in any case it is new' (quoted in Dujardin, p. 90). Though he acknowledged his literary debt to Dujardin by attaching a dedicatory letter to his novel *The Lake*, Moore differentiated his own narrative method from that of his friend, even whilst pursuing a similar psychological interest.

In Kawabata's *The Lake*, various sensorial impressions – auditory, visual and tactile – invoke memories which often unfold through visual images. Nakamura compares this characteristic style of narrative development in Kawabata's *The Lake* with Proust and other French writers of the modern period:

James Joyce, by Jacques-Emile Blanche (1861–1942), 1935. (*Peter Barritt/Alamy*)

> Just as in Proust's novels, we are, by a chance encounter with trivial matters, led to another incident of a completely different time. And then, as that incident (or rather, that fragment) would be a very Kawabataesque, lyrical and sensual image, the novel as a whole would present an appearance like that of a patchwork of gorgeous pieces of cloth. Traditionally such a novel never had existed. If one would seek its likes, then one has to search the modern works of experimental French novelists. (Nakamura 183, my translation)

I, however, argue that we can also find a remarkable likeness in the stylistic experiment of an Irish writer at the turn of the twentieth century.

George Moore was a writer who took a serious interest in, and very consciously explored, the mysterious mental processes by which hidden thoughts are suddenly and unexpectedly brought to the surface. Jayne Thomas points out that Moore, 'deliberately engaging with contemporaneous psychological theory' (p. 105), portrayed the workings of the unconscious 'as early as *Mike Fletcher* (1889)' (Thomas, p. 104), in which, 'significantly, thoughts and visions rise "into" consciousness and "out" of the unconscious' (Thomas, p. 104). And in *The Lake* (1905), which is dedicated to Édouard Dujardin, Moore foregrounds his preoccupations with psychological mechanisms. In this novel, we are not told the story of the protagonist Oliver Gogarty's life by a third-person narrator in any linear, explanatory way. Rather, we are allowed to follow the threads of his thought, which, under the influence of outward stimulants or by associations of memories, reveals his mental life through fragmentary though often vividly visual and sensuous images, so that we can relive parts of his life with him. Passing, for the first time in many years, his native town Tinnick, for example, Oliver is suddenly reminded of a woman he used to glance at as a boy:

> No one spoke of them now; Father Oliver had not given them a thought these many years; he might never think of her again. Therefore he wondered what could have put thoughts of this dead woman in his mind. Was it the sight of the ugly cottages about the market-place, without cleanliness and without light? She [the woman loved by a friend of her husband] had done nothing to alleviate the lives of these

> poor folk, and it might have been those cottages that had put thoughts of her in his mind.
>
> (Moore, *The Lake*, p. 84)

Here, the representation of the comings and goings of memories between the realms of the conscious and the unconscious indicates the associationist views of mental processes, according to which, 'all thoughts are imperishable' (Coleridge, p. 76) and are always stored somewhere, either in one's consciousness or in the unconscious. Therefore, Oliver contemplates: 'True, the coming of a thought into the consciousness is often unexpected, but if the thought were not latent in the mind, it would not arise out of the mind' (p. 45).

In Kawabata's *The Lake*, when Gimpei gets his chest pinched by a passing prostitute, he feels 'freshness as if he were blown by a breeze on the shore of the lake' (p. 29), 'perhaps because it was after he almost felt like breaking the window-pane of the flower shop as large as the lake; a frozen lake was visualised in his mind – the lake of his mother's native village' (p. 29):

> Gimpei tempted out Yayoi, a cousin on his mother's side, rather than inviting her, to walk out on the ice on the lake. He cherished an evil hope that the ice underneath would break so that Yayoi would fall into the lake under the ice.

We can detect resemblances between the way the cutaneous sensation leads to Gimpei's boyhood memories and the mental processes described in Moore's *The Lake*. However, one might think that the comparison of the window-pane to the lake is unusual and abrupt, giving an impression that Kawabata wants to introduce the symbolism of the 'lake' just for the sake of it. The lake belongs to one of Gimpei's recurrent mindscapes, but why does Kawabata stick to this lake image so tenaciously? One possible explanation is that it can be utilised as a symbolic mirror reflecting what passes through the protagonist's mind. In his study of Kawabata's *The Snow Country* (Yukiguni), pointing out Kawabata's frequent usage of mirror images, Mimbu Kawamura argues: 'The act of creation is, so to speak, an attempt to present the real world through the gaze of the unreal. The projected image of the world, therefore, would assume the aspect of an unreal mirror-world' (Kawamura, p. 224, my translation). This statement would also apply to Kawabata's *The Lake*. In addition, it is at least possible that Kawabata might in some way have come into contact with Moore's *The Lake*, to know its content and narrative style. This speculation might not be so preposterous as it would appear, for, Jun'ichiro Tanizaki, another leading figure in the literary world of Kawabata's time, highly evaluated George Moore's later autobiographical and novelistic works, including *Heloïse and Abelard* (1921), mainly from the viewpoint of stylistics (Tanizaki, pp. 24–5; Akase, p. 128) as early as 1927, the year when an edition of Moore's *Confessions of a Young Man* was published in the Kenkyusha English Classics series, with a long introduction and 189 pages of notes by Minoru Toyoda. Kawabata, who later transferred himself to the Japanese literature department, had originally been enrolled at Tokyo Imperial University as an English undergraduate, and his serious interest in stylistic innovations in English literature shows itself in his fascination with Joyce's *Ulysses*. While he read it in Japanese, Kawabata also consulted Joyce's *Ulysses* in the original English version (Mebed 2003, p. 14). Though Kawabata was not on very close terms with Tanizaki (Koyano, pp. 112–13), it is not unlikely that Kawabata also took an interest in Moore's works such as *Heloïse and Abelard* and *The Lake*. It could be noted that the dominant theme of *Heloïse and Abelard*, the illicit relationship between the teacher and the pupil and their separation, seems to find an echo in the relationship between Gimpei and Hisako in Kawabata's *The Lake*.

Both versions of *The Lake* employ a wandering solitary male protagonist endowed with a keen aesthetic sensibility, and the recurrent image of the lake often associated with death.[9] 'Gimpei's father died in the lake', and 'it remains undetermined whether he was drowned, committed suicide, or was thrown into the water after being murdered' (p. 104). In Moore's *The Lake*, Father Oliver Gogarty, a Catholic priest in Ireland, 'weary of life', thinks of putting an end to his life by skating 'recklessly without trying to avoid the deeper portion where the ice was likely to be thin' (p. 249). At the beginning of the novel, Oliver fears that the beautiful music teacher Rose Leicester – whom he virtually banished from his parish when he found out that she was pregnant without being married – might have drowned herself: 'She might be lying at the bottom of the lake, and some day a white phantom might rise from the water and claim him' (p. 39). Later, suffering from his unrequited love for Rose, Oliver wonders 'if madness would be the end of his suffering, or if he would go down to the lake and find rest in it' (p. 246). Also in Moore's story, the 'lake' on whose side Oliver was brought up and still takes his daily walk as a priest, is compared to 'a blue sheet of glass' (p. 159); it is likened to a mirror when it first appears in the novel ('[t] he lake lay like a mirror that someone had breathed upon' [I]), and it functions as a mirror reflecting the internal visions of each human being: 'Yes, the lake reminds one of one's guilt. "Every man has a lake in his heart." He [Oliver] had not sought the phrase, it had come suddenly into his heart' (p. 57).

There are also other notable similarities between Kawabata's and Moore's protagonists. By the time the story commences, Gimpei has already lost his job as a teacher, his love affair with his student Hisako having been revealed by Miss Onda. Likewise, in Moore's *The Lake*, Rose Leicester has been banished from the parish for becoming pregnant while unmarried. One might draw a parallel between the disgust Oliver shows towards 'that detestable Mrs. O'Mara' (Moore, *The Lake*, p. 33), who reports to him Rose's love affair and supposed pregnancy, and the antipathy Gimpei feels towards Onda, whom he denounces as being 'impure' 'as if centipedes, slugs, or scorpions were crawling inside [her] intestines' (Kawabata, *The Lake*, p. 118). 'Loneliness begets sleeplessness, and sleeplessness begets a sort of madness' (Moore, *The Lake*, p. 241), Oliver writes to Rose, and also, 'Human life is a lonely thing' (p. 241): Gimpei would agree. 'He could sink no deeper. But he could; we can all sink deeper. Now what would the end be?' Oliver wonders (Moore, *The Lake, p.* 245). 'I will fall to the bottom of the world' (Kawabata, *The Lake*, p. 145), Gimpei says to Hisako. Moreover, Father Oliver, a Catholic priest who has to observe the vow of chastity, succumbs to his desire for Rose Leicester in sleep despite being able to suppress it by day: he takes a somnambulistic walk in the wood in search of the soul of Rose. The way Oliver is 'drawn' automatically – without being conscious – is comparable to Gimpei's loss of his 'sense of self 'in following a beautiful woman, 'totally immers[ing] himself' (p. 89) in a stranger:

> He was drawn from glade to glade through the underwoods, and through places so thickly overgrown that it seemed impossible to pass through, but even thorn-bushes gave way before him. For he was no longer alone. He had found her. She had descended from the trees into his arms, white and cold.
>
> (Moore, *The Lake*, p. 225)

In this passage, the description of Oliver's struggle through the 'underwoods' reflects objective reality, but later it is his subconscious desire that conjures up the spectral figure of the woman. Nevertheless, the narrative does not make any distinction between the two realms. Rather, it represents what is being conceived by Oliver as reality at that particular moment, and the reader cannot tell at first sight where the subjective vision begins. This narrative strategy is very similar to the one adopted by Kawabata in *The Lake* when he allows Gimpei's hallucinatory visions to intrude upon the external world:

> 'Hey!' Gimpei called out and raised himself. His baby was crawling from the other side of the earth surface, on which Gimpei was crawling. Just like crawling on the surface of a mirror, Gimpei's palm nearly touched that of the baby – a cold palm of the dead.
>
> (p. 160)

Here the narrator simply reports Gimpei's experience, without commenting upon its nature, upon whether it is illusory or not.

The male protagonists' thoughts on women constitute a leitmotif which compellingly drives the narratives and the plots. '[A]s all roads are said to lead to Rome, so do man's thoughts lead to the woman that lives in his heart' (Moore, *The Lake, p.* 223): so many of Oliver's solitary hours are imbued with his thoughts of Rose. Likewise, Gimpei's mind incessantly recurs to the women he has had relationships with in the past, especially Hisako. After the somnambulistic walk mentioned above, Oliver ceases to try to 'conceal from himself the fact that he love[s]' Rose (p. 245). This, of course, would be enough to disqualify him as a priest; what is more, he realises he has lost his faith. As a symbolic gesture absolving him of his social obligations, he swims across the lake all naked, to aim for America. On the other hand, in Kawabata's *The Lake*, Gimpei, looking into the eyes of Machie, feels that 'the girl's eyes started to seem like a black lake' (p. 97) and then desires to 'swim in those pure eyes, swim naked in the black lake' (p. 97). This pattern of imagery harks back to Moore's *The Lake*.

Now I would like to point out an intriguing coincidence in the protagonists' names, which bear chromatic associations. Gimpei's surname 'Momoi' literally means 'Peach Well': the noun 'momo' can refer to the fruit 'peach' as well as the colour pink.

Gimpei's discovery of the sky being 'momo-iro' – 'peach colour', which reminds us of his name – is emphatically described over two pages. 'When he saw the sky being peach-coloured for the first time, Gimpei had already lost his teaching job; Hisako had been transferred to another school, and it was a secret rendez-vous' (p. 113).

In Moore's *The Lake*, the name of the female protagonist is Rose Leicester, and Oliver sees the colour rose in the sky (p. 311). Is there any special symbolism attached to the colour 'rose' or 'peach'?

For Moore, who spent his formative years in Paris, the colour 'rose' might have been placed midway between red (rouge) and white (blanc), just as rosé wine stands between red and white wine. It is known that Moore wrote *Esther Waters*, another novel featuring a heroine giving birth to an illegitimate child, in rivalry with Thomas Hardy's *Tess of the d'Urbervilles* (1891–2) (Frazier, p. 229). In Hardy's *Tess*, as Tony Tanner has pointed out, the patterning of the colours red and white is a recurrent motif throughout the novel: white is associated with the heroine's initial virginal innocence, and red, the colour of blood, is an omen foreshadowing and connoting the rape and the cruel destiny that awaits her. Even though Hardy must have intended to criticize sexual double standards through his work, the stark colour contrast suggests the limit of his liberalism: for he seems to insist that while Tess' body has been stained, her spirit remains pure and innocent. To emphasise that argument, Tess' ability to dissociate her spirit from her physicality is repeatedly mentioned (Hardy, *Tess of the D'Urbervilles* pp. 135–6, 401). I would surmise that when writing *The Lake* and addressing the problem of illegitimacy, Moore had this influential precedent in mind and attempted to develop his social criticism much further than Hardy did, by radically deconstructing the body/spirit dichotomy in Hardy's work.[10]

In Moore's *The Lake*, Father Oliver, on learning of Rose's illegitimate pregnancy, first assumes a superior position as her spiritual authority and denounces her conduct. However, under the influence of Rose, whom he comes to regard as 'a cure for religion' (p. 281), he is eventually led to question the moral teachings of Christianity; and the conclusion he ultimately reaches is that 'body and mind' (p. 280) are 'not two things, but one thing' (p. 280); and also, 'the mysterious lights of instincts are alone worth following' (p. 279). From such a perspective, any conventional moral judgement is to be nullified. The colour symbolism underlying the heroine's name 'Rose' implies that conventional morality will no longer apply to her.

Returning to Kawabata, we find that his is also a godless world; as Tomioka says:

> A modern novelist in the Western world said, 'if there were no God, all would be forgiven,' and in this 'lake' which flashes up in the lightening tearing the gloom of the night, God does not exist. This is Kawabata's Makai.
>
> (Tomioka, p. 155)

And in this magical and evil world without God, Gimpei, to whom the colour pink is given as a defining attribute, cannot but follow the 'mysterious' workings of his 'instincts' (Moore, *The Lake,* p. 280) as Oliver does. Curiously, Kawabata employs pink as a colour that suggests amorality, or the rejection of conventional morality, in some other works as well. In his short story 'A White Flower' (Shiroi Hana), the sexuality of the nameless heroine is repeatedly associated with the word 'Momo-iro' (peach colour). To her own surprise, this heroine has found out that she cannot understand chastity; having 'kept her eyes on her own death since childhood' (p. 64), 'she does not believe in time, the continuity of time. Therefore, there is no such thing as chastity for her' (p. 64).

As we have seen, there are some notable resemblances between Moore's and Kawabata's *The Lake*. There might have been some direct lines of influence, but this is almost impossible to verify. In any case, their similarities could be ascribed to the similar ideological and cultural situations in which the authors found themselves. As Dujardin insists, '[a] new technique has its origins in the necessities of the period from which it emerges' (p. 131).

Moore's work reflects the ongoing collapse of existing belief systems and institutional religions, while the experience of the misery of the Second World War underlies Kawabata's notion of Makai (Tomioka, pp. 12–13). No longer believing in any absolute authority or ultimate source of values, these authors, who turned to continental European literature for their stylistic innovations, ceased to regard human existence as stable and solid. Even before the Second World War, Kawabata was a leading member of a literary movement called the 'New Sensualist School' (Shin-Kankakuha) (Koyano, p. 158), and the publication of *The Lake*

(1905) took place in what is called Moore's 'Impressionistic' period. Both of these novelists attempted to approach the essence of human nature by recording their protagonists' sensory experiences and mental fluctuations, paying special attention to the workings of the unconscious – both Gimpei and Oliver unwittingly betray their troubled minds by slips of the tongue: the former mentions a 'buried baby' to Hisako (p. 143) and the latter, by mumbling to Father Moran that 'woman is life' (p. 287), almost reveals his secret love for Rose.

Without any external moral guidance to subscribe to, these male protagonists act according to their 'instincts'. But here, we also feel a tonal difference between the two novels. Whereas Moore's *The Lake* concludes with a positive vision that Oliver will hereafter lead a fuller life, no such hope is to be found in Kawabata's Makai. Perhaps Moore, under the influence of Rousseau, had an implicit faith in human nature, while Kawabata never attained any optimistic visions. Contrary to Oliver's case, neither Gimpei's instincts nor his aesthetic sensibility will serve as 'lights' or a spiritual guide to lead him onto the right track. Gimpei, without any sense of moral orientation, wanders on in the dark labyrinth of Makai, as an embodiment of the Schopenhauerian Immanent Will.[11]

Conclusion

All the three works we have considered feature a male protagonist whose solitude, though agonising, allows him to wander freely and to explore the inner depths of his soul. Another intriguing common feature is that female perspectives are introduced in each of these works (Gerty in the 'Nausicaa' episode; Miyako in Kawabata's *The Lake*; and Rose as a correspondent in Moore's *The Lake*), enabling a stereoscopic view of their fictional worlds.[12] While Kawabata was a writer who represented traditional Japanese aesthetic values, he was also enthusiastic about new possibilities of literary expression (Mebed 2003, p. 5). To explore fully and to grasp comprehensively the depths of human nature, he eagerly sought and absorbed the latest innovations in the Western world before developing them further. Though the 'Joycean technique disappeared almost completely from Kawabata's works after the publication of 'Crystalline Phantasmagoria'' (Mebed 2014, p. 150), Joyce seems to have remained a lasting and significant source of inspiration for Kawabata. Even the firefly scene, which Tomioka regards as 'miraculously climactic' (p. 169), can be said to reflect the influence of *Ulysses* in evoking a very similar atmosphere of mystery.[13]

There are also striking affinities between the literary worlds of Moore and Kawabata: one example is their sympathy toward nature, a sensibility shared by Irish and Japanese cultures. Like Father Oliver in Moore's *The Lake*, who is always 'interested' in trees (p. 54), several male protagonists of Kawabata's fictional works, including Shingo in *The Sound of the Mountain* (Yama no Oto, 1949) and Hisao in 'Bamboo Voices, Peach Blossoms' (Take no Koe, Momo no Hana, posthumously published in 1973) show serious botanical interests and love of trees and flowers. The memorable episode of 'bird augury' (Moore, *The Lake*, p. 271) suggests the natural sensibilities shared by Oliver, who imagines his own escape while viewing 'a curlew with its legs tied together' (p. 272), and Hisao, who sees the emergence of a hawk on the top of a dead pine tree as a sign of good fortune.

Even without any monotheistic authority presiding over them, their worlds are awash with supernatural and miraculous mysteries, and it is these mysteries that provide the rich soil upon which Kawabata's Makai is founded.

Acknowledgements

I should like to express my gratitude to Professor Stephen Clark at the University of Tokyo, who kindly and carefully read through an early version of this chapter and gave me helpful suggestions, to Professor George Hughes, who has always warmly encouraged my studies on Moore, to Takaaki Endo, a former student at Kitasato University, who made an insightful comment on the representations of 'instincts' in the works of Kawabata, and to the good students I encountered at Kindai University, including Kazuma Nakao, Mizuki Onishi, Haruka Toda, and Nana Toshikawa, with whom I enjoyed rereading and discussing Moore's text in class.

Bibliography

Akase, Masako, 'Jun-itiro Tanizaki and French Culture', *Intercultural Studies* 22 (2000), pp. 119–29.

Coleridge, Samuel Taylor, *Biographia Literaria, I*, 108–16, rpt. in Jenny Bourne Taylor and Sally Shuttleworth ed. *Embodied Selves: An Anthology of Psychological Texts 1830–1890* (Oxford: Oxford University Press, 1998), pp. 73–6.

Dujardin, Édouard, 'Interior Monologue: Its first appearance and origins, and its place in the work of James Joyce', in Anthony Suter (trans.), *The Bays are Sere and Interior Monologue* (London: Libris, 1991), pp. 81–145.

Frazier, Adrian, *George Moore, 1852–1933* (New Haven and London: Yale University Press, 2000).

Hardy, Thomas, *Tess of the D'Urbervilles* (Oxford: Oxford University Press, 2008) [1891–2].

Hijiya-Kirschnereit, Irmela, 'The Flesh and the Experiment: The Aesthetics of the Disabled in the Literature of Kawabata' (*Shintai to Jikken Kawabata Bungaku ni Okeru Katawamono no Bigaku*), in Sakai et al. (eds), *Kawabata Yasunari Studies* (Tokyo: Kasama Shoin, 2016), pp. 167–82.

Joyce, James, *Ulysses*, ed., Hans Walter Gabler (New York: Garland Publishing, 1984) [1922].

____, trans. by Sei Itoh and Sadamu Nagamatsu, *Ulysses* (Tokyo: Shinchosha, 1955).

Kawabata, Yasunari, 'A White Flower.' (Shiroi Hana), in *Palm Stories* (Tanagokoro no Shosetsu) (Tokyo: Shinchosha, 2014), pp. 62–6 [1923].

____, *The Sound of the Mountain* (Yama no Oto) (Tokyo: Shinchosha, 2016) [1949].

____, *The Lake* (Mizuumi) (Tokyo: Shinchosha, 2013) [1955]

____, 'Bamboo Voices, Peach Blossoms' (Take no Koe Momo no Hana), in Kotaro Tomioka (ed.), *Emergency/ A Cold Wind/ The Snow Country, Abridged* (Hijō/ Kampū/ Yukiguni Shō) (Tokyo: Kodansha, 2015), pp. 253–64 [1973].

Kawaguchi, Kyoichi, Ulysses *in the Early Years of the Showa Era* (Showa Shonen no *Ulysses*) (Tokyo: Misuzu Shobo, 2005.

Kawamura, Mimbu, *Eros & Agape* (Erosu to Agape Kyoen no Hikaku Bungaku) (Tokyo: Eihosha, 2014).

Koyano, Atsushi, *Yasunari Kawabata: A Man with Two Faces* (Kawabata Yasunari Sōmen no Hito) (Tokyo: Chuo-Koron Shinsha, 2013).

Li Shengjie, 'A study on 'Mizuumi' (the lake) by Kawabata Yasunari: toward the origin of evilness', in *Shagakuken Ronshu* 16 (2010), pp. 164–79: https://waseda.repo.nii.

ac.jp/?action=pages_view_main&active_action=repository_view_main_item_detail&item_id=16138&item_no=1&page_id=13&block_id=21 [Accessed 14 June 2017].

Mebed, Sharif, 'On the Reception of 'Stream of Consciousness' in the Early Showa Period: James Joyce's *Ulysses* and Yasunari Kawabata's 'The Needle, Glass and Mist'' (*Showa Shoki ni Okeru Ishiki no Nagare Juyo wo Megutte – James Joyce no* Ulysses *to Kawabata Yasunari no 'Hari to Garasu to Kiri'*) in Kotoba to Bunka 4 (2003), pp. 5–15. https://www.lang.nagoya-u.ac.jp/nichigen/issue/pdf/4/4-01.pdf [Accessed 14 June 2017].

____, 'Joyce's Influence in the Literature of Kawabata and the Free Association: with a Special Focus on 'Crystalline Phantasmagoria'' (*Kawabata Yasunari Bungaku ni Okeru Joyce no Eikyo to Jiyū Rensō: 'Suishō Gensō' wo Chushin ni*) *Journal of the Nanzan Academic Society* 95 (2014), pp. 131–52.

Moore, George, *The Lake* (London: Heinemann, 1905).

Nakamura, Shin'ichiro, 'Commentary' (*Atogaki*) on *The Lake* (Tokyo: Shinchosha, 2003), pp 253–64.

Shimokusu, Masaya, 'Rudy and the Repressed Image of Unbaptised Child in James Joyce's *Ulysses*', *Abstracts: IASIL Japan The 34th Conference* (2017), p. 2.

Suter, Anthony, 'Introduction' to Édouard Dujardin, *The Bays are Sere and Interior Monologue*. (London: Libris, 1991), pp. xi–lvii.

Tanizaki, Jun'ichiro, 'Blabbermouth Records' (*Jōzetsuroku*) in Shunji Chiba (ed.), *Literary, Too Literary* (Bungeiteki-na, Amarinimo Bungeiteki-na) (Tokyo: Kodansha, 2017) (1927).

Tanner, Tony, 'Colour and Movement in Hardy's *Tess of the d'Urbervilles*', *Critical Quarterly* 10 (1968), pp. 219–39.

Thomas, Jayne, 'George Moore and the Unconscious in *Evelyn Innes* and *Sister Teresa*: 'Shapes from an Underworld', in Maria Elena Jaime de Pablos and Mary Pierse (eds), *George Moore and the Quirks of Human Nature* (Oxford: Peter Lang, 2014).

Tomioka, Koichiro, *Yasunari Kawabata: The Literature of* Makai (Kawabata Yasunari Makai no Bungaku) (Tokyo: Iwanami Shoten, 2014).

The Pathos of Things

Seamus Heaney

Poetry is a domestic art, most itself when most at home. It has even been argued, famously, that poetry is what is lost in translation. But while it is true that poets depend for the most part on the hearth-life and home-sweet-homeness of their native tongue, they also tend to be the Oliver Twists of language, never satisfied with their allotted ration, always asking for more, inclined to feel that enough is not enough but only the start of it, that somewhere there is another word that will be the key to another world.

So when native traditions are rejuvenated by what we now call 'the shock of the new', it is often through contact with a foreign culture that the new possibilities suggest themselves. This, after all, is what happened in Japanese poetry at the end of the nineteenth century, when the so-called *shintaishi* or New-style Poetry began to be written. The introduction to *The Penguin Book of Japanese Verse* attributes this radical shift of style to the publication in 1882 of a volume of translations of miscellaneous English verse, including excerpts from work by Longfellow, Tennyson, Shakespeare's *Henry IV, Part 2* and *Hamlet*. The volume also included experimental poems by the compilers, and it was followed seven years later by another such anthology entitled *Omokage* (Semblances), which again featured translations of work by Shakespeare and several figures from the European Romantic movement, including Byron, Goethe and Heine.

I don't know if William Wordsworth was among the Romantic poets translated in those epoch-making anthologies, but Wordsworth is where I want to begin. It seems to me that the scenes which inspired his most characteristic poetry could well have inspired many of the great masters of Japan. The English and Japanese sensibilities respond in similar ways to the natural world, and landscapes which brought out the best in Wordsworth could equally well have provided the setting for a haiku by Basho. Significantly also, the English poet's work abounds in phrases which could be used to describe the general emotional impact of a certain kind of Japanese lyric – as when he speaks of being 'an inmate of this active universe', of being taught to feel 'the self-sufficing power of solitude' or a something in nature which is 'far more deeply interfused', and so on.

What is un-Japanese about Wordsworth, however – and you only need to remember a poem like 'The Prelude' or 'Tintern Abbey' to realise it – is the nimbus of introspection and ratiocination which surrounds the physical details of the scene. In this Romantic period, poetry in English typically allows itself greater scope for commentary and elucidation, tending to clarify where Japanese poetry would be content to imply; often eager to point out where Japanese poetry would be happy to sink in; tending to add where the Japanese would subtract.

Consider, for example, the following passage from 'The Prelude'. Wordsworth is remembering a schoolboy expedition that he and his companions once made on horseback, a day trip when they galloped off to visit the ruins of Furness Abbey on the shores of Cumberland. Once there, they absorb the atmosphere of the place, the carved stone effigies of knights and abbots scattered about the roofless chantry, the wind passing overhead and the sound of the sea ebbing and flowing in the background – until it is time for them to go back. Then:

> Our steeds remounted, and the summons given,
> With whip and spur we by the chantry flew
> In uncouth race, and left the cross-legged knight
> And the stone abbot, and that single wren
> Which one day sang so sweetly in the nave
> Of the old church that, though from recent showers

The earth was comfortless, and, touched by faint
Internal breezes, sobbings of the place
And respirations, from the roofless walls
The shuddering ivy dripped large drops – yet still
So sweetly mid the gloom the invisible bird
Sang to itself that there I could have made
My dwelling place, and lived forever there,
To hear such music.

The dripping ivy, the roofless walls, the song of a single wren: a Japanese poet is likely to have been content with those elements of the scene. He would have been drawn to the still centre of the moment. The narrative would probably have fallen away, or perhaps have been reported in a brief anecdotal prose interlude. Typically, the moment of pure perception would have been isolated, the psychological and philosophical implications remaining unspoken. What Wordsworth explicitly declares – 'I could have ... lived for ever there / To hear such music' the Japanese poet would most likely have suggested by one or two illuminating images.

Still, English poetry would soon enough learn the Japanese lesson. Only a couple of decades after the 'new-style poets' of the 1890s brought out their anthologies in Japan, new-style poems began to appear in little publications in London. By the second decade of the twentieth century, two Americans had arrived and were producing work that would leave its mark on much of the verse written in English since. Ezra Pound and T.S. Eliot landed as expatriates, seeking on the one hand to find in Europe the origins of their cultural tradition, and seeking on the other hand to shake that tradition up, revive it and retune it to other registers. It was Pound who produced the work that here concerns us most, when he wrote one of the briefest but most influential poems in his total *oeuvre*, the well-known 'In a Station of the Metro'. In one stroke, or rather two lines, Pound managed to banish, as it were, his inner Wordsworth, and demonstrated to others that they could do the same.

His famous note about the composition of 'In a Station of the Metro' tells how he had attempted to find words for sensations that he had experienced after a unique and mysterious vision of beautiful faces coming and going among the passengers in the Paris metro at Place de la Concorde. 'There came an equation

Matsuo Bashō (1644–94), artist unknown. [CPA Media/Alamy]

…' Pound wrote, 'not in speech, but in little splotches of colour.' He had begun by composing a thirty-line poem, but had destroyed it because it didn't achieve a satisfactory intensity of expression; six months then passed and he wrote one half that length; and a year later he produced what he called a 'hokku-like sentence':

> The apparition of these faces in the crowd:
> Petals on a wet, black bough.

'I dare say it is meaningless', Pound concluded, 'unless one has drifted into a certain vein of thought. In a poem of this sort one is trying to record the precise instant when a thing outward and objective transforms itself, or darts into a thing inward and subjective.'

The poem is far from meaningless, and it is largely thanks to its existence that readers (and writers) in English have drifted 'into a certain vein of thought'. Thanks to these fourteen words, we are now well attuned to the Japanese effect, the evocation of that precise instant of perception, and are ready to grant such evocation of the instant a self-sufficiency of its own. We don't require any labouring of the point. We are happy if the image sets off its own echoes and associations, if it speaks indirectly, as Issa speaks in his haiku: 'A good world – / dew drops fall / by ones by twos.'

By ones, by twos, ripples pulsed out from the image poem, so it was inevitable, especially given Pound's capacities as an operator on the literary scene, that the new Japanese effect should be integrated into the history of poetry in English as 'The Imagist Movement'. Moreover, once the aesthetic procedure was named, it was to a certain extent tamed, and like any other domesticated species, it began to breed and be taken for granted in its new setting – as in this other early example of the genre by T.E. Hulme:

> Old houses were scaffolding once
> And workmen whistling.

Neither Pound's poem nor Hulme's obeys the formal rules of the Japanese; the syllable count of five seven five is neglected and the 'seasonal' word is missing, but the sense of evanescence, of the transitoriness of things, of the stillness behind things into which they eventually pass, this essential quality is nevertheless present.

It might even be said that with the writing of these early image-based poems and with the formulation of the principles of imagism, the concept of mono no aware enters the English language, both in theory and in practice. Mono no aware is defined in a glossary of Japanese artistic terms as a literary and artistic ideal cultivated in the Heian period. Literally meaning 'pathos of things', it usually refers to sadness or melancholy arising from a deep empathic appreciation of the ephemeral beauty manifested in nature, human life or a work of art.

For curiosity, I went through the recently published *New Penguin Book of English Verse* in search of this effect in pre-imagist periods, but didn't discover anything. This is not to say, of course, that poetry in English is unaware or unexpressive of the underlife of feelings or the melancholy of things: since Anglo-Saxon times the elegiac mood has been a constant of the poetic literature. It's just that the means of expression are different. In 1869, for example, Matthew Arnold wrote this brief, untitled poem:

> Below the surface-stream, shallow and light,
> Of what we say we feel – below the stream,
> As light, of what we think we feel – there flows
> With noiseless current strong, obscure and deep,
> The central stream of what we feel indeed.

What the haiku/imagist form can do is to reach down into that noiseless, strong, obscure, deep central stream and give both poet and reader a sense of epiphany. It's worth noticing, indeed, that the word 'epiphany' becomes available as a literary term around about the time when Pound is coining the term 'imagism', James Joyce being the one who was responsible for this new extension and application of its meaning. In their different ways, Pound and Joyce felt a need to extend the alphabet of expressiveness, and found a way to articulate what T.S. Eliot would call 'the notion of some infinitely gentle / Infinitely suffering thing' – a thing which was also for Eliot inherent in certain 'images': 'I am moved by fancies that are curled / Around these images and cling.'

(opposite page) *Autumn Landscape*, hanging scroll by Yosa Buson (1716–83), *c.* 1780. (*Agefotostock/Alamy*)

東成謝寅

In the years since these early developments, the haiku form and the generally Japanese effect have been a constant feature of poetry in English. The names of Basho and Issa and Buson have found their way into our discourse to the extent that we in Ireland have learnt to recognise something Japanese in the earliest lyrics of the native tradition. The hermit poets who wrote in Old Irish in the little monasteries were also masters of the precise and suggestive:

Int én bec
ro léc feit
do rinn guip
glanbuidi:
fo-ceird fáid
ós Loch Laíg
Ion do chraíb
chairdbuidi.
[ninth-century Irish; translation]
The small bird
let a chirp
from its beak:
I heard
woodnotes, whingold, sudden:
the Lagan blackbird.

The economy of means, the sense of a huge encircling stillness, of swiftness and transience all at once, these qualities recall equally the traditional haiku and the twentieth-century imagist poem, and this single example will have to stand for many other lyrics that could be cited from the Old Irish canon.

Another quality which the Old Irish poet shares with his Japanese counterpart is a quality we might call 'this worldness' – both are as alert as hunters to their physical surroundings – and yet there is also a strong sense of another world within this 'this worldness', one to which poetic expression promises access. In each case it's as if the poet is caught between the delights of the contingent and the invitations of the transcendent, yet by registering as precisely and poignantly as possible his consciousness of this middle state he manages to effect what Matthew

Arnold would have called 'a criticism of life'. So you could argue that there is a direct line running from the startle of recognition in the work of the early Christian hermit as he renders the whole strangeness of the blackbird's song to the 'tinkle of china / And tea into china', as Derek Mahon contrasts the exquisite manners of those attending the snow party (in his poem of that name) with the savagery of contemporary European wars, including those being waged in Ireland 'in the service of barbarous kings'. Mahon's poem, one of the most durable written in the late twentieth century, constitutes in effect a proof of the contention by his friend Michael Longley – that other Hiberno-Japanese master – that the opposite of war is not peace but civilisation.

Yet Japanese poetry is not all snow parties and snow water. One of its most attractive features is the folk form known as *senryu*, more humorous and robust than the haiku, more down to earth and insinuating, and again you could make interesting juxtapositions of *senryu* with the Old Irish triads – or with brief merry poems by Iain Crichton Smith written first in Scots Gaelic and translated into English as 'Gaelic Stories', or with Paul Muldoon's 'Hopewell Haiku', or Michael Hartnett's 'Inchicore Haiku' or Cathal Ó Searcaigh's glosses from Gortahork.

So while it is true that our sense of the Japanese effect was heightened by Ezra Pound's imagism, it's also fair to say that from the start there has been a certain resemblance between vernacular Irish and traditional Japanese ways of looking at things. And it can be further said that in the course of the twentieth century, as empires and ideologies contended for supremacy, and atrocities were committed on a scale unprecedented in human history, poets became desperately aware of the dangers of rhetoric and abstraction. In these circumstances the poet's duty to be truthful became more and more imperative and, as it did, the chastity and reticence of Japanese poetry grew more and more attractive. Its closeness to common experience and its acknowledgement of mystery, its sensitivity to *lacrimae rerum*, to the grievous aspects of human experience, have made it a permanent and ever-more valuable resource to which other literatures can turn.

This reading was given at the Lafcadio Hearn Lecture in 2000 and is included in Irene De Angelis and Joseph Woods (eds), Our Shared Japan *(Dublin: Dedalus Press, 2007)*

Arts of Japan for Ireland at Home: An exhibition of Japanese prints from the collections of Sir Chester Beatty held for An Tóstal, 1955

Mary Redfern

On 9 January 2017, Minister Kishida presented his Foreign Minister's Commendation to the Chester Beatty in a ceremony at Iveagh House, Dublin. Culture and the arts have played a vital role in strengthening ties between Ireland and Japan over the last sixty years. The honour bestowed upon the Chester Beatty by Minister Kishida recognised the part this institution has played in deepening understanding of Japan through its unique collections. Turning the clock back a little more than sixty years, this essay focuses on one such initiative from the earliest years of the Chester Beatty: the exhibition of Japanese prints held during the An Tóstal celebrations of 1955.

The history of this particular exhibition of Japanese prints, all loaned from Chester Beatty's then growing collections, combines both a significant moment of collecting and the presentation of that collection to new audiences in Ireland. Held within a year of the public opening of the Chester Beatty Library on Shrewsbury

Road, this was also a critical period in the history of this institution. The prints at the heart of this story remain one of the jewels in the Chester Beatty collection, and have played their own part in furthering appreciation of Japanese art and culture within Ireland and beyond.

The formation of Beatty's Japanese collection

Born in New York in 1875, Alfred Chester Beatty made his fortune in mining. He moved to London after the death of his wife Ninette in 1911. Already a wealthy man, in 1914 Beatty founded the mining company Selection Trust. As his business interests grew, so, too, did his passion for art. Beatty amassed unique collections of Western illuminated manuscripts and exquisite Islamic texts, which joined the Chinese snuff bottles and small Japanese decorative arts he collected in his younger years.

In 1917, as he recovered from a bout of Spanish influenza, Beatty heeded the advice of his doctors and embarked upon a round-the-world voyage. Stopping in both China and Japan (where he spent three months), this trip set Beatty's collecting on a new path. As he travelled in Japan, the artworks Beatty saw captured his attention. Shipping invoices from the journey and memoranda written on hotel letterheads list Buddhist sutras and exquisite painted narrative handscrolls and albums that he was moved to acquire. His interests persisted beyond his return, with numerous works added to the collection in the years that followed.

A naturalised British citizen since 1933 and denizen of London for nearly forty years, Beatty's decision to move both his residence and his renowned collections to Dublin following his retirement in 1950 garnered some surprise. A combination of factors drove his decision, including – but not limited to – the landslide victory of the Labour Party led by Clement Attlee over Winston Churchill's Conservatives in the British general election of 1945 (an active supporter of Churchill, Beatty had been instrumental in securing strategic raw materials for the Allies during the war). Beatty's son had also already taken a residence in Ireland, and Beatty himself enjoyed Irish ancestry on his father's side.

This decision to move had huge ramifications for the future of Beatty's collections, but may also have been predicated on this precise concern. The Irish government worked to encourage Beatty in this endeavour. The outcome was the creation of a new institution: a stand-alone library in the suburbs of Dublin that would not only carry Beatty's name but, more importantly, preserve the integrity of his diverse collections while making them available to scholars and, later, the general public.

Although it can only be conjecture, had Beatty stayed in London the future of his collection may well have been very different. Beatty had already presented certain manuscripts from his Egyptian collections to the British Museum, for example. It is possible that much more of his collection may have followed a similar trajectory – that is, dispersed among the holdings of much larger institutions. As Beatty set the foundations for his new library in Dublin, he acknowledged certain 'gaps' that needed filling so as to render his collections more 'representative'. This would not have been so great a concern in other circumstances perhaps, but with the independent future of his collection decided, Beatty identified new priorities for collecting.

One particularly significant development occurred in 1954. With building work completed on his library in Shrewsbury Road, Beatty was presented with a unique opportunity to develop his Japanese holdings. Kegan Paul, Trench & Trubner (a London dealership with which Beatty was well acquainted) had secured a large collection of Japanese woodblock prints gathered together by one H.F.T. Cooper. Numbering more than 600 sheets in total, these prints spanned Japan's Edo period (*c.* 1603–1868), charting key developments in this important medium.

Although Beatty had previously acquired a few Japanese printed books and a small number of single-sheet prints, he had never before made any great efforts to collect the woodblock prints for which Japan was so famous. Even as he seized upon this unique opportunity, Beatty appears to have been somewhat equivocal about the works themselves. In a letter to his friend and fellow collector Wilfred Merton, Beatty notes, 'Mr Coles [of Kegan Paul] showed [the collection] to [J.V.S. Wilkinson, Beatty's librarian] … He tells me that he has gone "crackers" about Japanese prints. You evidently are crazy about them too: it only remains for me to go "crackers".'[1]

Correspondence surrounding the acquisition highlights the value of this purchase to Beatty. As he wrote to Merton, 'If we can add this to our collection of Siamese [manuscripts], Chinese [painted scrolls] and albums, Japanese [painted scrolls], [manuscripts] and woodblock books we will have a fine and representative collection of Eastern art.'[2] Convinced of the merits of the proposal, Beatty bought the Cooper collection for £4,250 on 12 May 1954. In one fell swoop he was able to acquire an established and 'representative' collection of excellent quality.

Beatty recognised from the outset that additional work would be needed, both in terms of cataloguing and supplementary acquisitions. Jack Hillier was approached to undertake this work. Hillier was a published scholar of Japan's printed arts. As consultant and cataloguer for Japanese artworks submitted for sale at Sotheby's, he was also uniquely placed to read the contemporary market and secure the final works needed to complete Beatty's collection.[3] With Hillier's specialist expertise and Beatty's developing enthusiasm, the collection was refined and augmented, adopting additional foci with regard to printed books and the privately printed and distributed woodblock prints known as *surimono*.[4]

Prints were bought from sales and dealers in London and Paris, examined by Hillier, and sent on their way to Dublin. Beatty had initially considered that a collection of 400 to 450 prints would probably be appropriate.[5] At the end of 1955, he reaffirmed this expectation to Hillier, observing that with 450 superb prints (a standard they were near attaining), 'we can have three exhibitions with no duplication'.[6] This figure now encompassed only the commercially published Japanese prints and not the *surimono* that were Beatty's new passion, but this remark demonstrates that the exhibition potential of the collection was of great significance to its formation.

From its commencement in 1954, the work undertaken to develop Beatty's collection of Japanese prints took a little under a decade. The result is a glorious collection comprising some 450 commercially published woodblock prints, approximately 375 single-sheet *surimono* (with additional examples bound into albums), and more than a hundred book titles embodying the exceptional standards of quality and condition that were fundamental criteria for Beatty as a collector. Upon his death in 1968, these works, the library building and its wider collections were bequeathed in trust to the people of Ireland: a magnificent legacy and an exquisite gift to the nation.

The 1955 exhibition

The exhibition of Japanese prints was part of the programme for the 1955 An Tóstal celebrations.[7] The prints were displayed at Regent House, Trinity College, from 10 to 29 May. A second exhibition drawing on Beatty's collections opened a week later in the library of Trinity College.[8] This exhibition featured thirty-two Western illuminated manuscripts from Beatty's collections alongside eight works from the college's own holdings. The exhibition of Japanese prints, however, drew exclusively on Beatty's growing collection.

The potential for such undertakings had been raised the year before. In 1954, as the public were first offered admittance to the newly built Chester Beatty Library, the *Irish Press* noted that Beatty also intended to lend items from the collections to universities and other institutions for exhibitions during periods such as An Tóstal.[9] Later, the library building itself was expanded to offer additional dedicated display space, but this statement shows that the proper exhibition of his collections within Ireland was an early concern for Beatty.

Carrying the meaning of a 'gathering', the title of the An Tóstal festival was given in English as 'Ireland at Home'. A national festival, inaugurated in 1953 and held annually until 1958, An Tóstal presented a diverse selection of social, cultural and sporting events across Ireland. In its first year, these included horse-racing, camogie and roller hockey, alongside orchestral performances, historical and artistic exhibitions, floodlighting of public buildings, parades and decorations. As the then minister for industry and commerce Seán F. Lemass declared in the official souvenir handbook, 'Ireland is keeping "open door" to men and women of Irish birth and origin from all parts of the world who have come home to renew their contacts with our country, and also to every stranger who may wish to join us'.[10]

The An Tóstal celebrations were intended to offer 'a permanent asset to the Irish tourist industry' (particularly in the springtime off-season).[11] Local and central councils arranged their own programmes of events under the An Tóstal banner. Writing for the 1953 souvenir handbook, Malachy Hynes observed that, although the events were organised independently by the councils, 'each alike is motivated by the same ideal in all their programmes, emphasising Irish-Ireland, the language and the cultural background that have guided our people's destiny from the earliest times'.[12] Amidst such goals, the selection of Japanese prints for exhibition two years later cannot but seem somewhat incongruous.

According to correspondence preserved in the archives of the Chester Beatty, the exhibition of Japanese prints was suggested by Beatty following a visit to the library by the Earl of Rosse (then president of the Friends of the National Collections of Ireland).[13] Rosse wrote to Beatty on 11 January 1955 to follow up on the suggestion, commenting on the Friends' possible involvement and matters of timing and venue.[14] Beatty responded on 5 February to say that he would be happy to cover the costs of the exhibition. Proceeds from the sale of exhibition catalogues and any donations would go to charity, and Beatty suggested these might be used for the purchase of wireless sets for the blind.[15] With regard to the content of the exhibition, Beatty wrote, 'I should think they would be interested in having an Exhibition of Japanese Prints, as there are so few fine exhibitions of that kind … It is simply a case of how keen they are in Ireland to have the Exhibition'.[16] He also maintained that it should be held during An Tóstal. On 21 February, Beatty's librarian, James Wilkinson, attended a meeting with the Friends of the National Collections at the An Tóstal offices, where all agreed that such an exhibition would be welcome.[17] The exhibition was organised in collaboration with the Friends of the National Collections of Ireland (represented by R. Figgis, honorary secretary) and the An Tóstal Visual Arts Committee (represented by James White). Although Jack Hillier was relied upon by Beatty for the collecting and cataloguing of his Japanese prints at this time, he was not directly involved in the exhibition project.[18] A memo records that Figgis and White were responsible for the initial selection of works, shortlisting some 160 prints from Beatty's growing collection.[19] The venue was settled as the historic Regent House at the College Green entrance to Trinity College. Wilkinson then prepared the exhibition catalogue. Using details already received from Hillier for the individual prints, he penned his own introductory essay, and White supplied the foreword.

The exhibition of Japanese prints from Beatty's collection was opened on 10 May 1955 by President Seán T. O'Kelly; ill health sadly prevented Beatty from attending.[20] The significance of the event was addressed by Wilkinson in notes prepared for the president's reference. He writes, 'A good many exhibitions of [Japanese] prints have been held in Paris and London in the last fifty years during which the interest has not abated, but it is believed that this is the first exhibition to be held in Dublin.' Whether this was indeed Ireland's first exhibition to focus solely on Japanese prints remains to be established (the collections at the National Museum of Ireland certainly included such material); even so, the *Irish Independent* had no qualms in describing it as 'an exhibition out of the ordinary, and one that should on no account be missed by anyone who has any interest in art'.[21]

According to 'An Irishman's Diary' in *The Irish Times*, 'So many people were present at the Japanese prints opening that it was virtually impossible to see the

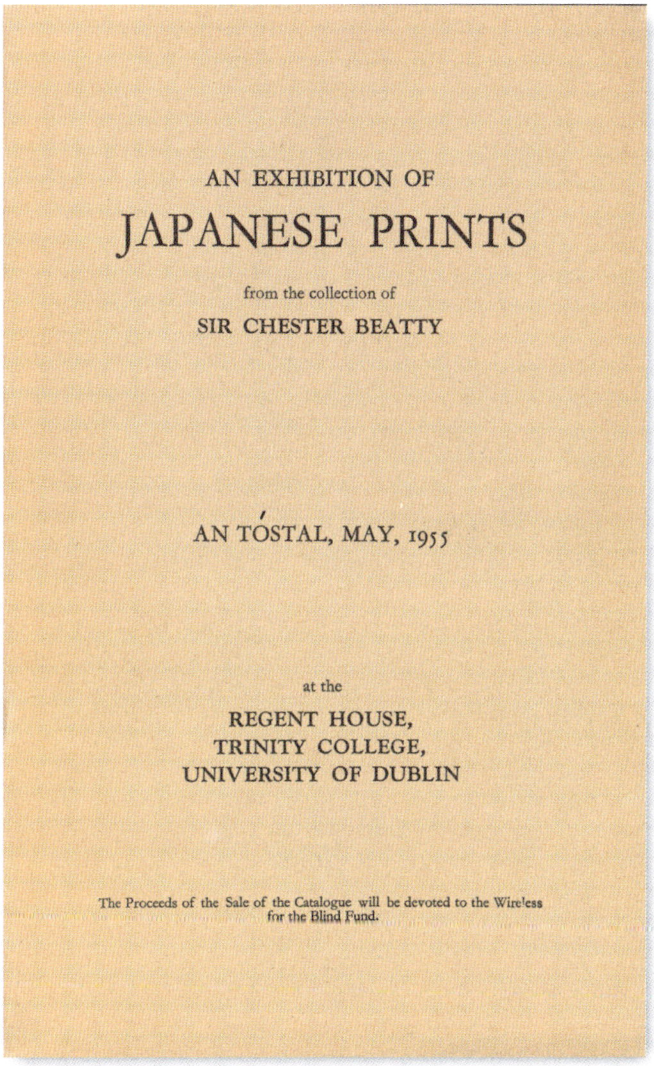

AN EXHIBITION OF

JAPANESE PRINTS

from the collection of

SIR CHESTER BEATTY

AN TÓSTAL, MAY, 1955

at the

REGENT HOUSE,
TRINITY COLLEGE,
UNIVERSITY OF DUBLIN

The Proceeds of the Sale of the Catalogue will be devoted to the Wireless for the Blind Fund.

Catalogue: *An Exhibition of Japanese Prints from the Collection of Sir Chester Beatty*, Trinity College, May 1955. (© *The Trustees of the Chester Beatty Library, Dublin*)

exhibits'.[22] Altogether, 132 prints were displayed. The exhibition was staged before the privately printed *surimono* had become a priority of Beatty's collecting, and as such only seven of these luxurious works were featured.[23] Mounted in card and cellophane, Beatty's prints were hung upon freestanding display units arranged

Installation of *An Exhibition of Japanese Prints from the Collection of Sir Chester Beatty*, Trinity College, May 1955. (© *The Trustees of the Chester Beatty Library, Dublin*)

within the room. Photographs of the installation show the sharp contrast these displays struck against the room's historic plaster mouldings.

Contemporary newspaper reports underscore that the exhibits were laid out chronologically. This didactic arrangement allowed the visitor to walk through the history of Japanese *ukiyo-e* prints from the early monochromatic and hand-tinted works of artists such as Hishikawa Moronobu (d. 1694) and Torii Kiyomasa I (*fl. c.* 1704–14), right through to the richly coloured prints of Katsushika Hokusai (1760–1849) and Utagawa Hiroshige (1797–1858). Wilkinson's catalogue essay further elaborated this history for the interested reader, detailing also the impact of these prints upon the artists of Europe.

Sales of the exhibition catalogue achieved £46 *6s 6d*.[24] Together with donations, the exhibition raised £58 17*s* 0*d* for the Wireless for the Blind Fund.[25] The qualitative impact of the exhibition, however, is harder to assess. For those who visited Regent House during the 1955 An Tóstal celebrations, a rare experience awaited. Whether visitors from overseas or local residents, each was offered a unique view of the art and culture of Japan's Edo period, captured with skilful artistry and rendered in glorious colour.

Mandarin Ducks in the Snow, by Utagawa Hiroshige (1797–1858), *c.* 1835. (CBL J 2725 © *The Trustees of the Chester Beatty Library, Dublin*)

Legacies

Unlike many of the events held during An Tóstal, the exhibition of Japanese prints from Beatty's collections did not hark towards an 'Irish Ireland' but, instead, showcased the quality of the artistic heritage being gathered within that nation's borders. While Beatty's library did not count among the National Collections – it was not until 1957 that he would write to the taoiseach, Éamon de Valera, to propose the formation of a trust to hold the library for the benefit of Ireland;[26] his decision to bring his collections to Ireland was warmly embraced. The Friends of the National Collections of Ireland was keen to work with Beatty to display the exquisite artworks he had assembled right in the heart of the city.

For Beatty's part, the exhibition of Japanese prints (and its sister exhibition of Western manuscripts) would surely have helped to raise the profile of the library, which had opened to the public less than a year before. In a letter to White, Wilkinson noted his hope that the print exhibition would be widely known and featured in the press.[27] Usually only open to the public on Wednesday afternoons, it was also agreed that the library at Shrewsbury Road would be open to the public every day during the An Tóstal celebrations, a matter publicised in the official festival programme.[28]

Cautiously optimistic, Wilkinson advised Miss Healy of An Bord Fáilte that they would not have the staff to cope with large parties of visitors in coaches.[29]

However, Beatty's willingness to support this exhibition extended beyond the desire for publicity. As he established his library in Dublin, he began to collect for an institution that would be his legacy (a legacy that would later be designated Beatty's gift to the Irish nation). When Beatty's collecting of Japanese prints is considered, the extent to which he took this legacy to heart is clear, allowing it to guide his selection of material with the goal of creating a representative collection. The readiness with which Beatty lent these works for the An Tóstal exhibition (as well as supporting its costs) further demonstrates that the display of his collections to the wider public and the fostering of partnerships with Dublin's cultural and academic institutions were of great importance to Beatty. These masterpieces of Japanese art had found a new home in Ireland.

In the sixty years since the exhibition of Beatty's Japanese prints at Trinity College, this collection has continued to offer a focal point for collaborative endeavours and for public engagement with the arts of Japan. Many of these collaborations have been direct partnerships between Ireland and Japan. Large parts of the collection were published in 1991 by the Japanese publisher Kodansha in its series *Ukiyo-e Masterpieces in Great European Collections*.[30] In more recent years, researchers from Ritsumeikan University's Art Research Centre have travelled to Ireland in order to photograph the museum's holdings of Japanese printed material as part of a project to digitise such collections across the world.[31] A number of exhibitions of the prints collected by Beatty and Hillier have been held at the Chester Beatty (in Shrewsbury Road, and since 2000 in its new home in the Clock Tower of Dublin Castle) and through touring internationally to introduce new audiences to the refinement of these exquisite artworks.[32]

Writing on the eve of the first An Tóstal celebrations in 1953, J.A. Nugent, chairman of An Bord Fáilte, wrote: 'Our efforts – whether reflected in the simple village pageant, or in the more ambitious programmes of the bigger towns and cities – are being made with the sincere desire to give pleasure. In all this, we are conscious of a proud inheritance, of our glorious past, and of our place amongst the Nations to-day.'[33] The collections of Sir Alfred Chester Beatty are now part of Ireland's proud inheritance. Today, as in 1955, they offer a place for us to gather with friends from all over the world.

Strongly Spent is Kept: A tradition of generosity

Taketoshi Furomoto

Many obituaries of Seamus Heaney referred to his generosity as one of his greatest virtues. During some public events I talked with him more or less formally, but private occasions provided me with an insight into how ready he was to offer guidance to his students. This readiness to make sacrifices, to put one's own convenience aside, can only be found in an excellent teacher.

Another gift of his was more literary. He gave me an anthology in which he wrote an inscription: 'Strongly spent is kept' (by Robert Frost). The quotation was from the preface to the Modern Library edition of Frost's poems, but Heaney's inscription turned the prose into something more like a line of poetry or an aphorism:

> Every single poem written regular is a symbol small or great of the way the will has to pitch into commitments deeper and deeper to a rounded conclusion and then be judged for whether any original intention it had has been strongly spent or weakly lost; be it in art, politics, school,

> church, business, love, or marriage – in a piece of work or in a career. Strongly spent is synonymous with kept.

It can be construed that what is being spent is not only the artist's energy – expended in the creation of a work of art that endures – but also the energy devoted to teaching lessons that will live on in the minds of students. In Frost's context, 'spent' and 'kept' allude figuratively to economic activity. Worthy spending can be a good way to get your money's worth.

But Heaney was very frank about how exhausting it was to create a work of art and to prepare for teaching. He himself examined closely what was happening in his mind. He could discuss this without any sense of self-pity; rather, he loved to talk about the process, like a confident magician who reveals his secrets. Being asked about his own remark that 'a poet can end up exhausted and hating the activity' at a poetry workshop, he replied:

> When I said that, I was simply acknowledging the wear and tear your spirit undergoes when you work intensely and closely with other people's hopes and inwardness. What wears you down is, on the one hand, a constant expectation of response, honest response presumably, an effort at truthful judgment, and on the other, a consciousness that nurture is called for also, and praise is being sought.
>
> (*Stepping Stones*, p. 275)

Here is a man who is eager to talk about truth as precisely as possible. He was quite right to point out the duality of a poet-teacher like his predecessor Robert Frost. More than once Heaney admitted that Frost had amalgamated two elements within himself: poet and teacher (or critic). This kind of person can move 'from talking about the poet, in the solitude box of writing, to the relationship between the work and the audience'. And in the latter capacity there are two types of critics: the 'appreciator' (who says, 'You really must have this, it's terrific') and the 'adjudicator' (who says, 'I really wonder if this is worth having at all'). Frost was 'a great teacher', Heaney said, because he was not only a poet per se but also a critic, combining these two functions to create a large audience (Stepping Stones, p. 458). To attract a large audience you have to have something to satisfy them, to teach them what is important, what is moving, what is worth keeping in memory and thinking over – in short, something that helps them think about how to live. Thus, an important characteristic of an excellent teacher is to be able to appreciate the need to satisfy the expectations of the audience. These expectations are nurtured in the daily processes of learning. Once satisfied, they will only become stronger and higher. So the mental mechanism will work both through the reader's longing and through the teacher's pleasure, complementarily and dialectically.

Seamus Heaney, 1998. (*Interfoto/Alamy*)

The poet-teacher or poet-critic who works in a liminal realm is also a theme of Heaney's Oxford lectures, entitled *The Redress of Poetry*. Ending the series of lectures, he admitted that what he had been talking about was 'somewhat analogous to Professor Roy Foster's proposition'. This is the passage by Foster he referred to: 'We need not give up our own claims on Irishness in order to conceive of it as a flexible definition. And in an age of exclusivist jihads to east and west, the notion that people can reconcile more than one cultural identity may have much to recommend it.' As a critic of Heaney, Eugene O'Brien points out that Foster's biography of Yeats was read by Heaney sympathetically. And O'Brien – quoting Heaney's review of the biography – emphasised the impact of Irish revisionism on history written from pluralistic points of view and with an 'inclusive consciousness'. In *Seamus Heaney* (2003), O'Brien cites Heaney's review (1997) and his Oxford lectures (1995) to suggest that the ideas Heaney was working on were closely connected. In his Oxford lectures, Heaney said:

> In other words, whatever the possibilities of achieving political harmony at an institutional level, I wanted to affirm that within our individual selves we can reconcile two orders of knowledge which we might call the practical and the poetic; to affirm also that each form of knowledge redresses the other and that the frontier between them is there for the crossing.
>
> (*The Redress of Poetry*, pp. 202–3)

At the end of the lecture, Heaney quoted his own poem recounting a mysterious encounter at Clonmacnoise monastery. There, a ship appears in the air, above the praying monks. The anchor rope is hooked onto the altar rails, bringing the ship to a standstill. A crew member comes down to unhook it, but in vain. So the abbot orders the monks to help him. The message of the story is that, in response to the

Temple Finghin and McCarthy's Tower at Clonmacnoise Monastery, County Offaly. (*Gareth McCormack/Alamy*)

prayers, a miracle has occurred; miracles can be seen with human eyes, but their occurrence is always a result of intervention and correspondence in our world. A miracle is a miracle only for those who can see it as such. The two orders converge for the benefit of both. Neil Corcoran says of the poem:

> The little miracle-tale, then, is emblematic of the way two orders of being – those of imagination and reality, or of religious faith and experience, or of poetry and event – may coexist and be interdependent, and may rely on each other in acts of mutually responsive generosity. The poem is the recommendation of a tolerant beneficence dependent on the recognition of, and fascination with, otherness.
>
> (*The Poetry of Seamus Heaney: A critical study* (1998), p. 168)

He was careful not to enter into theology, but to limit the implications to the aftermath of the incident. But I would like to propose the heterodoxical view that the miracle of the angelic mission is completed only with human collaboration. And after the work is done, 'The man climb[s] back out of the miracle.' The miracle can happen only here in our world, where the crew cannot stay long. Thus, the annals testify to what is witnessed by someone exceptional on each side. Of course, a variety of interpretations are possible, but what is important is that the two orders are inter-dependent – the boundary can be crossed and perhaps recrossed.

The function of an excellent teacher-poet is to act as a go-between so as to connect creation with appreciation. The teacher is expected to read carefully with imagination, think intensely with lucidity, and explicate persuasively with passion. Thus, the poet-critic bridges the two orders: the practical and the poetic, the utilitarian and the aesthetic. The words used for the first order are 'social' and 'functional', for the second 'authentic' and 'private'. The ability to talk about the mystery of the private world in socially creditable terms reminds us of W.H. Auden on Yeats:

> The social virtues of a real democracy are brotherhood and intelligence, and the parallel linguistic virtues are strength and clarity …
>
> (*The Public v. the Late Mr. William Butler Yeats*)

Frost was much like Yeats and Auden, and Heaney inherited a similar mentality: he praise the same virtues and handed them down to the next generation. Furthermore, an excellent teacher can cite evidence from his own lived experience. An interpretation of a line of poetry may show the trace of a mind working rapidly or slowly, regularly or abruptly. Thus it can be so much more instructive.

Heaney's son Michael said that his father's last words to his family were 'noli timere', which can be read not as a simple coercive imperative but as an invitation: 'let's try if possible', with humility, to go along the same route together. This attitude is that of a man who knows how difficult it is to pursue what he himself is proposing. And it is a secret of Heaney's that the message sounds more intimate when addressed to a reader or a listener.

Another mediating role of the critic is to make peace between two confronting groups. The critic's task is to find a string of peace in the predicament of communal reality, however thin that string may be. Some of the most impressive terms to me in the *Preoccupations* and *The Government of the Tongue* concern a poem's function of comforting our mind. In the first book, Heaney uses 'assuaging' (p. 17) and, in contrast, 'exacerbation' (p. 29), and in the latter 'appease' and 'massages rather than ruffles' (p. 121), so as not to exacerbate (p. xxii) the disturbances of the mind. These are quite natural ideas for a man from a conflict-torn country. But it does not mean that Heaney was ever compromising. As is well known, when necessary, he said a definite 'No', as in the case of the *Penguin Book of Contemporary British Poetry*; the capitalised No is also in the vocabulary of democracy, strength and clarity.

The two aspects of a poet-teacher's task are mysterious and persuasive. The first is almost impossible to imitate; one can do nothing but accept authoritative truth the poet tells us. But in the second he can be analytical and communicable so as to verbalise the process of the mystery. Readers and audiences are allowed to share the experience, and imitate and learn the process of thinking precisely. Thus we can enjoy the analysis in our own mind with interest. The joy and satisfaction of being taught in this way awakes in our mind a sense of gratitude to the teacher. And in this function Heaney's generosity makes us all the more strongly aware of the treasure lying in gratitude.

The Garden History Society: The Japanese Garden, Tully, Kildare

John Colleran and Eileen McCracken, 1977
Revised by Yvonne O'Conor, 2017

The Japanese garden at Tully is acclaimed as one of the oldest and finest examples of a Japanese garden in Europe.

Western European interest in the layout, composition and symbolism of Japanese gardens dates back to the 1850s. Since then, individual features necessary in a Japanese garden – such as pavilions, bridges, certain trees and plants, stone lanterns and flowing water – have been introduced into many gardens. However, in isolation or in haphazard arrangement they do not make a Japanese garden. The Japanese garden is a unit incorporating all these components as symbols, and the arrangement of the garden in a framework of water, stone and plants follows certain oriental principles.

There are three basic types of Japanese garden: water garden, dry garden and tea garden. The tea garden at Tully symbolises the embodiment of the spirit/soul and its journey through this human stage of existence. The Tully Japanese Garden, now state property, is magnificently maintained and is visited by over 120,000 visitors annually.

香蝶楼
国貞画
極

The Tully estate was bought by Colonel William Hall-Walker (created Baron Wavertree of Delamere in 1919) in 1900. By 1915, when he presented Tully to the state, he had established the stud farm and had also created the Japanese garden that lies adjacent to the farm. From 1915 to 1943, Tully was owned by the British National Stud, and for part of this time a nursery was maintained in the stud grounds. By the time the Irish National Stud Company took over the Tully estate, the Japanese garden was in quite a dilapidated state, and it was not until the appointment of a gardener from the National Botanic Gardens (Paddy Doyle) in 1946 that things began to improve. In 1973, John Colleran took over the supervision of the garden, and continuing to this day there has always since been a horticulturist overseeing the continued restoration of the garden.

Colonel Hall-Walker – a Conservative politician and businessman with an interest in art – knew Japan well, and recognised that the swampy site at Tully, with natural springs, could be developed as a Japanese garden. In 1906, he commissioned Tassa (Saburo) Eida (whom records lead us to believe was an art dealer) to design and oversee the construction of this garden. We have no idea if Eida had any formal training in horticulture, but we do know that he was involved in designing gardens for the Japan-British Exhibition in London in 1910.

It took forty labourers four years to lay out the garden, at a cost of £38,000. Hundreds of tonnes of rock were carted from the Silliot hills, and large, mature Scots pines transplanted from Dunmurray. Eida's brother lived in Japan at this time, and between them they organised a chartered cargo from Japan to bring stone lanterns, plants, bonsai, a tea house and a miniature village, the various parts of the latter carved in Fujiyama lava. Crevasses in the individual pieces of lava from which the village was cut have been used to grow dwarfed conifers and azaleas.

The plants used in the Tully garden include spring-flowering species of cherry blossom, flowering almond and plum, with Japanese azaleas and camellias forming a canopy over St Bridget anemonies, and other spring bulbs. In summer the hostas, ferns, Japanese anemonies and Tibetan poppies provide a lovely shaded tranquillity beneath the tree canopy. Autumn is perhaps the most spectacular season, with the wonderful diversity of autumn colour on the Japanese maples.

(opposite page) *Gatherer of Herbs*, by Utagawa Kunisada (1786–1865). (*© National Museum of Ireland*)

(left) Stone lantern, or 'toro', meaning 'light basket' (Japanese Garden, Tully, County Kildare). (*Photo courtesy of Yvonne O'Conor*); (right) Stone lantern, or 'toro', meaning 'light basket' (Japanese Garden, Tully, County Kildare). (*Photo courtesy of Yvonne O'Conor*)

Many of the original bonsai *Larix kaempferi* and *Chamaecyparis obtusa*, in particular, are still growing in the garden, but although still pruned to give the appearance of bonsai, they have long since burst their pots, and are rooted into the ground (one of the results of that obscure period from 1915 to 1946).

The Japanese Garden at Tully covers about one and a quarter acres, with about a fifth of the area occupied by a lawn that represents the end of the saga the garden depicts. The original wall next to the public road is capped with a timber Japanese-style fence, and in 2014 a similar wall was constructed along the interior boundary of the garden. This was done out of necessity as the *Thuja plicata* hedge that formed this boundary was very badly damaged during the severe winter of 2010, and was beyond recovery.

The Tully tea garden portrays the journey of the spirit/soul through its human existence. The 'pilgrim soul' enters through the Gateway of Oblivion … our birth is but a sleep and a forgetting. A small rock cave crowned by a flowering cherry symbolises the womb and the beginning of life. From the cave a sunken path paved with irregularly placed stones depicting the tottering steps of childhood leads to a dark twisting rock tunnel, the Tunnel of Ignorance, which signifies a child's lack of understanding. Halfway along the Tunnel of Ignorance are stone steps leading upwards, the Steps of Learning. These lead to a mound topped by a Scots pine, the Hill of Knowledge. Here a Pitfall can trap the too self-assured. From the Hill of Knowledge two paths lead to adulthood, one smooth and easy, the other a rugged path of adventure. Once adulthood is attained there is a choice of three paths: the first smooth and easy, flanked by flowering cherries, symbolising temptation; the second, the lonely road of austere living or bachelorhood; and the third, the middle path, leads to marriage. The path to marriage crosses water by stepping stones to the Island of Joy and Wonder, where the young person meets their future partner and the two leave the island by way of a small bridge, the Bridge of Engagement. A bush of clipped boxwood represents a table set for the pre-nuptial feast. Beyond this Wedding Table is the Marriage Bridge, made of two slabs of stone set in opposite banks of a stream but meeting over midstream to lie side by

The tea house viewed from the 'honeymoon path' (Japanese Garden, Tully, County Kildare). (*Photo courtesy of Yvonne O'Conor*)

The tea house viewed from the flat bridge at the base of the Hill of Ambition (Japanese Garden, Tully, County Kildare). (*Photo courtesy of Yvonne O'Conor*)

side, symbolising the union of matrimony. The honeymoon path is an easy, wide path by the side of the stream, where the newly-weds walk side by side happily until they encounter an obstacle that causes their paths to diverge temporarily; this represents their first disagreement. Soon after, they are reunited and together seek the way to the Well of Wisdom. Disappointment is in store as they follow a very tempting path that leads under a trelliswork of wisteria to a dead end. They must retrace their steps and tread the rocky path that leads upwards towards the Hill of Ambition. Personality difficulties cause the man and woman to part and follow different routes, but they are united at the summit of the Hill of Ambition, which, like the Hill of Knowledge, is crowned with a Scots pine. From here they can look back along the garden and see only as far as the Bridge of Engagement, which indicates a general lack of memory of childhood. The Hill of Ambition is the peak of life and the highest point in the garden. From its summit a path leads down to a turbulent stream where there are statues of the Water Gods. Again, there is a choice of ways: a smooth and easy path or a set of difficult stepping stones across the waterfall. But both paths lead to a tea house and the Well of Wisdom. Now they come to the iconic curved red bridge that epitomises the Span of Life, and they move on to the flat lawn of Peace and Contentment, bordered by a tranquil river and trees. At the entrance to the lawn is a box-topiary figure of a chair, the Chair of Old Age. From here one partner watches the other cross the lawn on the irregularly placed flagstones that represent the tottering steps of old age and which lead to the Hill of Repose. Here the old man or woman is laid to rest under the weeping trees. The human life story complete, the soul goes forth through the Gate of Eternity.

While in Tully, Eida also designed and planted an area that is now considered as National Stud grounds rather than part of the Japanese garden. Two artificial lakes were excavated, the upper lake of spring water, controlled by sluice gates, flowing by a narrow stream to the lower lake, whose sluice gates in turn control the flow of water into the tea garden. These two lakes were representative of the oldest of Japanese landscape styles, which go back to the Nara period (646–794) when the land-and-island theme emerged as the earliest theme of Japanese classical design. This style was further developed on the estates of the feudal lords during the Edo period. Edo, renamed Tokyo in 1869, was originally the site of the castle belonging to the shogun, and has given its name to the historic period. The islands

An original bonsai, a Japanese larch (*Larix leptolepis*), approximately 150 years old (Japanese Garden, Tully, County Kildare). It has burst its pot and is rooted. (*Photo courtesy of Yvonne O'Conor*)

of the upper lake were planted with dogwood under willows, while on the lower lake's largest island a rustic thatched house was built to shelter the lake's swans. This house is now gone, but the upper-lake area has been developed into a new water-and-rock garden symbolising Ireland through the ages, with sunken forests and beehive huts. This garden was designed by Martin Hallinan in 1999 and is dedicated to St Fiachra, the patron saint of gardeners.

The following poem by Helen Sevrez (from *Men Call it Love and Other Poems* (1926)) describes the Japanese Garden at Tully:

Within this garden of Japan I sought
In symbol Earth to mark from Youth to Age
Such of Life's meaning as old time has taught
And point the pathways of our pilgrimage.

From Forest gloom the paths of Beauty rise
From rocks of gate spring little flowers of flame
So that our steps be steadfast and our eyes
Be not too blindly raised to heights of fame.

Here spreads the panorama of Desire
Of cherry blossom rapture and allure,
And here the path where wisdom shall aspire
To nobler heights and bliss that shall endure.

Here leads to Joy the mystic path of Pain
Life's hilltop reached, then languor, then release,
That brings the soul oblivion once again
Mid flowering glory of Elysian peace.

Below, the species of Japanese maples and cherry/almond blossoms in the garden are itemised.

Japanese Maples

Japanese maples (*Acer palmatum*) have been cultivated in Japan for centuries. These beautiful trees include hundreds of named cultivars with a variety of forms, colours and leaf types. Heights of mature specimens range from 0.5m to 25m, depending on type. The trees are particularly suitable for borders and ornamental paths because the root systems are compact and not invasive. Many varieties of *Acer palmatum* are successfully grown in containers.

Well-drained soil is essential as they will not survive in soggy waterlogged soil. Trees should only be lightly fertilised, preferably using slow-release fertiliser. Nitrogenous lawn fertilizer should be avoided in the immediate vicinity of these trees as excessive nitrogen can cause overly vigorous growth that is prone to infection.

Japanese maples naturally self-prune any foliage that does not receive enough light, such as internal branches that are overly shaded by their own canopy. The form of the tree, especially without leaves in winter, can be of great interest, and it can be pruned to highlight this feature. Trees heal readily after pruning without the need for aftercare. This species should not be pruned like a hedge but shaped by carefully choosing individual branches to remove.

Most cultivars of Japanese maples are individually hand-selected from specific seedlings that show particularly striking characteristics. The selected cultivar is then propagated, usually by grafting.

In Japan the Japanese maple is used as an accent tree providing gentle shade in summer and beautiful colours in autumn. Many cultivars have characteristics that come into prominence during different seasons, including the colour of new or mature leaves, beautiful autumn colour, or unusual bark marking or colouring. Sometimes cultivars can scarcely be distinguished from others, and if trees are grown from seed, each one that grows will be very different from the others (seedling variation).

There are more than a thousand cultivars of Japanese maples, and in the Japanese Garden we are privileged to have some of the most beautiful.

Here is a list of some of the cultivars of Japanese maples that we have at the Japanese Garden:

Acer palmatum Dissectum Atropurpureum	Lawn inside Gate of Oblivion and Well of Wisdom

Acer palmatum Dissectum Viride	Lawn inside Gate of Oblivion
Acer palmatum 'Garnet'	Lawn inside Gate of Oblivion
Acer palmatum 'Sango kaku'	Lawn inside Gate of Oblivion
Acer palmatum 'Osakazuki'	Hill of Ambition, Water Gods, Easy Path
Acer palmatum 'Shishigashira'	Wall side of Easy Path
Acer palmatum 'Suminagashi'	Wall side of Path of Adventure
Acer palmatum 'Shigitsu sawa'	Marriage Bridge
Acer palmatum 'Sango kaku'	Left-hand side Hill of Ambition, seat at wall
Acer palmatum 'Shaine'	Steps at tea house
Acer palmatum 'Iroha momiji'	Behind tea house

There are multiples of many of the above cultivars in this garden, and the sites listed above only give an idea of where there are individual specimens.

Cherry blossom varieties you will find in the Japanese Garden

Prunus shirofugen	Lawn inside Gate of Oblivion
Prunus serrulata tai – haku (great white cherry)	Rockery to the right approaching the Cave of Birth
Prunus Kanzan	Cave of Birth
Prunus incisa Kko jo no-mai (dwarf)	Hill of Learning
Prunus shirotae 'Mount Fuji'	Hill of Learning
Prunus amanagowa	Left-hand side, Path of Adventure

Prunus umineko	Wall (Bachelor) Path
Prunus kanzan	Island of Joy and Wonder
Prunus Pink perfection	Right-hand side Marriage Bridge
Prunus serrula tibetica	Pond edge past the Parting of the Ways
Prunus ichiyo	Behind the tea house on the rockery

Many of the above varieties occur more than once through the garden, so we have selected the most typical of each variety to give an idea of their growth habit and flowering.

In the stud grounds you will see a good avenue planting of *Prunus kanzan*.

Bear in mind also that you are looking at trees of varying age, as some of the older trees have had to be replaced.

Coke Fuji (height 71cm x width 51cm). Coca-Cola rises to a great height, the symbol of fast food and convenience.

Thirty-Six New Views of Mount Fuji

Seisai (Peter MacMillan)

The thirty-six new views of Mount Fuji presented in this volume take their starting point from Katsushika Hokusai's *Thirty-Six Views of Mount Fuji*, a series of colour woodblock prints depicting Mount Fuji from thirty-six different perspectives, although there are forty-six images in both Hokusai's series and my own. The prints collected here juxtapose an idealised historical view of Mount Fuji and Japanese culture with the reality of contemporary society. Some years ago, I began to compile selections of poetry and prose about Mount Fuji for a book entitled *One Hundred Literary Views of Mount Fuji*. The manuscript is now in the final stages. As I compiled and translated these works, I became very conscious of the gaps that have opened up between the world of classical Japanese, on the one hand, in which man exists in harmony with nature, and contemporary consumer society, on the other hand, in which he increasingly does not. In the present volume, I seek to evoke this growing gap through images of Mount Fuji that that are sometimes mournful, yet often playful and satirical.

The disparities – some subtle, some rather less so – between the original and the recomposed images invite the viewer to reflect upon the differences between traditional and contemporary Japanese culture. The series also celebrates the granting of World Heritage Site status to Mount Fuji by having her travel overseas and make many new friends, including in my own homeland of Ireland.

Mount Fuji is a sacred mountain of great cultural significance and has been depicted widely in literature and art since the seventh century. The *Thirty-Six New Views of Mount Fuji* aims to reveal the cultural importance of this sacred mountain to people both in Japan and around the world.

Seisai is my artist name. It is an homage to Hokusai, whose own name means 'study in the north'; Seisei means 'study in the west'. The prints are mixed media, combining lithography, offset printing, hand-painting and gold leaf applied by hand.

Highway Fuji (height 51cm x width 71cm). Road construction was one of the pillars on which Japan's post-war economy was built, but will all the roads end up at the peak of sacred Fuji?

Before the Great Wave (height 51cm x width 71cm). As the Arctic ice melts, water levels rise throughout the world.

When the great wave of Hokusai
strikes up to the sky,
avalanches into the sea,
Fuji may suddenly disappear.

– Kitahara Hakushu

Cup Noodle Fuji (height 51cm x width 71cm). Cup noodles, the epitome of Japanese fast-food culture. This image is based on a motif from a painting of Mount Fuji by Yokoyama Taikan.

Flag Fuji II (Cherry Blossom) (Height 87cm x Width 136cm). This image depicts the friendship between Japan and the United States.

Maid Fuji (Height 51cm x Width 71cm). A comment on costume play and the famous maid cafés of Japan. The motif is borrowed from a painting of Mount Fuji by Yokoyama Taikan.

Mandara Fuji (Height 71cm x Width 51cm). In the Edo period, a religion called Fujiko was devoted to the worship of Mount Fuji, and many people climbed the sacred mountain in pilgrimage. This image depicts Japanese businessmen of today climbing the great mountain. The traditional decorations of the sun and the moon have been replaced by coins.

The Peak of Fuji (height 51cm x width 71cm). The red circle represents Fuji's peak while the surrounding lines depict the actual contours of the mountain. This work was created to commemorate Mount Fuji's registration as a World Heritage Site.

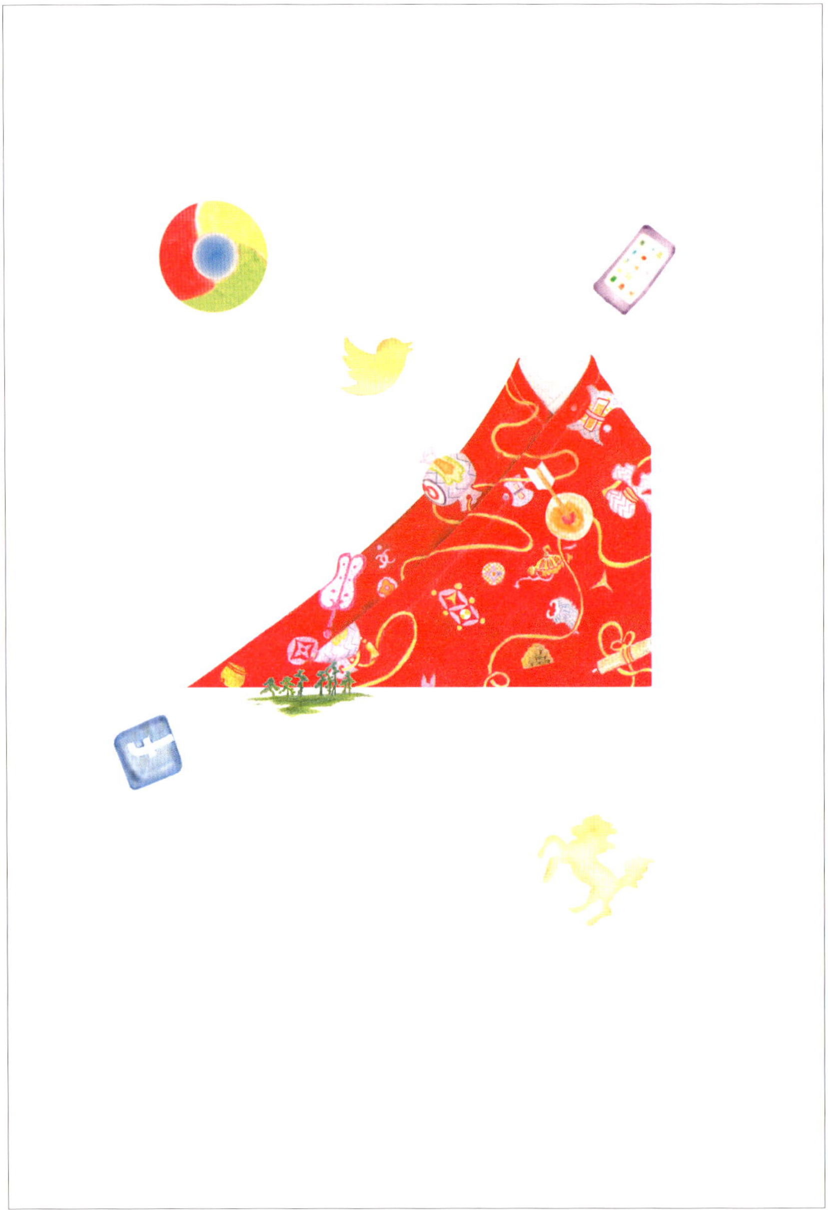

Hagoromo Fuji II (height 66cm x width 46cm). This image celebrates Mount Fuji's connection with the Noh play Hagoromo (A Robe of Feathers), which is set in Miho no Matsubara, not far from the mountain. Mount Fuji wears the costume used in the play, decorated here with depictions of traditional and contemporary treasures.

The Traditional Seven Treasures Plus One Irish Treasure

Small Mallet – To ensure your wishes come true.

Weight – The symbol of wealth, weight is used for weighing gold.

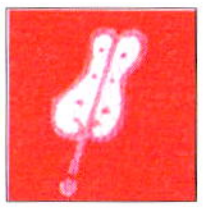

Referee's Fan – A fan used to declare the victor in a contest.

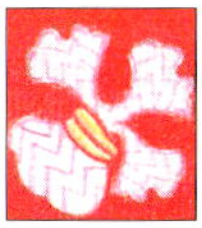

Money Bag – A pouch containing treasure.

Scroll – The symbol of wisdom and knowledge.

The Seven Treasures – The seven treasures of the world of Buddhism.

Sedge Hat/Straw Cape – A cape and hat to conceal and protect the wearer from danger.

The Pot of Gold – The Leprechaun's pot full of gold found at the foot of a rainbow.

Present-Day Treasures

Twitter

Facebook

Smart phone

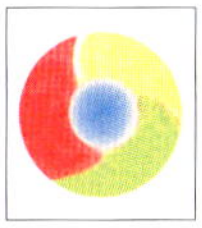

Google

Porsche

Mercedes Benz

BMW

Chanel

Louis Vuitton

Symbol of the Japanese Lottery

Money

Single Pine Fuji (height 71cm x width 51cm). After the Great East Japan Earthquake of 2011 only a single pine remained on the beach of Rikuzen Takada. It became a symbol of hope for Japan.

Irish Fuji (height 36cm x width 51.5cm) This image celebrates the bonds between Ireland and Japan. The mountain in the image looks like Fuji but is really Croagh Patrick, a sacred mountain where St Patrick is said to have performed religious practices. The cogon grass ring is used for purification in Japan, as at the festival at which Mount Fuji is opened to climbers for the summer. Here it symbolises the entering of a different dimension: the world of the magical and supernatural that exists in the everyday in Ireland and Japan. Both countries share folk tales with closely related motifs, such as Tír na nÓg and Urashimataro. In both tales, a young man goes to the land of eternal youth for 300 years and when he returns he ages suddenly. In the Japanese tale, he travels on a turtle, which appears in a prominent position in this image. The turtle here travels between Ireland and Japan, sharing myths and the magical elements of everyday life. The six-sided shapes here are from the turtle's back. They often appear in shrine decorations and are a symbol of good fortune in Japan. Ireland, meanwhile, is famous for the six-sided rocks of the Giants Causeway, a World Heritage Site, which consists of about 40,000 interlocking basalt columns, the result of an ancient volcanic eruption.

The shamrock is a symbol of Ireland recognised around the globe. The colours of the image are inspired by the Irish tricolour: green, white and orange. The Celtic Triskelion is taken from the astronomical calendar at the famous megalithic tomb of Newgrange in Ireland, built around 3200 BC. A version of the same symbol (mitsudome), a visual representation of a vortex, has been widely used in Japan since ancient times.

Crane Fuji I (height 46cm × width 66cm). The crane is a symbol of celebration and longevity, and in this image the body of the crane is Mount Fuji. This is a work created to commemorate the naming of Mount Fuji as a World Heritage Site and it taking flight around the world to disseminate Japanese culture.

Tuna Fuji (height 71cm x width 51cm). A tuna becomes Mount Fuji.

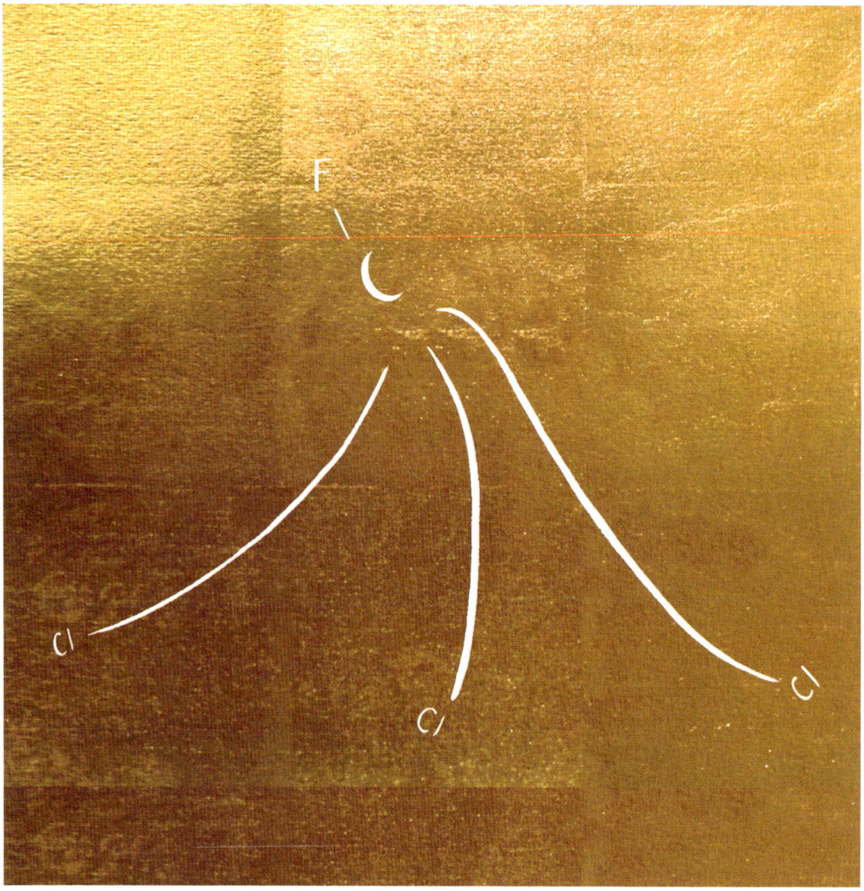

Freon Fuji (height 71cm × width 51cm). This image depicts Mount Fuji and the three-day moon and, at the same time, portrays the chemical structure of freon gas.

Plastic Fuji (Height 71cm x Width 51cm). The universality of Mount Fuji is a theme of the series. In contemporary consumer society, what is more universal than plastic?

Vuitton Fuji (Height 71cm x Width 51cm). Mount Vuitton represents the popularity of the famous brand in consumerist Japan. The Louis Vuitton logo is said to be based on a traditional Japanese family-crest design.

Justice Fuji (Height 71cm x Width 51cm). What is the place of justice in society? This image portrays the scales, in delicate Japanese colours, with Icarus falling into the sea unnoticed. It follows the depiction of the suffering of others in the painting *Landscape with the Fall of Icarus*, which is also described in W.H. Auden's poem 'Musée des Beaux-Arts'.

Lacquer Wave Fuji (height 78cm x width 58cm). Celebrating the art of lacquer ware. Or is it an oil spill?

Kilimanjaro Fuji (height 66cm × width 31.5cm). Mount Fuji makes friends with Mount Kilimanjaro in Tanzania. How many Fujis can you find hidden in the image? And can you find Kilimanjaro on the neck of the giraffe? *Kirin* is also the Japanese word for giraffe, so the name is a pun on the 'kilim' of Kilimanjaro. A giraffe called Fuji-ko was acquired by Hirakawa Zoo, Kagoshima, in 1952.

Spin Fuji (Height 68cm x Width 68cm). If one thinks of the centre of the axel as the peak of the mountain, then there is one Fuji spinning around; but one can also see five more Fujis, one within each of the metal frames.

Miyako Fuji (height 50cm x width 43cm). The famous ballerina Miyako Yoshida's tutu is made from the snow of the peak of Fuji.

Detail from volume 3 of the *Tales of Ise* (Ise monogatari), artist unknown, late sixteenth century. (CBL J 1050.3,

Poetry

詩

ŌE's Yeats

Kenzaburō Ōe

From 'Led by Poets' in I A Novelist's Way of Writing (*Shinchousha Bunko Heisei 13*)

> … as for preparedness, as an example of being never converted, W.B. Yeats taught me a lot. On one of the cards of the draught of my translation inserted among the pages of the *Collected Poems of Yeats* is that of the Choice.

What I learnt from Yeats was an attitude of a poet, who, though no believer in any cult, is always considering and gazing at 'the Heavenly mansion'. In the writers' world in this country now we find many utterances from those writers or critics who have a belief in a religious principle, either Protestant or Catholic. Especially from those novices who have only recently found faith, the support of the church may look too optimistically authoritative. On the other hand we the common citizen, though revealing somewhat similar optimism, cannot pass the boundary between the belief and non-belief so off-handedly for we contrast our 'raging in the dark' with their conclusive argument …

In case of Yeats the process is discussed more directly in Kathleen Raine's Blake studies and Yeats studies, at the back clearly connected with Jewish-Christian inheritance and its context of wider tradition of religious feeling, imagery and the outlook of the universe. I have been guided by these preceding speculations. My *Blazing Green Tree* may have shown these influences rather undisguisedly.

Now, in this way I have written many stories based on what has been inspired by these poets. All of them came from absorbed reading of the poets indeed, and they made up surely happy experiences. Yet when I recall the concrete spot of each birth, contrarily to the happiness, more often than not hard memory comes back vividly… (pp. 77–8)

Poetry and Politics Should be Separated: A Rhapsody

Masazumi Toraiwa

Poetry and politics, like church and state, should be separated. And for the same reasons: mysteries distort the rational processes which ideally prevail in social relations; while ideologies confiscate the poet's special passport to terra incognit.

(from Edna Longley, *Poetry in the Wars*)

And poetry and pottery also should be separated
Like pot-and-pee because it quickly gets foul and stinky,
And of course you cannot keep poetry in the pot, can
you? I wish poetry and poverty would be separated for
good But it's a pity most poets are poverty stricken, For
poetry and pound are separated hopelessly.
Poor poets have nothing to eat but dry, hard bread and cheese
And drink cheap pint and smoke pot,

Only to keep imagining a ghostly tyger, tyger, burning bright,
And to find out dry-hard images and useless rhyme and rhythm.
Unfortunately I cannot but conclude 'poverty is mother of poetry.'
And since music has nothing to do with poetry
They also should be separated like wife and husband,
Though they believe united each other after meeting so often.
Plato and poetry are different things to be separated
And Plato has left so many mischievous lies in philosophy
And expelled those emotional and crazy liars from his Republic;
So poetry should be separated from politics all right.
But Plato should be absolutely separated from potato,

Though they tend to stick to each other through rhyming power. But potato and fish are easily combined to be "fish and chips" Even so they must be separated because fish is not potato, you know. Significant 'fish' is arbitrarily combined with 'potato' To make a new sign of "fish and chips" in deep oil,

And once they are combined in the wrapping old newspaper, You cannot separate these two like two pages of a sheet of paper.

Poetry is printed on a page but still they should be separated
Like a child dragged out from a mother in the pool of blood.

As poetry should be pure and posh, especially for the academics, So poetry and punk should be separated like pudding and pie. And poets and pubs should be separated by all means Like sewing-machine and umbrella on the table.

However crazy they look, poets are in fact sober up all the time To make brilliant poems full of idiotic images.

It's really, really sad to say poetry and play should be separated For we love to play with words and poetry as crazily as possible.

Needless to say poetry and pentagon, like bomber and bombs, Should be separated, to kill hungry children on the streets. By the way, even if you might think it's cruel to declare President and pretzel should be separated like chew and choke, And like brainless ape in the bush and *Homo sapiens*, *Linné*.

That's the lesson a mother can tell to her silly son, not grown up yet.
Pure poetry constructed with purely verbal signs,

Under the tent of intensive care of doctors and nurses, To cut off germs and noises for art for art's sake: But alas, all these should be separated like pest and patient, Poesie puree should be separated from tomato puree.

Poetry comes out flowing from the poet's pen,

Printed on the paper to bring it out in the pocket To please poor penniless pauper; But again all these should be separated.

And poets are totally entitled to mock and jibe the rogues,
President or king, dead or alive, if they dare to tum over the world.
Poetry is just powerless before the coward ape-like monster.
But can you walk away from the dying children from hunger?
Can you imagine tears and smiles burning in your napalm-bombs?
Can you hear children weep under your blast bombs?

You cannot separate poetry from pumpkin and picnic and ping-pong And from everything including politics and peace, can you? Can you? Can you?

Roman mosaic showing Plato (seated second from left) among students and other philosophers. (*World History Archive/Alamy*)

White metal-girder bridge, Biei, Hokkaido, Japan. (*Scott Sim/Alamy*)

Gensuke-bashira

John FitzGerald

The long white bridge with its pillars of iron is recognisably modern

Lafcadio Hearn

But the townsfolk couldn't bring themselves
to cross, fearing another pact with the gods,
that crimson glow on moonless nights.

Last time, they'd buried a good man
live into the sandy bed to appease the flood-spirits
who wouldn't let the fill-stones settle.

And when they fixed the pillars in
one sank deeper down, yet shouldered the road
ably over three centuries.

Red-crowned crane.
(David Tipling Photo Library/Alamy)

Poems

Michael Longley

To Otomo Yakamochi

on receiving the inaugural Yakamochi Medal

You, Otomo Yakamochi,
Poet and governor, and I
Minor bureaucrat, and poet too,
Meet across thirteen hundred years
To talk about birds and flowers.

Lover of cuckoos and wisteria,
For you I have saved meadowsweet
And willowherb and loosestrife
And the meadow pipit's few notes
And the skylark's aria.

We gaze on our soul-landscapes
More intensely with every year –
Small boats passing Inishbofin,
Small boats on the Nago Sea,
Wokami River crimson-lustrous.

Barnacle geese our messengers
Across space and time, Otomo –
Tormentil closed by the rain
And centaury, tiny boxes
Yellow and pink, Japanese.

Anything however small
May make a poem, a snail, say,
Tucked into the marram grass,
In the distance Tateyama
Or Mweelrea, holy mountains.

I picture you at the White Strand
Galloping through the breakers,
Spring-tide and rain and spray
Kicked up by your horse's hooves
Drenching bridle and stirrups.

A small townland becomes my life,
Carrigskeewaun, grandchildren
Wading in the tidal channel –
Otomo, my soul's a currach
Disappearing behind the waves.

The Anthologist

Otomo Yakamochi,
Earliest anthologist,
Listened to thousands of poems
And listened to cranes calling
Their mating calls back and forth,
To songbirds among blossoms,
And listened to grasshoppers
And frogs in the harvest fields,
And listened as girls chatted
Up to their knees in shallows
Gathering rock-weed to sell,
And all summer long the snow
Remained on Tachi Mountain,
Sure sign of its divinity.

Grass of Parnassus

High up on Tateyama
(Of Japan's holy mountains
Yakamochi's favourite)
We find by a stony path
A solitary overlooked
Grass of Parnassus in flower
And stoop to decipher
Engraved petals, and to share
Across the millennium
With the flower-loving poet
The white gleam we first noticed
Amid eyebright and speedwell
At far-off Carrigskeewaun
Years ago, and still in bud.

Platinum Anniversary

Sinéad Morrissey

The two of us wound
into borrowed kimonos
on the temple steps

my heavy headgear
dagger tucked into my waist-
band should you ever

undress another
one flick of my ivory
wrist and I'd collapse

in the wet of my
small intestine my stomach
bridles soon enough

A *maiko* dances. (*Andrew Linscott/Alamy*)

over uncooked eggs
at the airport and you you
star you crucible

my teeth are yours I
think my ribs removable
your unwavering

lantern frown above
my ice bed bloody sheets your
trousseau in my dream

I see our future
daughter driving a ragtop
and then I wake or

don't and there's this trick
your skin still does if I brush
my thumb along it

thronged notes spun into
one held hum by a gesture
all the hares lie down

and the two of us
just under half our lives and
this glitch we ride in

space together I
see precisely no one else
inside a shrinking

bubble of light the
minuscule part of matter
that's matter splitting

apart from itself
bright you singing on the stair-
way there's only you

Bashō in Kinsale

Derek Mahon

Samurai cries from
Enthusiasts in the gym
As I wander home.

Dithery rain lines;
Crows glisten in the branches
Of listening pines.

Culls in the clear air,
Hawthorn snow in the hedges;
Soon you will be here.

March, evening shadow
On pine and quiet dockyard
Here in Hokkaido.

Clouds obscure the night
Giving our eyes a rest from
The intense moonlight

Rough sea after dark;
Blazing over the harbour
The fierce zodiac.

A heron voice harsh
Above us after midnight
Like a lightning flash.

Walking each evening
At a slower pace, we hear
The dark river sing.

A morning of mist;
No light source but a hidden
Sun burns in the east.

A cove, flies and fleas,
Wrack magic in salt sea air
And the faintest breeze.

The seal surfaces.
Around her in the water
A cloud disperses.

Actors as Samurai, by Katsukawa Shunsho (1726–92). (*World History Archive/Alamy*)

White Heron and Purple Iris, by Utagawa Hiroshige (1797–1858), c. 1830. (*World History Archive/Alamy*)

These old childish things,
Big blisters at the shoreline,
Are my water wings.

Blown sand and no talk,
Even the most northern road
An easier walk.

Watching us, the earth
Has all the time in the world
For death and rebirth.

Desert island books:
Homer and Rachel Carson,
Durable hardbacks.

Sketch of a sail race,
The work of many summers:
A few lines in space.

Detail from scroll 2 of 'Song of Lasting Sorrow' (*Chōgonka gakan*), by Kanō Sansetsu (1589–1651), late 1640s. (CBL J 1158.2, © *The Trustees of the Chester Beatty Library, Dublin*)

Memoir

伝記

伝記

'Under the Cherry Tree, There Are No Strangers': Adventures of an Irishwoman in Japan

Dearbhla Kelly

Dearbhla Kelly was a JET participant 1991–3, Kobe University masters student 1993–5, English lecturer Wakyama Shin Ai and Osaka Womens' College, 1995–9

How did I come to Japan?

It all began with a book that cast its spell over me. On its cover was a soaring temple set in silhouette against a red vibrant sky. Its inner pages – Japanese rice paper speckled with gold and silver – teemed with vibrantly beautiful Japanese pottery, ikebana (flower arrangements), meticulously arranged *bento* (lunch boxes), formidable Japanese castles and mysterious temples. Something about the aesthetic sensibility of that fascinating book piqued my interest and struck a chord in my heart.

It was called *The Dawns of Tradition*, and I discovered it as a grey-uniformed, sixteen-year-old in the sleepy library of the Abbey Vocational School in Donegal town. I held on to that book and never let it go. Thirty years later it still serves as a reminder of life-changing events.

After secondary school, I went to the University of Ulster to study media studies, geography and French. I struggled with French, but in a library – everything important always happens in libraries – met a mature student who oddly suggested that I switch to Japanese as Japanese was far easier … hmm, unlikely. I did not know then that the student, David McNeill, would later go on to become the Japanese correspondent of *The Irish Times*.

Women under
the cherry tree.
(*New York Public Library*)

Young and impulsive, I leapt into a sea of *kanji* (Japanese characters), *hiragana* and *katakana*. I had only one career aim in mind: to travel to Japan. In my interview for the Japan Exchange and Teaching (JET) programme, I told the panel that I would, by hook or by crook, go to Japan.

I arrived in Tokyo on 28 July 1991. It was 37°C and I was hit by a wall of humidity and surrounded by a sea of sweat-moistened, white-shirted, black-haired salary men (the Japanese term for businessmen).

We stayed in the forty-seven-floor Keio Plaza Hotel in the heart of Tokyo and I was star struck: skyscrapers all around me, feeling as if the windows of the world were opening up to me. I was introduced to JETs from America, Canada, New Zealand, Australia, the UK and Ireland. I began practising the art of bowing and displays of respect to my seniors in Japanese society.

I experienced Japanese beer gardens on rooftops and belted out Beatles and Elvis songs at karaoke. My playmate and roommate was Maureen Moore; we were both assigned to the Iburi Board of Education in a town called Muroran. Maureen was a UK JET, from Belfast.

We received lavish Japanese hospitality, both from the Ministry of Education and the Irish embassy in Tokyo. I recall Gatsby-esque banquets with splendid flower arrangements and swan sculptures crafted from ice and platters of sushi accompanied by *Kampai* cheers. The air was filled with possibilities of future meaningful exchanges.

As I had just turned twenty-one, I was the youngest Irish JET of that year, and came under the wing of Richard Kelly, who had been assigned to work in swanky Ashiya in central Japan. Richard was mindful of the fact that I was the only Irish JET and that I had been assigned to work in Hokkaido in the far north of Japan.

We left the bright lights of *Blade Runner*-bedazzling Tokyo and took a two-hour flight to Hokkaido. It was there, on Japan's most northern island, that I truly embraced a new language, a new culture, a new apartment, a new job, new friends, and even new climates. From the moment my feet touched Hokkaido soil, I became 'Keri-Sensei' (Kelly Teacher). From that point on, dear Dearbhla was called everything from Debra to Zebra.

Over the next two years, I sampled all that Hokkaido had to offer. I began with a three-hour tea ceremony where ladies played homage to tea while kneeling on the floor.

Maureen and I were a double act. We took part in the town float for the *Obon Matsuri*, the Festival of the Dead. We visited geisha playing the *shamisen* (Japanese banjo). We went to temples, whale-watched and went to *onsens* (hot springs). We enjoyed the neatly delineated four seasons and Hokkaido's spectacular scenery.

In winter we learnt to ski. Our predecessor was an Olympic-standard skier from Calgary, Canada. The Japanese were perplexed as to why we fell about on our skis, asking us 'Isn't Iceland cold?' We replied that we were from *Ireland*, but by the time we started to explain about the North Atlantic Gulf Stream (*Danryu aru kara yuki ga nai)*, we had already lost them. Maureen and I were like the Jamaican bobsleigh team in the film *Cool Runnings*. We joined the local speed skiing team. For safety reasons and due to our lack of speed, we were always the last to set off; we were even placed after the three-year-old kindergarten kids, who bombed down the ski slopes ahead of us.

Then we got a call from a local volcanic mountain village to represent Ireland in an international cross-country skiing marathon. We had never tried cross-country skiing before, but why should that stop us? We proudly requested the Irish flag from the embassy in Tokyo, and embraced the opportunity to fly it high. We were joined by Austrians, Finns, Swedes and Swiss, all in their latex gear, and displaying world-class proficiency. That day we were humbly beaten by an eighty-four-year-old Japanese man and a child from kindergarten. But, win or lose, at every opportunity I flew the flag for Ireland.

And if we were chilled to our bones, there was always time to enjoy the *kotatsu* (heated table) and share meals and stories with Japanese friends. I stayed with around thirty Japanese home-stay families as I wanted to get to know the people around me. I also visited around thirty schools, and often went to schools in mountain villages for overnight stays.

In Yubari, a mountain village famous for its mouth-watering melons, the entire village greeted me on arrival, and the mayor and all the teachers had a little party for me in the traditional *ryokan* hotel. They put on a splendid feast of Hokkaido crab, lobster, sushi and sashimi. The sense of welcome was outstanding.

In these rural mountainous outposts, they rarely ever met a *gaijin* (foreigner). When I arrived at a local school it was as if a rock star had descended from the heavens and all the kids started shouting 'Madonna' – because of my blonde hair and blue eyes, albeit without the conical breasts – and requested my signature.

I really enjoyed teaching English and bringing a sense of fun into their lessons.

'When in Rome do as the Romans do', so I got stuck into local customs and, putting my feminist credentials on hold, made green tea and served more than thirty Japanese male office workers at tea time when the tea lady was off sick. And I then became great friends with the tea lady and her friends. I went on nights out with my co-workers, sang karaoke, and filled their glasses with beer.

My fellow office workers loved my efforts to learn Japanese and my *niggiaka* lively personality. I participated in the *giri choco* – obligatory chocolates given to men on Valentine's Day – and always brought gifts (*omiyage*) back from my travels. We learnt the rules of seniority and how that permeated everything, including going home at the close of day. We could only leave the office after the senior-ranking officials went home. The officials went home in descending order of rank. 'Would they *ever* leave?' I sometimes wondered.

I also became involved in the local community, joined the local parish church, and became great friends with a family called the Katos as well as the Mary Knoll Missionaries, many of them of Irish descent. I helped to organise a St Patrick's Day party for a hundred guests and introduced the traditional Irish dances 'The Walls of Limerick' and 'The Waves of Tory'. We all danced like waves on the sea, and even more tempestuously after I sourced Irish whiskies, Baileys and – together with the local Japanese ladies – made stew and porter cakes for our hundred guests.

In my determination to showcase Ireland, I even mistakenly sold samples of Avoca and Tara pottery and some jewellery from a company in Tokyo. Mortified at my mistake, I could only repeatedly apologise, purchase back the samples, and return them.

In my second year, I joined Síle Ní Fhearraigh and Colm Ó Baoill in Tokyo and got stuck into the preparations for the first Irish St Patrick's Day parade in 1992.

This was Japan in the pre-Internet era: no Skype, emails, WhatsApp or FaceTime. The main mode of communication with home was by mail. I would wait in anticipation for letters from my mother, and I always called round to my neighbour who owned a corner shop-cum-sake store and snack bar. I asked them every day if the postman had arrived, and they in return would invite me in for tea. Over time I was adopted by a granny living there called Fumiko. She became my honorary *obaasan* granny. Fumiko always wore a kimono and a smile. She had a great spirit of fun and downed three bottles of sake every night!

The JET programme gave me memories, photos and friends in abundance. Twenty-six years later I am still great friends with Maureen and am godmother to her son Rory. I still holiday with UK JETs Alex and Jim. This year I am off to walk the Ring of Kerry with a UK JET from Hokkaido.

The Katos are still my friends and they have made two trips to Ireland. Hiromi Kato stayed with us in Donegal for three weeks. Over the years, the Kato family treated me like the daughter they never had.

I hosted my line manager Fukuzawa's wife in Donegal and in Milton Malbay for the Willie Clancy traditional-Irish music festival. My line manager's wife fell in love with Ireland and took up the tin whistle after our stint in Japan. Since then I have hosted at least six other Japanese friends in Donegal.

I was not ready to end my love affair with Japan after two years of JET. Thanks to Professor Richard Kelly's guidance, I went on to study at Kobe University and deepened my knowledge of Japan. I took a masters in sociology at Kobe, researching Japanese management in multinational enterprises in Ireland, such as NEC, Asahi Kasei, Fujitsu, Munekata, Noritake and so on. During my research I held interviews with both Japanese and Irish management and employees. My main research focused on examining the transfer of Japanese management style within organisational cultures. My research looked at the pillars of Japanese management techniques in the 1990s, such as the Japanese emphasis on *nemawashi* (consensus building) and *ringi* (shared decision-making), as well as so-called 'just in time' production, *kaizen* (continuous improvement) and bottom-up style of management.

These techniques were looked at through the lens of organisational culture using Edgar Schein's model that defines a culture through its artefacts, behaviours, espoused values and underlying basic assumptions. My research concluded that a hybrid of Japanese and Western styles of management exists in the Japanese companies in Ireland. The culture of many organisations, I concluded, employs a mix of Japanese practices within an Irish context.

When I was a student, I was taught the importance of honour, loyalty and seniority. At Kobe University I made great friends with my classmates and my *sempai* (seniors) and, leaving the safety net of JET, jumped into the deep end of Japanese culture. I was the only Westerner in my classes, and was expected to observe certain codes of behaviour. For example, I had to respect and defer to my *sempai* – those that were in the year ahead of me.

Tokyo. (*Didier Zylberyng/Alamy*)

I was assigned a tutor, Shoko Hirai, who was a year ahead of me, and our *sempai–kohai* (senior–junior) relationship began. Shoko and I became very close, and she advised me on various nuances of Japanese behaviour. Shoko also brought me to her family in Nara, and I have fond memories of staying in her traditional Japanese home with her mother, father and grandmother. Her mother even gifted me a string of pearls, and I was invited to sing at Shoko's wedding to one of my classmates. I was drawn into her intimate circle.

I was also assigned, like an apprentice to a master, to the care of my supervisor, Professor Ohno. I salute Professor Ohno's patience with me as I really struggled learning sociology in Japanese. Every Monday, Professor Ohno spent three hours with me explaining sociological concepts while I nodded back like a bewildered rabbit.

Throughout my time at Kobe University I learnt that the group supersedes the individual. We coordinated all activities as a group, from organising conferences to the licking of an envelope. I truly came to understand the quintessentially Japanese aphorism that 'The protruding nail will be hammered down.' It was important for me to grasp this concept as Western or Irish culture tends to be based more on the individual (*kojinshugi*) than on the group (*shudanshugi*). Looking back, I really appreciate the immense patience and understanding my professors, seniors and classmates showed me. Their patience went beyond words.

When I was in Kobe I lived in a dormitory with people of sixteen other nationalities and gained an insight into cultures in South East Asia, South America, India, Pakistan, Burma and so on. These experiences of multicultural crossings have enriched my life and broadened my perspectives on the world.

The most affecting experience during my time in Japan was the Kobe earthquake of 1995. At that time, Professor Richard Kelly, Ciarán Quinn, Graeme Knowd (all JETs in 1991) and I were living in the Kobe area. The earth shuddered violently from below, causing mass destruction. More than 6,500 people died. I can still remember looking at the houses that were toppled and flattened. People were forced to live in community halls and fires destroyed everything around us. There was a huge sense of loss, grief and pain. Despite all the loss and post-traumatic stress, the Japanese society group spirit (*shudanshugi*) was unmistakable. At that time, the Irish embassy in Tokyo organised an ambassadorial visit to the Irish people who were caught up in the earthquake. The Irish ambassador, James

Sharkey, and his wife Sattie gave us great support. They organised an evening for all of us with the president of Ireland, Mary Robinson, in Osaka following the earthquake. We were all very touched by the way the Irish embassy reached out to us.

That time really inspired both me and my Japanese friends, fellow students and lecturers, as well as my Irish and American friends. It was then that I really encountered the Japanese spirit of *gambarre*: that *fighto* spirit of never giving up and rising to the occasion. I can vividly remember looking at my Japanese professor, Professor Ohno (who passed away last year), and thinking that this is what the samurai code of honour is all about. Like a samurai, he made the journey on foot from Nara to Kobe on a daily basis through mangled roadways and collapsed bridges, all for the love of his university and students.

Japan has shaped the course of my life and has left its imprint on my heart. I have been in love with Japan since the age of sixteen. I went to Japan as an immature girl and came back as a woman. Japan offered me a journey of exploration and self-discovery that in turn encouraged me to pursue a career counselling others on finding their true vocation and purpose.

This process of self-discovery through the exploration of a foreign culture reminds me of the great Irish author Lafcadio Hearn's early writings on Japan in 'My First Day in the Orient'. Hearn (1850–1904) describes his journey up mountains and cliffs to a shrine, and then describes what he finds within the small, old grey temple on the rocky height:

> Then I reach the altar, gropingly, unable yet to distinguish forms clearly. But the priest, sliding back screen after screen, pours in light upon the gilded brasses and the inscriptions: and I look for the image of the deity or presiding spirit between the altar groups of convoluted candelabra. And I see – only a mirror, a round pale disk of polished metal, and my own face therein; and behind this mockery of me a phantom of the far sea.
>
> Only a mirror! Symbolizing what? Illusion? Or that the universe existed for us solely as the reflection of our own souls? Or the old Chinese teaching that we must seek the Buddha only in our own hearts? Perhaps some day I shall be able to find out all these things.

For Hearn, Japan was a journey to discover his own self and see his own true face.

It is twenty-six years since my own first days in the Orient. In my own career journey I was fortunate to meet and work with Japanese students when I worked as a careers advisor in Trinity College, Dublin, and I felt I came full circle when I taught the JET participants basic Japanese there. I attended their farewell party at the Japanese ambassador's residence in Foxrock in Dublin, and enjoyed the fanfare of the beat and pulsating energy of the *kodo* drum concert.

Japan's culture of honour and respect has stayed with me. The art of bowing still influences me. I also enjoy the custom of gift-giving when visiting houses and the importance of paying attention to form and politeness. I have treasured my lifelong friendships with my Japanese friends and fellow JET participants.

My story is just one of many since the Japan Exchange and Teaching programme invited third-level graduates from Ireland to participate in international exchange and foreign-language education throughout Japan. According to the Japanese embassy in Dublin, the programme was established in 1986 and has earned a prestigious reputation, both in Japan and overseas, for its progress in social and cultural exchange, and has become one of the largest exchange programmes in the world. As of July 2016, there are over 4,952 international participants from forty countries on the programme.

More than 1,200 Irish people have contributed to and enjoyed the programme. Forty-one Irish JETs departed for Japan in 2016, and more than a hundred Irish JETs are currently living and working in Japan. The JET programme has been a pivotal key to crossings between both countries, placing young Irish graduates and qualified teachers in schools, boards of education and government offices as either assistant language teachers or as coordinators for international relations. Since the establishment of the JET programme, more than 61,000 global participants have worked in Japan and engaged in international exchanges.

The renowned haiku poet Kobayahi Issa once said, '花の陰赤の他人はなかりけり – Hana no kage aka no tanin wa narikeri.' This translates as: 'Under the cherry tree there are no strangers.' In many ways the JET programme has been like that cherry tree. In writing this essay, the eyes of my imagination see the countless people who show up to celebrate the shade of the cherry tree and the companionship the cherry-tree blossoms affords.

I am grateful for the flourishing friendships between Ireland and Japan that sprang up under the shade of its cotton candy-pink umbrella! It is no wonder I fell in love with this country and spent eight years living, studying and working in Japan.

Thanks to Sinead Silva and Harriet Sheridan at the JET desk of the Japanese embassy in Dublin for their support. Thanks also to Damian Flanagan, author and critic, for his suggestions. A most sincere thanks to Professor Richard Kelly for his guidance and invitation to contribute to *Crossings*.

Bibliography

Embassy of Japan in Ireland, http://www.ie.emb-japan.go.jp/itprtop_en/index.html.

Hearn, Lafcadio, 'My First Day in the Orient', in idem, *Glimpses of Unfamiliar Japan*, vol. 1 (1894).

Irish JET Alumni Association, https://ijetaa.wordpress.com.

Japan Exchange and Teaching Programme, http://jetprogramme.org/en/arigatojet.

Pink lotus flower at World Expo Park, Osaka, 2019. (*Tang Wai Chung/ Truphotos.com/Alamy*)

Japan: A memoir

James A. Sharkey

I want to thank Dr Richard Kelly for giving me the chance to contribute this memoir as part of the 'Crossings' initiative on the occasion of the sixtieth anniversary of diplomatic relations between Ireland and Japan. Richard is one of Ireland's great advocates in Japan, and I got to know something of his tenacity and courage when we worked together in the days after the tragic Hanshin earthquake in 1995. We have been friends ever since.

I was privileged to be Ireland's ambassador in Japan during a particularly fruitful and intense period of bilateral relations (1989–95). At the political level, there were exchange visits for the first time between our ministers of foreign affairs and ministers of trade and industry. Future prime ministers Bertie Ahern and Albert Reynolds both had opportunities to come to Tokyo, as did many other Irish ministers and senior politicians. The future Japanese foreign and trade and industry minister, Kabun Muto, led a parliamentary delegation to Ireland, and Makiko and Naoki Tanaka, both senior political figures, visited officially and even took time to make the historic pilgrimage to Glendalough. My term in Japan ended with a high-profile, extended state visit by President Mary Robinson, which brought her to Hiroshima, Nara, Kyoto, Matsue, Osaka and Tokyo.

In contrast, at the popular level in Japan, at the level of everyday awareness and appreciation, there seemed to exist very few points of reference or familiarity between the Japanese and Ireland. This was in the years before the spectacle and acoustic exuberance of *Riverdance* set the heartbeat of the world racing. Certainly, Ireland had more than its fair share of superstars in Japan who had achieved quite substantial popularity – namely U2, Sinéad O'Connor and Enya – but, curiously, none of these, at least at the beginning, not even Enya, were perceived as distinctively or exclusively Irish. Even Lafcadio Hearn/Koizumi Yakumo, arguably the most acclaimed foreigner in Japan, was often seen as solely Greek and Japanese until my predecessor, Ambassador Sean Ronan, began the crusade to change this perception and subsequently charged me with the same task. This problem of limited recognition and poor definition in Asia is a common and persistent one for many small European countries, where geographic distance and the absence of substantial historical or political ties can frequently produce blurring and identity confusion.

Why was it important to try to address this awareness deficit? Well, if only for reasons of national pride, the Irish have an urge to make Ireland better known wherever we are. Furthermore, trade, tourism and job-making investment were priorities for Ireland in Japan, and our semi-state bodies reported that lack of familiarity with Ireland and things Irish could hinder their efforts to promote closer economic cooperation. There was also a problem, not uncommon in those years, that far afield and for all the wrong reasons, Belfast was sometimes a better-known Irish city than Dublin. More fundamentally, many Irish visitors to Japan had the feeling that if only the Japanese could get to know us better, this would reveal a common sensibility, a convergence of instinct and outlook on a range of issues; ethical, aesthetic and international. This may have been unduly optimistic, given differences of scale, geography and history, but the high status of literature in both societies and similarities in the texture and preoccupation of our early nature poetry seemed a good starting point.

This was, of course, still the age of the Japanese economic miracle, before the crash of the mid-Nineties and the so-called 'lost decade'. It was Japan in those days, not China, that was the centre of international attention and economic envy. It was the place where everyone wanted to do business and, though a formidably difficult market place, the belief was, to paraphrase a popular song, that if you could make it there, you could make it anywhere. It was also a time when Japan-bashing was reaching fever pitch in the US Congress. American frustration at their growing trade deficit as well as permanent American anxiety about their global decline produced a library of books and publications, scholarly and not so scholarly, forecasting (ominously, it would always seem) the rise of Japan as the world's next superpower. The Japanese are relieved that this is all now a distant memory.

For Irish businessmen and for 'Ireland Inc.', shortly to pool their energies within Tokyo Ireland House, Japan was undoubtedly an important economic and investment partner, but in a context where international competition for the time and the attention of the Japanese was relentless. When the Industrial Development Authority (IDA) opened its first office in Tokyo in the early 1970s, there were very few others lobbying for the investment surplus of the Japanese. By the 1990s, virtually every European and Asian country had investment offices in Japan, as had many of the individual states of the US and several of the provinces of Canada. Clearly, it was important for Ireland to find ways to stand out from the crowd, or at least make an effort to do so, and, indeed, to challenge the distorted, myopic stereotype of Japan as a cold and distant, robotic, industrial powerhouse.

In moving forward with this objective, 'Ireland Inc.' could draw on the encouragement and energy of a small but enthusiastic resident Irish business community that was determined to raise Ireland's visibility in Japan. They were eager to prioritise an image of Ireland as a green and peaceful island, in contrast to stories of violence from the North, and to show us as a nation that combined beauty, tradition and a distinct culture with a young and innovative population looking to the future. This had been the theme of Ireland's engagement in the 1990 Osaka Garden Expo, and it proved popular and successful. There followed a range of initiatives that combined a spirit of audacious optimism with not insignificant risk-taking.

The Irish in Japan, with their Japanese friends, rose wholeheartedly to the challenge of organising a St Patrick's Day parade in Tokyo, a city where very few could even imagine who St Patrick was. To the delight and wonder of the onlooking Japanese, the first parade set off in a fanfare of green, and a flurry of banners and piping, and children in pushchairs from the ambassador's residence in Roppongi to the nearby Wave record shop that had opened for the occasion a special section on Irish music. In the next year, the parade moved to fashionable Omotesando, and the rest is history. There are now ten parades in cities across Japan.

My wife and her friends decided it was time to hold a high-profile St Patrick's Day ball in Tokyo inspired by the annual high-society Cherry Blossom Ball, something up to then unthinkable and even brazen for a small country like Ireland to contemplate. The result was the inaugural Emerald Ball in 1993, attended by the Irish and their Japanese friends with the gracious participation of the Japanese imperial family. Phil Coulter was musical guest. The resplendent image of an elegant Princess Akishino dancing in a lovely green gown was captured on TV and seen across Japan.

So fertile was the creative drive, a Celtic Festival was established (before the arrival of *Riverdance*) to bring to the Japanese Ireland's distinctive Celtic heritage and to profile Irish and other Celtic musical traditions. This helped open doors into Japan for a range of Irish performers, including Mary Black, Paul Brady, the Chieftains, De Danaan and the Hothouse Flowers. From Scotland, the renowned Capercaillie were early guests of the festival. This was in many ways the precursor of the contemporary 'I love Ireland' festival that has proved such a great success and which has engaged the loyalty of a new generation of young Irish expatriates in Tokyo, of whom my son Colm was happily a part.

More and more, Irish ambassadors have made a point of embracing the goodwill and activism of local Irish communities overseas, and have found in their support an invaluable underpinning of our diplomacy.

On an entirely different level, Ireland draws immeasurable strength from the force field of energy that is the achievement and international acclaim of our great writers, and the literary networks of friendship and scholarship that they inspire. Although the impact is necessarily at the level of literature and thought, as distinct from popular awareness and appreciation, it is a power source that is ever present for Irish diplomats; uplifting, prestigious and virtually cost-free. It is also an energy that we can encounter in the most unexpected ways, as I discovered on many occasions in Japan.

Once, shortly after I arrived, when only myself and my PA were holding the fort at the embassy (officially closed during lunchtime), the doorbell rang. I was presumably struggling at the time to complete some inevitably urgent and overdue report for HQ when my PA came in and told me that there was a young lady requesting help in finding on the map a location in Ireland. My first instinct was to wonder if she could not wait until the embassy opened properly, but instead,

Famous Views of Edo, Flowers in the Rain by the Sumida River, by Utagawa Hiroshige (1797–1858). (*© National Museum of Ireland*)

rashly, I asked what the name of the place was. My PA came back and told me it was located in County Derry, a place called Mossbawn. Naturally, I was hooked. I then spent something like an hour in the company of a Japanese university student guiding her through the townlands of Bellaghy, Castledawson and Kilrea, familiar to me as the home place of so many boarders at St Columb's College in Derry, where both myself and Seamus Heaney had gone to school and now familiar to a wider world as the foundational landscape of some of Heaney's greatest poems. I was overwhelmed with the thought that it was extraordinary that students in Japan, a country on the other side of the world from Ireland, should take an interest in and spend time poring over Ordnance Survey maps of the parishes of mid-Ulster. And though we tend to take it all for granted in Ireland, it is something truly exceptional and inspirational that the lakes and hills of County Sligo, the streets and taverns of downtown Dublin, and the farmlands of rural Derry should have become part of the imaginative inheritance of the world.

It was undoubtedly the poet William Butler Yeats who was the first major Irish writer to capture the literary imagination of the Japanese. The probability is, moreover, that Yeats first came to the notice of the Japanese through the interest of

Lafcadio Hearn when he was professor of English at Tokyo Imperial University. *The Wind Among the Reeds* was the collection of poems that attracted Hearn to Yeats, and Hearn prized in his library the 1900 third edition of the book. However, it was not Hearn but a loyal friend of the temperamental Hearn, Ernest Fenollosa, who, through the intermediary of his wife and Ezra Pound, embedded the imagination of Yeats irretrievably in Japan. I spoke about this in an interview in 1995 with the great *Noh* actor Kanze Hideo, who had worked with both the Abbey Theatre and Trinity College, Dublin. I was intrigued in particular by his following recollection:

> The secret of Yeats's attraction to *Noh* is, I think, this book by Fenollosa. Fenollosa translated about fifty *Noh* plays. He was studying Buddhist statues and at the same time he was learning about *Noh*. In this regard, Fenollosa translated the dialogues and explained each action on the stage as well. Yeats was able to learn even the actions on the stage through Fenollosa's translations. And this again is an extraordinary coincidence; it was my own grandfather who taught *Noh* to Fenollosa.

In Japan, as in Ireland, the past is never very far away.

In 1994, the year before Seamus Heaney won his Nobel Prize, the recipient was the Japanese writer and critic Kenzaburō Ōe. Lovers of Irish literature in Japan were surprised and heartened that in his Stockholm acceptance address Ōe made a point of acknowledging Yeats as one of his special influences and 'the writer in whose wake I would like to follow'. Although in his later novels it was Samuel Beckett who served as inspiration for Kenzaburō Ōe, it was always and assuredly the guardian spirit of Yeats who guided the Japanese to a fuller encounter with Irish literature.

One of my first public engagements, after arriving in Japan, was to be guest of the Yeats Society in Hokkaido, meeting in the beautiful fishing and wetlands country of Kushiro, whose red-crowned cranes are one of the recurring images in Japanese traditional painting, symbolising longevity, good fortune and strength. The Yeats Society, founded in 1965 by Waseda Professor Shotaro Oshima, together with its younger sister, the International Association for the Study of Irish Literatures (IASIL), has played an indispensable role in promoting Irish studies in Japanese universities and in bringing Irish poets and writers closer to the heart and soul of Japan, never far away for those who seek them out. Michael Longley and I were special guests of the Yeats Society in a memorably wet and mist-covered retreat high in the mountains above Nagoya. Michael relished this encounter with Yeats, the isolation and the shifting climate of the mountains, and the experience inspired the title of one of his finest collections of poems, *The Weather in Japan*, in which he wrote 'Makes bead curtains of the rain/Of the mist a paper screen.' Other prominent visitors in those years included Paul Muldoon, Richard Murphy, Nuala Ní Dhomhnaill, Julia O'Faolain, James Simmons, Ulick O'Connor, Peter Fallon and, of course, Seamus Heaney.

Like Yeats, James Joyce and Samuel Beckett have had a notable impact on Japanese literary thought, in Joyce's case stretching back to the fervour of the early Taisho era when *Portrait of the Artist* came to the notice of the famed novelist Yone Noguchi, coincidentally a patron of the Hearn family and the author of one of the first books on Hearn. *Ulysses* was translated into Japanese first in 1931 and at least six times since then, an extraordinary statement of the fascination Joyce holds for literary Japan. For Beckett, whose *Godot* was very favourably received, much to the disapproval of Yukio Mishima, there was an unavoidable tendency to be drawn into the slipstream of Japanese traditional theatre. It is no coincidence that several members of the Kanze *Noh* family, including Hideo, have had a close association with the interpretation of Beckett's work. Beckett on his side, of course, has been a stern defender of orthodoxy in stage presentation, and the Beckett estate was moved to deter over-experimental *Noh*-influenced adaptations of the plays.

In celebration of Joyce's achievement in Japan, I sought early on in my stay to inaugurate an annual Bloomsday reading. Little did I think that my guest of honour at the residence in our second year would be the translator of *Finnegans Wake*, Naoki Yanase, who sadly died in July 2016. Yanase had not only introduced an Irish masterpiece to the Japanese public but, in the process, created a new acclaimed Japanese work of art: something like a novel in its own right for which Joyce's work provides the architecture, the inspiration and the justification. One of Yanase's many admirers, attracted by the clever word play of the translation and its restoration of long unused *kanji* characters to convey Joyce's multi-layered meanings, was the head of the powerful Japanese business organisation, the Keidanren. Semi-state colleagues and I were able to share several long meals with Yanase and the Keidanren president, with an empty chair always kept for James

Osaka Street, *c.* 1920–9. (*New York Public Library*)

Joyce. Thus, thanks to *Finnegans Wake*, art and business found an unexpected but pleasant gastronomic reconciliation.

Probably, my main contribution to the celebration of Lafcadio Hearns' Irish background and influences was an article I provided to the *Yomiuri Shimbun*, arguably the largest circulating newspaper in the world. This was after a visit to the remote Oki islands, off the coast of Shimane Prefecture, which I made with my family, following in the footsteps of Lafcadio Hearn who had visited there a hundred years earlier. The reaction to my article was embarrassingly warm, partly because I had been the first foreign emissary to visit the islands 'since the time of the gods', and partly because the translation of my original English text into Japanese by Professor Marie Kai (a translator of Brian Friel) was as flattering as it was superb. As a consequence, I was briefly embraced by those in Japan who regard Hearn as a Shinto apostle. I was invited to the centennial reconstruction ceremonies for the revered Ise shrine, something unusual for a foreigner, and introduced to the great Sumo champion, Akebono, who it turned out was of

Hawaiian-Irish extraction. The English-language text of my article was eventually published in a compendium of essays on Hearn edited by Ambassador Sean Ronan, which was at least some reassurance that I had managed to fulfil the charge he had assigned me.

I left Tokyo in the summer of 1995 and returned to headquarters in Dublin, unsure as to whether any of the initiatives in which we had engaged, including the high-level visits, had enlarged the generalised appreciation of Ireland in Japan. In diplomacy, however, it is an old saying that we take up the baton from our predecessors and, when the time comes, pass it on to those who come after to do even better things. In this respect both Ireland and Japan have been fortunate to be the beneficiaries of the committed service of those who preceded and inspired me, and of the dedication and imaginative contribution of the colleagues who followed after.

Seamus and Marie Heaney were guests of IASIL in 1990 and stayed at the residence, where we had a chance to renew old friendships. Seamus has been a dedicated champion of Irish causes, and always gave generous support to projects in which I was involved in America, Russia and Denmark as well as Japan. With customary kindness he had printed and hand-signed in 1993 several hundred copies of his *Villanelle of Northwest Orient Flight 4* for distribution at the inaugural Emerald Ball. Without question, no Irish poet has ever given more time to Japan than Seamus Heaney, and certainly no foreign poet will be remembered with such warm affection, delightful anecdote and assured respect and admiration. He touched the imagination of the Japanese at the very highest level, and will remain an abiding and inspiring presence. It is only right that we should give Seamus the last word and end with a quote from his *Northwest Villanelle*, written with ironic good humour and self-effacing modesty following his first visit to Japan:

> Their word for Mister is the suffix-san.
> Their cherry blossom is a perfect pink
> Haikus in English hardly ever scan
> The bard should know. The bard was in Japan.

Donegal, July 2017

Sr Clothilde Anamizu. (*Image supplied by the author*)

Crossings: An adventure with God

Sr Clothilde Anamizu

In the East and the West alike, human life is often compared to a journey or a pilgrimage; a walk from birth to death. The path may be wide or narrow, smooth or rough, level or steep, straight or sinuous. No matter what it is like, one continues to walk, crossing rivers, fields, borders and mountain passes; some of us even have to cross oceans and entire continents.

When I look back on my life's journey, several crossings spring to mind. I was invited to share some of these with you. I want to call my journey 'An adventure with God'.

*****

I was born to middle-class parents in Tokyo, the third girl in the family. When I was born, Japan was in the midst of the Second World War. My earliest memory is hearing the siren warning of an air raid. Covering our heads with cotton and wool hoods made by our mother, and picking up our toy boxes, my two sisters and I crossed the lawn and made our way to the air-raid shelter that had been dug in our garden.

The atomic bombs brought the Second World War to a close. Tokyo was devastated, desolated and burnt down. Soon the US army came to occupy the city; at the same time missionaries also arrived, with a lot of support materials from abroad.

Meanwhile, we reached school age. Our mother wanted us to go to the missionary school for girls run by the Congregation of the Sisters of St Paul of Chartres. There, I met and played with many good friends. (After a half century, I am still in touch with some of them.) One of my friends was from a Catholic family. We used to take turns staying at each other's houses at weekends. When it was my turn to stay at her house, we all went to Mass on Sundays in a big van converted into a family car. I felt envious because they could go up in a line to receive Holy Communion while I alone was staying in my seat. The best way to be with friends after school was to join the catechism class, which all Catholics, as well as non-Catholics who wished to be baptised, had to attend. All other pupils had to go home immediately after school. There was a free hour before the catechism class – that is, an hour during which we could play together. How could I have missed this opportunity! I stayed after school and played with my friends, then attended the catechism class: I can remember almost nothing about the class itself.

My next memory is this. During the Feast of the Immaculate Conception, I was dressed in a long white robe, with a veil and a crown of flowers, standing among a dozen newly baptised adults and students. I was in my last year of elementary school. Thus, the gratuitous gift of God accepted a child from a pagan family into His household. A crossing made possible by grace.

The following April, the start of a new academic year, we crossed the boundary that separated the elementary school from the junior high school at the same missionary institution. We had a new English class taught by a new teacher from abroad. While we sat waiting for our first ever English class, the door opened and there appeared a tall, strong-bodied sister with blue eyes and rosy cheeks, in a black religious garment with an old white cornette. She smiled to us in silence and put her hand into her spacious pocket on one side of her robe. She produced a big red apple and, holding it high, said, 'An apple.' This was my first encounter with the Irish sister. She loved us, and we all enjoyed her class.

I was a slow-maturing girl. I went to school in order to play with friends; most of the classes were boring. I enjoyed the breaks, playing ball and skipping ropes, and so on.

After I entered high school, it all happened. My carefree, happy, joyful childhood suddenly came to an end, just like a dream. One morning, while in class, I had a severe stomach ache and was sent back home. My mother was alarmed and called the family doctor; I was diagnosed with acute appendicitis.

The following day I was lying in the operating theatre and felt that it was becoming harder and harder to breathe. I shouted, moving my head right and left: 'Help! I'm suffocating.' The doctor pinched my cheek. Ouch! He pinched my neck. Ouch! He pinched my chest, no feeling. There arose a commotion in the operating theatre, and I heard 'Oxygen!' I lost consciousness. When I woke up with pain and nausea, I found myself back in my room. That day I made a crossing from a happy, carefree dreamland full of love to life's merciless realities. I realised that I existed. Why did I exist? Who was I? What was the meaning of my life? All of these questions welled up in my mind one after another. Nevertheless, one thing was clear: I knew, deep in my heart, that there existed someone who had given me 'life', someone who would always love and care for me. The ultimate key to my questions was: what did He want me to be, and what was His plan for me?

The missionary institution did not have a university. My family advised me to transfer to my father's university, which had an affiliated girls' high school. Transferring from a Catholic school to a most liberal and secular high school was no mean crossing. At the end of my time there, I received an offer from the department of science and technology at the university. Softly but insistently, my inner voice was telling me, 'What would become of your faith if you went to that secular university? You would lose your religion.' At that time there were only two Catholic universities in Tokyo: Sophia University, run by the Jesuits, and the University of the Sacred Heart, run by the Society of the Sacred Heart. When I revealed my concerns to my father, he immediately rejected Sophia, saying, 'It is a university for monks, not for you.' About Sacred Heart he was reluctant, but he eventually allowed me to go for its scholarship examination, for at that time Michiko Shoda, one of the graduates of the Sacred Heart, was chosen to become crown princess, now empress. We, as students of that affiliated high school, were not prepared for the ordinary university entrance examinations. I made a deal with God: 'If you really want me to go to the Catholic university, you have to let me pass the examination. For my part I will study as hard as I possibly can for four weeks until the exam.' I had never studied as hard in my life. The day of announcements came. My mother asked me: 'Why are you not going to see the result?' 'I don't think it's necessary. I'm sure I did not pass', I replied. Persuaded by my mother, I went up to the university. When I entered the hall and saw my number on the board, I said to God, 'You won the bet. I admit defeat.'

It was another crossing: from a secular, popular and famous university to a smaller and stricter Catholic university for women. The four years at the University of the Sacred Heart, nonetheless, reminded me of the 'Hound of Heaven'.[1] My every effort to muffle the inner voice – which gently but persistently invited me to 'come and follow Him' – proved to be in vain. On the one hand, I spent my time participating in social activities, joining the tennis club and the drama club, not missing any of the pleasant events that my college had to offer. At the same time, I frequently visited the college chapel and enjoyed just being there. Gradually, it became clear deep in my heart that my true happiness and peace consisted only in giving myself to the One who had given me 'life'. A religious vocation was an undeniable reality toward the end of my senior year.

I stopped running away and yielded to the Heavenly Hound. But there were further questions to ponder.

They say that even God does not know how many congregations of religious sisters exist in the world. The first question was: to which convent should I go? The second thing to consider was that I was the only Catholic in my family. None of them practised any religion. How should I reveal my intention and get their approval?

God always opens up what is apparently a dead end in an unexpected way. His is a father's delight to surprise his children with a sudden gift. One evening my father asked me, 'What are you going to say to Mr X?' My family had introduced me to several men, hoping to get me married off. I gave no answer. He became a bit irritated that night and said, 'You have been silent so far. It is time to decide. Do not let him wait. It is not polite. Why can't you decide? Unless you are going to a nunnery.' 'Going to a [Buddhist] nunnery' is a common expression for the action of a 'broken-hearted girl'. I answered quietly: 'Yes, father, that is exactly what I am thinking. I want to enter the convent.' That was the declaration of a cold war between my family and me. In order to change my mind, my father threatened to disown me. On the day of my graduation, we were having dinner at home. My father stood up and opened a bottle of wine. He walked around the table and came to me. Pouring wine into my glass, he said quietly: 'No matter what, you are still my daughter.'

Sr Clothilde Anamizu. *(Image supplied by the author)*

Having decided to try a teaching career, I went to the boarding school of the Sacred Heart two hours away from Tokyo. This was the first time I had left home. I had made a crossing from a cosy home to the outside world. There I met an old Irish nun, Sister Duff, who was ninety years old. I accompanied her to every class from first to sixth grade and served as her interpreter when required, since she did not speak Japanese. I still remember vividly her reading *The Tablet* whenever she was free. She was very kind to me and cared for me just like a grandmother.

I enjoyed teaching. I taught classes from nursery school to junior college. The more my physical activities were appreciated, the more intense my inner search and discernment of God's will became.

I carried on my journey. In the ten years that followed, my journey was full of even more difficult crossings. I crossed swampy fields without seeing any dry land before me. I climbed over steep mountains, only to see yet another path winding upwards ahead of me. I crossed many lands shrouded in mists or darkness, barely able to see beyond the next step.[2] But now I can say that throughout these crossings, it was not me walking, but it was the merciful Father who was carrying a small, feeble child on his shoulders.[3] And He finally put me down at the gate of a Cistercian monastery, commonly called Trappistine, near Kobe.

At the early stages, my family was strongly against my entering religious life and tried every possible means to frustrate my attempt. When all their efforts proved in vain, they reluctantly let me go and do what I had decided to do. I left the world, family and friends behind and crossed the threshold of the Cistercian monastery, Our Lady of Nishinomiya.

In the monastery I had very limited contact with my family and friends. A couple of years later, my father passed Kobe on business. He dropped in to see me for the first time. While we were walking together in the garden, he put out his hand. I took it and we made peace. Two years later, in his prime of life, he was

Sr Clothilde Anamizu at St Mary's Abbey, Glencairn, County Waterford. (*www.glencairnabbey.org*)

suddenly diagnosed with a rare cancer and died after nine months. Twenty years later, an intimate friend of his told me what he had said upon his deathbed: 'She [meaning me] is the happiest of my daughters.'

My twenty-five years in the monastery went by quietly, peacefully, steadily, without any upheaval. Our Lady of Nishinomiya was at that time one of the three biggest Cistercian monasteries for nuns. When I arrived, the Abbess told me: 'you are the eighty-fifth member of the community.' We received solid monastic teachings, and life in that well-established community was uneventful.

Then it appeared as if God had thought it better to shake this self-contented community. I felt my powerlessness, unable to find the answers. When the abbot general visited us, I consulted him and asked if I could go to another monastery outside Japan, since the problem was partly in conjunction with other Japanese monasteries. To my surprise he immediately agreed to my request and recommended two monasteries: one was in the US, which was well known and of good reputation, and the other, as he said, was in 'Glencairn, in Ireland' – I knew the name but nothing else. I asked him to describe 'Glencairn' a bit more. He said, 'Well, Glencairn is the community, open and free.' I heard the voice inside me and said: 'Let me go there, Reverend Father.'

Looking at the address of Glencairn in County Waterford, Ireland, the Japanese travel agency found an airport near Waterford city. They arranged my flights: from Tokyo to London, and then from London to Waterford. I crossed the vast Eurasian continent and arrived at London Heathrow for the first time. Where was Stansted Airport? I had to travel across London city with two suitcases, big and small, in rain. I nearly missed the train for Stansted. The plane waiting for me was very small; on board were only ten or twenty passengers. Even though it was a jet aircraft, it flew very low and rather slowly. I enjoyed looking down on the beautiful blue-green water while crossing the Irish Sea. When we landed, there was no one checking the passengers' passports. I simply picked up my suitcases and walked towards a priest waving at me. I found out later that Waterford airport was mainly for cargo, and no sisters in Glencairn knew that there was an airport in Waterford. The chaplain, Fr Patrick, picked me up and drove me to Glencairn, where I received a warm Irish welcome. Thus terminated my longest crossing, from Japan in the Far East to Ireland in the far west. It was at the dawn of the new millennium, in January 2000.

A full seventeen years have elapsed without any physical crossings made. My vow of stability[4] is helping me become more and more deeply rooted in Glencairn. But my inner journey – that inner crossing from Japan to Ireland – continues. There is a big difference between physical crossings and inner spiritual crossings. For the former, I have left one place for another. In the course of the latter kind of crossing, however, I have never denied nor turned my back on Japanese culture, Japanese mentality, the Japanese language, and anything else that I imbibed in Japan. The wonderful reality is that inner crossings retain what is original while enriching our lives through new encounters. I am vitalised more and more by the visible and invisible beauty of Ireland. While my journey goes on, my expectation is rising: the expectation of the final, ultimate, true crossing, from this temporal dwelling place to the true, eternal homeland of the children of God.[5] There will no longer be any distinctions between Irish and Japanese: we will all be one in love and praise the Lord of love and life for ever and ever.[6] When will He call out to me, 'Come'?

The Suns on the Horizons: Reflections on the Celtic connections with Japan

Alan Titley

This is a dim memory. I worked as a very young teacher/lecturer in Nigeria in the late 1960s. I had gone there straight out of college in a spirit of adventure and discovery. While there, we had very little connection with the outside world. News of what was happening out beyond us was particularly thin, and even more so because the Biafran–Nigerian war was raging and a tight censorship reigned. But I do recall, either in an Irish newspaper smuggled in or left behind by a priest who had been at home, a brief account of a visit which the then taoiseach, Jack Lynch, made to Japan in 1968.

This may be just an invention of mine, but it is hard to know why such an imaginative flight would have stuck if it had not some basis. The taoiseach spoke, and I only remember the phrase, of 'the close cultural connections between Ireland and Japan'. I chuckled, and even chortled at the time, thinking yes, of course we could talk up the close cultural ties between Ireland and France, or Spain, or Italy, or Britain or the US, but ... Japan?

There were the obvious open doors, of course. Yeats' *Noh* drama inspired by the great fascist poet Ezra Pound. Neither Pound nor Yeats knew Japanese, but they were creative artists and not translators, and literature works along its own airy channels without the straightjacket of theory. That strange and wonderful man, Lafcadio Hearn, was another obvious entry point, but he is far better known in Japan than he is in Ireland, and has to be dragged into the discussion for most Irish people. I became aware over the years of journals dealing with Irish or Celtic literature and studies, but necessarily these were directed at a fairly specialised readership.

My own main interest is in the Irish Gaelic tradition and, thus, I began to surmise how it interacted or intersected with Japan. There were not any obvious connections. It might be argued in the best tourist-speak that Japan is the Land of the Rising Sun, and Ireland that of its setting. This does not get us too far, however. On the other hand, literacy in Irish and in Japanese began to grow and to flourish around the same time, and if Irish is one of the oldest continuous vernacular literatures in Europe, the same can be said of Japanese in eastern Asia.

There was the further observation made by Theodore W. Goosen in his introduction to *The Oxford Book of Japanese Short Stories* (1997) that 'modernism' came late to Japan and that writers of the new fiction were often dismissed as frivolous or even vulgar. He added:

> A new language for literature, which would reflect how people actually spoke, and which could be used to express exciting new concepts like 'love' and 'individualism', had to be created from scratch. Finally, it was necessary to grapple with the literary forms – the novel, the short story, the poem – that had been developed in the West.

What struck me immediately were the similarities in forging a new Irish literature in a language cut off not so much, like Japan, by edict, but by the impoverishment and degrading of its speakers for 200 years.

Debates raged in Irish about whether the new literature should be based on the classical prose of the seventeenth century or just on *caint na ndaoine*, the speech of the ordinary people. Much energy was expended on whether a short story had to begin in the traditional manner (*Bhí fear ann fadó*/Once upon a time) or

Yosa Buson, artist unknown. (*History and Art Collection/Alamy*)

could jump into *medias res* as the new-fangled fashions demanded. There was a kindergarten of thought that promoted the folk novel as the only genuine article, but all critical positions were superseded by a new and vigorous practice. I have to imagine that similar contention arouse around Japanese literature, contested territories finally conquered by the act of writing itself.

Shortly after the independent Irish Free State was founded in 1922, it set up a government publishing company in order to speed up the provision of books in Irish. This was known as An Gúm (The Scheme), and one of its tasks was to translate works of literature from other languages into Irish. The work it did was prodigious. Many of the world's classics appeared in Irish as well as current best-sellers and shock schlocks. Books were turned from French, German, Italian, Russian, Polish, Spanish, English and other European languages into Irish, nearly always directly without any intermediary or bridging translation. To my knowledge there were none from any Asian language and nothing from Japanese. This was not surprising as the number of Irish speakers who knew Japanese was probably zilch, and even if they did, the chances of their being willing to undertake a work of literary translation was more zilchful still.

On the other hand, the tradition begun by An Gúm has been continued by independent publishers until today, and thus the Japanese connection has been made. An example of this is Seán Ó Dúrois' *Rashoomon*, a collection of stories by Ryūnosuke Akutagawa published in 1995. The title story is quite famous because of the wonderful film directed by Akira Kurosawa, although it is based more on a different story 'I bhFáschoill' (In a Grove), which is also included in the collection. I had the pleasure of 'teaching' this collection of stories to my class in university, partly because I wanted to introduce them to world literature, but more seriously because the stories were great. One student queried why we should be studying Japanese literature as we had plenty of our own native stuff to be examining. I replied that Irish literature was bigger than Ireland and belonged to the world, just as the world belonged to us.

The great German scholar Kuno Meyer once made the pertinent observation: 'Like the Japanese, the Celts were always happy to take an artistic hint; they avoid the obvious and the commonplace; the half-said thing to them is dearest.' While whatever we mean by Celtic literature encompasses everything from the anorexic wafer to the wild abandon of excess verbiage and does not have a deep heart's core, he was specifically referring to those brief and aphoristic poems that Irish monks penned to the edge of their manuscripts when they grew tired of copying biblical texts or twisting birds' necks into fancy letters for their illuminated books. An example might be the famous few lines about the blackbird of Belfast Lough scratched ever before ugly stanchions scraped the sky above its beautiful bay.

Int én bec
ro léic feit
do rind guip
glanbuidi.
Fo-ceird faíd
ós Loch Laíg
lon do chraíb
charrbuidi.

Or in Frank O'Connor's translation:

What little throat
Has framed that note?
What gold beak shot
It far away?
A blackbird on
His leafy throne
Tossed it alone
Across the bay.

It was written, probably, in the eighth century, and is only one example of a particular kind of terseness that is really only found in the haiku. Modern Irish poetry from the seventeenth century onwards can be verbose and bosky, piling adjective upon adjective, while contemporary poetry is not much different from its neighbours in Europe and the world. The present muse will generally eschew traditional metres and wander with the best or worst that is available elsewhere. The new will generally mean being like in theme and form with what is being written in Britain, America, France or sometimes Italy.

One poet, however, jumped across the normal suspects and headed east. Gabriel Rosenstock quickly divined the truth of Meyer's comment, and forged a link between this very early Irish clarity of simple vision and the bright bulb of the haiku. It might be said that he almost single-handedly brought this classical Japanese form into Irish, and is still its foremost practitioner. He has written or translated hundreds of haiku, including those of the great Japanese masters.

One of these is Yosa Buson, the eighteenth-century poet and painter, and one of the three acknowledged masters of haiku, along with Issa and Basho, whom he has also translated.

> Crithloinnir
> Feithidí gan ainm
> Is caolrian bán ina ndiaidh.
> [Heat shimmers –
> Nameless insects
> Leaving a faint white trail.]

And you sometimes begin to imagine that these could have been written in Old Irish, for which numerous resemblances and parallels could be easily provided:

> Gealach gheimhridh –
> Ag umhlú do mhanach
> Ar an droichead.
> [Winter moon –
> Bowing to a monk
> On the bridge.]

This rejuvenation of the dew-sharp quality of our early lyrics through its marriage to the Japanese haiku is one of the great literary experiments in Irish, and has come to us as a seamless garment, a bridge across time and place. It now seems like the most natural thing in the world, but it took a poet of courage and international openness to recognise and remake it.

It should be said that translation goes both ways. While we revere the brevity and aphoristic sharpness of the haiku, there is also in every tradition a wilder shore. One of the greatest and most famous poems in Irish is Brian Merriman's 'Cúirt an Mheon-Oíche' (The Midnight Court) composed in the late eighteenth century. It has been an endless source of speculation as to 'what it is about', but it is certainly about having literary and verbal fun around men and women, and the stuff that we do or do not. It has been translated into English more than a dozen times, and into many other European languages in whole or in part. Only two years ago

The Issa Soju Memorial Hall in Nagareyama commemorates Issa Kobayashi, a renowned Japanese haiku poet in the eighteenth and nineteenth centuries, and Soju Akimoto, a brewer of mirin. (*John Lander/Alamy*)

a translation into Japanese was made as 'Buraian Meriman Mayonaka no Hótei: Júhasseiki Airurandogoshi no Shihó', and remarkably this was rendered directly from Irish with the assistance and guidance of Liam P. Ó Murchú, the foremost authority on the poem and its provenance. It must be hoped that this translation gives a different idea of Irish culture beyond the folksy and the ordinary.

One of the great commonalities of the human mind is found in folk tales. Although often touted as being particularly native, that is to say, Irish or Serbian or Kikuyu or whatever, it is the one product of the human mind in which our narrative clamps us together. This is a paradox as the Aarne-Thompson-Uther classification system for folk tales can more or less assign any story to a certain type with recurring motifs. While this does not deny creativity or individual expression or the numberless sub-twists in any tale, it does seem to argue that there is a deep bedrock of story on which we bounce our own.

While Irish gods and heroes are certainly not Japanese ones, we can read their myths and stories with a certain embedded understanding. This may be why Lafcadio Hearn renderings of Japanese tradition became so popular, and it just might be that his own Irish background had its own influence. The Irish scholar Tomás de Bhaldraithe wrote an essay on Hearn in the influential literary journal *Comhar* in 1985 which he entitled 'Ar Thóir Uí Chonaire na Seapáine' (In Search of the Ó Conaire of Japan). The 'Ó Conaire' he refers to was one of the first modernist writers in Irish, and helped to fashion the short story and the novel. De Bhaldraithe, however, draws more attention to the vagrant and itinerant life that they both lived, their mental independence, and their sympathy for ordinary people rather than to their writings.

Hearn's work is not unknown in Irish, however. Or rather, I should say in one of the Irishes. While Irish is often referred to as Gaelic, this is historically incorrect, and even what is now called Gaelic in Scotland was regularly spoken of as Irish. Having no wish to get involved in linguistic terminological colonialism, it is perfectly correct today to refer to the Celtic language of Scotland as Gaelic; and beyond that, the native language of the Isle of Man as Manx. This Manx language is, of course, a form of Irish or of Gaelic, although written in its own unique orthography. It is through this Manx language that we have the stories and tales of Hearn, although he is correctly called Koizumi Yakumo in its title. These appeared as *Jeih Skeealyn Scaanjoon* (Ten Spectral Stories), 'Er nyn jyndaa gys Gaelg liorish

R.W.K. Teare' (Translated into Manx by R.W.K. Teare), which was published in 2007. They make ghostly reading in their own way: traditional stories written in Japanese by an Irishman translated into Manx Gaelic by a native of that island. All of the stories are entertaining and instructive, often enacting how humanity deals with its own dilemmas beyond the simple jacket of reductionist psychology. For example, 'Gialdin Freilt' (A Promise Kept) tells how a man fulfilled his promise to return to his brother and his home on a particular date. He is, however, detained by a nasty lord, and the only way he can keep his word is by becoming a ghost, since *tama yoku ichi nichi ni sen ri wo yoku*, or *foddee annym dooinney troailt meeilley meeilley ayns un laa*, or indeed, 'a person's soul can travel a thousand miles in one day.'

The Harp: Journal of Irish literatures began as a publication of the International Association for the Study of Irish Literatures in 1985, and became the *Journal of Irish Studies* in 2001. While it ranges wide in its subject matter, it is heavily weighted towards what used to be known as Anglo-Irish literature. There is, however, another Japanese learned journal which specialises in Celtic literature, *Studia Celtica Japonica.* It is published by the Celtic Society of Japan, and has appeared both regularly and intermittently in its new form since the 1980s. Although it deals with all the Celtic languages, the greater part is given over to Irish. It is also remarkably catholic in its subject matter, accepting essays on broad historical, literary, mythological or philosophical matter, as well as what might be seen as arcane linguistic probings to the uninitiated. For example, more or less at random, volume 6 (new series), published in 1994, contains the following: 'The Journey Across the Wilderness: Structural analysis of the three Welsh Arthurian romances' by Satoko Ito-Morino;'The River Boyne and the Ancient Seers' by Dáithí Ó hÓgáin; 'The Scope of Landscape: Some contrasts and realignments within the topographical vocabulary of Early Irish' by Liam Mac Mathúna; 'The Threefold Death in Early Irish Sources' by Tomás Ó Cathasaigh; 'The Extent of Royal Patronage on Irish High Crosses' by Peter Harbison (including photographs); and 'The Present State and Future Tasks of Celtic Studies in German-speaking Countries' by Karl H. Schmidt. This is simply a snapshot of every and any edition, but is nonetheless representative of them all.

Studia Celtica Japonica is a serious academic journal depending on the goodwill of a few dedicated scholars. It has certainly attracted the best Celtic scholars from around the world, and has added to the sum of our wisdom in a confined but vital field.

Thus, while Japan and Ireland may represent the rising and the setting sun respectively, it may be that while the sun shines in the sky they both illuminate one another.

Mo ghean an mhaidin bhán
Mo ghean duibhe na hoíche;
Mo ghean an ghrian ag éirí orainn
Is ag dul faoi riamh is choíche.

Irish Tales, Trails from Afar

Ciarán L. Quinn

Sunday

Ice cubes in a glass seem separate, have form. The sun shines; where have they gone? Nothing has been taken away. Their separateness is only form and only apparent, a temporary, illusionary state. Plants have consciousness. If there is reincarnation, and we are reincarnated as plants, our consciousness is different; ie. that of a plant. Our present body does not continue. Our consciousness according to theory would be different, i.e. that of a plant. Thus there is nothing left of the ice cube. We are all nothingness.

Another week

I told Takeo-san my answer. He said I was enlightened. Wonderful!

(Maura 'Soshin' O'Halloran, *Pure Heart, Enlightened Mind: The Zen journal and letters of an Irish woman in Japan* (published posthumously, 1994))

In 1979, a young woman, after spending a week in San Francisco with friends, set flight to Tokyo en route through Hawaii. Maura O'Halloran (1955–82), born in Boston and raised in Dublin from age four, having graduated with top distinctions in mathematical economics/statistics and sociology from Trinity College, embarked on a singular, spiritual and life-changing journey to the Far East. Engendered with a sense of social justice, acute to the obstacles laid by institutions to human development, detached from materialism, shabby but chic, Maura, a young woman who had wandered the world, the Americas and Europe, now found herself anew in the Orient. There, Maura was tonsured and entered a traditional Zen Buddhist monastery, Toshoji Temple in Tokyo, only to venture north to Kannonji Temple in more remote Iwate Prefecture:

> I thought about the alternatives that confronted me when I first came to Japan last November – the usual job as an English teacher didn't interest me. Either monastic renunciation or sensory wallowing drew me. A soul seeking surrender? It was either accident or providence that the former happened first. Either way was a search for liberation – freedom from inhibition, from other people's values, from their suffocating puritan ethic born from the delusion of a retributory hereafter. Or else the other option, spiritual liberation, but from what? This one was hazier. Those who suffer want liberation from suffering, but I seldom suffer. My life has been wonderful, blessed. Who could enslave me? I did as I wished when I wished. Now I feel gratitude that this Zen way took me, because I consciously, fervently, could not be said to have taken it. Now I feel there is no turning back.

Maura underwent three years of training at the temples, the selfless and ceaseless rigours of the cold, cooking, cleaning, gardening and begging, meditation and meandering through the confines and corridors of a male-dominated monastery, after which she was endowed with the Buddhist name Soshin. Hers was the devotional practice of both *zazen* (meditation) and the Bodhisattva Way of Zen (sacrifice).

But Maura yearned to travel back to Ireland, although her monastery did not want her to leave. It was not only meant to be an emotional return to family and

Kannonji Temple, Iwate Prefecture, Japan. (*John Lander/Alamy*)

friends but also a spiritual return to Ireland – to set up a Buddhist monastery in Ireland. But on a trip through northern Thailand, tragedy struck:

> In October of 1982, Maura finally set out to return to the West. Before going to Ireland, however, she planned to tour for two months in southeast Asia, then spend Christmas with her family in Maine. The temple people didn't want her to leave … She was one of the last passengers to board the bus for the overnight trip so she sat at the front near the driver. When he fell asleep near dawn the bus went off the road killing Maura, the driver, and two other passengers. Although her passport and journal were stolen with her luggage, the police were able to identify her by means of a ticket stub they found in the pocket-like sleeve of her monk's robe … Maura's ashes are interred beside her father's in Mt. Hope Cemetery in Lewiston, Maine.
>
> Scott O'Halloran

(a letter of condolence from Tetsugyu Ban to the O'Halloran family):

> On December 8th, 1979, Maura O'Halloran joined Toshoji Doairyo … Our grand master Dogen went to China and to the Tendo mountain for one thousand days, working hard all day, he sat in meditation at night. He slept two or three hours in the sitting position. Maura did the same. She was the modern Dogen … Then she left this life immediately to start the salvation of the masses in the next life! Has anyone known such a courageously hard working Buddha as Maura? …
>
> Ban Tetsugyu, 27 October, 11.00 p.m. as I watch the eleventh day moon

A statue stands today at Kannonji Temple commemorating Maura in her posthumous name 'Great Enlightened Lady, of Same Heart and Mind as the Great Teacher Buddha.'

Monday, 6 August 1945

> Suddenly there was a huge bang in the sky, just above the city. We were all thrown from our seats onto the ground. Realizing that it was a bomb, we quickly picked ourselves up and made a run for cover in the direction of the convent.
>
> We had only just taken shelter inside the convent when the entire building began to shake and give way.
>
> We turned and rushed outside again, the convent collapsing at our heels. The convent wall collapsed before our eyes and beyond where the wall had stood until a few seconds before lay the remains of our neighbourhood.
>
> There was hardly a building left standing. Everywhere people lay either dying or dead, burned – I was to learn later – was a flash of radiation.
>
> (Adrian Millar in interview with Sr Julia Canny)

At 8.15 a.m. on 6 August 1945, 'Little Boy', the first atomic bomb used in wartime, was dropped by an American B-29 bomber, the *Enola Gay*, on the city of Hiroshima in western Japan. In an instant, an estimated 70,000 people were killed, mostly civilians, including some 2,000 Korean slave labourers, and some 20,000 Japanese combatants. By that year's end, between 90,000 and 166,000 people had died either through injury or exposure to radiation.

Sr Julia Canny, born in Clonbur, County Galway, in 1894, joined the order of the Sisters of the Holy Souls aged thirty-nine. In 1939, she boarded the last boat from San Francisco to Japan before Japan and the US were to go to war. When she disembarked, Japanese authorities sent her to a concentration camp, suspecting her of being an American spy. The Swiss ambassador intervened, and six months later she was released on proof of her Irish citizenship.

Adrian Millar, a writer, carries further the telling of her story with him:

> 70 years ago … my friend Julia was sitting in her garden when she saw a huge blinding flash of light in the sky and was thrown off her chair … She had just witnessed the world's first atomic bomb, its epicenter a mere 1.7 kilometres away.

I met Julia for the first time some 40 years later. She was 92 and I was 24. I was a student of Japanese at the University of Waseda in Tokyo, and we immediately fell in love. She was holed-up – bedridden, effectively – in a convent house in Tokyo and didn't have a word of Japanese. It was 1984.

I was her 'television' because I brought her news of the outside world – and I was Irish, a 'boon' – a gift to her at the end of her life.

Julia never managed to return home. She wasn't in Clonbur when her parents died or for her sisters' marriages.

In the summer of 1985, I came home in her place, returning to Tokyo with photos of her octogenarian sisters, her parents' graves and her former school.

'Oh, my God, they have running water!' she said. She cried bittersweet tears.

On her down days, she would raise the palms of her hands pleadingly to me and tell me that she was suffering from the effects of the radiation – her palms reddened.

I would cajole her back to life.

When she was hospitalized at the age of 93, I was at her bedside everyday demanding her to live. She finally died one month short of her 94th birthday, in 1987. It was All Saints' Day.

Julia was my little saint, living by the simple tenet: 'Whatever you do to the least of these, you do onto me.'

Thursday, August 9, 1945

... came a frighteningly loud but rather flat explosion which was followed by a blast of hot air. Some of this could be felt even by us as it came through the shelter openings, which were very rarely closed owing to the poor ventilation.

(Bob Jackson, *A Doctor's Sword: How an Irish doctor survived war, captivity and the atomic bomb* (Cork: Collins Press, 2016))

Bockscar, the American B-29, released the second atomic bomb, 'Fat Man', upon the southern Japanese city of Nagasaki, and the largest and most destructive force the world has ever encountered was unleashed: between 40,000 and 80,000 were dead within months. Dr Aidan MacCarthy – an officer in the British Royal Air Force (RAF) and a prisoner of war (POW) imprisoned with others underground about a mile from the epicentre – crawled out to witness the utter devastation. He was to describe later this near-death experience – among others he endured in wartime – in modest but stark and succinct terms in his memoir, *A Doctor's War* (Robson Books, 1979), as in the case of the nearby Mitsubishi factory:

> Nearly five hundred girls had been working in these offices, and when the building had been hit, they had been catapulted out. They were spread in a human carpet up to a distance of nearly a thousand feet, giving the impression of a nightmare factory.

Aidan MacCarthy (1913–95) was born in the small coastal town of Castletownbere in west Cork. The town became strategically important as a naval base from the onset of the First World War in 1914 until 1938, when the Royal Navy seceded sovereignty over its base there to the Irish state. The MacCarthy family maintained a bar and grocery (established in 1860, still prominent in the town today) that benefited commercially from the shipping trade and from which they invested in their children's education. Aidan, a strong swimmer and a keen rugby player, trained as a doctor at University College, Cork in 1931. In 1938, he graduated from his medical studies and, without prospect of employment in Ireland, emigrated to London just as war was looming on the European continent. On 3 September 1939, Britain declared war on Germany, and the following day he volunteered for the RAF. He was commissioned as senior medical officer to Group 14 in northern France. In May 1940, German forces unleashed a *blitzkrieg* offensive, driving and surrounding British and French forces; the Allied forces initiated a humiliating retreat, evacuating across the English Channel from the beach at Dunkirk under the lethal onslaught of submarines and the dive-bombing German Luftwaffe. On the first day, only 7,669 men were evacuated, but by the end of the eighth day a total of 338,226 soldiers had been rescued by a hastily assembled flotilla of over 800 boats; Aidan MacCarthy had to wait three long days in a foxhole before receiving orders to move.

In July, Aidan was stationed at RAF Honington, a squadron leader of Bomber Command in Suffolk. Although life was safe and routine for medical staff such as Aidan, on average only 30 per cent of airmen would survive their first flying mission; about 10 per cent would survive their second; more than 55,000 died by war's end, the highest casualty rate of any Allied fighting force. One night in May the following year, a Wellington bomber on its captain's first mission returning from a night raid still carrying hundreds of 500-pound bombs crashed on the runway and burst into flames. Aidan and Captain John Gray leapt into action and dragged three crew out alive from the burning plane; both MacCarthy and Gray were awarded the George Medal for their bravery by King George VI at Buckingham Palace in November.

On 8 December 1941, Aidan boarded a ship on the Clyde in Scotland for north Africa as senior medical officer with a spitfire unit; on the same day the US declared war on Japan. However, the ship sailed on to Sierra Leone in west Africa, then to South Africa and towards Singapore, where a growing crisis was unfolding, as Japanese forces were encroaching upon the British colony. The ship was diverted to Batavia (now Jakarta) in Java, Indonesia. By February, Japanese forces had begun raiding Java, and by 8 March Allied forces in Java surrendered. Aidan was to spend a total of 1,257 days in captivity, enduring disease, malnutrition, and torture, both physical and psychological; in German POW camps the mortality rate of prisoners was 4 per cent, in the Japanese POW camps it stood at 27 per cent.

In May 1944, Aidan and some 1,200 Dutch, Australian, American and British were crowded into the holds of a small Japanese cargo vessel bound for Japan, where they were to work as involuntary labour for the Japanese war effort. Docking at Singapore, the prisoners were marched aboard a large cargo ship laden with aluminium ore. At Taiwan (formerly Formosa), surviving weary men, dishevelled and emaciated, were stowed in the holds of a ship that had been used to transport horses and mules. Only some twenty-five miles off the coast of Nagasaki, an American submarine detected the small convoy racing at full speed, and opened fire with torpedoes:

> In the hold of the *Tamahoku Maru*, MacCarthy was trying to sleep. He had wrapped his mosquito netting around his feet to protect them from the rats that infested the area where the prisoners slept ... Suddenly he felt

> a rat close to his feet: it was stuck in the netting. He sat up terrified, trying to disentangle himself from the rat … On board the *Tamahoku Maru* MacCarthy did not know whether he or the rat was more frightened. Then the torpedo struck. [1]

The ship sank in minutes; it was to be one of the deadliest recorded submarine attacks of the war. Survivors clinging to flotsam further endured the bombardment of depth charges by Japanese naval planes. The survivors were rescued by a Japanese destroyer twelve hours later; there were probably 212 survivors.

The prisoners were placed in a POW camp in Nagasaki and assigned to work at the Mitsubishi Steel and Arms Works nearby. They endured fleas, lice, maggots, beatings, filth and sewage, the heat and humidity, the stench, the daily work shift, the lack of sleep:

> For MacCarthy, Christmas 1944 passed with a greater sense of dread and homesickness than he had ever known. In his diary he noted: 'We had a parcel on Xmas Eve but it was not the same as being home for Xmas.'[2]

Occasionally the POWs were permitted to write postcards home, which were censored. In May 1945, a letter written in English by Aidan was broadcast on radio by the propagandist 'Tokyo Rose': 'Dearest Mom and Dad and all the family, hello …'[3] This was when his family first learned that he had survived the shipwreck the year previous.

In the aftermath of the Nagasaki atomic-bomb explosion, Aidan and others (*hibakusha*; atomic-bomb survivors) headed for mountains among the many that surround the city, witnessing on their way the horrors of death strewn at their feet, the horrific wounds and illnesses inflicted by the explosion, and the ensuing and lingering radiation. Aidan – while not knowing the origin, the nature of the nuclear cataclysm – noted the symptoms of sufferers as he fled, the first doctor in medical history on such a scale at close and immediate quarters to do so. He tried to treat those injured who had taken to the hills in caves, but without medicines and medical tools his efforts would prove exasperating.

A few days later, the POWS were marched back to camp, and on 15 August – after hearing on radio Emperor Hirohito's voice for the first time – unconditional surrender was announced to a nation wearied by war. Within hours, the frightened commandant of the camp, Lieutenant Kusuno, presented Aidan with his military sword, a gift, but the veritable spiritual symbol of his nationhood; the ashes of his ancestors were embedded in the sword handle. POWs remained in their camps for several weeks, fed and supplied by Allied airdrop parcels. One day, Superintendent Kobayashi, a local police chief in nearby Fukuoka Prefecture, and his wife, approached Aidan MacCarthy, pleading through an interpreter for help for his young daughter sick with pneumonia. Coincidentally, a new discovered drug, penicillin, had been dropped among the medicines to the POW camps, and Aidan administered the drug to the sick child.

It took three months for Aidan to arrive home to Ireland. En route he happened upon an American naval officer in a bar in Hawaii; he was Richard O'Kane, captain of the *Tang*, the submarine that had sunk the *Tamahoku Maru* transport ship, who was later to be captured as a POW himself.

By November's end, Aidan had reached Castletownbere, the odyssey ended. His mother died on Christmas Eve the following month. A few weeks later, Aidan returned to England and work at the RAF. In 1948, he married Kathleen, who was from County Galway. Among his RAF postings were several years spent in France and Germany. He experienced the joy of bringing into the world two young daughters, Nicola and Adrienne. Many the summer was spent in west Cork. When Aidan passed away, a remarkable life, a remarkable story, had unfolded:

> On 11 October 1995, Dr Aidan MacCarthy OBE, GM, MB, BCH, BAL, Knight of St Sylvester, Air Commodore RAF (retired) and hibakusha, died …
>
> Lucky to survive Dunkirk, lucky to be sent to the Bandung POW camp instead of another, to be woken by a rat before a torpedo struck, not to be dumped at sea by the Japanese whalers, was in the bomb shelter when the atomic bomb struck, was not closer to the bomb, the list goes on and on …

In 1999, Bob Jackson, a lecturer in Tralee, heard the story of Aidan MacCarthy for the first time. A few months later, Bob found himself sauntering into a bar called MacCarthy's in Castletownbere. A woman behind the counter pointed him to a framed article telling him that it was about her father. By the time Bob finished reading, Adrienne MacCarthy, Aidan's daughter, had placed a samurai sword on the counter. In July 2013, an album of memorabilia accidentally fell out of a suitcase of old books from on top of a wardrobe; there was a photo of a Japanese officer holding the same sword. A TV documentary ensued (2014), and Bob and Adrienne travelled to Nagasaki to commemorate the sixty-eighth anniversary of the atomic-bomb explosion on 9 August. That day, contact was made with Satoshi Kusuno, grandson of Lieutenant Kusuno, and both families met at his graveyard the following evening; Satoshi's grandfather had never talked about his wartime experiences, and here they learned for the first time of his samurai sword now in a bar in Ireland.

1868

In 1866, while en route to Hong Kong at the request of his cousin, Sir Richard Graves Mac Donnell, governor of Hong Kong, Francis Brinkley (1841–1912) stopped off at Nagasaki in southern Japan. Here, Brinkley – who had recently graduated as an artillery officer from the Royal Military Academy at Woolwich – witnessed a duel between samurai warriors. Upon the death of his opponent, in accordance with *bushido*, the moral code by which warriors abided, the victor covered the body with his haori jacket, kneeling with hands clasped in prayer. So impressed was Brinkley by this chivalric act that he resolved to return soon, and was to go on to reside in Japan, serving an impressive career both as military advisor and journalist to life's end in the Land of the Rising Sun.

Francis Brinkley was born at Parsonstown House, County Meath, the youngest of Matthew Brinkley and Harriet Graves' thirteen children. His family's legacy belies illustrious twists before and beyond:

- John Brinkley, paternal grandfather, last bishop of Cloyne, first Royal Astronomer of Ireland.
- Richard Graves, maternal grandfather, dean of Ardagh, Senior Fellow at Trinity College, Dublin.
- Cyril Connolly, author and critic, grand-nephew of Francis Brinkley.

Brinkley was to return to Japan the following year and never to leave. He came as a member of the British–Japanese legation, having been appointed assistant military attaché to the Japanese embassy. In 1871, he resigned and was appointed as foreign advisor to the Meiji government. The Meiji Restoration period (1868–1912) ushered in constitutional monarchy and a new era in Japanese history, a great upheaval structurally in society, politics, economics, foreign relationships and militarily. In a few short decades, Japan was to advance from the end of the Edo period (1603–1868) – a period of strong economic and cultural growth but isolationist feudalistic society under the rule of the Tokugawa shogunate, its geo-polity of some 300 *daimyō* (feudal lords) and samurai – to become a major protagonist on the international stage. Francis Brinkley had arrived in a 'brave new world'.

Brinkley took to the task of integrating into his newly adopted, newly emerging Japan with alacrity. He was soon to master the Japanese language fluently, both written and spoken, and marry Yasuko Tanaka, daughter of a former samurai, having two daughters and a son. Having instructed the Imperial Japanese Navy on artillery strategies and techniques, by 1878 he was lecturing in mathematics at what was later to become Tokyo Imperial University. In 1881, he became owner and editor of the *Japan Mail* (which later merged with *The Japan Times*); the newspaper was sponsored by the Japanese government and maintained a very pro-Japanese stance. Brinkley was also appointed war correspondent for *The Times* of London, for which he reported on both the First Sino-Japanese War (1894–5) and the Russo-Japanese War (1904–5). A fervent advocate for Japanese policies, he was awarded honours by the Emperor Meiji for his contributions to Anglo-Japanese relationships.

In a private capacity, among his other numerous hobbies Brinkley collected Japanese art and pottery, most of which was destroyed during the Great Tokyo earthquake (1923) and the Second World War. He also wrote books on the Japanese language for English-language beginners and grammar books, and compiled an influential English–Japanese dictionary. Immersed in the culture, he wrote on Japanese art and history, his *History of the Japanese People* published posthumously in 1915.

1868

In 2006, Toshio Akiyama, conductor and head of the Japanese Band Directors' Association, placed a notice in the *Daily Telegraph* appealing for information about events in the later life history of John William Fenton (1828–90). In 2008, Matthew

Emperor Meiji (1852–1912), by Eduardo Chiossone (1833–98), 1888. (*Pictorial Press Ltd/ Alamy*)

Zealear, a descendant of Fenton, and his wife, Lauri, after having responded to his appeal, travelled from California to Japan for Matthew to conduct the Central Band of the Maritime Self-defence Force at Myōkōji Temple, Yokohama. Mr Akiyama's ten years of searching had come to an end.

In 1868, John Fenton of Kinsale, County Cork – bandmaster in Britain's 10th Foot Regiment, 1st Battalion – disembarked in Japan. The regiment had been dispatched to protect the newly established small foreign community at Yokohama amidst the turbulent transition from the end of the Tokugawa shogunate era to the Meiji Restoration. When Japanese naval cadets heard in passing the band practising, they asked Fenton to form and teach their own brass band, the first in Japan; Fenton ordered the instruments from London.

In 1869, upon realising that the state – newly fledged on the international stage – lacked symbols representative of its rich culture and long heritage, John Fenton proposed to military leaders the need for a national anthem. Working with Captain Oyama Iwao, son of a *samurai* and military officer of the very southerly Satsuma clan who was educated both in Japanese and Chinese literature, they set upon finding verse for lyrics and musical notes for the tune. For the lyrics, Oyama-san selected a tenth-century poem that petitions for the health and long life of the Lord; it appears that Oyama requested Fenton to compose the accompanying melody. With only three weeks to complete his task, Fenton's aspiration to an anthem was performed in the presence of the emperor in 1870; however, this original version of 'Kimi ga Yo', the Japanese national anthem, proved short-lived. In 1880, the melody was modified at the request of the Imperial Household Agency; this version, the final and contemporary version, was composed by another bandmaster, Franz Eckert. Today, it maintains a mode of traditional Japanese court music infused stylistically with the traditions of Western Christian hymns but within which strains of Fenton's original arrangement still waft.

Although his regiment left Japan in 1871, Fenton stayed on as bandmaster to the Japanese navy first and later to the imperial court. His first wife, Anna Maria, died in 1871, and was interred in Yokohama. Then he married Anna Pilkington from Philadelphia, and they set sail for San Francisco in 1877. Census records reveal that between 1881 and 1890 the Fenton family resided in Montrose, Angus, Scotland, before returning to the US. John Fenton was interred at Santa Cruz, California.

John Fenton and Captain Oyama may not be the authors and composers of 'Kimi ga Yo', the Japanese national anthem as it played today, but they were its instigators; Myōkōji Temple, in memory of their former bandmaster John Fenton, plays their original version annually.

But John Fenton's true legacy to Japan lies not with its anthem but with every tune played every day by any and every Japanese band – he is the father of band playing. The All Japan Band Association holds its contest annually: it is probably the largest music contest in the world in terms of active contestants, with roughly 800,000 contestants, members of more than 14,000 bands.

My Experiences of Ireland

Hiroshi Miyoshi

As a young man, Miyoshi was the owner-breeder at Miyoshi Farm in Japan and bought many stud horses from Ireland, one of which won nine Japan Racing Association races. Now, he has passed the running of the farm to his daughter and her husband and left the Japan Racing Society, enjoying his retirement.

I am now retired as a horse owner and breeder at Miyoshi Farm in Japan, but when I was young and in the business, I wondered how to buy good horses and bring them back to Japan from abroad. A Japanese businessman, vice-director at Ozawa Organization working as an import agent in London, told me about a horse farm in Ireland run by a second-generation Japanese man, from whom horses could be bought at a far lower price than those paid for Godolphin horses (one of the largest and most famous thoroughbred horseracing stables and breeding operations in the world). The only condition was that the vice-director would be the broker who worked on the transfer of any good horses to Japan. This is how I came to meet with Mr Nakano, the owner of Nakano Stud Farm in Ireland.

To tell the truth, when I first heard of the plan, I was beset with doubts, but nonetheless accompanied the agent to the farm. Generally speaking, when a person is second-generation Japanese it usually means they can speak a few Japanese words such as *ohayo* (good morning), *konbanwa* (good evening) and *sayonara* (goodbye) and I expected Mr Nakano to be such a speaker of broken Japanese. However, to my great surprise, he talked to me in very fluent Japanese and, furthermore, sold me a horse as good as a Godolphin at 70 per cent of the price of a Godolphin.

This horse adapted well to the Japan Racing Association and he won nine times, earning 133,260,000 Yen in prize money. As a result, from this time onward, I have bought 40 per cent of my horses from Nakano Farm, up to ten horses a year (twenty-five horses in total), and now I have bequeathed the job of owner-breeder to my daughter who buys, on average, two horses every year from Nakano Farm as broodmares.

This was my introduction to Ireland through horses. Whenever I visited Ireland to buy new horses, my working friends accompanied me; people such as Hashimoto, Miyamoto and Kunihide Matsuda, trainers, and Michiaki Morisawa, my intimate friend and manager of Miyoshi Farm. As I wanted to take my children with me on a future trip, so that they might enjoy themselves, I found time to look for good beaches for their summer vacation.

To my regret, I have not yet realised my dream of taking my wife and children to Ireland. My son and daughter are grown up now with their own partners and already have their own children, my grandchildren. Thus, as they are busy now with their own families, it seems unlikely that I will take them to Ireland, but I hope they will take their own children.

Ireland is known as the Emerald Isle – a place where nature is fertile and the people are warm, a place filled with wonderful historic buildings and ruins. It is a country that is fascinating to foreigners, especially the Japanese people. I have heard all about St Patrick's Day, when the streets are crowded with people who are said to be dressed all in green, though, to my regret, I have never seen it. Would that St Patrick had given me the chance to experience it!

One of my favourite things about my trips was Irish cuisine. Irish dishes are unique in that they have found so many ways of cooking beef and mutton; Irish beef, especially, is said to be the best in Europe. This suited me, as I am particularly fond of beef. Therefore, let me introduce the foods and the cooking I particularly enjoyed on my trips to Ireland. These are based on my own experiences, which I admit does not vary too much.

As I have not drunk alcohol since 1975, I will begin by recalling what I enjoyed when I was younger. In general, so far as European beer is concerned, I like bitter ones. I particularly enjoyed Irish stout, Guinness, as well as Murphy's and Beamish from Cork. The beer I consider truly Irish is ale, which is extremely tasty. Other brands that come to mind are Kilkenny and Mystic Knot (coffee stout). Though not beer, the most wonderful drink enjoyed in the Irish summertime is Bulmer's Apple Cider. As for Irish whiskey, as a young drinker I often tasted Jameson, distilled in Dublin, and Bailey's Irish cream liquor is also well known.

To return to the topic of food: I like to eat and have always enjoyed my food – which is probably why I own seven French restaurants! –and like to try all sorts of things. I enjoyed soda bread every morning at the hotel breakfast, simple and natural bread made with baking soda in place of yeast, bread one can happily eat very morning. As for the main course, since Ireland, like Japan, is a country surrounded by the sea, the sea food is reliably delicious.

Finally, I would like to list some of my favourite dishes, as well as delicious souvenirs and sweets. Here are some Irish dishes that I particularly enjoyed:

- salad of red cabbage and pecan nuts
- casserole of corned beef and cabbage (I was infatuated with this!)
- omelette filled with mashed potato, very delicious
- boiled stew of potato and green onion (I was infatuated with this, too)
- Irish lasagna
- Guinness and honey pork loin (roast pork in Japan)
- colcannon soup: mashed potato with kale and cabbage to which milk is added, it is then flavoured with butter, salt and pepper, the whole of which is put into a blender to make a potage-like dish (this is especially delicious)
- Irish roast salmon (delicious, and different from the Japanese style of cooking salmon)
- Butlers: the first-rate Irish brand of chocolate
- banoffee pie, particularly the one created by the restaurant Hungry Monk in a small town named Greystones in the east of Ireland
- apple cake
- trifle
- Rhubarb crumble, a sweet and slightly bitter cake made of rhubarb
- old-fashioned whiskey cake
- Irish barmbrack (traditional fruit loaf)

Detail from *Tale of Muramatsu*
(*Muramatsu monogatari emaki*),
style of Iwasa Matabei (1578–1650),
1600–1650. (CBL J 1127.3, © *The Trustees*

Notes

注

Notes

Michelle P. Brown

1 This paper builds upon a theme of comparing the experiences of reception of incoming literate faiths by the island archipelagos of Britain and Ireland and Japan, which I introduced as the epilogue to an exhibition I curated at the British Library, London, in 2003. See the exhibition booklet, M.P. Brown, *Painted Labyrinth: The world of the Lindisfarne Gospels* (London: British Library, 2003). I should like to dedicate it to my good friend, Professor Richard Kelly.

2 M.P. Brown, *How Christianity Came to Britain and Ireland* (Oxford: Lion Hudson, 2006); B. Yorke and N. Yates, *The Conversion of Britain: Religion, politics and society in Britain, 600–800* (London: Pearson, 2006); M. Carver (ed.), *The Cross Goes North: Processes of conversion in northern Europe, AD 300–1300* (York: University of York/York Medieval Press, 2003).

3 M. Ryan, *Treasures of Ireland: Irish art, 3000 B.C.–1500 A.D.* (DUBLIN: RIA, 1985); S. Youngs, *The Work of Angels: Masterpieces of Celtic metalwork: 6th to 9th centuries* (London: BM, 1989); D. Ó Cróinín, *Early Medieval Ireland, 400–1200* (London and New York: Longmans, 1995); T. Ó Carragáin, *Churches in Early Medieval Ireland: Architecture, ritual and memory* (New Haven, CT: Yale University Press, 2010).

4 M.P. Brown, *The Book and the Transformation of Britain, c. 550–1050: A study in written and visual literacy and orality* (London and Chicago: BL and Chicago University Press, 2011); W.W. Farris, *Population, Disease, and Land in Early Japan, 645–900* (Cambridge, MA: Harvard University Press, 1985), pp. 84 ff.; J.W. Hall and J.P. Mass (eds), *Medieval Japan: Essays in institutional history* (Stanford: Stanford University Press, 1974), pp. 97 ff.

5 M.P. Brown and L. Webster (eds), *The Transformation of the Roman World* (London: British Museum Press, 1997).

6 M.P. Brown, 'Imagining, Imaging and Experiencing the East in Insular and Anglo-Saxon Cultures: New evidence for contact', in J.D. Niles et al. (eds), *Anglo-Saxon England and the Visual Imagination: Proceedings of the ISAS conference, Madison, 2012, ACMRS Essays in Anglo-Saxon Studies 6* (Arizona, NV: Arizona Univ. Press, 2016), pp. 49–88.

7 É. Ó Carragáin, *Ritual and the Rood: Liturgical images and the Old English poems of the Dream of the Rood Tradition* (London and Toronto: British Library and University of Toronto Press, 2005); R.J. Kelly and C.L. Quinn, *Stone, Skin and Silver: A translation of the Dream of the Rood* (Cork: Litho Press and London: Sheed and Ward, 1999; rev. edn and e-book, 2014).

8 M.P. Brown, *Art of the Islands: Celtic, Pictish, Anglo-Saxon and Viking visual culture c. 450–1050* (Oxford: Bodleian, 2016).

9 M.P. Brown, *The Lindisfarne Gospels and the Early Medieval World* (London: British Library, 2011); and idem, *Art of the Islands*; B. Meehan, *The Book of Kells* (London: Thames & Hudson, 1995).

10 The monk Hui Shen (慧深), Book of Liang, seventh century.

11 C.G. Leland, *Fusang or the Discovery of America by Chinese Buddhist Priests in the Fifth Century* (London: Curzon, 1973).

12 R.J. Bowring, *The Religious traditions of Japan, 500–1600* (Cambridge: Cambridge University Press, 2005), pp. 15–17.

13 W.T. De Bary, *Sources of Japanese Tradition* (New York: Columbia University Press, 2001), p. 100.

14 P. Watt, 'Japanese Religion' (2003), http://spice.fsi.stanford.edu/docs/japanese_religions (accessed 18 May 2017).

15 D. and A. Matsunaga, *Foundation of Japanese Buddhism, Vol. 1: The aristocratic age* (Los Angeles and Tokyo: Buddhist Books International, 1996); R. Buswell et al., *The Princeton Dictionary of Buddhism* (Princeton, NJ: Princeton University Press, 2013); J. Snelling, *The Buddhist Handbook: A complete guide to Buddhist teaching and practice* (London: Century Paperbacks, 1987); T. Yoshiro Tamura, *Japanese Buddhism: A cultural history* (Kosei Publishing Co., 2005).

16 On this and the following outline, see Barbara O'Brien, *Buddhism in Japan: A brief history*, https://www.thoughtco.com/buddhism-in-japan-a-brief-history-450148 (accessed 17 May 2017).

17 Snelling, *The Buddhist Handbook*, p. 178.

18 Ibid.

Richard Kelly

1 An authoritative biography of St Francis Xavier is G. Schurhammer, *Francis Xavier: His Life, His Times*, trans. M.J. Costelloe (Rome: Jesuit Historical Institute, 1973).

2 Anjiro's only account of himself is recorded in his one extant letter, a Spanish translation of the lost Portuguese original: 'Goa, 29 November 1548'; the letter is edited by J. Wicki in *Documenta Indica*: *Momunmenta Historica Societatis Iesu* (Rome: MHSI, 1948), vol. 1, sec. 2, pp. 332–41.

3 This article follows the historical timeline of Christianity in Japan as documented by G.D. Laman, 'Our Nagasaki Legacy: An examination of the period of persecution of Christianity and its impact on subsequent Christianity in Japan', *Northeast Asia Journal of Theology*, nos 28–9 (March/September 1982), pp. 94–141.

4 See J. Laures, *Kirishitan Bunko: A manual of books and documents on the early Christian missions in Japan*, 3rd edn (Tokyo: Sophia University, 1957), esp. pp. 1–26, for a comprehensive overview of the Christian texts that were translated into Japanese from the mid-sixteenth century to the contemporary era.

5 There are several historical studies of Christianity in Japan; the most significant are C.H. Boxer, *The Christian Century in Japan: 1548–1650* (Berkeley, CA: University of California Press, 1967); J. Jennes, *A History of the Catholic Church in Japan from its Beginnings to*

the Early Meiji Era (1549–1873): A short handbook (Tokyo: Oriens Institute for Religious Research, 1973); and S.H. Moffett, *A History of Christianity in Asia*, vol. ii (Maryknoll, NY: Orbis Books, 2005).

6 R. Lee, *The Clash of Civilizations: An intrusive gospel in Japanese civilization* (Harrisburg, PA: Trinity Press International, 1999), offers an insightful understanding into the contextualisation of Japanese society and culture. His discussion of the Japanese emperor system, identity and modernisation sheds much light on the challenges that St Francis Xavier endured during his short sojourn in Japan.

7 For a biography of Ōuchi, see M. Yonehara, *Ōuchi Yoshitaka: Meishō ga hanahirakaseta Yamaguchi bunka*, Chūsei Bunshi Sensho 20 (Tokyo: Ebisu Kōshō Shuppan, 2014).

8 On the lexicographical issues of the translation of biblical writings (*lingua sacra*) into Japanese, see N. Suzuki, *Seisho no Nihongo: Hon'yaku no rekishi* (Tokyo: Iwanami Shoten, 2006).

9 On the Court of Ōtomo, see M.H. Takao, 'Francis Xavier at the Court of Ōtomo Yoshishige: Representations of religious disputation between Jesuits and Buddhists in la conversione alla santa fede del re di Bungo giaponese (1703)', *Journal of Jesuit Studies*, vol. 3 no. 3 (2016), pp. 451–74; and M. Takita, *Ōtomo Shiryō: Ōtomo Ke monjoroku* (Ōita: Kin'yōdō Shoten, 1937).

10 See C.R. Boxer, *Jan Compagnie in Japan, 1672–1674: Anglo-Dutch rivalry in Japan and Formosa* (Tokyo: Asiatic Society of Japan, 1931).

11 A standard critical edition is J. Swift, *Gulliver's Travels*, ed. A.J. Rivero, Norton Critical Series (New York and London: W.W. Norton, 2002).

12 See M.O. Johnson, M. Kitagaki and P.E. Williams, *Gulliver's Travels and Japan: A new reading* (Kyoto: Amherst House, Doshisha University, 1977).

13 For a comprehensive analysis of Japan's Hidden Christians, see S.R. Turnbull, *Japan's Hidden Christians, 1549–1999* (Surrey: Japan Library; Tokyo: Synapse, 2000).

14 On the Thirty Years War, see R. Bonney, *Thirty Years' War: 1618–1648* (London and New York: Bloomsbury, 2002).

15 For a historical account of this rebellion, see J. Clements, *Christ's Samurai: The true story of the Shimabara Rebellion* (London: Robinson, 2016).

16 On the pontificate of Pope Paul V, see J. Loughlin, 'Pope Paul V', *Catholic Encyclopedia*, vol. 11 (New York: Robert Appleton Company, 1911).

17 On the trial of Galileo, see T.M. Mayer, *The Roman Inquisition: Trying Galileo* (Philadelphia: University of Pennsylvania Press, 2015).

18 For a comprehensive biography of Tokugawa, see A.L. Sadler, *The Maker of Modern Japan: The life of Tokugawa Ieyasu* (Hoboken: Taylor and Francis, 2013).

19 On the laws and justice of the Tokugawa Shogunate, see J.H. Wigmore, *Law and Justice in Tokugawa Japan: Materials for the history of Japanese law and justice under the Tokugawa shogunate, 1603–1867*, vol. 6: *Property: Legal precedents* (Tokyo: University of Tokyo Press, 1981).

20 See J.M. Suarez Japon, *Yoko Maeda: Mi amiga Japonesa* (Coria del Río [Sevilla]: Asociación Hasekura DL, 2016).

21 Letter of Hasekura to his son, written during his stay in the Philippines, Sendai City Museum, document 243.

22 This extract is referring to *Bankoku no monogoto, Rokuuemon monogatari no omomuki, kikai saita shi*「蛮国ノ物事、六右衛門物語ノ趣、奇怪最多シ」 (*Date Osamu-ka kiroku*) (伊達治家記録) ('Records from the House of Date').

23 Letter of Fr Angelis, dated November 1620 in T. Gonoi, *Hasekura Tsunenaga* (Tokyo: Yoshikawa Kōbunkan, 2003), p. 231. This letter is part of the China–Japan Collection of the Jesuit archives in Rome.

24 Letter of seventeen prominent Japanese Christians from Sendai to the pope, 29 September 1621, cited in Gonoi, *Hasekura Tsunenaga*, p. 229.

25 Letter of Masamune Date, dated 18 October 1620, cited in Gonoi, *Hasekura Tsunenaga*, p. 234.

26 A translation from Latin of L. Sotelo, *Ad Urbanum Octavum Pont. Max. de Ecclesiae Iaponicae Statu Relatio*, Rome, 1634: 16. On the missionary activity of Soleto in Japan, see L. Pérez and C.R. Boxer, *Apostolado y Martirio del Beato Luis Sotelo en el Japón* (Madrid: Imprenta Hispánica, 1924).

27 On this second diplomatic mission, see I. Nish, *The Iwakura Mission in America and Europe: A new assessment*, Meiji Series 6 (London: Routledge Curzon, 2004); and K. Kume, G. Healey, M.B. Jansen and M. Collutt, *The Iwakura Embassy, 1871–73: A true account of the ambassador extraordinary & plenipotentiary's journey of observation through the United States of America and Europe*, 5 vols (Chiba, Japan: Japan Documents / Richmond: Curzon, 2002).

28 Sakitsu Catholic church is beautifully documented in T. Kobayashi and T. Watanabe, *Amakusa Kirishitan kikō: Sakitsu, Ōe, Kirishitan yukari no chi* (Fukuoka-shi: Gen Shobō, 2016).

Hiroyasu Fujisawa

1 Ryūnosuke Akutagawa (1892–1927), born in Tōkyō, is known as a master of the Japanese short story. As a graduate of the Department of English at Tōkyō Imperial University, he was able to read foreign literature in English as well as Japanese literature and Chinese classics. The chief feature of his creative style is that he retold old stories in his own way. In the early years of his literary career, he borrowed topics from ancient Japanese stories in the Heian and Edo periods and produced such masterpieces as 'Rashōmon' and 'The Spider Thread' ('Kumo no Ito'), both of which gave inspiration to Akira Kurosawa's film, *Rashōmon* (1950). In later years, Akutagawa shifted his focus from old Japanese literature to Christianity and wrote several works influenced by it. He died of an overdose in 1927. Kunito Higuchi, whose pseudonym was Kōnosuke Hinatsu (1890–1971), was born in Nagano and studied at Waseda University. He published four collections of poems written in his 'Gothic-Roman style' and taught as a professor of English at Waseda University and Aoyama Gakuin University. Besides poems, he also published about 100 critical works and translations such as the complete poems of Oscar Wilde and Edgar Allan Poe's 'The Raven'. For his two-volume *History of Poetry in the Meiji and Taishō Periods* (Meiji Taishō Shi Shi, 1927) published by Shinchōsha, Hinatsu was awarded the first Yomiuri Literary Award in 1950. His learned, sometimes even

pedantic, literary style had a significant influence upon such authors as Yukio Mishima and Tatsuhiko Shibusawa.

2 The essay that contains the quotation first appeared in a Kyushū newspaper, *Nishinippon Shimbun*, on 17 April 1954 and was later reproduced in Hinatsu's collection of essays, *Drops of Water* (Kenteki) (Iida: the City Library of Iida, 1968), pp. 205–7.

3 Yaso Saijō (1892–1970) graduated from Waseda University with a degree in English and published many poems. After studying French literature in France, he became a professor of French at Waseda. In Japan, he is well known not only as a symbolist poet but as a popular-music lyricist.

4 A journal, *The Mask*, was issued by a group of students passionate about literature at Waseda University from 1913 to 1915, replacing its predecessor, *The Holy Grail* (Seihai, 1912–13). Hinatsu himself edited the July issue of *The Holy Grail* in 1913, which featured W.B. Yeats.

5 Yaso Saijō, 'My Curriculum Vitae' ('Watashi no Rirekisho') in *The Complete Works of Yaso Saijō* (Saijō Yaso Zenshū), Volume 17 (Tōkyō: Kokushokankōkai), p. 451.

6 *Kokuchō* (The Black Current) is a literary journal published from 1916 to 1918, to which Ryūnosuke Akutagawa contributed some short stories. For the postcard, see Ryūnosuke Akutagawa, *The Complete Works of Ryūnosuke Akutagawa* (Akutagawa Ryūnosuke Zenshū), Volume 18, eds. Toshirō Kōno, Eiji Ebii, and Tōru Ishiwari (Tōkyō: Iwanami Shoten, 2008), pp. 178–9.

7 As an English teacher, Ryūnosuke Akutagawa earned his living by working for the Naval Engineering College in Yokohama from 1916 to 1919. Hinatsu also lived in Kamakura in Kanagawa Prefecture in almost the same period. Kōnosuke Hinatsu, 'Akutagawa's Literature as a Will' in *The Complete Works of Kōnosuke Hinatsu* (Hinatsu Kōnosuke Zenshū), Volume 5 (Tōkyō: Kawade Shobō Shinsha, 1978), p. 335. Hinatsu also mentions the 'book of Mary' in his essays such as 'A Genius Is Dead' ('Shum'mō Horobu'), *The Complete Works*, Volume 8 (Tōkyō: Kawade Shobō, 1978), p. 152.

8 An unknown fourteenth-century writer, *The Life of Saint Mary Magdalen*, trans. Valentina Hawtrey with an Introduction by Vernon Lee (London: John Lane, the Bodley Head, 1906); hereafter cited as *The Life*.

9 Kōnosuke Hinatsu, *Virgin Mary Draped in Black* (Tōkyō: Ars, 1921).

10 See *The Sabbath*, Issue 1, Volume 4, Reprint Edition (Tōkyō: Bokushinsha, 1967 [1927]). In this part of the translation, the author describes the beauty of Mary Magdalen, introduces her family members, and mentions her betrothal to John the Evangelist and its cancellation due to his becoming one of Jesus Christ's followers.

11 The discovery of *The Life* as Akutagawa's 'book of Mary' and of Hinatsu's manuscript was reported by Hideki Komatsu in a local newspaper in Nagano, *Shinano Mainichi Shimbun*, on 27 December 2016.

12 It is tempting to imagine why such a productive author as Hinatsu stopped translating the entirety of *The Life* into Japanese. His fragile health, busy writing schedule and editorial work for journals such as *Pantheon* might have prevented him concentrating on this task. Is it a mere coincidence, however, that 1927, during which he stopped publishing his serial

translations of *The Life*, was the very year in which Ryūnosuke Akutagawa committed suicide? Hinatsu did not go on to translate the entire book perhaps because he had lost the only reader that could fully appreciate the significance of the translation.

13 See 'Preface' in *The Life*, p. vii.

14 Vernon Lee, *Renaissance Fancies and Studies* (London: Smith, Elder, & Co., 1896), pp. 55–8.

15 Domenico Cavalca, *Vite dei Santi Padri*, Volume 2, ed. Carlo Delcorno (Firenze: Edizioni del Galluzzo per la Fondanzione Ezio Franceschini, 2009). Domenico Cavalca, *Vorgrizzamento delle Vite de' Santi Padri di Fra Domenico Cavalca* (Milan: Silvestri, 1854).

17 See Kōnosuke Hinatsu, *The Complete Works*, Volume 3 (Tōkyō: Kawade Shobō, 1975), p.747. 18 See Ryūnosuke Akutagawa, Volume 6, *The Complete Works of Ryūnosuke Akutagawa* (Tōkyō: Iwanami Shoten, 1996), pp. 80–7.

18 See Yoshitoshi Kuzumaki (ed.), 'Mary Magdalena' ('Magdarena no Maria'), *Ryūnosuke Akutagawa's Unfinished Manuscripts* (Akutagawa Ryūnosuke Miteikōshū) (Tōkyō: Iwanami Shoten, 1968), pp. 158–63.

19 See Akutagawa's postcard to Wake in *The Complete Works of Ryūnosuke Akutagawa*, Volume 18 (Tōkyō: Iwanami Shoten, 2008), p. 310.

20 In her essay presented at the symposium of The First Conference of International Society for Akutagawa [Ryunosuke] Studies, Cho Saok (曺 紗玉) succinctly points out the connections between Jin Hua and Mary Magdalene but she does not mention *The Life* in her argument. See Chao Saok, 'Mary Magdalene in "Christ in Nanjing"', *Akutagawa Review* 1 (2007), pp. 15– 24.

21 *The Complete Works of Ryūnosuke Akutagawa*, Volume 6 (Tōkyō: Iwanami Shoten, 2007), p. 252; English translation mine.

22 Critics have explored the topic of Akutagawa and Mary Magdalen, but it seems that no one has ever taken *The Life* into account.

23 The Man in the West is generally said to imply Jesus Christ. See '15 Women' in *The Complete Works of Ryūnosuke Akutagawa*, Volume 15 (Tōkyō: Iwanami Shoten, 1997), pp. 254–5.

24 See *Drops of Water*, p. 206. At the end of this obituary, Hinatsu writes about Akutagawa movingly: 'I hated people in the literary world but I liked him exclusively. So I am still waiting for him alone.' *Drops of Water*, p. 207.

Mimbu Kawamura

1 Masaru Toda, *A 'Transmigrating' Story – the World of Koizumi Yakumo's Kwaidan* (Shinyosha, 2011).

2 Shinichi Matsumura, 'Hearn's "Yuki-Onna" and Ur-"Yuki-Onna" in *Yakumo*' (Koizumi Yakumo Kenshoukai, No. 11).

3. Yoko Makino, 'Lafcadio Hearn's "Yuki-Onna" and Baudelaire's "Les Bienfaits de la Lune"', *Comparative Literature Studies*, vol. 28, no. 3, East–West Issue, 1991 (Penn State University Press).

4. Sukehiro Hirakawa (ed.), *Koizumiyakumo, Kaidan & Kidan* (Koudansha-Gakujyutu-bunko, 2013), p. 83. The English quotations from 'Yuki-Onna' are all taken from the text of Lafcadio Hearn, *Kwaidan: Stories and Studies of Strange Things* (Kegan Paul & Co., 1904).
5 Toshiaki Komura, "Translations and Transformations of Snow Women as Exiles: Lafcadio Hearn's "Yuki-Onna" and Anne Sexton's "Snow White and the Seven Dwarfs"' (Fuji Women's University, Department of Literature Bulletin, 51, 2014), pp. 6–7.
6. Julia Kristeva, *Strangers to Ourselves*, Leon Roudiez, trans. (Columbia University Press, 1991), p. 3.
7. David Leeming, *Mythology* (Tokyo: Kinseido,1984), pp. 12–13.
8. Ibid., *Mythology, pp.* 16–17.
9. Oscar Wilde, 'The Star-Child' in *A House of Pomegranates* (1891). The following quotations from the story are all taken from http://www.eastoftheweb.com/short-stories/UBooks/StaChi.shtml.
10. Edward Larocque Tinker, *Lafcadio Hearn's American Days* (New York: Dodd, Mead and Company, 1924), p. 2. To support my argument, I may here refer to Hearn's first marriage, to Althea Foley, 'a pretty, well-made octoroon girl', violating Ohio state's 'law against miscegenation' (Ibid., pp. 27–8).
11. Theodore Watts-Dunton, *The Coming of Love and Other Poems* (John Lane, The Bodley Head, 1898).
12. Charles Baudelaire 'Les Bienfaits de la Lune', http://www.beverymatherne.com/Blessings-of-the-moon.html.
13. 'Studies on Extraordinary Prose', *Interpretations of Literature*, ed. John Erskin (New York: Dodd, Mead & Co.,1915) 2, p. 84.
14. Oscar Wilde, *Salomé* in *The Portable Oscar Wilde*, eds. Richard Aldington, Richard and Stanley Weibtraub (Penguin Books, 1981), p. 393.
15. Sukehiro Hirakawa (ed.), *Lafcadio Hearn's Dictionary* (Kobunsha,2000), pp. 323–4.
16. George Hughes, *Looking Forward and Looking Back: Essays on Hearn and Teaching in Japan*, trans. by Hiraishi Takaki & Tamai Akira (Kenkyusha, 2002), p. 135.

Bon Koizumi

1. *Writings of Lafcadio Hearn* (Houghton Mifflin Company, 1922), vol. 15, p. 333.
2. W.B. Yeats, *Wheels and Butterflies* (London: Macmillan, 1934), pp. 106–7.
3. Later, the name of the gardens was changed to Lafcadio Hearn Japanese Gardens.

Akiyo Suzuki

1 Kikuchi Kan, 'Thinking of Lafcadio Hearn', *Chūgai Nippō*, 2 August 1914.
2 Ibid.

3 Koizumi Bon, 'Lafcadio Hearn's adoption of and carrying on oral culture', in *The Water Veins of Celt Oral Culture* (Tokyo: Chūō University Press, 2006).
4 Paul Murray, Fantastic Journey: *The Life and Literature of Lafcadio Hearn* (London and New York: Routledge, 1993).
5 George Hughes, 'W.B. Yeats and Lafcadio Hearn: negotiating with ghosts', in Sukehiro Hirakawa (ed.), *Rediscovering Lafcadio Hearn: Japanese Legends, Life & Culture* (Folkestone: Global Books, 1997).
6 Nishi Masahiko, *Lafcadio Hearn's Ears, expanded edn.* (Tokyo: Iwanami Shoten, 1988).
7 Barbara Hayley, 'Lafcadio Hearn, W.B. Yeats and Japan', in Robert Welch and Suheil Badi Bushrui (eds), *Literature and the Art of Creation* (Totowa, NJ: Barnes, 1988), pp. 43–60.
8 George Hughes, 'Lafcadio Hearn: between Britain and Japan', trans. Tamai Akira, *Eureka* April 1995.
9 Honma Hisao, 'Recent currents in thought: a new theory regarding Lafcadio Hearn', *Waseda bungaku*, July 1914.
10 Doi Bansui, 'At Koizumi Yakumo Sensei's 25th memorial ceremony', *Tōkyō Nichi Nichi Shinbun*, 26 September 1929.
11 'News from world of literature', *Bunshō sekai*, January 1914.
12 Kikuchi Kan, 'Foreign authors that influenced me', *Theatre (Teatoru)*, May 1926.
13 Ernest Renan, *Poetry of the Celtic Races, and Other Essays*, trans. William G. Hutchison (London: Walter Scott, 1896), p. 9.
14 Kikuchi Kan, 'Synge and Ireland's thought', *Shinchō*, December 1917.
15 Matthew Arnold, *On the Study of Celtic Literature and Other Essays* (London and New York: J.M. Dent & Sons, 1910), p. 104.
16 Kikuchi Kan, 'Literature chat: the Irish and the Japanese', *Shinshosetsu*, June 1920.

Akiko Manabe

1 Tetsuro Sano's Japanese translation of *The Cat and the Moon* was used in the world premiere performance directed by Kaoru Matsumoto at Kobe Gakuin University in December 2015. Based on Hearn's *Chin Chin Kobakama*, Sengoro Shigeyama XIV wrote and will direct a new *kyogen* play in 2017.
2 Interestingly, Yeats did not have a complete command of the Irish language, and Hearn's Japanese was far from satisfactory. However, they caught the gist of the stories and songs they collected. They used their five senses to the fullest extent to capture the meaning of these classical tales, which were often taken for granted and therefore frequently forgotten.
3 *Kyogen* actors also play important parts in *Noh* plays called *ai* or *ai-kyogen*; they sometimes play narrators, explaining the whole scene, or as reporters giving information to the main characters, or as comical characters doing something foolish, often becoming a key to a crucial turning point in a play. *Ai kyogen* characters are integral parts of the drama, but at the same time contribute an unusual objectivity from quite a different perspective. But in this paper,

when I say *kyogen*, I mean an individual play performed between *Noh* plays, not *ai kyogen*.

4 13 June 2009: Symposium, 'Exchange Through Silk in Hikone– From Tomikoka Silk Mill to Hikone Silk Mill and Omi Silk Factory', *Kinto Zaemon* by Shime Shigeyama and Masakuni Shigeyama; 17 October 2009: Symposium, 'Traditional Culture and International Exchange in Modern Hikone', *Suo Otoshi* by Sengoro Shigyama XIII, Shime Shigeyama and Kaoru Matsumoto; and 8 November 2009: Symposium, 'Road to the Revival of Local Brand: Takashima Textile and Future of Hikone', *Tachi Ubai* by Masakuni Shigeyama, Kaoru Matsumoto and Moriyuki Yamashita. In 2016 Masakuni Shigeyama, who played the Blind Beggar in *C and M*, succeeded his late grandfather, a designated national treasure, and his father; he adopted the formal stage name of Sengoro XIV.

5 Masakuni Shigeyama as a Fox/Priest and Shigeru Shigeyama as a Hunter.

6 Pound drew on Ernest Fenollosa's manuscripts as a primary source for *Nogaku*. They contain a *zato kyogen*, *Kikazu Zato*, in which a blind person and a deaf person are ordered to look after a house while their master is away. Being alone in the house together, they mock each other's blindness and deafness, using abusive language and behaviour, but through their dance and song – which is both comical and graceful – the theatre is filled with warm joviality.

7 Though in Yeats's *C and M* only two characters are on the stage and the Saint appears only by voice – in fact, a musician on the stage speaks for him – director Kaoru Matsumoto decided that the Saint would appear as a third character on the stage because 'in *kyogen*, every character on the stage has to have physicality and appear as a human being. Even gods, a Buddha, spirits, fairies, goblins, even animals have to look like human beings to appear on the stage' (Matsumoto). Therefore, the Saint appears as a third character on the stage in the Shigeyama *kyogen* version.

8 Below are their profiles, based primarily on information from the website 'The Open Mind of Patrick Lafcadio Hearn – Coming Home', http://hearn2015.sanin-japan-ireland.org/reading, with additional information by Sano.

Actor, Shiro Sano, raised in Matsue, was a founding member of the 'Shakespeare Theatre', a troupe established in 1975. In 1980 he joined another troupe, the Gekidan Jokyo Gekijō, headed by Juro Kara. He made his screen debut in 1986, and has acted in more than 110 productions, including foreign movies. In 1999 he produced his first movie, *Karaoke*. In 2006 he directed, acted and wrote the script for the short film *A Drop of Dew*, which combined photographs of Shoji Ueda with the words of Hearn. In 2013, for Czech director Jiří Barta's animated film *Yuki Onna* [*Snow Woman*] – based on Hearn's story – he worked as a co-producer as well as voice actor. Interested in the fantastic since childhood, he has long been fascinated with the works of Hearn, many of which are related to Matsue. Through his activities and engagement with visual works, he has developed a deep interest in, and passion for, the world of Hearn. He began 'The Lafcadio Hearn Reading Performance' in Matsue in 2006, and this project has now come to occupy a central place in his life and work. His partner in this performance is the guitarist Kyoji Yamamoto. Sano and Yamamoto were classmates at Matsue Minami High School, and deepened their friendship through their mutual affection for music. In 2009 Shiro donated a first edition of *The Writings of Lafcadio Hearn* in sixteen volumes to the American College of Greece.

Guitarist/musician Kyoji Yamamoto was born and raised in Matsue. He began playing the guitar at the age of fifteen, and enrolled in the Yamaha Nemu Music Conservatory three years later. His reputation as an extremely talented guitarist was established from the start of his career, and he was appointed as the lead guitarist and vocalist of BOW WOW. The band quickly gained popularity through touring with both Aerosmith and Kiss. Kyoji's dynamic playing and exceptional technique led him to become one of the forerunners of the Japanese rock scene. He later formed VOW WOW. Based in London, the band recorded and performed in the United Kingdom, around Europe and the United States for four years. Acknowledged internationally, Yamamoto has influenced some world-famous artists, and is ever active on the global stage, demonstrating his wide range of musicianship. In addition to releasing several instrumental albums, he holds sessions with jazz-fusion musicians, performs in acoustic recitals, and creates the music for the 'Lafcadio Hearn Reading Performance' in collaboration with Shiro Sano. He is also a renowned producer for other international artists.

9 I should point out here that the theme of this particular story caught the attention of a young female director, Kihi Sugino, and in 2016 she – with insight and a peculiar sense of beauty – created a new film. Sano played two important roles in this film, and also provided significant creative feedback to Sugino. Another amazing occurrence is that a Japanese calligrapher of the highest calibre, Shiro Nakamura, stimulated by the reading performance held in Hikone, proceeded to create a brand new kind of artistic work. This is yet another example of a long line of artists, representing many different fields, who have been creatively stimulated by Hearn's pioneering literary achievement.

Hideaki Sato

* A sotōba generally means a 'stupa' in English. In Japan, a sotōba is usually used to commemorate the dead in the form of a long, thin board set up behind a tombstone, but in performances of 'Sotōba Komachi' it is often represented as a bench in a park, which makes it possible for the Old Woman to sit on it.

1 See Yukio Mishima, *Modern Noh Plays* (Tokyo: Shinchōsha, 1956). The book originally included five plays, among which was 'Sotōba Komachi', but it was later revised, and another four were added. One of the plays, 'Genji Kuyō', was later removed by the author, and the Shinchō Library edition of *Modern Noh Plays* includes only eight plays. In this paper, all quotations from 'Sotōba Komachi' are from Yukio Mishima, *Five Modern Noh Plays*, translated by Donald Keene (Tokyo: Tuttle Publishing, 1957), pp. 1–30.

2 Yukio Mishima, *Letters*: *The Definitive Edition of the Complete Works of Yukio Mishima*, vol. 38 (Tokyo: Shinchōsha, 2004), p. 921.

3 Yukio Mishima, 'My years of literary pilgrimage', letter to Makoto Mitani, 19 May 1945; in

this letter Mishima also writes, 'I am translating part of Yeats's one-act play every night.' See *The Definitive Edition of the Complete Works of Yukio Mishima*, vol. 38 (Tokyo: Shinchōsha, 2004), p. 921.

4 See 'My years of literary pilgrimage', in *The Definitive Edition of the Complete Works of Yukio Mishima*, vol. 32 (Tokyo: Shinchōsha, 2003), p. 28.

5 *Letters: The Definitive Edition of the Complete Works of Yukio Mishima*, vol. 38. (Tokyo: Shinchōsha, 2004). p. 756.

6 Keiko Wells, 'Ono no Komachi who became the moon – translation of *Noh* by Pound and Fenollosa and Pound's image of Komachi', *Literature* (*Bungaku*), no. 3 (1992), p. 133.

7 Regarding *Shite hitori shugi* (a dramatic principle that only one protagonist (*shite*) should control a whole Noh play), see Toyoichirō Nogami, *Noh:A Study and Discovery* (Tokyo: Iwanami Shoten, 1930), pp. 1–42.

8 Takako Abe, 'Yukio Mishima's "Sotōba Komachi" and W.B. Yeats, with special reference to the problem of the argument concerning the process of artistic production', *Bulletin of the Society of Japanese Language and Japanese Literature of Niigata University*, no. 45 (2003), pp. 1–11.

9 'Sailing to Byzantium', ll.1–6.

10 'Sotōba Komachi', *Five Modern Noh Plays*, p. 11.

11 See Yukio Mishima, *The Sun and the Iron*: *The Definitive Edition of the Complete Works of Yukio Mishima*, vol. 33 (Tokyo: Shinchōsha, 2003), p. 517.

12 'Sotōba Komachi', *Five Modern Noh Plays*, p. 12.

13 Ibid.

14 Komachi's age tells us that the story of 'Sotōba Komachi' is set around 1936, and that it speaks to a world fourteen years later, taking into consideration that the year of its first performance was 1952. It seems to me, however, that this time setting is almost meaningless. 'Sotōba Komachi' was performed at Bungakuza Atelier 19–25 February 1952.

15 Yukio Mishima's 'The Rokumeikan' first appeared in the 2 February 1956 issue of *Literary World* (*Bungakukai*) and was published by Tokyo Sōgensha in book form in 1957, pp. 5–20. It contains the statement, 'Hide! Cheat foreigners and all the world!'

16 See Masaaki Kōsaka, *Prime Minister Shigeru Yoshida* (Tokyo: Chuō Kōronsha, 1968), pp. 33–7.

17 For the script of 'Cathleen Ní Houlihan', I consulted 'Cathleen Ní Houlihan', in W.B. Yeats, *The Collected Plays of W.B. Yeats* (London: Macmillan, 1969), pp. 75–88.

18 'Éire, completely independent', *Asahi Shimbun*, 18 April 1949; 'Éire, completely independent', *Mainichi Shimbun*, 19 April 1949.

Shaun Richards

1 W.B. Yeats, 'Introduction', *The Classic Noh Theatre of Japan* (New York: New Directions, 1959), pp. 151, 155. This is a revision of Pound's '*Noh' or Accomplishment* (London, 1916),

which added his own introduction to the initial publication of *Certain Noble Plays of Japan* by Cuala Press, Dublin, which had been established in 1908 by Yeats's sister Elizabeth.

2 Daniel Albright, 'Pound, Yeats, and the Noh Theater', *Iowa Review*, vol. 15, no. 2 (spring/ summer 1985), p. 37.

3 Min Tian, "Alienation Effect' for Whom? Brecht's (Mis)interpretation of the classical Chinese theatre', *Asian Theatre Journal*, vol. 14, no. 2 (fall 1997), pp. 203–4.

4 R.F. Foster, *W.B. Yeats: A life II: The arch poet* (Oxford: Oxford University Press, 2003), p. 35

5 Maurice Maeterlinck, 'The Tragical in Daily Life', in Claude Schumacher (ed.), *Naturalism and Symbolism in European Literature, 1850–1918* (Cambridge: Cambridge University Press, 1996), p. 92.

6 Arthur Symons, *The Symbolist Movement in Literature* (London: W. Heinemann, 1899), p. 158.

7 Arthur Symons, *Studies in Seven Arts* (London: Archibald Constable & Co., 1906) p. 356.

8 Richard Allen Cave, 'Time for a Yeatsian Revolution', *Theatre Ireland*, no. 22 (spring 1990), pp. 24, 26.

9 Fintan O'Toole, 'Coca-Cola Yeats Could be the Real Thing', *The Irish Times*, 16 September 1989, p. 6.

10 Yasuo Nakamura, *Noh: The classical theatre* (New York: Weatherhill, 1971), pp. 154–5.

Akemi Yoshida

1. Translations from Tomioka's work used in quotation in this article are my own.
2. Mebed also points out that Kawabata's still earlier attempt at stylistic assimilation of *Ulysses* could be found in his short story 'The Needle, Glass and Mist' (Harito Garasu to Kiri, 1931), in which the style of the 'Circe' episode of *Ulysses* is imitated.
3. It might be intriguing also to note the resemblance of the title of one of Kawabata's representative works *The Sound of the Mountain* (Yama no Oto, 1954) to that of George Moore's short story 'The Voice of the Mountain' (1904), though they seem to share little in common as to the content.
4. All translations from Kawabata's texts in this article are my own.
5. It would be interesting to note that this combination of deformed feet and outstanding aesthetic sensibility is also employed as a dominant motif in E.M. Forster's *The Longest Journey* (1907), in the characterisation of the male protagonist and his aunt. Kawabata is known to have been familiar with Forster's works (Mebed 2003, p. 5), so the latter could have been a common source of inspiration for both Joyce and Kawabata.
6. Though I have not yet had the opportunity to have a look at the earliest version of the Japanese translation of *Ulysses* by Sei Itoh which Kawabata perused, I had access to the revised version published in 1955, where the word adopted for 'glow-worm' is *hotaru*, identical to the one Kawabata used for 'fireflies' in *The Lake*. Kawabata might not have been aware that the image of gleaming insects employed in *Ulysses* is not that of fireflies, the species more

commonly seen in Japan and regarded as one of the seasonal charms of summer.

7. Mebed has also drawn a parallel between the images of the dead child in *Ulysses* and Kawabata's early work 'Needle, Glass and Mist,' whose protagonist is traumatised by the death of her baby (2003, p. 11), pointing to Kawabata's interest in Freudian psychoanalysis.
8. Though certain resemblances might be found between the narrative style adopted in the earlier part of the 'Nausicaa' episode which seemingly takes the third-person narrative and the style throughout Kawabata's *The Lake*, the former should be regarded as what Dujardin calls an 'indirect interior monologue' (p. 142), in which Gerty is unfolding a monologue about herself that is highly sentimental, subjective, and decorative, in the form of a third-person narrative. The third-person narrators in Kawabata's *The Lake* and Moore's *The Lake*, on the other hand, are neutral mediators who, without giving any judgement, verbally and objectively translate what the protagonists perceive.
9. In a later work *Beauty and Sadness* (Utsukushisa to Kanshimito, 1965), Kawabata again gives an important role to a lake, making Lake Biwa the scene of a revengeful murder.
10. Moore's colour symbolism here is comparable to that used by George Egerton, a 'New Woman' writer with Irish connections who was active around the *fin-de-siècle* period and whose works Moore must have been familiar with. In *Keynotes* (1893), her first short story collection which created a sensation among the reading public, Egerton notably employed unconventional heroines clad in grey, as if to show that they are beyond the existing moral criteria and should not be subjected to the black/white binary.
11. Kawabata familiarised himself with the philosophy of Schopenhauer when he was a student at Tokyo Imperial University (Mebed 2003, p. 5).
12. At the annual meeting of Japan-Ireland Society on 3 December 2017, Hiroyuki Yamasaki, in his lecture entitled 'The Revivalists' Reception of O'Grady: The Solitary Image of Cuchulain Transformed,' has pointed out the image of the solitary and contemplative hero Cuchulain, presented by Standish James O'Grady, has become a prototype of the modern individual, an ideal to be pursued thereafter. The protagonists dealt in this chapter could probably be said to belong to the same lineage.
13. The original serialised version of Kawabata's *The Lake* (1954) had a cyclic structure (Li, 1645). That might evoke the famously cyclic structure of Molly's monologue in *Ulysses*, which commences and concludes with the same word: 'Yes'.

Mary Redfern

1. Letter, A.C. Beatty to W. Merton, 15 April 1954; CBP 1500.
2. Ibid.
3. Hillier's wife, Mary, also worked on the cataloguing of Beatty's *netsuke*.
4. For further discussion of the formation of Beatty's collection of Japanese prints, see Mary Redfern, *The Art of Friendship: Japanese Surimono prints* (Dublin: Chester Beatty Library, 2017). A complete catalogue of the library's *surimono* collection was published in 1985: Roger

Keyes, *The Art of Surimono: Privately published Japanese woodblock prints and books in the Chester Beatty Library, Dublin* (London: Sotheby, 1985).

5. Letter, A.C. Beatty to W. Merton, 11 April 1954; CBP 1500.
6. Copy of letter, A.C. Beatty to J. Hillier, 27 December 1955; CBP 922.2.
7. *An Exhibition of Japanese Prints from the Collection of Sir Chester Beatty* (Dublin, 1955).
8. *A Loan Collection of Western Illuminated Manuscripts from the Library of Sir Chester Beatty* (Dublin: Friends of the Library of Trinity College, 1955).
9. *Irish Press*, 12 August 1954.
10. Seán Lemass, Foreword, *An Tóstal: Official souvenir handbook* (Dublin: Fógre Fáilte, 1953).
11. Malachy Hynes, 'An Tóstal, 1953', *An Tóstal: Official souvenir handbook* (Dublin: Fógre Fáilte, 1953), p. 96.
12. Ibid.
13. The catalogue notes that the exhibition was proposed by the Friends of the National Collections of Ireland: James White, Foreword, *An Exhibition of Japanese Prints from the Collection of Sir Chester Beatty* (Dublin: 1955). The Earl of Rosse was president of the Friends, and may have approached Beatty regarding an exhibition of his collections; alternatively, it may be that it was the Friends who took the idea forward to the An Tóstal committee. The suggestion for an exhibition of Japanese prints certainly belonged to Beatty. Copy of letter, Earl of Rosse to A.C. Beatty, 11 January 1955; CBP 149; copy of letter, A.C. Beatty to Earl of Rosse, 5 February 1955; CBP 425.
14. Copy of letter, Earl of Rosse to A.C. Beatty, 11 January 1955; CBP 149.
15. Copy of letter, A.C. Beatty to Earl of Rosse, 5 February 1955; CBP 425.
16. Ibid.
17. Memo, J.V.S. Wilkinson, [February] 1955; CBP 425.
18. Copy of letter, J.V.S. Wilkinson to J. Hillier, 5 April 1955; CBP 922.2.
19. Memo, J.V.S. Wilkinson, [March] 1955; CBP 425.
20. *Irish Press*, 11 May 1955.
21. *Irish Independent*, 11 May 1955.
22. *The Irish Times*, 12 May 1955.
23. *Catalogue: An exhibition of Japanese prints from the collection of Sir Chester Beatty.*
24. Receipt, National Council for the Blind of Ireland, 31 May 1955; CBP 425.
25. Receipt, National Council for the Blind of Ireland, 29 June 1955; CBP 425.
26. Brian Kennedy, *Alfred Chester Beatty and Ireland, 1950–1968: A study in cultural politics* (Dún Laoghaire: Glendale Press, 1988), p. 110.
27. Copy of letter, J.V.S. Wilkinson to J. White, 6 April 1955; CBP 425.
28. *An Tóstal 1955: National programme* (Dublin: 1955), pp. 13–14.
29. Copy of letter, J.V.S. Wilkinson to J. Healy, 27 April 1955; CBP 425.
30. Narazaki Muneshige (ed.), 秘蔵浮世絵大観（別巻）チェスター・ビーティ／ケルン／アムステルダム：ヨーロッパ浮世絵蒐集ガイド [Ukiyo-e Masterpieces in Great European Collections: vol. 13] (Tokyo: Kodansha, 1991).
31. Akama Ryō (ed.), イメージデーターベースと日本文化研究 [Image Database and

Studies for Japanese Arts and Cultures] (Kyoto: Nakanishiya Shuppan, 2010).

32. For examples, see Ushioda Yoshiko, *Twelve Hundred Years of Japanese Woodblock Prints from the Chester Beatty Collection* (Dublin: Chester Beatty Library, 1981); Roger Keyes, *Surimono from the Chester Beatty Collection* (Alexandria, VA: International Exhibitions Foundation, 1987); Clare Pollard, *The Art of Hokusai: Masterpieces of Japanese printing in the Chester Beatty Library* (Dublin: TownHouse, 2003); Redfern, *The Art of Friendship.*
33. J.A. Nugent, 'Foreword', *An Tóstal: Official souvenir handbook* (Dublin: Fógre Fáilte, 1953).

Sr Clothilde Anamizu

1. A poem, 'Hound of Heaven' by Francis Thompson.
2. 'Lead Kindly Light', hymn by John Henry Newman.
3. Deuteronomy 1:31.
4. One of the three monastic vows promising to stay in the same monastery until death.
5. Matthew 18:3.
6. Galatians 3:28.

Ciarán L. Quinn

1. Bob Jackson, *A Doctor's Sword: How an Irish doctor survived war, captivity and the atomic bomb* (Cork: Collins Press, 2016).
2. Ibid.
3. Ibid.

Appendices

Irish Ambassadors to Japan	
Name	**Dates**
Christopher Peter Fogarty	September 1973 to March 1976
David Neligan	March 1976 to December 1978
Charles Victor Whelan	December 1978 to September 1984
Sean Ronan	September 1984 to March 1989
Jim Sharkey	August 1989 to August 1995
Declan O'Donovan	August 1995 to October 2001
Padraig Murphy	October 2001 to August 2005
Brendan Scannell	September 2005 to September 2010
John Neary	September 2010 to August 2014
Anne Barrington	September 2014 to April 2018 (retire)
Paul Kavanagh	September 2018 to

Japanese Ambassadors to Ireland	
Date	**Diplomat**
January 1964	Yujiro Iseki
February 1968	Bunshichi Hoshi
March 1971	Nisshi Sato
April 1973	Sigeaki Yamashita
January 1976	Nobuyasu Nishimiya
December 1978	Ryoukou Ishikawa
March 1982	Minoru Takeda
May 1985	Yoshinao Odaka
March 1988	Yoshifumi Ito
August 1990	Yuzo Hatano
July 1993	Kiyoshi Furukawa
November 1995	Takanori Kazuhara
December 1998	Kazuko Yokoo
March 2002	Takeshi Kagami
September 2005	Keiichi Hayashi
January 2008	Toshinao Urabe
April 2011	Chihiro Atsumi
December 2015	Mari Miyoshi
August 2019	Mitsuru Kitano

Index

Note: Page locators in **bold** refer to illustrations, prints and photographs.